CHRIST  ;HTS

D1388406

Combining Jewish, Greek, and Roman teachings with the radical new teachings of Christ and St. Paul, Christianity helped to cultivate the cardinal ideas of dignity, equality, liberty, and democracy that ground the modern human rights paradigm. Christianity also helped shape the law of public, private, penal, and procedural rights that anchor modern legal systems in the West and beyond. This collection of essays explores these Christian contributions to human rights through the perspectives of jurisprudence, theology, philosophy, and history. The authors also analyze Christianity's contribution to the special rights/claims of women, children, and the environment, and document the church's repeated failures to live up to the human rights ideals it has long advocated. With contributions from leading scholars, including a foreword by Archbishop Desmond Tutu, this book provides an authoritative treatment of how Christianity shaped human rights in the past, and how Christianity and human rights continue to challenge each other in modern times.

JOHN WITTE, JR. is Jonas Robitscher Professor of Law, Alonzo L. McDonald Family Foundation Distinguished Professor, and Director of the Center for the Study of Law and Religion at Emory University. His previous publications include *The Sins of the Fathers: The Law and Theology of Illegitimacy Reconsidered* (Cambridge, 2009), *Christianity and Law: An Introduction* (with Frank S. Alexander, Cambridge, 2008), *The Reformation of Rights: Law, Religion, and Human Rights in Early Modern Calvinism* (Cambridge, 2007), and *Law and Protestantism: The Legal Teachings of the Lutheran Reformation* (Cambridge, 2002).

FRANK S. ALEXANDER is Sam Nunn Professor of Law and Founding Director of the Center for the Study of Law and Religion at Emory University. His previous publications include *Georgia Real Estate Finance and Foreclosure Law* (5th edn, 2009), and, with John Witte, Jr., *The Teachings of Modern Christianity on Law, Politics and Human Nature*, 2 vols. (2006) and *The Weightier Matters of the Law: Essays on Law and Religion* (1988).

CAMBRIDGE UNIVERSITY PRESS
Cambridge, New York, Melbourne, Madrid, Cape Town, Singapore,
São Paulo, Delhi, Dubai, Tokyo, Mexico City

Cambridge University Press
The Edinburgh Building, Cambridge CB2 8RU, UK

Published in the United States of America by Cambridge University Press, New York

www.cambridge.org
Information on this title: www.cambridge.org/9780521143745

First published 2010

Printed in the United Kingdom at the University Press, Cambridge

A catalogue record for this publication is available from the British Library

Library of Congress Cataloguing in Publication data
Christianity and human rights : an introduction / [edited by] John Witte, Jr.,
Frank S. Alexander.
p.   cm.
Includes index.
ISBN 978-0-521-19441-9 (hardback)
1. Human rights–Religious aspects–Christianity.   2. Christianity–Influence.
3. Human rights–History.   I. Witte, John, 1959–
II. Alexander, Frank S., 1952–
BT738.15.C47525   2010
261.7–dc22
2010039006

ISBN 978-0-521-19441-9 Hardback
ISBN 978-0-521-14374-5 Paperback

To Alonzo L. McDonald
Christian Visionary, Moral Exemplar, Generous Friend

Contents

Contributors

FRANK S. ALEXANDER is Sam Nunn Professor of Law and
Founding Director of the Center for the Study of Law and Religion
at Emory University.

DAVID E. AUNE is Walter Professor of New Testament and
Christian Origins at the University of Notre Dame.

ROBERT N. BELLAH is Elliott Professor of Sociology Emeritus at the
University of California at Berkeley.

† DON S. BROWNING was Alexander Campbell Professor of Ethics
and the Social Sciences Emeritus at the University of Chicago
Divinity School and Senior Fellow of the Center for the Study of
Law and Religion at Emory University.

CHARLES DONAHUE, JR. is Paul A. Freund Professor of Law at
Harvard Law School.

SILVIO FERRARI is Professor of Law at the University of Milan.

RICHARD W. GARNETT is Professor of Law and Associate Dean at
the University of Notre Dame Law School and Senior Fellow of the
Center for the Study of Law and Religion at Emory University.

M. CHRISTIAN GREEN is Alonzo L. McDonald Family Senior
Lecturer and Senior Research Fellow at Emory University.

KENT GREENAWALT is University Professor at Columbia Law
School.

T. JEREMY GUNN is Associate Professor of International Studies at
Al Akhawayn University, Morocco, and Senior Fellow of the Center
for the Study of Law and Religion at Emory University.

ix

J. BRYAN HEHIR is Parker Gilbert Montgomery Professor of the Practice of Religion and Public Life at the Kennedy School of Government at Harvard University and Secretary for Social Services in the Archdiocese of Boston.

R. H. HELMHOLZ is Ruth Wyatt Rosenson Distinguished Service Professor of Law at the University of Chicago.

JOHN A. MCGUCKIN is Ane Marie and Bent Emil Nielsen Professor in Late Antique and Byzantine Christian History at Union Theological Seminary, Professor of Byzantine Christian Studies at Columbia University, and Senior Fellow of the Center for the Study of Law and Religion at Emory University.

JOHN COPELAND NAGLE is John N. Matthew Professor of Law at University of Notre Dame Law School.

DAVID NOVAK is J. Richard and Dorothy Shiff Chair of Jewish Studies, Professor of the Study of Religion, and Professor of Philosophy at the University of Toronto.

ROBERT A. SEIPLE is Former President of World Vision and Former Ambassador-at-Large for International Religious Freedom at the Department of State.

DESMOND M. TUTU is Anglican Archbishop of Cape Town, South Africa.

JEREMY WALDRON is University Professor at New York University School of Law and Chichele Professor of Social and Political Theory, Oxford University.

JOHN WITTE, JR. is Jonas Robitscher Professor of Law, Alonzo L. McDonald Family Foundation Distinguished Professor, and Director of the Center for the Study of Law and Religion at Emory University.

NICHOLAS P. WOLTERSTORFF is Noah Porter Professor of Philosophical Theology Emeritus at Yale University, Senior Fellow at the Institute for Advanced Studies at the University of Virginia, and Senior Fellow of the Center for the Study of Law and Religion at Emory University.

Acknowledgements

In this volume, twenty leading scholars explore the contributions of Christianity to the development of human rights in the West. Combining Jewish, Greek, and Roman teachings with the radical new teachings of Christ and St. Paul, Christianity helped to cultivate the cardinal ideas of dignity, equality, liberty, and democracy that ground the modern human rights paradigm. Christianity also helped to shape the law of public, private, penal, and procedural rights that anchor modern legal systems in the West and beyond. The pages that follow explore these Christian contributions to basic human rights through the lenses of jurisprudence, theology, philosophy, and history. They also explore Christian contributions to the special rights claims of women and children, the poor and the needy, prisoners and enemies, nature and the environment. No author ignores the church's own checkered human rights record over the centuries and the many failings of Christians to live up to their own human rights ideals. Nor does anyone pretend that Christianity has had or should have a monopoly on rights talk – let alone on the legal structures that implement rights. But every author believes that Christian ideas and institutions are essential to the cultivation of human rights today – and a few of them, starting with Archbishop Tutu, offer pointed injunctions on how to live out the ideals of human rights in thought, word, and deed.

This volume is part and product of an ongoing project on Christian Legal Studies, undertaken by our Center for the Study of Law and Religion at Emory University in Atlanta. This project, which has involved 200-plus scholars over twenty-plus years, explores the historical and contemporary influence of Christian ideas, institutions, and individuals on Western law, politics, and society. In its earlier phases, this project analyzed some of the Christian foundations and fundamentals of Western constitutionalism, democracy, and religious liberty, yielding a score of volumes that have appeared in a score of languages. In its current phase, the project has commissioned thirty new volumes on the past and potential contributions of Catholic, Protestant, and Orthodox Christianity to the hard legal and political questions that are now challenging and dividing church, state, and society.

This volume – and the broader project of Christian legal studies of which it is a part – was made possible by generous grants from the Alonzo L. McDonald Family Foundation and the Henry Luce Foundation, Inc. We express our profound gratitude to Alonzo, Peter, and Suzie McDonald, and Robert Pool of the McDonald Foundation and to Michael Gilligan and his Luce colleagues for their generous and genial support. We express our warm thanks to our Center colleagues – April Bogle, Linda King, Anita Mann, and Amy Wheeler – for their effective and efficient administrative work on this volume and related projects. We thank the *Emory International Law Review* for permission to reprint Desmond Tutu's essay herein. And we thank Kate Brett and Laura Morris and their colleagues at Cambridge University Press for taking on this volume and bringing it to print with their usual excellence and professionalism.

This volume is dedicated to Dr. Alonzo L. McDonald, Christian visionary, moral exemplar, and generous friend to so many.

John Witte, Jr. and Frank S. Alexander

The first word: to be human is to be free

Desmond M. Tutu

There is a story, which is fairly well known, about when the missionaries came to Africa. They had the Bible and we, the natives, had the land. They said "Let us pray," and we dutifully shut our eyes. When we opened them, why, they now had the land and we had the Bible. It would, on the surface, appear as if we had struck a bad bargain, but the fact of the matter is that we came out of that transaction a great deal better off than when we started. The point is that we were given a priceless gift in the Word of God: the Gospel of salvation, the good news of God's love for us that is given so utterly unconditionally. But even more wonderful is the fact that we were given the most subversive, most revolutionary thing around. Those who may have wanted to exploit us and to subject us to injustice and oppression should really not have given us the Bible, because that placed dynamite under their nefarious schemes.

The Bible makes some quite staggering assertions about human beings which came to be the foundations of the culture of basic human rights that have become so commonplace in our day and age. Both creation narratives in Genesis 1–2 assert quite categorically that human beings are the pinnacle, the climax, of the divine creative activity; if not climactic, then central or crucial to the creative activity. In the first narrative the whole creative process moves impressively to its climax which is the creation of human beings. The author signals that something quite out of the ordinary is about to happen by a change in the formula relating to a creative divine action. Up to this point God has merely had to speak "Let there be …" and by divine fiat something comes into being *ex nihilo*. At this climactic point God first invites his heavenly court to participate with him, "Let us create man in our image" (Gen. 1:26). Something special has come into being.

Remarkably this narrative is, in fact, in part intended to be a jingoistic propaganda piece designed to lift the sagging spirits of a people in exile whose fortunes are at a low ebb, surrounded as they are by the impressive

I

We cannot properly praise or blame someone who does what he or she cannot help doing, or refrains from doing what he or she cannot help not doing. Moral approbation and disapproval have no meaning where there is no freedom to choose between various options on offer. That is what enables us to have moral responsibility. An automaton cannot be a moral agent, and therein lies our glory and our damnation. We may choose aright and therein is bliss, or we may choose wrongly and therein lies perdition. God may not intervene to nullify this incredible gift in order to stop us from making wrong choices. I have said on other occasions that God, who alone has the perfect right to be a totalitarian, has such a profound reverence for our freedom that He had much rather we went freely to hell than compel us to go to heaven.

An unfree human being is a contradiction in terms. To be human is to be free. God gives us space to be free and so to be human. Human beings have an autonomy, an integrity which should not be violated, which should not be subverted. St. Paul exults as he speaks of what he calls the "glorious liberty of the children of God" (Rom. 8:21) and elsewhere declares that Christ has set us free for freedom. It is a freedom to hold any view or none – freedom of expression. It is freedom of association because we are created for family, for togetherness, for community, because the solitary human being is an aberration.

We are created to exist in a delicate network of interdependence with fellow human beings and the rest of God's creation. All sorts of things go horribly wrong when we break this fundamental law of our being. Then we are no longer appalled as we should be that vast sums are spent on budgets of death and destruction, when a tiny fraction of those sums would ensure that God's children everywhere would have a clean supply of water, adequate health care, proper housing and education, enough to eat and to wear. A totally self-sufficient human being would be subhuman.

Perhaps because of their own experience of slavery, the Israelites depicted God as the great liberator, and they seemed to be almost obsessed with being set free. And so they had the principle of Jubilee enshrined in the heart of the biblical tradition. It was unnatural for anyone to be enthralled to another, and so every fifty years they celebrated Jubilee, when those who had become slaves were set at liberty. Those who had mortgaged their land received it back unencumbered by the burden of debt, reminding everyone that all they were and all they had was a gift, that absolute ownership belonged to God, that all were really equal before God, who was the real and true Sovereign.

The first word: to be human is to be free

Desmond M. Tutu

There is a story, which is fairly well known, about when the missionaries came to Africa. They had the Bible and we, the natives, had the land. They said "Let us pray," and we dutifully shut our eyes. When we opened them, why, they now had the land and we had the Bible. It would, on the surface, appear as if we had struck a bad bargain, but the fact of the matter is that we came out of that transaction a great deal better off than when we started. The point is that we were given a priceless gift in the Word of God: the Gospel of salvation, the good news of God's love for us that is given so utterly unconditionally. But even more wonderful is the fact that we were given the most subversive, most revolutionary thing around. Those who may have wanted to exploit us and to subject us to injustice and oppression should really not have given us the Bible, because that placed dynamite under their nefarious schemes.

The Bible makes some quite staggering assertions about human beings which came to be the foundations of the culture of basic human rights that have become so commonplace in our day and age. Both creation narratives in Genesis 1–2 assert quite categorically that human beings are the pinnacle, the climax, of the divine creative activity; if not climactic, then central or crucial to the creative activity. In the first narrative the whole creative process moves impressively to its climax which is the creation of human beings. The author signals that something quite out of the ordinary is about to happen by a change in the formula relating to a creative divine action. Up to this point God has merely had to speak "Let there be …" and by divine fiat something comes into being *ex nihilo*. At this climactic point God first invites his heavenly court to participate with him, "Let us create man in our image" (Gen. 1:26). Something special has come into being.

Remarkably this narrative is, in fact, in part intended to be a jingoistic propaganda piece designed to lift the sagging spirits of a people in exile whose fortunes are at a low ebb, surrounded as they are by the impressive monuments to Babylonian hegemony. Where one would have expected the author to claim that it was only Jews who were created in the image of God, this passage asserts that it is all human beings who have been created in the divine image.

That this attribute is a universal phenomenon was not necessarily self-evident. Someone as smart as Aristotle taught that human personality was not universally possessed by all human beings, because slaves in his view were not persons. The biblical teaching is marvelously exhilarating in a situation of oppression and injustice, because in that situation it has often been claimed that certain groups were inferior or superior because of possessing or not possessing a particular attribute (physical or cultural). The Bible claims for all human beings this exalted status that we are all, each one of us, created in the divine image, that it has nothing to do with this or that extraneous attribute which by the nature of the case, can be possessed by only some people.

The consequences that flow from these biblical assertions are quite staggering. First, human life (as all life) is a gift from the gracious and ever-generous Creator of all. It is therefore inviolable. We must therefore have a deep reverence for the sanctity of human life. That is why homicide is universally condemned. "Thou shalt not kill" would be an undisputed part of a global ethic accepted by the adherents of all faiths and of none. For many it would include as an obvious corollary the prohibition of capital punishment. It has seemed an oddity that we should want to demonstrate our outrage that, for example, someone had shown scant reverence for human life by committing murder, by ourselves then proceeding to take another life. In some ways it is an irrational obscenity.

The life of every human person is inviolable as a gift from God. And since this person is created in the image of God and is a God carrier, a second consequence would be that we should not just respect such a person but that we should have a deep reverence for that person. The New Testament claims that the Christian person becomes a sanctuary, a temple of the Holy Spirit, someone who is indwelt by the most holy and blessed Trinity. We would want to assert this of all human beings. We should not just greet one another. We should strictly genuflect before such an august and precious creature. The Buddhist is correct in bowing profoundly before another human as the God in me acknowledges and greets the God in you. This preciousness, this infinite worth, is intrinsic to who we all are and is inalienable as a gift from God to be acknowledged as an inalienable right of all human persons.

The Babylonian creation narrative makes human beings have a low destiny and purpose – as those intended to be the scavengers of the gods. Not so the biblical *Weltanschauung* which declares that the human being created in the image of God is meant to be God's viceroy, God's representative in having rule over the rest of creation on behalf of God. To have dominion, not in an authoritarian and destructive manner, but to hold sway as God would hold sway – compassionately, gently, caringly, enabling each part of creation to come fully into its own and to realize its potential for the good of the whole, contributing to the harmony and unity which was God's intention for the whole of creation. And even more wonderfully this human person is destined to know and so to love God and to dwell with the divine forever and ever, enjoying unspeakable celestial delights. Nearly all major religions envisage a post mortem existence for humankind that far surpasses anything we can conceive.

All this makes human beings unique. It imbues each one of us with profound dignity and worth. As a result, to treat such persons as if they were less than this, to oppress them, to trample their dignity underfoot, is not just evil as it surely must be; it is not just painful as it frequently must be for the victims of injustice and oppression. It is positively blasphemous, for it is tantamount to spitting in the face of God. That is why we have been so passionate in our opposition to the evil of apartheid in South Africa. We have not, as some might mischievously have supposed, been driven by political or ideological considerations. No, we have been constrained by the imperatives of our biblical faith.

Any person of faith has no real option. In the face of injustice and oppression it is to disobey God not to stand up in opposition to that injustice and that oppression. Any violation of the rights of God's stand-in cries out to be condemned and to be redressed, and all people of good will must willy-nilly be engaged in upholding and preserving those rights as a religious duty. Such a discussion as this one should therefore not be merely an academic exercise in the most pejorative sense. It must be able to galvanize participants with a zeal to be active protectors of the rights of persons.

The Bible points to the fact that human persons are endowed with freedom to choose. This freedom is constitutive of what it means to be a person – one who has the freedom to choose between alternative options, and to choose freely (apart from the influences of heredity and nurture). To be a person is to be able to choose to love or not to love, to be able to reject or to accept the offer of the divine love, to be free to obey or to disobey. That is what constitutes being a moral agent.

We cannot properly praise or blame someone who does what he or she cannot help doing, or refrains from doing what he or she cannot help not doing. Moral approbation and disapproval have no meaning where there is no freedom to choose between various options on offer. That is what enables us to have moral responsibility. An automaton cannot be a moral agent, and therein lies our glory and our damnation. We may choose aright and therein is bliss, or we may choose wrongly and therein lies perdition. God may not intervene to nullify this incredible gift in order to stop us from making wrong choices. I have said on other occasions that God, who alone has the perfect right to be a totalitarian, has such a profound reverence for our freedom that He had much rather we went freely to hell than compel us to go to heaven.

An unfree human being is a contradiction in terms. To be human is to be free. God gives us space to be free and so to be human. Human beings have an autonomy, an integrity which should not be violated, which should not be subverted. St. Paul exults as he speaks of what he calls the "glorious liberty of the children of God" (Rom. 8:21) and elsewhere declares that Christ has set us free for freedom. It is a freedom to hold any view or none – freedom of expression. It is freedom of association because we are created for family, for togetherness, for community, because the solitary human being is an aberration.

We are created to exist in a delicate network of interdependence with fellow human beings and the rest of God's creation. All sorts of things go horribly wrong when we break this fundamental law of our being. Then we are no longer appalled as we should be that vast sums are spent on budgets of death and destruction, when a tiny fraction of those sums would ensure that God's children everywhere would have a clean supply of water, adequate health care, proper housing and education, enough to eat and to wear. A totally self-sufficient human being would be subhuman.

Perhaps because of their own experience of slavery, the Israelites depicted God as the great liberator, and they seemed to be almost obsessed with being set free. And so they had the principle of Jubilee enshrined in the heart of the biblical tradition. It was unnatural for anyone to be enthralled to another, and so every fifty years they celebrated Jubilee, when those who had become slaves were set at liberty. Those who had mortgaged their land received it back unencumbered by the burden of debt, reminding everyone that all they were and all they had was a gift, that absolute ownership belonged to God, that all were really equal before God, who was the real and true Sovereign.

That is the basis of the egalitarianism of the Bible – that all belongs to God and that all are of equal worth in His sight. That is heady stuff. No political ideology could better that for radicalness. And that is what fired our own struggle against apartheid – this incredible sense of the infinite worth of each person created in the image of God, being God's viceroy, God's representative, God's stand-in, being a God carrier, a sanctuary, a temple of the Holy Spirit, inviolate, possessing a dignity that was intrinsic with an autonomy and freedom to choose that were constitutive of human personality.

This person was meant to be creative, to resemble God in His creativity. And so wholesome work is something humans need to be truly human. The biblical understanding of being human includes freedom from fear and insecurity, freedom from penury and want, freedom of association and movement, because we would live ideally in the kind of society that is characterized by these attributes. It would be a caring and compassionate, a sharing and gentle society in which, like God, the strongest would be concerned about the welfare of the weakest, represented in ancient society by the widow, the alien, and the orphan. It would be a society in which you reflected the holiness of God not by ritual purity and cultic correctness but by the fact that when you gleaned your harvest, you left something behind for the poor, the unemployed, the marginalized ones – all a declaration of the unique worth of persons that does not hinge on their economic, social, or political status but simply on the fact that they are persons created in God's image. That is what invests them with their preciousness and from this stems all kinds of rights.

All the above is the positive impact that religion can have as well as the consequences that flow from these fundamental assertions. Sadly, and often tragically, religion is not often in and of itself necessarily a good thing. Already in the Bible there is ample evidence that religion can be a baneful thing with horrendous consequences often for its adherents or those who may be designated its unfortunate targets. There are frequent strictures leveled at religious observance which is just a matter of external form when the obsession is with cultic minutiae and correctness. Such religion is considered to be an abomination, however elaborate the ritual performed. Its worth is tested by whether it has any significant impact on how its adherents treat especially the widow, the orphan, and the alien in their midst. How one deals with those who have no real clout and who can make no claim on being given equitable and compassionate treatment, becomes a vital clue to the quality of religiosity.

We must hang our heads in shame, however, when we survey the gory and shameful history of the Church of Christ. There have been numerous wars of religion instigated by those who claimed to be followers of the One described as the Prince of Peace. The Crusades, using the cross as a distinctive emblem, were waged in order to commend the Good News of this Prince of Peace amongst the infidel Muslims, seeking to ram down people's throats a faith that somewhere thought it prided itself on the autonomy of the individual person freely to choose to believe or not to believe. Religious zealots have seemed blind to the incongruity and indeed contradiction of using constraint of whatever sort to proclaim a religion that sets high store by individual freedom of choice. Several bloody conflicts characterize the history of Christianity, and war is without doubt the most comprehensive violation of human rights. It ignores reverence for life in its wanton destruction of people. It subverts social and family life and justifies the abrogation of fundamental rights.

Christians have waged wars against fellow Christians. St. Paul was flabbergasted that Christians could bring charges against fellow Christians in a court of law. It is not difficult to imagine what he would have felt and what he would have said at the spectacle of Christians liquidating fellow Christians as in war. Christians have been grossly intolerant of one another as when Christians persecuted fellow Christians for holding different views about religious dogma and practice. The Inquisition with all that was associated with it is a considerable blot on our copybook. The church has had fewer more inglorious occasions than those when the Inquisition was active. Christians have gone on an orgy of excommunicating one another just because of disagreements about doctrine and liturgy, not to mention the downright obscurantism displayed in the persecution of the likes of Galileo and Copernicus for propounding intellectual views that were anathema to the church at the time.

Slavery is an abominable affront to the dignity of those who would be treated as if they were mere chattels. The trade in fellow human beings should have been recognized as completely contrary to the central tenets of Christianity about the unspeakable worth and preciousness of each human person. And yet Christians were some of the most zealous slave owners who opposed the efforts of emancipators such as William Wilberforce. The Civil War in the United States of America in part happened because of differences of opinion on the vexed question of slavery. Devout Christians saw no inconsistency between singing Christian hymns lustily and engaging in this demeaning trade in fellow humans. Indeed one of the leading hymn writers of the day was also an enthusiastic slave owner.

Christians have been foremost supporters of anti-Semitism, blaming Jews for committing deicide in crucifying Jesus Christ. A devastating chapter in human history happened with Hitler's final solution culminating in the Holocaust. Hitler purported to be a Christian and saw no contradiction between his Christianity and perpetrating one of history's most dastardly campaigns. What is even more disturbing is that he was supported in this massive crime against humanity by a significant group called German Christians. Mercifully there were those like Dietrich Bonhoeffer and others who opposed this madness, often at great cost to themselves as members of the confessing church. Christianity has often been perversely used in other instances to justify the iniquity of racism. In the United States the rabid haters of blacks, the Ku Klux Klan, have not balked at using a flaming cross as their much-feared symbol. One would have to travel far to find a more despicable example of blasphemy. Apartheid in South Africa was perpetrated not by pagans but by those who regarded themselves as devout Christians. Their opponents, even though known to be Christians, were usually vilified as communists and worse. Many conflicts in the world have been started and certainly been made worse by religious and sectarian differences, as we see in many of the conflicts in Northern Ireland, in Sudan, in the Indian sub-continent, and in the Middle East. Religious differences have exacerbated the horrendous bloodletting in Bosnia euphemistically described as ethnic cleansing.

Religion should produce peace, reconciliation, tolerance, and respect for human rights but it has often promoted the opposite conditions. And yet the potential for great good in the impact and influence of religion remains. I can testify that our own struggle for justice, peace, and equity would have floundered badly had we not been inspired by our Christian faith and assured of the ultimate victory of goodness and truth, compassion and love against their ghastly counterparts. We want to promote freedom of religion as an indispensable part of any genuinely free society.

Introduction

John Witte, Jr.

The world has entered something of a "Dickensian era" in the past three decades.[1] We have seen the best of human rights protections inscribed on the books, but some of the worst of human rights violations inflicted on the ground. We have celebrated the creation of more than thirty new constitutional democracies, but lamented the eruption of more than thirty new civil wars. We have witnessed the wisest of democratic statecraft and the most foolish of autocratic belligerence. For every South African spring of hope, there has been a Yugoslavian winter of despair, for every Ukrainian season of light, a Sudanese season of darkness.

These Dickensian paradoxes of the modern human rights revolution are particularly striking when viewed in their religious dimensions. On the one hand, the modern human rights revolution has helped to catalyze a great awakening of religion around the globe. In regions newly committed to democracy and human rights, ancient faiths once driven underground by autocratic oppressors have sprung forth with new vigor. In the former Soviet bloc, for example, numerous Buddhist, Christian, Hindu, Jewish, Muslim, and other faiths have been awakened, alongside a host of exotic goddess, naturalist, and personality cults. In post-colonial and post-revolutionary Africa, these same mainline religious groups have come to flourish in numerous conventional and inculturated forms, alongside a bewildering array of Traditional groups. In Latin America, the human rights revolution has not only transformed long-standing Catholic and mainline Protestant communities but also triggered the explosion of numerous new Evangelical, Pentecostal, and Traditional movements. Many parts of the world have seen the prodigious rise of a host of new or newly minted faiths – Adventists, Bahi'as, Hare Krishnas, Jehovah's

---

[1] The phrase is from Irwin Cotler, "Jewish NGOs and Religious Human Rights: A Case Study," in Michael J. Broyde and John Witte, Jr., eds., *Human Rights in Judaism: Cultural, Religious, and Political Perspectives* (Northvale, NJ: Jason Aronson, 1998), 165.

Witnesses, Mormons, Scientologists, Unification Church members, among many others – some wielding ample material, political, and media power. Religion today has become, in Susanne Rudolph's apt phrase, a major "transnational variable."[2]

One cause and consequence of this great awakening of religion around the globe is that the ambit of religious rights has been substantially expanded. In the past three decades, more than 150 major new statutes and constitutional provisions on religious rights have been promulgated – many replete with generous protections for liberty of conscience and freedom of religious exercise, guarantees of religious pluralism, equality, and non-discrimination, and several other special protections and entitlements for religious individuals and religious groups. These national guarantees have been matched with a growing body of regional and international norms, notably the 1981 *UN Declaration on Religious Intolerance and Discrimination Based Upon Religion and Belief* and the 1992 *UN Declaration on the Rights of the Persons Belonging to National or Ethnic, Religious, and Linguistic Minorities.*

On the other hand, this very same world democratic and human rights revolution has catalyzed new forms of religious and ethnic conflict, oppression, and belligerence, often of tragic proportions. In some communities, such as the former Yugoslavia, Chechnya, and Iraq, local religious and ethnic rivals, previously kept at bay by a common oppressor, converted their new liberties into licenses to renew ancient hostilities, with catastrophic results. In other communities, such as Sudan, Rwanda, and the Central African Republic, ethnic nationalism and religious extremism conspired to bring violent dislocation or death to hundreds of rival religious believers each year, and persecution, false imprisonment, forced starvation, and savage abuses to thousands of others. In other communities, most notably in Canada, France, and Belgium, political secularism, laicization, and nationalism have combined to threaten a sort of civil denial and death to a number of believers, particularly "sects" and "cults" of high religious temperature or of low cultural conformity. In still other communities, from Asia to the Middle East, Christians, Jews, and Muslims, when in minority contexts, have faced sharply increased restrictions, repression, and martyrdom. And, in many parts of the world today, Islamicist terrorists have waged their distorted and destructive theory of jihad against all manner of enemies, real and imagined.

---

[2] Susanne Hoeber Rudolph and James Piscatori, eds., *Transnational Religion and Fading States* (Boulder, CO: Westview Press, 1997), 6.

In parts of Russia, Eastern Europe, Africa, and Latin America, this human rights revolution has brought on something of a new war for souls between local and foreign religious groups. With the political transformations of these regions in the past two decades, foreign religious groups were granted rights to enter these regions for the first time in decades. Beginning in the early 1990s, Silvio Ferrari's chapter shows, these foreigners came in increasing numbers to preach their faiths, to offer their services, to convert new souls. Initially, local religious groups – Orthodox, Catholic, Protestant, Sunni, Shi'ite, and Traditional alike – welcomed these foreigners, particularly their foreign co-religionists with whom they had lost contact for many decades. More recently, local religious groups have come to resent these foreign religions, particularly Christian groups from North America and Western Europe who assume a democratic human rights ethic. Local religious groups resent the participation in the marketplace of religious ideas that democracy assumes. They resent the toxic waves of materialism and individualism that democracy inflicts. They resent the massive expansion of religious pluralism that democracy encourages. They resent the extravagant forms of religious speech, press, and assembly that democracy protects. The same charges of proselytism, exploitation, and cultural obtuseness are sounding anew against foreign missionaries and disaster relief groups who have been helping victims of war, tsunamis, hurricanes, and earthquakes around the world.

A new war for souls has thus broken out in many regions of the world, a war to reclaim the traditional cultural and moral souls of these new societies, and a war to retain adherence and adherents to local faiths. In part, this is a theological war, as rival religious communities have begun to demonize and defame each other and to gather themselves into ever more dogmatic and fundamentalist stands. The ecumenical spirit of the previous decades is giving way to sharp new forms of religious Balkanization. In part, this is a legal war, as local religious groups have begun to conspire with their political leaders to adopt statutes and regulations restricting the constitutional rights of their foreign religious rivals. Beneath shiny constitutional veneers of religious freedom for all and unqualified ratification of international human rights instruments, several countries of late have passed firm new anti-proselytism laws, cult registration requirements, tightened visa controls, and various other discriminatory restrictions on new or newly arrived religions. Indeed, many parts of the world seem bent on creating new Islamic or Christian religious establishments.

Such Dickensian paradoxes have exposed the limitations of a secular human rights paradigm standing alone. They also have inspired the earnest search for additional resources to deter violence, resolve disputes, cultivate peace, and enhance security through dialogue, liturgical healing, reconciliation ceremonies, and other means. Human rights principles are as much the problem as they are the solution in a number of current religious and cultural conflicts. In the war for souls in Russia, Africa, and Latin America, for example, two absolute principles of human rights have come into direct conflict: the foreign religion's free exercise right to share and expand its faith versus the local religion's liberty-of-conscience right to be left alone on its own territory. Or, put in Christian theological terms, it is one group's rights to abide by the Great Commission – "Go ye therefore, and make disciples of all nations" – versus another group's right to insist on the Golden Rule – "Do unto others as you would have done unto you" (Matt. 28:19–20, 7:12; Mark 16:15–18; Acts 1:8). Further rights talk alone cannot resolve this dispute. Likewise, some of the nations given to the most belligerent forms of religious oppression have ratified more of the international human rights instruments than the United States has, and have crafted more elaborate bills of rights than what appears in the United States Constitution. Here, too, further rights talk alone is insufficient.

These paradoxes of the modern human rights revolution underscore an elementary, but essential lesson – that human rights norms need a human rights culture to be effective. "[D]eclarations are not deeds," Judge John T. Noonan, Jr. reminds us. "A form of words by itself secures nothing ... [W]ords pregnant with meaning in one cultural context may be entirely barren in another."[3] Human rights norms have little salience in societies that lack constitutional processes that will give them meaning and measure. They have little value for parties who lack basic rights to security, succor, and sanctuary, or who are deprived of basic freedoms of speech, press, or association. They have little pertinence for victims who lack standing in courts and other basic procedural rights to pursue apt remedies. They have little cogency in communities that lack the ethos and ethic to render human rights violations a source of shame and regret, restraint and respect, confession and responsibility, reconciliation and restitution. As we have moved from the first generation of human rights declaration following World War II to the current generation of human rights implementation, this need for a human rights culture has become all the more pressing.

---

[3] John T. Noonan, Jr., "The Tensions and the Ideals," in Johan D. van der Vyver and John Witte, Jr., eds., *Religious Human Rights in Global Perspective: Legal Perspectives* (The Hague: Martinus Nijhoff, 1996), II:594.

These paradoxes, when viewed in their religious dimensions, further suggest that religion and human rights need to be brought into a closer symbiosis. On the one hand, as Robert Bellah's chapter demonstrates, human rights norms need religious narratives to ground them. There is, of course, some value in simply declaring human rights norms of "liberty, equality, and fraternity" or "life, liberty, and property" – if for no other reason than to pose an ideal against which a person or community might measure itself, to preserve a normative totem for later generations to make real. But, ultimately, these abstract human rights ideals of the good life and the good society depend on the visions and values of human communities and institutions to give them content and coherence – to provide what Jacques Maritain once called "the scale of values governing [their] exercise and concrete manifestation."[4] It is here that religion must play a vital role. Religion is an ineradicable condition of human lives and human communities. Religions invariably provide many of the sources and "scales of values" by which many persons and communities govern themselves. Religions inevitably help to define the meanings and measures of shame and regret, restraint and respect, responsibility and restitution that a human rights regime presupposes. Religions must thus be seen as indispensable allies in the modern struggle for human rights. To exclude them from the struggle is impossible, indeed catastrophic. To include them, by enlisting their unique resources and protecting their unique rights, is vital to enhancing the regime of human rights and to easing some of the worst paradoxes that currently exist.

Conversely, religious narratives need human rights norms both to protect them and to challenge them. There is, of course, some value in religions simply accepting the current protections of a human rights regime – the guarantees of liberty of conscience, free exercise, religious group autonomy, and the like. But passive acquiescence in a secular scheme of human rights ultimately will not prove effective. Religious communities must reclaim their own voices within the secular human rights dialogue, and reclaim the human rights voices within their own internal religious dialogues. Contrary to conventional wisdom, the theory and law of human rights are neither new nor secular in origin. Human rights are, in no small part, the modern political fruits of ancient religious beliefs and practices – ancient Jewish constructions of covenant and *mitzvot*, classic Christian concepts of *ius* and *libertas*, freedom and covenant, and more.

---

[4] Jacques Maritain, "Introduction," in UNESCO, *Human Rights: Comments and Interpretations* (New York: Columbia University Press, 1949).

AN EMERGING HUMAN RIGHTS HERMENEUTIC

A number of religious traditions of late have begun the process of reengaging the regime of human rights, of returning to their traditional roots and routes of nurturing and challenging the human rights regime. This process has been incremental, clumsy, and controversial – at times even fatal for its proponents. But the process of religious engagement of human rights is now under way in Christian, Islamic, Judaic, Buddhist, Hindu, Confucian, and Traditional communities around the world. Something of a new "human rights hermeneutic" is slowly beginning to emerge among modern religions.

This is, in part, a hermeneutic of confession. Given their checkered human rights records over the centuries, religious bodies have begun to acknowledge their departures from the cardinal teachings of peace and love that are the heart of their sacred texts and traditions. Christian churches have taken the lead in this process – from the Second Vatican Council's confession of prior complicity in authoritarianism, to the contemporary Protestant and Orthodox churches' repeated confessions of prior support for communism, racism, sexism, fascism, anti-Semitism, and other systemic violations of human rights.

This is, in part, a hermeneutic of suspicion, in Paul Ricoeur's famous phrase. Given the pronounced libertarian tone of many recent human rights formulations, it is imperative that we not idolize or idealize these formulations. We need not be bound by current taxonomies of "three generations of rights" rooted in liberty, equality, and fraternity. Common law formulations of "life, liberty, and property," canon law formulations of "natural, ecclesiastical, and civil rights," or Protestant formulations of "civil, theological, and pedagogical uses" of rights might well be more apt classification schemes. We need not accept the seemingly infinite expansion of human rights discourse and demands. Rights bound by moral duties, by natural capacities, or by covenantal relationships might well provide better boundaries to the legitimate expression and extension of rights.

This is, in part, a hermeneutic of history. While acknowledging the fundamental contributions of Enlightenment liberalism to the modern rights regime, we must also see the deeper genesis and genius of many modern rights norms in religious texts and traditions that antedate the Enlightenment by centuries, even by millennia. The Western tradition knew "liberty long before liberalism"[5] and had human rights in place long

---

[5] Quentin Skinner, *Liberty Before Liberalism* (Cambridge: Cambridge University Press, 1998).

before it fought democratic revolutions in their name. We must retrieve these ancient sources and reconstruct them for our day. In part, this is a return to ancient sacred texts freed from the casuistic accretions of generations of jurists and freed from the cultural trappings of the communities in which these traditions were born. In part, this is a return to slender streams of theological jurisprudence that have not been part of the mainstream of the religious traditions, or have become diluted by too great a commingling with it. In part, this is a return to prophetic voices of dissent, long purged from traditional religious canons, but, in retrospect, prescient of some of the rights roles that the tradition might play today.

And this is, in part, a hermeneutic of law and religion. A century of legal positivism in the Western academy has trained us to think that law is an autonomous discipline, free from the influence of theology and the church. A century of firm laicization and strict separation of church and state have accustomed us to think that our law and politics must be hermetically and hermeneutically sealed from the corrosive influences of religion and belief. An ample body of new scholarship has emerged, however, to show that law and religion need each other, and that institutions like human rights have interlocking legal and religious dimensions. Religion gives law its spirit and inspires its adherence to ritual and justice. Law gives religion its structure and encourages its devotion to order and organization. Law and religion share such ideas as fault, obligation, and covenant and such methods as ethics, rhetoric, and textual interpretation. Law and religion also balance each other by counterposing justice and mercy, rule and equity, discipline and love. This broader understanding of the interaction of law and religion has particular pertinence for understanding human rights.

In this volume, we apply and illustrate the budding new human rights hermeneutic of the Christian tradition. The Christian story of human rights can be told in different ways. It could focus on the rights contributions of seminal figures from Christ's day to our own. It could analyze the complex rights theories and laws of discrete Christian groups or denominations in different social and political contexts around the world. It could rehearse the distinct contributions of Christianity to discrete rights, such as those protecting religious freedom, education, or social welfare. It could rehearse great human rights cases, statutes, or constitutional texts in which Christianity played seminal roles or had much at stake. All these approaches and others now populate the literature. Some of the best of such literature is cited in the "Recommended Reading" sections that follow each chapter in this volume.

To provide an accessible introduction to this vast topic of "Christianity and Human Rights," we have divided this volume into two main parts. First, we analyze the foundations of rights talk in the first millennium of the common era, and the gradual development of rights ideas and institutions within the mainline Catholic, Protestant, and Orthodox traditions. Thereafter, we address several modern human rights themes and issues that are of central importance to persons of (the Christian) faith today. The balance of this Introduction provides an overview of the historical development of human rights within the three main branches of Christianity, with running references to the more expansive discussion of several topics in the individual chapters that follow.[6]

BIBLICAL AND CLASSICAL FOUNDATIONS

The Bible has long been the anchor text for Christian teachings on human rights. The Bible is no human rights textbook, of course, nor were the ancient Hebrew, Greek, and Roman cultures in which the Bible was forged human rights cultures, by any definition. But the Bible is filled with critical passages that have long inspired deep theological insights into the nature of rights. And some ancient Greek and Roman teachings and laws were important prototypes for later Western rights talk.

Foremost among the biblical texts is the Genesis account of the creation of men and women: "Then God said, 'Let us make man in our image, after our likeness; and let them have dominion over the fish of the sea, and over birds of the air, and over the cattle, and over all the earth, and over every creeping thing that creeps upon the earth.' So God created man in his own image, in the image of God he created him; male and female he created them. And God blessed them, and God said to them, 'Be fruitful and multiply, and fill the earth and subdue it'" (Gen. 1:26–8). Desmond Tutu, Jeremy Waldron, and Nick Wolterstorff all underscore how the idea of humans created in the image of God forms the deep ontological foundation of a Christian theory of human dignity, human worth, and human rights. Don Browning and Christy Green both emphasize further how

---

[6] These next sections are adapted in part from the following sources, each with detailed bibliography: John Witte, Jr., *The Reformation of Rights: Law, Religion, and Human Rights in Early Modern Calvinism* (Cambridge: Cambridge University Press, 2007); Witte, *God's Joust, God's Justice: Law and Religion in the Western Tradition* (Grand Rapids, MI: Wm. B. Eerdmans, 2005); Witte, *Law and Protestantism: The Legal Teachings of the Lutheran Reformation* (Cambridge: Cambridge University Press, 2002); John Witte, Jr. and Joel A. Nichols, *Religion and the American Constitutional Experiment*, 3rd edn (Boulder, CO and London: Westview Press, 2011).

the admonition of the first man and the first woman to "be fruitful and multiply" provides a foundation for the rights of spouses, parents, and children, a teaching amplified many times over in later biblical passages on the importance of marriage as an enduring "one flesh" union and the marital household as a symbol of God's love for his people. John Nagle's chapter underscores how humans are created as caretakers and cultivators of the natural order, with rights and duties to "dress and keep" the beauties of the Garden of Paradise even as they build toward the splendors of a Golden City in the eschaton.

Also fundamental to Christian understandings of human rights is the Mosaic law, which was based on a series of covenants between God and ancient Israel. David Novak's chapter uncovers the many reciprocal rights and duties embedded in the Mosaic law, and their amplification both by the Prophets of the Hebrew Bible and the Rabbis of the Talmud. He also works out a complex taxonomy of rights around the reciprocal covenants between and among God, the community, and individuals. This early Judaic understanding of rights inspired the later Church Fathers and medieval scholastics, but even more the sixteenth- and seventeenth-century Protestants. As my chapter herein elaborates, early modern Calvinists in particular used the Decalogue as an organizing framework for their understanding of fundamental religious and civil rights, and harvested from the Mosaic law and the New Testament a number of other basic public, private, penal, and procedural rights that would become axiomatic for the civil law and the common law traditions of the West.

The New Testament is heavily peppered with a number of strong texts on Christian freedom. "For freedom, Christ has set us free." "You were called to freedom." "Where the Spirit of the Lord is, there is freedom." "For the law of the Spirit of life in Christ has set [you] free from the law of sin and death." "You will know the truth, and the truth will make you free." "You will be free indeed." You all have been given "the law of freedom" in Christ, "the glorious liberty of the children of God." You must all now "live as free men" (Rom. 8:2, 21; John 8:32, 36; 1 Pet. 2:16). These passages, together with the many apostolic instructions on Christian ethics, have long inspired Christians to work out the meaning of Christian freedom within their church communities. Already in the early centuries after Christ, John McGuckin shows, the Greek Fathers and church councils worked out detailed canon laws for the codification and elaboration of Christian liberty, and these early Orthodox laws had parallels in the budding apostolic canons of the West. Throughout the second millennium, these strong biblical passages on liberty provided endless inspiration for Christian freedom fighters on both sides of the Atlantic.

The New Testament also calls for a much greater equality among humans than prevailed in either the Jewish or Graeco-Roman cultures of Christ's day. St. Paul's manifesto to the Galatians is the most famous statement: "[I]n Jesus Christ, you are all sons of God through faith. For as many of you as were baptized into Christ have put on Christ. There is neither Jew nor Greek, there is neither slave nor free, there is neither male nor female; for you are all one in Christ Jesus" (Gal. 3:26–8; see also Col. 3;11; Eph. 2:14–15). As David Aune's chapter demonstrates, this radical Christian message of human equality trumped conventional Graeco-Roman hierarchies based on nationality, social status, gender, and more. St. Peter amplified this call to equality with his admonition that all are called to be prophets, priests, and kings: "You are a chosen race, a royal priesthood, a holy nation, God's own people" (1 Pet. 2:9; cf. Rev. 5:10, 20:6). Though these New Testament passages were qualified by other biblical texts, they were critical to the gradual development of women's rights in the West, as Christy Green shows. Moreover, as Kent Greenawalt shows, these passages eventually became critical sources for the modern march to equal protection and treatment of all persons before the law, and to domestic and international guarantees of freedom of all from discrimination based on gender, race, culture, ethnicity, social or economic status.

The New Testament is even more radical in its call to treat the "least" members of society with love, respect, and dignity. Christ took pains to minister to the social outcasts of his day – Samaritans, tax collectors, prostitutes, thieves, traitors, lepers, the lame, the blind, the adulteress, and others. "He who is without sin, cast the first stone," he instructed a stunned crowd ready to stone an adulteress (John 8:7). "Today you will be with me in Paradise," he told the contrite thief nailed on the cross next to his (Luke 23:43). Even the duly convicted criminal deserves mercy and love was the point. Echoing the Hebrew Bible, Christ called his followers to feed and care for the poor, widows, and orphans in their midst, to visit and comfort the sick, imprisoned, and refugee. "Whatever you do for one of the least of these brothers of mine, you do for me," he told them (Matt. 25:40). Christ and St. Paul also called believers to share their wealth, to shore up those in need, to give up their extra clothes and belongings even to their creditors. They furthermore called believers to "love their enemies," to give them food and water, to turn their cheeks to those who strike them, to forgo lawsuits, vengeance, and retributive measures, to be peacemakers

in expression of the radical demands of Christian discipleship (Matt.
5:21–6; Rom. 12:9–21). Many Christians over the centuries – monks and
nuns, ascetics and Anabaptists, missionaries and peacemakers and various others – have sought live out these Christian ideals, often in intensely
Christian communities. Desmond Tutu and Robert Seiple in their chapters see in these biblical passages and historical exemplars, strong foundations for the rights of the poor and needy in society and the correlative
duties of all to support and protect them as they have means.

Finally, the New Testament calls Christians to "render to Caesar the
things that are Caesar's and to God the things that are God's" (Matt.
22:21) and reminds them that God has appointed "two swords" (Luke
22:38) to rule this life, the spiritual and the temporal. Christians are called
to "remain separate" from "worldly temptations" to be "in the world, but
not of it," and not "conformed" to its secular ways. For Christians are, at
heart, "strangers and foreigners on the earth"; their "true citizenship is
in heaven" (Rom. 12:2; 2 Cor. 6:14–18; Col. 3:1; Phil. 3:20). The Bible also
speaks frequently about building and rebuilding "walls" to foster separation. In the Hebrew Bible, these walls separated the City of Jerusalem
from the outside world, and the temple and its priests from the commons
and its people.[7] In the New Testament, St. Paul spoke literally of a "wall of
separation" interposed by the law of God (Eph. 2:14). These passages and
others have inspired Christians over the centuries to develop dualistic theories of religion and politics, church and state – two ways, two cities, two
powers, two swords, two kingdoms, two institutions, two realms. Today
such images, Jeremy Gunn and Rick Garnett show, are captured in constitutional rights of religious individuals and groups and constitutional
injunctions of separation of church and state.

While the Bible provided ample inspiration for the later development
of rights in the West, classical Roman law provided ample illustration of
what rights actually looked like in a sophisticated legal system. As Charles
Donahue's chapter herein shows, Roman jurists, both before and after the
Christianization of the Roman Empire in the fourth century, used the
Latin term "ius" to identify a "right" in both its objective and subjective
senses. (*Ius* also meant law or legal order more generally.) The objective
sense of *ius* – to be in proper order, to perform what is right and required,
"to give to each his due" (*ius suum cuiuque tribuere*) – dominated the
Roman law texts, both before and after the Christian conversion of the
Roman Empire in the fourth century. But these texts also occasionally

---

7 1 Kgs. 3:1; Jer. 1:18–19, 15:19–21; Ezek. 42:1; Neh. 3:1–32, 4:15–20, 12:27–43.

used *ius* subjectively, in the sense of a person "having a right" (*ius habere*) that could be defined, defended, and vindicated. Many of the subjective rights recognized at classical Roman law involved private property: the right to own or co-own property, the right to possess, lease, or use property, the right to build or prevent building on one's land, the right to gain access to water, the right to be free from interference with or invasion of one's property, the right or capacity to alienate property, the right to bury one's dead, and more. Several texts dealt with personal rights: the rights of testators and heirs, the rights of patrons and guardians, the rights of fathers and mothers over children, the rights of masters over slaves. Other texts dealt with public rights: the right of an official to punish or deal with his subjects in a certain way, the right to delegate power, the right to appoint and supervise lower officials. Others dealt with procedural rights in criminal and civil cases.

The classical Roman law also occasionally referred to subjective rights using the Latin term "libertas," which roughly translates as liberty, freedom, privilege, or independence. At its most basic level, *libertas* was, as Justinian put it, "the natural ability [*facultas*] to do anything one pleases, unless it is prohibited by force or law."[8] The nature and limits of one's *libertas* at Roman law turned in substantial part on one's status in Roman society. Men had more *libertas* than women, married women more than concubines, adults more than children, freemen more than slaves, and so on. But each person at Roman law had a basic *libertas* inherent in his or her social status. This included a basic right to be free from subjection or undue restraint from others who had no right (*ius*) to or possessory claim (*dominium*) over them. Thus the wife had *libertas* from sexual relations with all others besides her husband. The child had *libertas* from the direction of all others save the paterfamilias or his delegates. Even the slave had *libertas* from the discipline of others besides his or her master.

Some *libertas* interests recognized at Roman law were cast more generally, and were not necessarily conditioned on the correlative duties of others. A good example was the freedom of religion guaranteed to Christians and others under the Edict of Milan (313) passed by Emperor Constantine. This included "the freedom [*libertas*] to follow whatever religion each one wished"; "a public and free liberty to practice their religion or cult"; and a "free capacity" (*facultas*) to follow their own religion and worship as "befits the peacefulness of our times."[9]

---

[8] Institutes, I.III.

[9] Lactantius, *De Mortibus Persecutorum [c. 315]*, 48.2–12, ed. and trans. J. L. Creed (Oxford: Oxford University Press, 1984), 71–3.

Echoes of both *ius* and *libertas* recurred occasionally in later Frankish and Anglo-Saxon texts. By the late ninth and early tenth centuries, Anglo-Saxon texts variously translated these terms as "ryhtes," "rihtes," and "rihta(e)."[10] The careful Roman law differentiation of objective and subjective senses of right, however, seems to have been lost in the last centuries of the first millennium CE – though a systematic study of the possible rights talk of the Germanic texts of this period is apparently still a desideratum. And what is also apparently still needed is a close study (at least in a Romance language) of the possible rights talk of Muslim and Jewish scholars in this same period. After all both Muslim and Jewish scholars had access to the ancient Roman law texts that were lost in the West after the sixth century, and both worked out a refined theological jurisprudence in the eighth through tenth centuries CE

HUMAN RIGHTS AND ROMAN CATHOLICISM

The rediscovery of the ancient texts of Roman law in the late eleventh and twelfth centuries helped to trigger a renaissance of subjective rights talk in the West. As R. H. Helmholz's chapter shows, medieval church lawyers, called canonists, differentiated all manner of rights (*iura*) and liberties (*libertates*). They grounded these rights and liberties in the law of nature (*lex naturae*) or natural law (*ius naturale*), and associated them variously with a power (*facultas*) inhering in rational human nature and with the property (*dominium*) of a person or the power (*potestas*) of an office of authority (*officium*). The early canonists repeated and glossed many of the subjective rights and liberties set out in the Roman law – especially the public rights and powers of rulers, the private rights and liberties of property, and what the great canonist Gratian in *c.* 1140 called the "rights of liberty" (*iura libertatis*) enjoyed by persons of various stations in life and offices of authority.[11] They also began to weave these early Roman law texts into a whole complex latticework of what we now call rights, freedoms, powers, immunities, protections, and capacities for different groups and persons.

This renaissance and expansion of Western rights talk was part and product of the Papal Revolution fought in the name of "freedom of the

[10] *OED*, s.v. "right"; Alfred Kiralfky, "Law and Right in English Legal History," in *La formazione storica de diritto moderno in Europa* (Florence: Leo S. Olschki, 1977), III:1069–86.

[11] C. 16, q. 3, dictum post c. 15, quoted in Brian Tierney, *The Idea of Natural Rights: Studies on Natural Rights, Natural Law, and Church Law, 1150–1625* (Grand Rapids, MI: Wm. B. Eerdmans, 1997), 57.

church" (*libertas ecclesiae*). In the later eleventh and twelfth centuries, Pope Gregory VII (1073–85) and his successors led the Catholic clergy in throwing off their royal and civil rulers and establishing the church as an autonomous legal and political corporation within Western Christendom. For the first time, the church successfully claimed jurisdiction over such persons as clerics, pilgrims, students, Jews, and Muslims and over such subjects as doctrine and liturgy; ecclesiastical property, polity, and patronage; marriage and family relations; education, charity, and inheritance; oral promises, oaths, and various contracts; and all manner of moral and ideological crimes. The church predicated these jurisdictional claims in part on Christ's famous delegation of the keys to St. Peter (Matt. 16:18) – a key of knowledge to discern God's word and will, and a key of power to implement and enforce that word and will by law. The church also predicated these new claims on its traditional authority over the form and function of the Christian sacraments. By the fifteenth century, the church had gathered around the seven sacraments whole systems of canon law rules that prevailed throughout the West.

The medieval canon law was based, in part, on the concept of individual and corporate rights (*iura*, the plural of *ius*). Most important to the medieval canonists were the rights needed to protect the "freedom of the church" from the secular authorities. The canonists thus delineated in some detail the rights of the church to make its own laws, to maintain its own courts, to define its own doctrines and liturgies, to appoint, support, discipline, and remove its own clergy. They stipulated the exemptions of church property from civil taxation and takings, and the right of the clergy to control and use church property without interference or encumbrance from secular authorities. They also guaranteed the immunity of the clergy from civil prosecution, military service, and compulsory testimony, and the rights of church entities like parishes, monasteries, charities, and guilds to form and dissolve, to accept and reject members, and to establish order and discipline. These early formulations of religious group rights against secular authorities would become axiomatic for the later Western tradition.

In the twelfth and thirteenth centuries, the canon law gradually refined the internal rights structure of the church and its offices and members as well. It defined the rights of church councils and synods to participate in the election and discipline of bishops, abbots, and other clergy. It defined the rights of the lower clergy vis-à-vis their superiors. It defined the rights of the laity to worship, evangelize, maintain religious symbols, participate in the sacraments, travel on religious pilgrimages, and educate their

children. It defined the rights of the poor, widows, and needy to seek sol-
ace, succor, and sanctuary within the church. It defined the rights of husbands and wives, parents and children, masters and servants within the
household. The canon law even defined the (truncated) rights that Jews,
Muslims, and heretics had in Christian society. These medieval canon law
rights were enforced by a hierarchy of church courts and other administrative offices, each with distinct rules of litigation, evidence, and judgment,
and with rights of ultimate appeal to Rome.

These medieval rights formulations were often narrowly defined in
scope and severely limited in application. Medieval Christendom was
hardly a liberal democracy or a modern social welfare state – as the blood
of too many martyrs can attest. But a great number of basic public, private, penal, and procedural rights came to be formed in this period. And
these basic rights formulations were gradually made more widely applicable to others and deepened theoretically through the work of such
scholars as William of Ockham (*c.* 1285–*c.* 1349), John Wycliff (d. 1384),
Conrad Summenhart (1465–1511), Richard Fitzralph (d. 1360), Jean Gerson
(1363–1429), Bartolomé de las Casas (1484–1566), Francisco de Vitoria (*c.*
1486–1546), Fernando Vázquez (n.d.), Francisco Suarez (1548–1617), and
others. Particularly the formulations of the Spanish neo-scholastics in
the sixteenth century, most of them Dominicans, were of monumental
importance to the evolution and expansion of Western rights talk. Early
modern Catholic, Protestant, and Enlightenment jurists and philosophers
alike drew on these neo-scholastic sources in developing their rights formulations. Vitoria was particularly prescient in pressing for the rights of
Indians and other indigenous peoples as well as the rights of soldiers and
prisoners of war – both critical topics of international human rights law.
Vitoria and Suarez also worked out an intricate natural law and natural
rights theory of the family based on Aristotelian and Thomistic principles;
Don Browning shows the enduring importance of this natural theory
of the family for the development of the 1948 Universal Declaration of
Human Rights.

The medieval canon law formulations of rights and liberties had some
parallels in medieval common law of England and the civil law of the
Continent. Particularly notable sources of rights and liberties were the
thousands of treaties, concordats, and charters that were issued from
the eleventh to the sixteenth centuries by various authorities in Western
Europe. These were often detailed, and sometimes very flowery, statements
of the rights and liberties to be enjoyed by various groups of clergy, nobles,
barons, knights, municipal councils, citizens, universities, monasteries,

and other corporate entities. A famous example was the Magna Carta (1215), the great charter issued by the English Crown at the behest of the church and barons of England. The Magna Carta guaranteed that "the Church of England shall be free [*libera*] and shall have all her whole rights [*iura*] and liberties [*libertates*] inviolable" and that all "free-men" (*liberis hominibus*) were to enjoy their various "liberties" (*libertates*). These guarantees included sundry rights to property, marriage, and inheritance, to freedom from undue military service, and to freedom to pay one's debts and taxes from the property of one's own choosing. The Magna Carta also set out various rights and powers of towns and of local justices and their tribunals, various rights and prerogatives of the king and of the royal courts, and various procedural rights in these courts (including the right to jury trial).[12] These medieval charters of rights became important prototypes on which early modern democratic revolutionaries, both Catholic and Protestant, would call to justify their revolt against tyrannical authorities.

It was, in part, the perceived excesses of the sixteenth-century Protestant Reformation that closed the door to the Catholic Church's own secular elaboration of this refined rights regime. The Council of Trent (1545–63) confirmed, with some modifications, the internal rights structure of the canon law, and these formulations were elaborated in the writings of Spanish and Portuguese neo-scholastics. But the church left it largely to non-church bodies and non-Catholic believers to draw out the secular implications of the medieval human rights tradition. The Catholic Church largely tolerated Protestant and humanist rights efforts in the later sixteenth century and beyond, which built on biblical and canon law foundations. The church grew increasingly intolerant, however, of the rights theories and political attacks of the Western Enlightenment.

Part of the Enlightenment attack was political, as Catholic civil authorities, like their Protestant counterparts, made ever-deeper cuts into the authority of the canon law and church courts, eventually isolating national Catholic churches from Rome and dissolving any lingering aspiration for the restoration of a universal Western Christendom. Part of the attack was philosophical, as Enlightenment philosophers advocated material and scientific theories of law, politics, and society in place of traditional biblical and theological teachings, and pressed for secular control of the universities and lower schools long chartered and controlled by the church. Part of the attack was sociological, as various groups protested the heavy

---

[12] *The Statutes at Large of England and of Great Britain from the Magna Carta to the Union of the Kingdoms of Great Britain and Ireland*, 20 vols. (London: G. Eyre and J. Strahan, 1811), I:1.

Catholic tone of public life in Catholic lands, and the active involvement of Catholic clerics and monastics in marriage, education, charity, and other vital social services. Part of the attack was economic, as both public and private parties encroached ever more heavily on the church's vast lands, endowments, banks, and chartered companies. During the French Revolution in the 1780s and 1790s, these attacks reached genocidal proportions – with more than 30,000 priests and untold tens of thousands of Catholic laity killed or exiled from France, massive numbers of church properties defaced, destroyed, or confiscated, and much priceless religious art, literature, and statuary stolen or destroyed. These Enlightenment attacks on the church, which were spread from France to other lands by Napoleon's military campaigns, were codified in sweeping legal reforms such as the Frederician Code (1791) of Prussia, the Code Napoleon (1804) of France, and many later ordinances that reflected the new Enlightenment ideology.

For much of the nineteenth century, the Catholic leadership pronounced anathema on this radical Enlightenment project and its new ideas of liberty, democracy, and separation of church and state – and called the faithful back to the ideals of a unified Christendom under the moral and legal authority of the papacy. The blistering Syllabus of Errors of 1864 was only the most famous of a whole series of such bitter denunciations. But beginning with Pope Leo XIII in his 1879 encyclical *Aeterni Patris*, and escalating in the twentieth century, the Catholic Church leadership eventually found a way to reconcile its cardinal theological teachings with modern theories of democracy, human rights, and separation of church and state – and, indeed, to become a champion of these theories around the world. The driving intellectual engine of this movement was the church's reconstruction of the philosophical wisdom of Thomas Aquinas (1225–74) and the jurisprudential sophistication of the medieval canonists. The rehabilitation and universalization of Catholic rights talk was a critical part of this new Catholic social teachings movement, as Bryan Hehir's chapter shows.

This neo-Thomist movement culminated in the work of the Second Vatican Council (1962–5). Among many other things, Vatican II transformed the Catholic Church's theological attitude toward human rights and democracy. In a series of sweeping new doctrinal statements – from Pope John XXIII's *Mater et Magistra* (1961) onward – the church came to endorse many of the very same human rights and democratic principles that it had spurned a century before. First, the church endorsed human rights and liberties – not only in the internal, canon law context but also now in a global, secular law context. Every person, the church taught in its famous decree, *Dignitatis Humanae*, is created by God with "dignity, intelligence and free will ... and has rights flowing directly and simultaneously from his very nature." Such rights include the right to life and adequate standards of living, to moral and cultural values, to religious activities, to assembly and association, to marriage and family life, and to various social, political, and economic benefits and opportunities. The church emphasized the religious rights of conscience, worship, assembly, and education, calling them the "first rights" of any civic order. The church also stressed the need to balance individual and associational rights, particularly those involving the church, family, and school. Governments everywhere were encouraged to create conditions conducive to the realization and protection of these "inviolable rights" and encouraged to root out every type of discrimination, whether social or cultural, whether based on sex, race, color, social distinction, language, or religion. Second, as a corollary, the church advocated limited constitutional government, disestablishment of religion, and the separation of church and state. The vast pluralism of religions and cultures, and the inherent dangers in state endorsement of any religion, in the church's view, rendered mandatory such democratic forms of government.

Vatican II and its progeny transformed not only the theological attitude but also the social actions of the Catholic Church respecting human rights and democracy. After Vatican II, Bryan Hehir emphasizes, the church was less centralized and more socially active. Local bishops and clergy were given greater autonomy and incentive to participate in local and national affairs, to bring the church's new doctrines to bear on matters political and cultural. Particularly in North America and Europe, bishops and bishops' conferences became active in cultivating and advocating a variety of political and legal reforms. Likewise, in Latin America, the rise of liberation theologies and base communities helped to translate many of the enduring and evolving rights perspectives of the church into intensely active social and political programs. The Catholic Church was thereby transformed from a passive accomplice in authoritarian regimes to a powerful advocate of democratic and human rights reform. The Catholic Church has been a critical force in the new wave of political democratization that has been breaking over the world since the early 1970s – both through the announcements and interventions of the papal see, and through the efforts of its local clergy. New democratic and human rights movements in Brazil, Chile, Central America, the Philippines, South Korea, Poland, Hungary, the Czech Republic, Ukraine, and elsewhere owe much of their inspiration to the teaching and activity of the Catholic Church.

The Catholic Church has thus come full circle. The Catholic Church led the first human rights movement of the West at the opening of the second millennium. It is leading the universal church's next human rights movement of the world in this opening of the third millennium – equipped with a refined theology and law of human rights and more than a billion members worldwide. The Catholic Church offers a unique combination of local and global, confessional and universal human rights strategies. Within the internal forum and the canon law, the church has a distinctly Catholic human rights framework that protects especially the second generation rights of education, charity, and health care within a sacramental and sacerdotal context. Within the external forum of the world and its secular law, however, the church has a decidedly universal human rights framework that advocates especially first generation civil and political rights for all.

HUMAN RIGHTS AND PROTESTANTISM

While "Freedom of the Church" was the manifesto of the twelfth-century Papal Revolution, "Freedom of the Christian" was the manifesto of the sixteenth-century Protestant Reformation. Martin Luther (1483–1546), Thomas Cranmer (1489–1556), Menno Simons (1496–1561), John Calvin (1509–64), and other leading sixteenth-century reformers all began their movements with a call for freedom from the medieval Catholic Church – freedom of the individual conscience from intrusive canon laws and clerical controls, freedom of political officials from ecclesiastical power and privileges, freedom of the local clergy from central papal rule and oppressive princely controls. "Freedom of the Christian" became the rallying cry of the early Reformation. It drove theologians and jurists, clergy and laity, princes and peasants alike to denounce canon laws and ecclesiastical authorities with unprecedented alacrity, and to urge radical constitutional reforms in the name of human rights. The church's canon law books were burned. Church courts were closed. Monastic institutions were confiscated. Endowed benefices were dissolved. Church lands were seized. Clerical privileges were stripped. Mandatory celibacy was suspended. Indulgence trafficking was condemned. Annates to Rome were outlawed. Ties to the pope were severed. Appeals to the papal rota were barred. Each nation, each church, and each Christian was to be free.

Left in such raw and radical forms, this early Protestant call for freedom was a recipe for lawlessness and license, as Luther learned the hard way during the Peasants' Revolt of 1525. Luther and other Protestants soon came to realize that structures of law and authority were essential to protecting order and peace, even as guarantees of liberties and rights were essential to preserving the message and momentum of the Reformation. The challenge for early Protestants was to strike new balances between authority and liberty, order and rights on the strength of cardinal biblical teachings.

One important Protestant contribution to Western rights talk, which was common to early Lutherans, Calvinists, Anglicans, and Anabaptists, was to comb through the Bible in order to redefine the nature and authority of the family, the church, and the state vis-à-vis each other and their constituents. Most Protestant Reformers regarded these three institutions of family, church, and state as fundamental orders of creation, equal before God and each other, and vested with certain natural rights and duties that the other authorities could not trespass. To define these respective offices clearly not only served to check the natural appetite of the *paterfamilias*, *patertheologicus*, and *paterpoliticus* for tyranny and abuse. It also helped to clarify the rights and liberties of those subject to their authority, and to specify the grounds on which they could protest or disobey.

A second major contribution was the Protestant Reformers' habit of grounding rights in the duties of the Decalogue and other biblical moral teachings. The First Table of the Decalogue prescribes duties of love that each person owes to God – to honor God and God's name, to observe the Sabbath day and to worship, to avoid false gods and false swearing. The Second Table prescribes duties of love that each person owes to neighbors – to honor one's parents and other authorities, not to kill, not to commit adultery, not to steal, not to bear false witness, not to covet. The Reformers cast the person's duties toward God as a set of rights that others could not obstruct – the right to religious exercise: the right to honor God and God's name, the right to rest and worship on one's Sabbath, the right to be free from false gods and false oaths. They cast a person's duties toward a neighbor, in turn, as the neighbor's right to have that duty discharged. One person's duties not to kill, to commit adultery, to steal, or to bear false witness thus give rise to another person's rights to life, property, fidelity, and reputation. Nick Wolterstorff's chapter shows how this understanding of duty-based rights still persists in many Protestant circles.

A third major Protestant contribution to Western rights talk was its effort to develop new understandings of the relationship of church and state. The Protestant Reformation permanently broke the unity of Western Christendom under central papal rule, and thereby laid the foundations for the modern constitutional system of confessional pluralism.

The Lutheran Reformation territorialized the faith through the principle of *cuius regio, eius religio* ("whose realm, his religion") established by the Peace of Augsburg (1555). Under this principle, princes or city councils were authorized to prescribe the appropriate forms of Evangelical or Catholic doctrine, liturgy, and education for their polities – with religious dissenters granted the right to worship privately in their homes or to emigrate peaceably from the polity. After decades of bitter civil war, the Peace of Westphalia (1648) extended this privilege to Reformed Calvinists as well, rendering Germany and beyond a veritable honeycomb of religious plurality for the next two centuries – though a community still decidedly inhospitable to Jews, Muslims, and Orthodox Christians.

The Anglican Reformation nationalized the faith through the famous Supremacy Acts and the Act of Uniformity (1559) of the Church and Commonwealth of England. Citizens of the Commonwealth were required to be communicants of the Church of England, subject to the final ecclesiastical and political authority of the Monarch. The Toleration Act (1689) extended a modicum of rights to some Protestant dissenters. But it was not until the Jewish and Catholic Emancipation Acts of 1829 and 1833 that the national identity of the Church and Commonwealth of England was finally broken.

The Anabaptist Reformation communalized the faith by introducing what Menno Simons once called the *Scheidingsmaurer* – the wall of separation between the redeemed realm of religion and the fallen realm of the world. Anabaptist religious communities were ascetically withdrawn from the world into small, self-sufficient, intensely democratic communities, governed internally by biblical principles of discipleship, simplicity, charity, and Christian obedience. When such communities grew too large or too divided, they deliberately colonized themselves, eventually spreading the Anabaptist communities from Russia to Ireland to the furthest frontiers of North America.

The Calvinist Reformation congregationalized the faith by introducing rule by a democratically elected consistory of pastors, elders, and deacons. In John Calvin's day, the Geneva consistory was still appointed and held broad personal and subject matter jurisdiction over all members of the city. By the seventeenth century, most Calvinist communities in Europe and North America reduced the consistory to an elected, representative system of government within each church. These consistories featured separation among the offices of preaching, discipline, and charity, and a fluid, dialogical form of religious polity and policing centered around collective worship and the congregational meeting.

A fourth major Protestant contribution to the Western rights talk was its new emphasis on the role of the individual believer in the economy of salvation. The Protestant Reformation did not invent the individual, as too many exuberant commentators still maintain. But sixteenth-century Protestant reformers, more than their Catholic contemporaries, gave new emphasis to the (religious) rights and liberties of individuals at both religious law and civil law. This new emphasis on the individual was true even in the more intensely communitarian traditions of Anglicanism and Anabaptism. The Anglican *Book of Common Prayer* was designed, in Thomas Cranmer's words, as a "textbook of liberty." The daily office of the lectionary, together with the vernacular Bible, encouraged the exercise of private devotion outside the church. The choices among liturgical rites and prayers within the Prayer Book encouraged the exercise of at least some modest clerical innovation within the church, with such opportunities for variation and innovation increasing with the 1662 edition of the Prayer Book, and even more with the gradual development of national Anglican churches in different parts of the Commonwealth.

The Anabaptist doctrine of adult baptism gave new emphasis to a voluntarist understanding of religion, as opposed to conventional notions of a birthright or predestined faith. The adult individual was now called to make a conscientious choice to accept the faith – metaphorically, to scale the wall of separation between the fallen world and the realm of religion to come within the perfection of Christ. Later Free Church followers converted this cardinal image into a powerful platform of liberty of conscience, free exercise of religion, and separation of church and state – not only for Christians but eventually for all peaceable believers. Their views had a great influence on the formation of constitutional protections of religious liberty in eighteenth- and nineteenth-century North America. And it would come to new expression in twentieth-century international human rights instruments that guaranteed the right freely to choose and change one's religion.

The Lutheran and Calvinist branches of the Reformation laid the anthropological basis for an even more expansive theory and law of rights. Classic Protestant theology teaches that a person is both saint and sinner. On the one hand, a person is created in the image of God and justified by faith in God. The person is called to a distinct vocation, which stands equal in dignity and sanctity to all others. The person is prophet, priest, and king and responsible to exhort, minister, and rule in the community. Every person, therefore, stands equal before God and before his or her neighbor. Every person is vested with a natural liberty to live, to believe, to serve God and neighbor. Every person is entitled to the vernacular Scripture, to education, to work in a vocation. On the other hand, the person is sinful and prone to evil and egoism. He needs the restraint of the law to deter him from evil and to drive him to repentance. He needs the association of others to exhort, minister, and rule him with law and with love. Every person, therefore, is inherently a communal creature. Every person belongs to a family, a church, a political community.

These social institutions of family, church, and state, Protestants believe, are divine in origin and human in organization. They are created by God and governed by godly ordinances. They stand equal before God and are called to discharge distinctive godly functions in the community. The family is called to rear and nurture children, to educate and discipline them, to exemplify love and cooperation. The church is called to preach the word, administer the sacraments, educate the young, aid the needy. The state is called to protect order, punish crime, promote community. Though divine in origin, these institutions are formed through human covenants. Such covenants confirm the divine functions, the created offices, of these institutions. Such covenants also organize these offices so that they are protected from the sinful excesses of officials who occupy them. Family, church, and state are thus organized as public and transparent institutions, accessible and accountable to each other and to their members. Particularly the church is to be organized as a democratic congregational polity, with a separation of ecclesiastical powers among pastors, elders, and deacons, election of officers to limited tenures of office, and ready participation of the congregation in the life and leadership of the church.

Protestant groups in Europe and America cast these theological doctrines into democratic forms designed to protect human rights. Protestant doctrines of the person and society were cast into democratic social forms. Since all persons stand equal before God, they must stand equal before God's political agents in the state. Since God has vested all persons with natural liberties of life and belief, the state must ensure them of similar civil liberties. Since God has called all persons to be prophets, priests, and kings, the state must protect their natural freedoms to speak, to preach, and to rule in the community. Since God has created persons as social creatures, the state must promote and protect a plurality of social institutions, particularly the church and the family. Protestant doctrines of sin were cast into democratic political forms. The political office must be protected against the sinfulness of the political official. Political power, like ecclesiastical power, must be distributed among self-checking executive, legislative, and judicial branches. Officials must be elected to limited terms of office. Laws must be clearly codified, and discretion closely guarded. If officials abuse their office, they must be disobeyed; if they persist in their abuse, they must be removed, even if by force.

These Protestant teachings helped to inspire many of the early modern revolutions fought in the name of human rights and democracy. They were the driving ideological forces behind the revolts of the French Huguenots, Dutch Pietists, and Scottish Presbyterians against their monarchical oppressors in the later sixteenth and seventeenth centuries. They were critical weapons in the arsenal of the revolutionaries in England, America, and even France. They were important sources of the great age of democratic construction in later eighteenth- and nineteenth-century America and Western Europe. In the twentieth century, Protestant ideas of human rights and democracy helped to drive the constitutional reformation of Europe in the post-war period, and some of the human rights and democratic movements against colonial autocracy in Africa.

The role of Protestant missionaries in nineteenth- and twentieth-century Africa is particularly notable. Protestant mission churches sometimes served as "zones of liberty" in colonial African society.[13] They were organized democratically, with ecclesiastical authority distributed among pastors, elders, deacons, and teachers. Communicant members elected the clergy to their offices and had ready access to those who were elected. Churches served as centers of poor relief, education, health care, and social welfare in the community. Churches catalyzed the formation of voluntary associations, like youth groups, women's groups, and business associations. Churches provided a sanctuary for political dissidents and a sanction for movements of political reform and renewal. By so doing, churches provided both models of democracy and vindicators of rights in parts in Africa.

Christian teachings further helped to "lower" political officials and to "elevate" political subjects in African cultures. Many traditional African religions, as Desmond Tutu's chapter references, "sacralized" political rulers, viewing them not only as preeminent authorities in the present but also preeminent interpreters of the past, of an ancestral tradition that had to be obeyed. Christianity "desacralized" politics by showing that all human authorities are subordinate to and empowered by divine authority.

---

[13] The phrase is from Richard Joseph, "The Christian Churches and Democracy in Contemporary Africa," in John Witte, Jr., ed., *Christianity and Democracy in Global Context* (Boulder, CO and London: Westview Press, 1993), 231–48.

Christianity also "dignified" political subjects by giving each person access to the ancestral wisdom of the vernacular Scripture. The Scripture liberated Africans both from their political rulers and from their Christian missionaries. It gave the Africans a common point of departure and reference to create a new belief system that combined Scripture with native traditions and a new political system that combined Christian political doctrines with indigenous lore.

These cardinal Protestant teachings and practices have much to offer to the regime of human rights in the twenty-first century, as Nicholas Wolterstorff's chapter outlines. Protestant theology avoids the reductionist extremes of both libertarianism that sacrifices the community for the individual and totalitarianism that sacrifices the individual for the community. It avoids the limitless expansion of human rights claims by grounding these norms in the creation order, divine callings, and covenant relationships. And it avoids uncritical adoption of human rights by judging their "civil, theological, and educational uses" in the lives of both individuals and communities. On this foundation, Protestant theology strikes unique balances between liberty and responsibility, dignity and depravity, individuality and community, politics and pluralism.

HUMAN RIGHTS AND THE ORTHODOX TRADITION

The Orthodox churches, rooted in Greek Christianity and the Byzantine Empire, ground their human rights theology less in the dignity of the person and more in the integrity of the natural law and the liberty of the canonical Christian community. To be sure, several fourth-century Greek Fathers, notably Gregory of Nyssa (335–94) and John Chrysostom (347–407), sounded familiar Western themes of liberty of conscience, human dignity, and free exercise of religion. Such sentiments have echoed in the Orthodox tradition ever since – particularly in the modern transplanted Orthodox communities of Western Europe and North America.

What has rendered the historical Orthodox human rights understanding unique, however, is its distinct natural law foundations. Already the early Greek Orthodox Fathers emphasized that God has written His natural law on the hearts of all persons and rewritten it on the pages of Scripture. This natural law, which finds its most sublime source and summary in the Ten Commandments, prescribes a series of duties that each person owes to others and to God – not to kill, not to steal, not to bear false witness, not to swear falsely, not to serve other gods, and others. Humanity's fall into sin has rendered adherence to such moral duties imperative to the survival of the human community. God has called church and state alike to assume responsibility for enforcing by law those moral duties that are essential to such survival.

According to classic Orthodox theology, human rights are the reciprocals of these divinely ordained moral duties. One person's moral duties not to kill, to steal, or to bear false witness give rise to another person's rights to life, property, and dignity. A person's moral duties not to serve other gods or to swear falsely give rise to his right to serve the right god and to swear properly. For every moral duty taught by natural law there is a reciprocal moral right. On the strength of this ancient biblical ethic, Orthodox theologians endorse a three-tiered system of rights and duties: (1) a Christian or "evangelical" system of rights and duties, based upon the natural law principles of Scripture, which are enforced by the canon law and sacramental theology of the church; (2) a "common moral" system of rights and duties, based upon universal natural law principles accepted by rational persons in all times and places, which are enforced by moral agents within the community; and (3) a legal system of rights and duties, based upon the constitutional laws and social needs of the community, which are enforced by the positive laws of the state. The church is responsible not only to maintain the highest standards of moral right and duty among its subjects, but also to serve as a moral agent in the community, to cultivate an understanding of "common morality," and to admonish pastorally and prophetically those who violate this common morality.

Particularly during the long winter of Marxist-Leninist rule in the twentieth century, Orthodox churches throughout the world let their pastoral and prophetic voices be heard in endorsement of human rights and in condemnation of their violation. The World Congress of Orthodox Bishops (1978), for example, greeted the thirtieth anniversary of the United Nations Declaration of Rights with the call:

We urge all Orthodox Christians to mark this occasion with prayers for those whose human rights are being denied and/or violated; for those who are harassed and persecuted because of their religious beliefs, Orthodox and non-Orthodox alike, in many parts of the world; for those whose rightful demands and persistence are met with greater oppression and ignominy; and for those whose agony for justice, food, shelter, health care and education is accelerated with each passing day.[14]

---

[14] Statement by Standing Conference of Canonical Orthodox Bishops in the Americas, *Archdiocesan Archives* (Dec. 1978), quoted in Stanley Harakas, "Human Rights: An Eastern Orthodox Perspective," *Journal of Ecumenical Studies* 19 (1982): 13, 21.

In 1980, the 25th Clergy-Laity Congress of the Greek Orthodox Archdiocese of North and South America pronounced:

[H]uman rights consist of those conditions of life that allow us fully to develop and use our human qualities of intelligence and conscience to their fullest extent and to satisfy our spiritual, social, and political needs, including freedom of expression, freedom from fear, harassment, intimidation and discrimination, and freedom to participate in the function of government and to have the guarantee of the equal protection of the law.[15]

They further called upon "totalitarian and oppressive regimes to restore respect for the rights and dignity of the individual and to insure the free and unhindered exercise of these vital rights by all citizens, regardless of racial and ethnic origin, or political or religious espousal."[16] "All people," the Orthodox Congress later declared, "have the God-given right to be free from interference by government or others in (1) freely determining their faith by conscience, (2) freely associating and organizing with others for religious purposes, (3) expressing their religious beliefs in worship, teaching and practice, (4) pursuing the implications of their beliefs in the social and political community."[17]

The Orthodox churches also moved gradually toward a greater separation of church and state – though seemingly more out of political necessity than theological conviction. Since the time of the Byzantine Empire, the Orthodox Church had a closer relationship with the Christian state, through an arrangement known as *symphonia*. This concept was, as John McGuckin describes it herein, "a harmony of powers whose very juxtaposition delineated precise limits of power: to each their own, and from each their proper sphere of accountability ... as near an evocation of later subsidiarity theory as we might hope to find in antiquity." To be sure, in some areas and eras, this *symphonia* of church and state subjected the Orthodox Church to substantial state control over its polities and properties, and substantial restrictions on its religious ministry and prophecy. But this arrangement also gave the Orthodox clergy a strong and singular spiritual voice in civil society. It allowed the clergy to teach the community through Orthodox schools and monasteries, Orthodox literature and preaching, often supported by generous state patronage. It allowed them

---

[15] Minutes, Decisions, Resolutions and Statements of the 25th Clergy-Laity Congress of the Greek Orthodox Archdiocese of North and South America in Atlanta, Georgia (June 27 – July 5, 1980), 114–15, quoted in Harakas, "Human Rights," 26.

[16] Minutes, Decisions, Resolutions and Statements, quoted in Harakas, "Human Rights," 26.

[17] Quoted in Alexander F. C. Webster, *The Price of Prophecy: Orthodox Churches on Peace, Freedom, and Security* (Grand Rapids, MI: Wm. B. Eerdmans, 1995), 148.

to nurture the community through the power and pathos of the Orthodox liturgy, icons, artwork, prayers, and music. It allowed them to advise officials on the moral dimensions of positive law.

This symbiotic relationship between church and state worked well enough when state authorities were themselves Orthodox, or at least openly supportive of Orthodoxy. Such was the case for much of the history of Russia, and other parts of Central Eurasia before the Bolshevik Revolution of 1917. This relationship did not work well, however, when political authorities had no Orthodox allegiances. Such was the case for most other Orthodox communities after the fifteenth century. With the Islamic conquest of the Byzantine Empire in the 1450s, and the expansion of the Ottoman Empire thereafter, the Orthodox Church could no longer readily depend upon the state for protection and support. Often consigned to restricted millets, local Orthodox communities turned to an increasingly stretched Patriarchate of Constantinople for their principal support. After the great wars of nationalist liberation in Greece, Bulgaria, Romania, and the Balkans in the eighteenth and nineteenth centuries, the depleted Patriarchate of Constantinople finally broke up the church into autocephalous national churches, which cooperated with local governments as best they could. Many of these new Orthodox churches saw separation from state control and state support as the safest policy, if not the best theology. Similarly, after the great emigrations of Orthodox believers to North America at the turn of the twentieth century, the transplanted autocephalous Orthodox communities were forced to survive with little support from local state officials. Here, too, separation of church and state became an expedient principle of ecclesiastical living. And similarly, after the Bolshevik Revolution of 1917 and the gradual Sovietization of Eastern Europe, the church came to endorse the Marxist-Leninist doctrine of separation of church and state, mostly out of the sheer need to survive. While individual theologians have sought to draw from these disparate experiences of Orthodox churches a new theology of separatism, no such systematic theory seems to have yet captured the field.

Today, the Orthodox Church's commitment to human rights and democratic principles is being tested more severely than ever before – particularly in Russia and Eastern Europe. The remarkable democratic revolution of the Soviet bloc following the lead of Mikhail Gorbachev brought not only new liberty to these long closed societies, but also new license. These societies have come to face moral degradation, economic dislocation, and human suffering of massive proportions. They have faced the renewal of ancient animosities among religious and cultural rivals previously kept at bay by the Communist Party. They have faced an enormous influx of foreigners – religious, cultural, and economic – offering beliefs and practices that are radically different from those held by the fallen socialist state and the struggling Orthodox churches.

The leadership of the Orthodox Church of late, while continuing to endorse democratic and human rights principles, has condemned bitterly the corrosive libertarian values that often accompany these principles. Local Orthodox clerics have often acquiesced in, if not prompted, provincial and local officials in the Russian Federation to crack down on many foreign traditions and practices. And they have stood behind the more strident policies of favoritism, if not reestablishment of Russian Orthodoxy in Russia. Where such a critical stand on human rights will lead the Orthodox Church is very much an open question. Orthodoxy has a strong, millennium-old foundation for an alternative Christian theology of duty-based rights and rights-based social action that holds great intellectual and institutional promise. Moreover, the Orthodox Church has immense spiritual resources, besides this, whose implications for human rights are only now beginning to be seen. These spiritual resources lie, in part, in Orthodox worship – the passion of the liturgy, the pathos of the icons, the power of spiritual silence. They lie, in part, in Orthodox church life – the distinct balancing between hierarchy and congregationalism through autocephaly, between uniform worship and liturgical freedom through alternative vernacular rites, between community and individuality through a Trinitarian communalism, centered on the parish, on the extended family, on the wizened grandmother (the "babushka" in Russia). And these spiritual resources lie, in part, in the massive martyrdom of millions of Orthodox faithful in the last century – whether suffered by Russian Orthodox under the Communist Party, by Greek and Armenian Orthodox under Turkish and Iranian radicals, by Middle Eastern Copts at the hands of various religious extremists, or by North African Orthodox under all manner of fascist autocrats.

These deep spiritual resources of the Orthodox Church have no exact parallels in Catholicism and Protestantism. How the Orthodox Church can apply them to the nurture of human rights is one of the great challenges, and opportunities, of this new century. It would be wise to hear what an ancient church, newly charred and chastened by decades of oppression and martyrdom, considers essential to the regime of religious rights. It would be enlightening to watch how ancient Orthodox communities, still largely centered on the parish and the family, will reconstruct social and economic rights. It would be prudent to see whether a culture, more prone to beautifying than to analyzing, might transform our understanding of cultural rights. It would be instructive to listen how a tradition, that still celebrates spiritual silence as its highest virtue, might recast the meaning of freedom of speech and expression. And it would be illuminating to feel how a people, that has long cherished and celebrated the role of the woman – the wizened babushka of the home, the faithful remnant in the parish pews, the living icon of the Assumption of the Mother of God – might elaborate the meaning of women's rights.

CONCLUDING REFLECTIONS

Rights are so commonplace today that the term is in danger of becoming cliché. Rights talk has become a dominant mode of political, legal, and moral discourse in the modern West, and rights protections and violations have become increasingly important issues in international relations and diplomacy. Most nation-states now have detailed bills or recitations of rights in their constitutions, statutes, and cases. The United Nations and various other groups of nation-states have detailed catalogues of rights set out in treaties, declarations, conventions, and covenants. Many Christian denominations and ecumenical groups, alongside other religious groups, have their own declarations and statements on rights as well. Thousands of governmental, intergovernmental, and non-governmental organizations are now dedicated to the defense of rights around the world, including a large number of Christian and other religious lobbying and litigation groups.

Various classes of rights are now commonly distinguished by Western jurists and philosophers. One common distinction is between public or constitutional rights (those which operate vis-à-vis the state) and private or personal rights (those which operate vis-à-vis other private parties). A second distinction is between the rights of individuals and the rights of associations or groups (whether private groups, like businesses or churches, or public groups, like municipalities or political parties). A third is between natural rights (those that are based on natural law or human nature) and positive rights (those that are based in the positive law of the state). A fourth is between substantive rights (those that create or confirm goods or entitlements) and procedural rights (those that guarantee subjects certain types of treatment by government officials). A fifth is between human rights (those that inhere in a human qua human) and civil rights (those that inhere in citizens or civil subjects). A sixth is between unalienable or non-derogable rights (those that cannot be given or taken away) and alienable or derogable rights (those that can be voluntarily given away or can be taken away under specified legal conditions like due process of law). A seventh is between will theories of rights (that emphasize the individual's rational choices and desires) and interest theories of rights (that focus on individual's needs and society's duties to meet those needs). International human rights jurists now also group these binary pairs differently into "first-generation" civil and political rights, "second-generation" social, cultural, and economic rights, and "third-generation" rights to peace, environmental protection, and orderly development.

Different types of legal claims and jural relationships are inherent in these various classifications of rights. Some scholars distinguish rights (something that triggers a correlative duty in others) from privileges (something that no one has a right to interfere with). Others distinguish active rights (the power or capacity to do or assert something oneself) and passive rights (the entitlement or claim to be given or allowed something by someone or something else). Others distinguish rights or privileges (claims or entitlements to something) from liberties or immunities (freedoms or protections from interference). This latter distinction is also sometimes rendered as positive liberty or freedom (the right to do something) versus negative liberty or freedom (the right to be left alone).

In all these foregoing formulations, the term "right" and its various synonyms and analogues is being used in a subjective sense – what is called a "subjective right," a "human right." The right is vested in a subject (whether an individual, group, or entity), and the subject usually can have that right vindicated before an appropriate authority when the right is threatened or violated. This subjective sense of right is quite different from right in an "objective sense" – what is called an "objective right." "Objective right" (or "rightness") means that something is the objectively right thing or action in the circumstances. Objective right obtains when something is rightly ordered, is just or proper, is considered to be right when judged against some objective or external standard. "Right" is here being used as an adjective, not as a noun. It is what is correct or proper – "due and meet" as the Victorians used to put it.

These subjective and objective senses of right can cohere, even overlap. You can say that "a victim of theft has a right to have his property restored" or that "it is right for a victim of theft to have his property restored." Knowing nothing else, these are parallel statements. But if the victim is a ruthless tycoon and the thief a starving child, the parallel is harder to draw. Even though the subject (tycoon) has a right, it might not always be objectively right to respect or enforce it. Sometimes the subjective and objective senses of right are more clearly dissociated. Even if it is object-ively right for someone to perform an action, it does not always mean the beneficiary of that action has a subjective right to its performance. Though it might be right for you to give alms to the poor, a poor person has no right to receive alms from you. Though it might be right for a parishioner to give tithes to the church, a church has no right to receive tithes from that parishioner.

This basic tension between the subjective and objective senses of the English term "right" has parallels in other languages. *Recht* in German, *droit* in French, *diritto* in Italian, *ius* in Latin, all can be used in both subjective and objective senses – and sometimes in other senses as well. And, like English, each of these languages has developed its own terms for privileges, immunities, powers, capacities, freedoms, liberties, and more, which are used to sort out various types of rights.

These linguistic tensions and tangles of our rights talk today are prod-ucts of a two-millennium-long evolution in the West in which Christianity has played a vital role. The intellectual history of Western rights talk is still very much a work in progress, with scholars still discovering and dis-puting in earnest the basic roots and routes of the development of rights concepts and structures. But the traditional story that the history of human rights began in the Enlightenment of the later seventeenth and eighteenth centuries is becoming ever harder to sustain. Our schoolboy and schoolgirl texts have long taught that human rights were products of the Western Enlightenment – creations of Grotius and Pufendorf, Locke and Rousseau, Montesquieu and Voltaire, Hume and Smith, Jefferson and Madison. Human rights were the mighty new weapons forged by American and French revolutionaries who fought in the name of political democracy, personal autonomy, and religious freedom against outmoded Christian conceptions of absolute monarchy, aristocratic privilege, and religious establishment. Human rights were the keys that Western liberals finally forged to unchain themselves from the shackles of a millennium of Christian oppression and Constantinian hegemony. Human rights were the core ingredients of the new democratic constitutional experiments of the later eighteenth century forward. The only Christians to have much influence on this development, we are told, were a few early Church Fathers who decried pagan Roman persecution, a few brave medieval-ists who defied papal tyranny, and a few early modern Anabaptists who debunked Catholic and Protestant persecution.

Historians have now made clear that there was ample "liberty before liberalism," and that there were many human rights in place before there were modern democratic revolutions fought in their name. Indeed, it is now quite clear that the Enlightenment was not so much a well-spring of Western rights as a watershed in a long stream of rights thinking that began nearly two millennia before. The Enlightenment depended fundamentally on critical rights developments in biblical times and classical Rome, in medieval Catholicism and canon law, and in early modern Catholic and Protestant formulations of civil law and common law. The Enlightenment inherited many more rights and liberties than it invented, and many of these were of Christian origin. Indeed, by 1650, on the eve of the Enlightenment, Christians on both sides of the Atlantic had defined, defended, and died for every one of the rights that would later appear in the 1791 US Bill of Rights. While they certainly made their own original and critical rights contributions, too, what Enlightenment philosophers contributed more than anything were new theoretical frameworks that eventually widened these traditional rights formulations into a set of universal claims that were universally applicable to all.

A number of distinguished commentators, including a good number of Christians, have recently encouraged the abandonment of the human rights paradigm altogether – as a tried and tired experiment that is no longer effective, even a fictional faith whose folly has now been fully exposed. Others have bolstered this claim with cultural critiques – that human rights are instruments of neo-colonization which the West uses to impose its values on the rest, even toxic compounds that are exported abroad to breed cultural conflict, social instability, religious warfare and thus dependence on the West. Others have added philosophical critiques – that rights talk is the wrong talk for meaningful debate about deep questions of justice, peace, and the common good. Still others have added theological critiques – that the secular beliefs in individualism, rationalism, and contractarianism inherent to the human rights paradigm cannot be squared with cardinal biblical beliefs in creation, redemption, and covenant.

Such criticisms properly soften the overly bright optimism of some human rights advocates. They properly curb the modern appetite for the limitless expansion and even monopolization of human rights in the quest for toleration, peace, and security. And they properly criticize the libertarian accents that still too often dominate our rights talk today. But such criticisms do not support the conclusion that we must abandon the human rights paradigm altogether – particularly when no viable alternative global forum and no viable alternative universal faith is yet at hand. Instead, these criticisms support the proposition that the religious sources and dimensions of human rights need to be more robustly engaged and extended. Human rights norms are not a transient libertarian invention, or an ornamental diplomatic convention. Human rights norms have grown out of millennium-long religious and cultural traditions. They have traditionally provided a forum and focus for subtle and sophisticated philosophical, theological, and political reflections on the common good and our common lives. And they have emerged today as part of the common law of the emerging world order. We should abandon these ancient principles and practices only with trepidation, only with explanation, only with articulation of viable alternatives. For modern academics to stand on their tenured liberties to deconstruct human rights without posing real global alternatives is to insult the genius and the sacrifice of their many creators. For now, the human rights paradigm must stand – if nothing else as the "null hypothesis." It must be constantly challenged to improve. It should be discarded, however, only on cogent proof of a better global norm and practice.

A number of other distinguished commentators have argued that Christianity and other religions can have no place in a modern regime of human rights. Religions might well have been the mothers of human rights in earlier eras, perhaps even the midwives of the modern human rights revolution. Religion has now, however, outlived its utility. Indeed, the continued insistence of special roles and rights for religion is precisely what has introduced the Dickensian paradoxes that now befuddle us. Religion is, by its nature, too expansionistic and monopolistic, too patriarchal and hierarchical, too antithetical to the very ideals of pluralism, toleration, and equality inherent in a human rights regime. Purge religion entirely, this argument concludes, and the human rights paradigm will thrive.

This argument proves too much to be practicable. In the course of the twentieth century, religion defied the wistful assumptions of the Western academy that the spread of Enlightenment reason and science would slowly eclipse the sense of the sacred and restore the sensibility of the superstitious. Religion defied the evil assumptions of Nazis, fascists, and communists alike that gulags and death camps, iconoclasm and book burnings, propaganda and mind controls would inevitably drive religion into extinction. Yet another great awakening of religion is upon us – now global in its sweep and frightening in its power.

It is undeniable that religion has been, and still is, a formidable force for both political good and political evil, that it has fostered both benevolence and belligerence, peace and pathos of untold dimensions. But the proper response to religious belligerence and pathos cannot be to deny that religion exists or to dismiss it to the private sphere and sanctuary. The proper response is to castigate the vices and to cultivate the virtues of religion, to confirm those religious teachings and practices that are most conducive to human rights, democracy, and rule of law.

Religion is an ineradicable condition of human lives and human communities. As Ecumenical Orthodox Patriarch Bartholomew reminds us, "faith is not a garment to be slipped on and off; it is a quality of the human spirit, from which it is inseparable."[18] Religion will invariably figure in legal and political life – however forcefully the community might seek to repress or deny its value or validity, however cogently the academy might logically bracket it from its political and legal calculus. Religion must be dealt with, because it exists – perennially, profoundly, pervasively – in every community. It must be drawn into a constructive alliance with a regime of law, democracy, and human rights.

The regime of law, democracy, and human rights needs religion to survive. For a democratic regime dedicated to human rights and rule of law is an inherently relative system of ideas and institutions. It presupposes the existence of a body of beliefs and values that will constantly shape and reshape it, that will constantly challenge it to improve. "Politicians at international forums may reiterate a thousand times that the basis of the new world order must be universal respect for human rights" and democracy, Czech President Václav Havel declared in 1994 after receiving the Liberty Medal in Philadelphia. "[B]ut it will mean nothing as long as this imperative does not derive from the respect of the miracle of being, the miracle of the universe, the miracle of nature, the miracle of our own existence. Only someone who submits in the authority of the universal order and of creation, who values the right to be a part of it, and a participant in it, can genuinely value himself and his neighbors, and thus honor their rights as well."[19]

RECOMMENDED READING

Brett, A. S. *Liberty, Right, and Nature: Individual Rights in Later Scholastic Thought.* Cambridge and New York: Cambridge University Press, 1997.

---

[18] Quoted in John Witte, Jr. and Michael Bourdeaux, eds., *Proselytism and Orthodoxy in Russia: The New War for Souls* (Maryknoll, NY: Orbis Books, 1999), 20.

[19] Václav Havel, "Speech on July 4, 1994 in Philadelphia, on Receipt of the Liberty Medal," reported and excerpted in *Philadelphia Inquirer* (July 5, 1994): A08; *Buffalo News* (July 10, 1994): F8; *Newsweek* (July 18, 1994): 66.

Davis, R. W., ed. *The Origins of Modern Freedom in the West.* Stanford: Stanford University Press, 1995.

Ehler, Sidney Z. and John B. Morrall, eds. *Church and State Through the Centuries: A Collection of Historic Documents with Commentaries.* Newman, MD: Newman Press, 1954.

Harakas, Stanley S. *Let Mercy Abound: Social Concern in the Greek Orthodox Church.* Brookline, MA: Holy Cross Orthodox Press, 1983.

Hohfeld, W. N. *Fundamental Legal Conceptions.* New Haven: Yale University Press, 1919.

Honoré, Tony. *Ulpian: Pioneer of Human Rights.* 2nd edn. Oxford: Oxford University Press, 2002.

Huber, Wolfgang and Heinz Eduard Tödt. *Menschenrechte: Perspektiven einer menschlichen Welt.* Stuttgart: Kreuz-Verlag, 1977.

Nurser, John. *For All Peoples and All Nations: Christian Churches and Human Rights.* Geneva: WCC Press, 2005.

Skinner, Quentin. *The Foundations of Modern Political Thought*, 2 vols. Cambridge: Cambridge University Press, 1978.

Tierney, Brian. *Religion, Law, and the Growth of Constitutional Thought, 1150–1650.* Cambridge: Cambridge University Press, 1982.

The Idea of Natural Rights: Studies on Natural Rights, Natural Law, and Church Law, 1150–1625. Grand Rapids, MI: Wm. B. Eerdmans, 1996.

Tuck, Richard. *Natural Rights Theories: Their Origins and Development.* Cambridge and New York: Cambridge University Press, 1979.

Villey, Michel. *Le droit et les droits de l'homme.* Paris: Presses universitaires de France, 1983.

Leçons d'histoire de la philosophie du droit. New edn. Paris: Dalloz, 1977.

Wirszubski, C. *Libertas as a Political Idea at Rome during the Late Republic and Early Principate.* Cambridge: Cambridge University Press, 1960.

Witte, John, Jr. *The Reformation of Rights: Law, Religion and Human Rights in Early Modern Calvinism.* Cambridge: Cambridge University Press, 2007.

Witte, John, Jr. and Johan D. van der Vyver, eds. *Religious Human Rights in Global Perspective*, 2 vols. The Hague: Martinus Nijhoff, 1996.

Foundations and developments
of human rights

CHAPTER I

The Judaic foundation of rights

David Novak

RIGHTS, DUTIES, AND LAW

There is a widespread assumption among scholars that neither natural law nor human rights is inherent to the biblically based Jewish tradition. Yet, as we shall see, these two normative institutions need to be integrated with each other. Human rights need to be structured by a universal law in order to be more than arbitrary local entitlements. Natural law is about the basically interpersonal, rational nature of human beings, of which rights are an essential component. I submit that both intertwined normative institutions are found in the Jewish tradition when it is examined philosophically, and that one cannot be properly understood without the other. Moreover, these intertwined normative institutions can be philosophically integrated with the revealed law (Torah) lying at the heart of Judaism.[1]

Many argue that the idea of natural law came out of ancient Greek philosophy and was only adopted by Judaism during the Hellenistic Age. This synthesis seems rather artificial, though, inasmuch as it does not seem cogently to connect a law revealed *by* God *to* humans to a law discovered *by* humans *through* the exercise of their natural discursive reason. In this view, anyway, the rational discovery of natural law is already one big move away from the faithful acceptance of revealed law; hence any synthesis of the two is inauthentic historically as well as philosophically. Moreover, many have argued that the idea of human rights was invented by modern philosophy in the seventeenth and eighteenth centuries as part of the progressive displacement of the authority of human nature by inventive human reason as the source of all political norms. In this view, anyway, proponents of modern Judaism only affirm human rights as a rhetorical device to gain cultural legitimization from modern liberal states.

---

[1] Indeed, the Talmud emphasizes the Torah as being the *raison d'être* of all creation. See *Babylonian Talmud* (hereafter "B."): Pesahim 68b re Jer. 33:25.

Here the difference between the modern idea of human rights and
the ancient idea of divine law, whether revealed or natural, is that law is
concerned with duty (what one *owes to* a higher authority as an *obligation*), whereas rights are what one human being may justifiably *claim from*
another human being (or other human beings) *with* whom one is more or
less equal. If one were to follow this kind of trajectory, Judaism is twice
removed from the institution of human rights as we understand it today,
for it was already left behind, so to speak, when natural law succeeded
revealed law in the Hellenistic Age, and it remains even further behind
when human rights succeed natural law in modernity.

All this prejudice, nevertheless, must be overcome if any Jewish rights
talk can be taken seriously today, let alone if the biblically based Jewish
tradition is to be taken as a cogent source of rights in the West.[2] Now that
does not require the elimination of the notion of human rights altogether
(which is politically unfeasible and needlessly reactionary). But it does
mean that we need the elucidation of a much more inclusive idea of rights,
and one that looks to a still-cogent metaphysics for its adequate foundation, a metaphysical foundation that Judaism can endorse in good faith.
That metaphysical endorsement makes Judaism more than a mere historical precedent for the idea of human rights.[3]

It would seem that a cogent Jewish rights theory will have to show that
rights as claims and duties as obligations are essentially related: every right
has a corresponding duty and every duty has a corresponding right. One
cannot see one without the other, so one should not argue for rights without their correlative duties, or for duties without their correlative rights.
Nevertheless, that correlation must begin from the point of rights and
then extend to the point of duty, but not vice versa. For a right always
elicits a duty as the correct response to the just or rightful claim it is making. But what many consider to be a "duty" is not necessarily elicited by a
rightful personal claim at all. Sometimes a duty is the response demanded
by an arbitrary, even tyrannical, potentate; but that is the exercise of raw,
unjustified political or military power.[4] And sometimes a duty per se is
one's self-motivation to achieve the private goal of self-fulfillment, or to

---

[2] See David Novak, "Religious Human Rights in Judaic Texts," in J. Witte, Jr. and J. D. van der Vyver,
    eds., *Religious Human Rights in Global Perspective: Religious Perspectives* (The Hague: Martinus
    Nijhoff, 1996), 175–201; Novak, *Covenantal Rights* (Princeton: Princeton University Press, 2000).
[3] See Hermann Cohen, *Religion of Reason Out of the Sources of Judaism*, trans. S. Kaplan (New
    York: Frederick Ungar, 1972), 63–4.
[4] See *Babylonian Talmud* [hereafter "B."] Shabbat 88a–b re Exod. 19:17 and Prov. 11:3; also
    Mekhilta: Yitro re Exod. 20:2, ed. Horovitz-Rabin, 219.

realize a public goal or ideal; but that is not a response to a claim of one person beckoning another person.[5] Indeed, one could well deny that these "duties" are what the Jewish tradition means by *duty* at all.

The correlation of rights and duties is structured and directed by law. Thus a right-bearer is the proper subject of lawful human action; a duty-bearer is the proper object of that action. Their relationship is a legitimate interpersonal *transaction*. Initially, the subject *acts upon* the object; only then does the object *react to* the initiating subject, thereby becoming a subject in return.[6] Moreover, God *entitles* rational human creatures to make justifiable claims upon each other, and gives them good reason to resist unjustifiable claims made upon each other. And, as we shall soon see, the covenant between God and God's creatures even entitles these creatures to make some claims upon God himself.

An authentically Jewish rights teaching will have first to show that natural law or justice (best designated by the biblical term "*mishpat*") concerns the rights-and-duties that are discovered *through* rational human interaction. It will also have to show that Torah law endorses those inter-human rights, then reveals *what* God immediately claims from humans as God's own right, then shows *how* humans are dutifully to respond to these uniquely divine claims.[7] One learns what are authentic inter-human rights and duties from the ordinary experience of natural human sociality, from the experience of humans justly claiming each other's just response. One learns what are the authentic divine-human rights and duties from the extraordinary experience of revelation, from the experience of being directly and systematically claimed by God's commandments (*mitsvot*). What God wants from us for himself could not be known without revelation. Both of these experiences, though, that of natural human sociality and that of revelation, produce law (*halakhah*).

The inter-human relationship and the divine–human relationship function in tandem, since the God–human relationship is primarily a covenant (*brit*). The covenant is God's relationship with a community of humans

---

[5] See Emmanuel Levinas, "The Rights of Man and the Rights of the Other," in Levinas, *Outside the Subject*, trans. M. B. Smith (Stanford: Stanford University Press, 1994), 116–25.

[6] The Hebrew word for "duty" – *hovah* – is based on the word for "debt" – *hov* (see, for example, *Mishnah* [hereafter "M."]: Ketubot 9.2; B. Berakhot 27b). To claim what one is owed is called a "plea" – *ta'anah* (see, for example, M. Shevuot 6.1) or a "summons" – *tevi'ah* (see, for example, M. Ketubot 5.2). These last two terms come closest to what we now mean by a "right." A legal entitlement or permission to act without legal restraint is called *reshut* (see, for example, M. Peah 7.5; B. Berakhot 27b).

[7] See David Novak, *Natural Law in Judaism* (Cambridge: Cambridge University Press, 1998), 27–61.

who are already related to one another in a lawfully structured society. Indeed, the revelation of unique divine claims can only be an act of intelligent acceptance when its recipients already have some prior human experience of what it means to be justifiably claimed by others and what constitutes a just response thereto, that is, when they have the experience of *lawfulness*. As such, there is no right/claim that does not come both *from* God *and* human others, and there is no duty/response that does not go back both *to* God *and* human others.

COVENANT: GOD, HUMAN PERSONS,
DIVINE—HUMAN COMMUNITY

When Judaism, especially in its legal or *halakhic* manifestation, is taken to be a system of rights and correlative duties, that system itself can be understood to govern the following relationships: (1) God and human persons; (2) human persons and God; (3) God and human community; (4) human community and God; (5) one human person to another; (6) human persons and their community; (7) human community and its personal members. This should be seen in contrast to most modern notions of rights that only recognize the rights of individual persons. That limitation of rights to individuals assumes that they are the only personal realities in the world, leaving them without any existential connection to either God or human community.

God and human persons. At the most primary level, humans experience the power of God the Creator as unlimited and terrifying. "See now that I, I am He, and there is no other power [*ein elohim*] along with me. I kill and I give life; there is no one who can escape My hand" (Deut. 32:39). At this level, human creatures cannot experience themselves as the bearers of duties, and all the more so as the bearers of rights, because like Job we are reduced to moral impotence by the Creator's challenge: "Where were you when I established earth?" (Job 38:4). When faced by God's overwhelming power, there is no ground anywhere in the world to stand upon to actively respond to God. One's response can only be one of abnegation. Such a person is surely too terrified to be the active subject of a divine command, much less a person capable of making an actual claim on anyone else. He or she is "but dust and ashes" (Gen. 18:27; Job 45:5).

That is why God could only exercise God's right or claim on a creature who is capable of being commanded, which means he or she is intelligent enough to understand *who* gave the command, *what* he or she is being asked to do, and *how* it is to be done. Then, this person must have enough freedom to choose whether to obey or disobey the One who has so commanded him or her, whether to keep or not keep what is being commanded, and to know how the commandment is to be practiced. As such, God has to limit God's raw power to make room (as it were) for at least one of God's creatures to answer back to God, either positively or negatively, though neither response can be made with impunity. Both obedience and disobedience have consequences, which are both known and unknown.

This intelligent, responsive freedom to obey or disobey a commandment could well be what Scripture means by "God created the human being [*adam*] in His image, in the image of God [*be-tselem elohim*] He made him, male and female He created them" (Gen. 1:27). When God says "let us [*na'aseh*] make the human being in our image" (Gen. 1:26), that might well mean that God and humans share together in the ongoing constitution of human life in the world.[8] Essential human action, which is the practice of the commandments, is unlike all other things that are *made* by the Creator; rather, it is done *with* the Creator who is now divine Lawgiver, Governor, and Judge.

This can be seen in the first time God addresses God's human creatures, which seems to be synonymous or almost synonymous with their being created. "And the Lord God commanded [*va-yitsav*] the human being saying: 'From all the trees of the garden you may surely eat, but from the tree of the knowledge of good and bad you may not eat, for if you do, on that day you will surely die'" (Gen. 2:16–17). In rabbinic exegesis, the human being is both spoken *to* and spoken *about* in this statement.[9] The Hebrew "*al ha'adam*" can mean both "to the human being" and "concerning the human being." In other words, the human being is both the subject and the object of this first divine commandment. Only in those commandments we would consider to be specifically "religious," like the commandment to pray to God, is God the object of the commandment addressed to human subjects.[10]

God is considered to be the ultimate if not the immediate object of every commandment, even those commandments that intend a human object. So, to benefit another human being is considered to be for God's

---

[8] See Franz Rosenzweig, *The Star of Redemption*, trans. B. E. Galli (Madison, WI: University of Wisconsin Press, 2005), 166–7.

[9] See B. Sanhedrin 56b; also Abraham Joshua Heschel, *Who Is Man?* (Stanford: Stanford University Press, 1965), 97–106.

[10] In fact, it is sometimes asserted that God himself keeps the commandments that pertain to God's relationship with Israel for the sake of covenantal intimacy. In this view, then, human observance of these commandments is *imitatio Dei*. See Exod. 20:11; *Palestinian Talmud*: Rosh Hashanah 1.3/57a–b re Lev. 22:9. See also Maimonides, *Mishneh Torah*: Blessings, 11.2.

sake in the end; and to harm another human being is considered to be directed against God in the end.[11] That is because the human being is God's image, God's worldly representative, as it were, about whom God surely cares.[12] Since one cannot benefit God directly inasmuch as God is not directly available, what better way is there to do so than to benefit God's representative image by respecting their rights? And since one cannot harm God directly for the same reason, isn't the only way to harm God, at last indirectly, to harm God's representative image by violating their rights?[13] Thus humans are included in what is done for God as long as their "junior partner" status in the covenant is acknowledged. That is why there is no commandment intending God as its object that does not have (however seemingly tangential) some human component; and there is no commandment intending another human being as its object that does not ultimately intend God (however tenuously).[14]

Human persons and God. The idea that God enables humans to be related to him through the acceptance and keeping of God's commandments leads to the idea that humans can claim justice from God, even though God can decide whether that claim is just or not, and if just, when and where to fulfill that human claim. That is because God is not only the cosmic Lawgiver, but just as much "the judge of all the earth" (Gen. 18:25), that is, the Governor of the cosmos who requires enforcement of the law and the cosmic Judge who enables either obedience or disobedience of the law to have consequences wherever and whenever God so chooses to realize them. Just as the law itself is considered good, so must its administration be good, and so must it lead to the ultimate judgment of good consequences. Without that assurance, the law is not a blessing, but a curse.

To claim justice from God is either to claim one has been the victim of injustice at the hand of God himself, or to claim one has been the victim of injustice at the hand of a fellow human person. In the case of a claim against God, one can answer with the rabbinic tradition that God will explain or rectify, either here or in a yet unforeseeable future, what now appears to be unjust to a human victim. The only rabbinic debate seems to be whether all divine justice will be in the world-yet-to-come (*olam ha-ba*) or that at least some of it can be experienced in this world

---

[11] See Prov. 17:5. Thus crimes against another human being require reconciliation with that other person, plus atonement from God. See M. Yoma 8.9 re Lev. 16:30; also *Sifra*: Vayiqra re Lev. 5:21, ed. Weiss, 27d (and comment of Ravad thereon).

[12] See M. Avot 3.14; *Palestinian Talmud*: Nedarim 9.3/14c.

[13] See B. Shabbat 50b and Rashi, s.v. "bi-shvil" re Gen. 9:5; *Midrash Vayiqra Rabbah* 34.3 re Prov. 11:16.

[14] See M. Avot 2.11; B. Berakhot 63a re Prov. 3:6.

here and now.[15] Anyone, though, who expects complete or even very much divine justice in this world is a fool, "who will soon say in his heart there is no divine Judge" (Ps. 53:2), and who will quickly conclude that without a divine Judge, there is no God-given law worth keeping.[16] In good faith, then, one can only complain, "Why does the way of the wicked prosper?!" (Jer. 12:1). That complaint seems to be about divine omission, what seems to be God's inaction in either preventing or at least rectifying undeserved human suffering in this world. (Needless to say, that complaint about divine inaction has become much more poignant after the Holocaust, especially when heard on the lips of those who survived it, but whose families perished.)

In the end, the human claim on divine justice is a cry to God for God to redeem us from the death and destruction of this world by establishing his heavenly kingdom (*malkhut shamayim*) on earth. Yet only those who have accepted biblical revelation, and who have become part of the community that has accepted that revelation as its law, only they have any basis to hope for that final redemption, since only that same revelation has promised this redemption to the covenanted community of which they are part.[17] And because God has promised that redemption, calling for it is not begging for divine mercy; it is claiming divine justice, even if humans in this world cannot determine the true location of that divine justice in the cosmos.

When one has been the victim of injustice at the hand of a human being, one can claim justice from God. Thus, at the time of the first crime recorded in Scripture, the murder of Abel by his brother Cain, Abel is portrayed as making a posthumous plea for justice for himself from God. As God informs Cain: "The voice of your brother's blood cries to me from the soil" (Gen. 4:11), which means that Abel's death calls for God to avenge it by punishing Cain who murdered Abel knowingly and willingly. And, after the flood, which was brought about because of the sin of publicly endorsed violence, God assures the survivors, Noah and his family, that justice will be done. "Indeed, your lifeblood I shall claim [*edrosh*] from the hand of every beast I shall claim it, from human hands I shall claim human life [*nefesh ha'adam*], even a man from his brother's hand" (Gen. 9:5).[18] This

---

[15] See M. Kiddushin 1.10; B. Kiddushin 39b and Tosafot, s.v. "matnitin."
[16] See *Midrash Ruth Rabba* 6.6. Cf. B. Hullin 142a.
[17] See B. Berakhot 4a re Ps. 27:13–14.
[18] This verse is interpreted in the Talmud (B. Baba Kama 91b) as including the prohibition of suicide. As such, there is no "right to die," even if one is both the subject and the object of homicide. See B. Avodah Zarah 18a; also David Novak, *The Sanctity of Human Life* (Washington, DC: Georgetown University Press, 2007), 112–41.

last clause about fraternal violence seems to suggest the primal crime of Cain against Abel. Nevertheless, humans are not to wait for God to effect justice. "Because in God's image He made humans" (Gen. 9:6), humans represent God not only when they are the objects of violence, but also when they are the subjects of active justice whenever they can do so. In this latter situation, humans are exercising a divine right by proxy, as it were. Indeed, to leave the execution of all justice to God, when there are opportunities for humans to act on God's behalf, is considered a sin of omission.[19]

God and community. In the biblical narrative, the original hope for a united humankind, for one human city on earth, is dashed by the arrogant attempt of the builders of the Tower of Babel to unite humankind against God. According to an ancient Jewish tradition, their grandiose attempt at complete human sovereignty in God's world also resulted in the wholesale violation of human rights, something modern totalitarian regimes with their totalizing agendas have surely reiterated.[20] Due to this crisis in the divinely ruled cosmic order, for the sake of God's sovereignty, "the Lord scattered them over all the earth" (Gen. 11:9). So, a truly united humankind acceptable to God will only come when God himself redeems the world, "when the kingdom will be the Lord's" (Obad. 1:21).

It seems that due to the inevitable fragmentation of humankind in this world, the biblical narrative quickly turns to God's relationship with one particular people. In God's choice of Abraham and his descendants and adherents (proselytes), God's direct covenant with at least some of humankind is now Scripture's primary concern. Nevertheless, the particularity of this covenant notwithstanding, it has universal human significance. Thus God informs Abraham (or "Abram" as he was still named), at the very inception of his election, that "all the families of the earth shall be blessed through you" (Gen. 12:3). To be sure, most of their uniquely national practices, especially pertaining to the God–human relationship rooted in election, are God's claims on this people alone. They are only meant for Israel. But the moral norms that pertain to their inter-human relations are frequently of universal significance.[21] And, as we shall see, these norms oblige the respect, protection, and vindication of universally valid human rights. In fact, Abraham's people are supposed to be active advocates of these rights.

---

[19] See B. Baba Kama 93a and Tosafot, s.v. "d'eeka"; B. Sanhedrin 6b re 2 Chr. 19:6.
[20] See Louis Ginzberg, *The Legends of the Jews*, trans. H. Szold (Philadelphia: Jewish Publication Society of America, 1909), I:179.
[21] See B. Sanhedrin 59a re Deut. 33:4 and Lev. 18:5.

Along these lines, God invites Abraham to a dialogue with God concerning the proposed punishment of the evil cities of Sodom and Gomorrah and all their citizens:

How can I conceal from Abraham what I am about to do? Abraham is to be a great and mighty nation through whom all the nations of the earth are to be blessed. For I know him intimately, and this is to lead to his commanding his children and household to follow after him, that they might keep the way of the Lord: to practice righteous judgment [*tsedaqah u-mishpat*]. (Gen. 18:17–19)

If "the way of the Lord" is to practice justice and to demand that God deal justly with all of humankind, then the greatness and importance of the Abrahamic people of Israel is not due to their material or military might. Their greatness in the eyes of the world is to be moral; it is their law and their practice of it, especially its advocacy of universal human rights. Thus Moses tells the people of Israel poised to enter the Promised Land of the universal significance of the law which God has given them:

For it is your wisdom and understanding in the eyes of the nations who will hear all these statutes and will say, "surely this nation is a wise and discerning people." For what great nation has God so close to them as we do when we call upon the Lord our God? And what great nation has such righteous statutes [*huqqim*] and ordinances [*mishpatim*] as this whole Torah. (Deut. 4:6–8)

For that reason, undoubtedly, the nations of the world will some day come to Jerusalem saying: "Let us go up to the mountain of the Lord, to the house of the God of Jacob, and from His way He shall direct us and we shall walk in His paths … He shall judge between the nations and admonish many peoples" (Isa. 2:3–4). Furthermore, this is not just a messianic desideratum; in rabbinic lore it is taught that even at the time of Moses, some of the nations of the world sent emissaries to take parts of the Torah back home with them for guidance (if not actual governance) there.[22] Undoubtedly, the moral parts of the Torah, dealing as they do with universal human rights, were assumed to be what these gentiles took from the Torah. That legend foretells the historical fact that Christianity to a greater extent, and Islam to a lesser extent, took the most basic moral norms of the Torah in developing their own conceptions of human rights. So, for example, Thomas Aquinas considered the Torah to be the best embodiment of the universal and perpetual norms of natural law.[23]

---

[22] See *Tosefta*: Sotah 8.6 B. Sotah 35b re Deut. 27:8.
[23] *Summa Theologiae*, 2/1, q. 103, a.3 ad 1.

Because of God's claim on God's covenanted community to exercise their duty to deal justly with each other, communally as well as individually, the greatest indictment of this community and its legal and political institutions by the Prophets was their perversion of the rights of the most helpless citizens of the polity by those with the power to do otherwise. Thus military defeat and political dissolution are promised unless "you seek justice [*dirshu mishpat*], rectify oppression, champion [*shiftu*] the orphan, and plead the cause of the widow" (Isa. 1:17). Inasmuch as the covenant is with the all-seeing God, no perversion of rights can hide behind the anonymity of faceless institutions. God's concern for the welfare of every human person created in the image of God makes God's right to demand proportional concern on the part of his covenanted community attractive to morally earnest humans. As such, they are motivated to imitate God in God's role as "father of orphans and advocate [*ve-dayyan*] for widows" (Ps. 68:6).[24]

God's own rights and God's endowing human creatures with their own rights create numerous duties for the community to uphold. Yet the issue of the just adjudication of human rights at times is so important that, when the covenanted community's legal authorities are either unable or unwilling to effect justice among the members of their own domain, Jews are then permitted to go to gentile authorities for justice. That is, when these gentile authorities engage in the due process of law in a system of evidently just laws, they are willing and able to enforce them and adjudicate according to them.[25]

Community and God. God's right to command numerous duties to God's elect community, prominent among them the duty to "pursue justice" (Deut. 16:20), does not mean that the covenanted community is only a duty-bearer vis-à-vis God. By being the subjects of God's covenant, Israel is now entitled even to demand from God that God not abandon them by annulling the covenant. The validity of the covenant is irrevocable, Israel cannot undo their election by God, and God may neither cancel Israel's election nor select another people to replace Israel. This comes out vividly in the way the Talmud interprets Moses's dialogue with God after Israel has worshiped the Golden Calf. "Remember Abraham, Isaac, and Israel Your servants to whom You Yourself took an oath" (Ex. 32:13). According to Rabbi Eleazar, Moses really said the following to God when advocating for the people Israel: "Master of the universe … you have taken an oath

---

[24] See B. Shabbat 133b re Exod. 15:2 (the opinion of Abba Saul).
[25] See Maimonides, *Mishneh Torah*: Sanhedrin, 26.7.

[*shevu`ah*] by your own name. Therefore, just as your great name lives and endures forever, so must your oath endure forever."[26]

This theological homily is based on the legal fact that in Jewish law an oath is a self-imposed obligation. Only an external higher authority can annul an oath, thus freeing the person who took the oath from the obligation the oath creates for him or her.[27] But God has not recognized any authority higher than God; indeed, were God to do so, God would no longer be God. And, were God to release himself from the sworn obligation to be forever covenanted with Israel, how could God ever be trusted by anyone else again? (This has profound meaning for those Christians who do not see themselves as having displaced the Jews as Israel.) As such, much of Jewish communal prayer in the form of requests of God (*baqashot*) is the claim on God to ever remember just who God's people are, and how they need to be preserved in both body and spirit. This is considered to be Israel's right. At times, it can be expressed quite angrily, just short of blasphemy.[28]

One human person to another. The rights humans may claim from each other, and the duties they owe to each other, emerge from the common world human persons have to share with each other. The idea of basic human mutuality and reciprocity comes out in one of the most famous passages in the Talmud. When a gentile asks Hillel the Elder, in preparation for conversion to Judaism, to "teach me the whole Torah while I stand on one foot," the Sage answers: "What is hateful to you, do not do to your fellow human [*le-haveirakh*]."[29] Of course there is much more to the Torah than just that, but what seems to be suggested here is that consideration of the basic rights and duties that emerge out of universally valid human mutuality and reciprocity is where to begin to appreciate the fuller and deeper range of rights and duties presented in the Torah. This is clearly what is meant by Hillel's concluding words to this would-be convert: "This is the whole Torah; now go and learn!"

The central concern with mutuality and reciprocity comes out in a comment by the great twelfth-century Jewish jurist, theologian, and philosopher, Moses Maimonides, on a rabbinic text that speaks of acts "of which the fruit is consumed in this world, even though the principle endures in the world-yet-to-come."[30] Maimonides explains in his commentary on this text that it pertains to those commandments that pertain to what is "between humans."[31] Unlike those commandments that pertain to what

---

[26] B. Berakhot 32a.   [27] See B. Nedarim 56b.
[28] See, for example, B. Gittin 56b re Exod. 15:11.   [29] B. Shabbat 31a.   [30] M. Peah 1.1.
[31] *Commentary on the Mishnah*: Peah 1.1, ed. Kafih, 1:55.

is "between humans and God," whose consequences are beyond our horizon, moral commandments have immanent consequences inasmuch as what I do on behalf of someone else is done with the justifiable expectation that as much is to be done for me were the tables turned. This is not a *quid pro quo*. When someone else does me a kindness, I have no right to expect to be repaid in kind in this world as some sort of rectifying justice from that very same person whom I have benefited. But I do have the right to expect the same kindness, when I actually need it, from someone who is now an unknown third party, someone who now owes me nothing. In rabbinic parlance, this is the "human dignity" (*kvod ha-beriyot*) that every human being created in the image of God is entitled to claim from every other human being anywhere at any time, here and now or there and then.[32]

Persons and community. Persons have duties to their community because their community has justifiable claims upon them. By "community" I mean the family (*mishpahah*) or the local community (*qehilah*) or the people (*ha`am*). Indeed, without the community and the duties it claims from its members, individual human rights would lose the only context in which they can be exercised with the force of law. Yet, in Jewish tradition, the community functions as much more than the mere arbitrator of the conflicting claims of individual citizens, which is its usual role in liberal societies.

Jewish law is replete with duties that the community claims from individuals. Most of these communal duties are formal legal obligations, and there are prescribed sanctions for refusal to obey them. The legislation of some of these communal duties also entails the simultaneous limitation of certain individual personal rights.[33] Such limitation is always justified by considerations of the common good that are supposed to override the private good that the exercise of an individual right intends. It is not to be done lightly or for any other reason than the true needs of the community.[34]

An example of such a rights limitation is the following:

Ulla said that the literal law of Scripture is that a debtor may pay his debt even with the poorest quality produce, as it says: "you [the claimant] are to stand outside [the dwelling of the debtor who] … shall bring the pledge out to you." (Deuteronomy 24:11) Now, what does one usually bring out?

---

[32] See B. Berakhot 19b and parallels.
[33] See, for example, B. Yevamot 89b re Ezra 10:8; B. Kiddushin 12b.
[34] See, for example, M. Arakhin 5.6; M. Gittin 9.8; also, Maimonides, *Mishneh Torah*: Sanhedrin, 24.10.

Is it not the least valuable stuff? Therefore, what is the reason the Sages rule that a debtor is to be paid with at least medium-quality produce? Is it not so that the door will not be closed in the face of borrowers?[35]

Here the assumption is that the full exercise of the right of debtors to readily unload items that are difficult to sell in the open market in payment of their debts will have the effect of stifling the easy lending of money or produce. As such, potential lenders (the richer members of the community) will increasingly avoid lending to those who need loans the most (the poorer members of the community) due to the low demand for the produce with which they have been repaid. Such a breakdown of responsibility for the common good on the part of borrowers will have bad consequences for the economy upon which the whole community depends for its overall livelihood.[36] Economic well-being depends on social well-being.

There are cases where the transfer of an individual right into a communal duty is not legislated, but only strongly encouraged by the community's jurists. (And, if they are politically astute, they will not encourage any such transfer of rights unless it already has strong popular approval.[37]) The following is a good example of this type of voluntary transfer of an individual right into a voluntary communal duty for the sake of the common good:

Rabbi Eliezer the son of Rabbi Yosē the Galilean says that it is forbidden [*asur*] to submit one's case to arbitration, and whoever does so is a sinner … but let the law [*ha-din*] pierce the mountain … Rabbi Joshua ben Korhah says that it is meritorious [*mitsvah*] to submit one's case to arbitration as Scripture says: "True and peaceful judgment [*emet u-mishpat shalom*] you shall adjudicate in your cities" (Zechariah 8:16) … But what kind of judgment contains peace? That is arbitration [*pesharah*].[38]

The phrase "let the law pierce the mountain" reminds one of the old Roman adage, "let justice be done even if the world perishes" (*fiat iustitia, pereat mundus*), namely, the letter of the law must be followed regardless of the social consequences. In this case, the law rules in favor of one party over the other: upholding the right of the party judged innocent to indemnification; enforcing the duty to the party judged guilty to indemnify the innocent party.

---

[35] B. Baba Kama 8a.
[36] See David Novak, *Jewish Social Ethics* (New York and Oxford: Oxford University Press, 1992), 206–24.
[37] See B. Avodah Zarah 36a and parallels.   [38] B. Sanhedrin 6b.

In the second opinion, though, there is the social issue of the peace of the community, which is a concern that should override the legal issue of who in a civil dispute is innocent and thus has the right to full compensation, and who is guilty and thus has the duty to compensate fully the party judged "injured." According to this opinion, the jurists must balance individual claims with the claims of the common weal (*shalom*). But, if only the rights of one party can be upheld, we then have a detriment to the common weal, since one party is a "winner" and the other a "loser." Moreover, one can assume that both the winner and the loser are usually members of the same local community, to which both will return after the adjudication of their conflict, and in which they will continue to interact socially and even commercially. Nevertheless, winners (and their relatives and friends) tend to be arrogant and self-righteous; losers (and their relatives and friends) have a tendency to be resentful. Inasmuch as the common weal is better served the less strife there is in a community, and since this "zero sum game" is likely to produce further strife in the community, a strictly legal solution to this civil conflict is not in the interest of the common weal. In fact, it might actually encourage further strife. So, promoting arbitration, where there is no winner and there is no loser, is the best solution for balancing the property rights of individuals and the rightful claim of the community on its individual members to compromise for the sake of the common weal, the common good, the public interest. The genuine rights of the community trump individual rights in cases of direct conflict between the two.[39]

Finally, even though no one is literally obligated by the law to agree to arbitration in lieu of an official court proceeding (*din torah*), thus in effect waiving his or her right to formal justice, later Jewish authorities used more and more social (if not strictly legal) pressure to get disputing parties to accept arbitration.[40] So, even though this did not become an individual duty, it did become a duty for the jurists to urge arbitration in lieu of an official court proceeding.[41]

Community and persons. The question of the rights of an individual person in relation to the duties of the community is the question of what are the just claims an individual person can make on the community. So,

---

[39] See David Novak, "Annulment in Lieu of Divorce in Jewish Law," in Novak, *Halakhah in a Theological Dimension* (Chico, CA: Scholars Press, 1985), 29–44.

[40] Maimonides, *Mishneh Torah*: Sanhedrin, 22.4–6; *Tur*: Hoshen Mishpat, 12.

[41] For the obligation of jurists to suggest strongly to litigants what they should do, even if the litigants are not legally obligated to do so, see M. Yevamot 12.6.

let us now look at the right to communal assistance, what we might call today a "welfare right."

The right to assistance in situations where a person is unable to provide basic necessities for himself or herself, like all rights, entails an individual duty. The basic commandment, "You shall love your neighbor as yourself" (Lev. 19:18), is one whose subject "yourself" (*kamokha*) is designated as singular. In fact, the most immediate form of such assistance, such as tending to the needs of the sick, is what the Rabbis call "acts of personal kindness" (*gemilut hasadim*).[42] These acts cannot be delegated to a third party; they must be performed on a person-to-person basis. Since society is that third party more abstractly, one certainly cannot claim such *personal kindness* from any social institution. And society itself cannot make these acts of personal kindness an enforceable duty with sanctions for non-compliance. Only God can do that.

Nevertheless, built upon this most immediate personal right is a right to monetary assistance (*tsedaqah*) when truly needed.[43] The duty that this right entails moves in a more abstract, less personal direction since it involves the transfer of money, which is itself a socially created abstraction. Just as money is an artificial social construction, so the distribution of what could be called "charity" has become a more impersonal social institution (though "welfare" is a better term than "charity," since charity implies that it is a matter of optional largesse and, as such, it is not something that can be commanded as a duty). But, since social welfare is a communal duty, those in real need of it have a right to it, that is, they can claim it from the community lawfully.[44] They are not begging for charity. Indeed, if the poor do have to beg, thereby humiliating themselves in the process, that is a moral disgrace to the community in which they have to do so.[45]

That the poor have a right to communal assistance is emphasized by the fact that welfare is not left to individual or even communal discretion. Thus the Talmud states about the various types of produce that Scripture decrees are to be left for the poor to come and gather for themselves, that "they are not the largesse [*tovat hana'ah*] of the owners [of the fields where the produce is to be left]."[46] As the eleventh-century commentator Rashi points out, "they [the communal authorities] force

---

[42] See Maimonides, *Mishneh Torah*: Mourning, 14.1.
[43] For the superiority of the more personal *gemilut hasadim* to the more impersonal *tsedaqah*, see B. Sukkah 49b.
[44] See Maimonides, *Mishneh Torah*: Gifts to the Poor, 10.2.   [45] See *ibid.*, 9.3.
[46] B. Hullin 131a–b re Lev. 23:22.

[*kofin*] him to give."[47] In fact, the right of the poor to these "gifts" is compared to the right of any member of the community to the institution of justice, which is clearly society's specific duty to perform on behalf of the innocent who have a right to it.

CONCLUSIONS

To be sure, Jewish thinkers need to do much more to develop larger notions of what individual persons can claim from their communities, and what they can claim from the secular societies in which almost all Jews today live and want to live. Nevertheless, too much rights talk today has emphasized individual rights at the expense of other rights. This has led to the assumption that individual rights are the only real rights at all, thus neglecting the fact that individuals are not the only manifestation of humanity in the world. This neglect in the end weakens the cause for individual rights because it makes them bear more social weight than they can handle; it asks of them more social benefit than they can possibly deliver. Indeed, without a primary connection to human community, human individuals become strangers competing against one another. And without connection to God, human persons have little reason to claim respect from each other.

Looking to Judaism, therefore, to learn from its doctrines a more adequate metaphysical foundation for rights, and to show us a more variegated development of rights theory and practice, that is surely good for giving Judaism a voice in contemporary ethical, political, and legal discourse. It is also good for our society's attempt to draw upon sources wider and deeper for the sake of strengthening the case for human rights by persuasion, for they are surely the hallmark of any constitutional democracy that seeks to practice justice at home and globally.

RECOMMENDED READING

Cohn, Haim H. *Human Rights in Jewish Law*. New York: KTAV, 1984.
Elon, Menachem. *Jewish Law*, 4 vols. Trans. B. Auerbach and M. J. Sykes. Philadelphia and Jerusalem: Jewish Publication Society, 1994.
Falk, Ze'ev W. *Law and Religion*. Jerusalem: Mesharim, 1981.
Fox, Marvin, ed. *Modern Jewish Ethics*. Columbus, OH: Ohio University Press, 1975.

---

[47] On B. Hullin 131b, s.v. "ein bahen." See B. Baba Batra 8a–b.

Goodman, Lenn E. *Judaism, Human Rights, and Human Values.* New York and Oxford: Oxford University Press, 1998.

On Justice. New Haven and London: Yale University Press, 1991.

Herzog, Isaac Halevi. *The Main Institutions of Jewish Law*, 2 vols., 2nd edn. London and New York: Soncino, 1965.

Konvitz, Milton R. *Judaism and Human Rights.* New York: W. W. Norton, 1972.

Novak, David. *Covenantal Rights.* Princeton: Princeton University Press, 2000.

Halakhah in a Theological Dimension. Chico, CA: Scholars Press, 1985.

The Jewish Social Contract. Princeton: Princeton University Press, 2005.

Jewish Social Ethics. New York and Oxford: Oxford University Press, 1992.

Natural Law in Judaism. Cambridge: Cambridge University Press, 1998.

The Sanctity of Human Life. Washington, DC: Georgetown University Press, 2007.

Walzer, Michael, ed. *The Jewish Political Tradition*, vol. I. New Haven and London: Yale University Press, 2000.

Ius *in Roman law*

Charles Donahue, Jr.

What did the Roman lawyers mean when they spoke of *ius*? The question is an important one not only for an understanding of Roman legal concepts but also for the history of Western law generally. Beginning in the twelfth century and extending to today, the texts of Roman law have been studied with an assiduity second only to that devoted to the Bible. A concept as fundamental as *ius* could not fail to have influenced Western legal thought, particularly because, in many periods, those who studied the Roman texts also sought to apply what they learned in those texts to the law of their own time. The question is not only important, it is also difficult. The word "ius" in Latin (like *droit* in French, *Recht* in German, etc.) is ambiguous. It can mean a whole body of normative rules, a legal order, as well as "right," in any of the many senses of the English word. (The absence of this ambiguity in English is more than compensated for by the notorious ambiguity of the word "law," which can mean either *lex*, in the sense of statute or rule, or *ius*, in the sense of the body of normative rules.)

Although the word "right" is not so ambiguous in English as is the word "ius" in Latin (and its counterparts in most Western languages), it is ambiguous. Early in the last century, Wesley Newcomb Hohfeld proposed that English speakers resolve the ambiguity, at least in precise legal language, by using the word "right" only where there was a correlative "duty" in another or others.[1] If there was no correlative duty, but simply an absence of right in someone else (a "no-right"), Hohfeld preferred to say that the subject had a "privilege." Hohfeld also proposed four other "fundamental legal categories": "power" (another word that is sometimes encompassed in "right"), "immunity," "liability," and "disability," categories that referred

---

[1] Wesley Newcomb Hohfeld, "Some Fundamental Legal Conceptions as Applied in Judicial Reasoning," *Yale Law Journal* 23 (1913): 16–59, reprinted in Hohfeld, *Fundamental Legal Conceptions* (New Haven: Yale University Press, 1919).

to the subject's ability or lack thereof to change the first set of categories. Perhaps the easiest illustration of all the categories may be seen in the context of tangible property, where the owner normally has the exclusive "right" to possession (others have the "duty" to stay off), the "privilege" of use (others have "no-right" to prevent it), and the "power" to convey this right and privilege (others being liable to or immune from the exercise of the power).

Hohfeld's proposed vocabulary has not been universally accepted, but his distinction between "rights" and "privileges" is well recognized. Other authors distinguish between "claim rights" and "liberty rights" or "passive rights" and "active rights." Whether the Romans saw these distinctions is a question that cannot be answered in this chapter. The important thing about Hohfeld's analysis for our purposes is that it firmly connected rights, privileges, powers, and disabilities with a given legal subject and defined them in terms of that subject's relationship to others. My contention in this chapter is that the Roman lawyers used the word "ius" in just the way that Hohfeld used the words "right," "privilege," and, occasionally, "power" to refer to a "jural relationship," in Hohfeld's language, in which another or others have a duty or obligation to the subject, no right to prevent the subject from acting, or are liable to or immune from the subject's changing their rights and privileges.

It is necessary to make this argument because the French scholar Michel Villey denied it in a series of works written in the middle of the last century.[2] Villey's contribution to the understanding of the language of the classical Roman lawyers was to emphasize in a way that had not been emphasized for some time that the word "ius" meant not only a body of normative rules, a legal order, and also (albeit in the strongest statement of Villey's view only in late or interpolated texts) a right of an individual (a right, privilege, or, perhaps, a power, in the Hohfeldian senses) but also an objective situation that was right, in the adjectival sense of the English word. When Ulpian tells us that "iustitia est constans et perpetua uoluntas ius suum cuique tribuendi," we should not translate "justice is the steady and enduring will to render unto everyone

---

[2] For example, Michel Villey, "L'Idée du droit subjectif et les systèmes juridiques romains," *Revue historique de droit français et étranger*, 4e sér. 24–5 (1946–7): 201–28; Villey, "Du sens de l'expression *jus in re* en droit romain classique," in *Mélanges Fernand de Visscher*, 2 (= RIDA, 1er sér. 3) (1949): 417–36; Villey, "Le 'jus in re' du droit romain classique au droit moderne," in *Conférences faites à l'Institut de droit romain en 1947* (Paris: Institut de droit romain de l'Université de Paris, 1950), 187–225. The last contains the strongest claim: "Le droit romain classique ignore, à mon avis, totalement l'idée de droit subjectif." "Le 'jus in re,'" 188.

his right," but "justice is the set and constant purpose which gives to every man his due."[3]

Where Villey went wrong was in arguing that the subjective meaning of *ius* did not exist, or barely existed, before the fourteenth century. All three definitions may be found from the twelfth century onward. Some authors, like Thomas Aquinas, omit the subjective meaning, but it is to be found in Thomas's predecessors and contemporaries, particularly among the lawyers, and, Villey to the contrary notwithstanding, it is not clear whether we can attribute much significance to Thomas's failure to mention it.[4] In this chapter, I am going to argue that the notion of subjective right was, in fact, quite fundamental to Roman law.[5] Hence, there was nothing particularly original about the canonists' and civilians' use of the idea in the twelfth and thirteenth centuries.

We confine ourselves here to the classical Roman jurists (roughly, 100 BCE to 250 CE), whose works, to the extent that they survive, are found, for the most part, in Justinian's *Digest.*[6] We will not find any general definition of *ius* in those works.[7] The classical Roman jurists are, however, notoriously chary of definitions (see D.50.17.202 [Iau., Ep. 11]). Hence, we cannot attach much significance to the fact that the classical jurists do not define the term "ius."

What is clear is that the classical jurists frequently used the word "ius" in a subjective sense. No fewer than 191 times in the *Digest* is someone

---

3 D.1.1.10pr (Ulp., Reg. 1); cf. JI.1.1pr. The first translation is that of Watson's group, the second that of the corresponding passage in the *Institutes* by J. B. Moyle, long before Villey. See Villey, "Suum jus cuique tribuens," in *Studi in onore di Pietro de Francisci* (Milan: Giuffrè, 1956), 361–71. (Hereafter, D [followed by book, title, fragment, and paragraph number with the original source in brackets] = *Corpus Iuris Civilis, Digesta* in *The Digest of Justinian*, ed. Theodor Mommsen and Paul Krueger, trans. ed. Alan Watson, 4 vols. [Philadelphia: University of Pennsylvania Press, 1985]; hereafter, JI [followed by book, title, and paragraph number] = *Corpus Iuris Civilis, Institutiones* in *The Institutes of Justinian*, ed. J. B. Moyle, 2 vols., 5th edn [Oxford: Oxford University Press, 1913].)

4 Brian Tierney, *The Idea of Natural Rights: Studies on Natural Rights, Natural Law and Church Law, 1150–1625* (Atlanta: Scholars Press, 1997), 58–67, 22–7.

5 This idea is not new. See Max Kaser, "Zum 'Ius'-Begriff der Römer," in *Essays in Honor of Ben Beinart*, 2 (= *Acta Juridica* [1977]), 63–81, with references to earlier work.

6 The argument of this chapter is based on Charles Donahue, "*Ius* in the Subjective Sense in Roman Law: Reflections on Villey and Tierney," in Domenico Maffei *et al.*, eds., *A Ennio Cortese* (Rome: Il Cigno, 2001), I:506–35. That article contains tables of all the texts relied on, extensive quotations from the Latin, and some discussion of possible interpolations. Except where noted, the translations here are mine.

7 The closest we come is D.1.1.11 (Paul., Sab. 14); cf. D.1.3.41 (Ulp., Inst. 2). Hence, we agree with the weak form of Villey's argument: "La notion de droit subjectif … n'est pas l'objet à Rome d'une véritable élaboration scientifique" (Villey, "Droit subjectif," 226). There is, however, a substantial gap between this claim and the claim (see n. 2) that it did not exist.

said to have *ius* (*ius habere*).[8] The range of *iura* so described is broad indeed. They include *iura* of both public and private law. They include *iura* in the law of persons, of things, and of actions. In the second category we find subjective *iura* in the area that we would call property more frequently than in the area of obligations, but the latter are not wanting.

Equally common is the expression that *ius* belongs to someone, expressed either by the verb "to be" with the dative (*ius esse alicui*) or with the possessive adjective or pronoun (*ius meum, tuum, suum, nostrum, alienum, eius, eorum, alterius*, etc.). Here, too, the range of *iura* so described is broad. A more technical variant of this usage is the phrase in the law of persons that someone is *sui iuris* "of his own right" or *alieni iuris* "of someone else's right," meaning that the person in question either has legal capacity on his own or is in the power, *manus*, or *mancipium* of another.

Let us examine a subset of these usages more carefully. Analysis of the 191 places in the *Digest* where someone is said to have *ius* (*ius habere*) and the 103 places in which a given *ius* is said to belong to someone (*ius esse alicui*) should give us a good idea of both the range and the possible limits of the Roman jurists' conception of subjective right. While analysis of a broader group – including, for example, the uses of *ius* in connection with the possessive noun, adjective, or pronoun – might change the proportion of different kinds of uses, an unsystematic examination of these uses indicates that it would not change them in broad outline.

RIGHTS IN THE THING OF ANOTHER
(*IURA IN RE ALIENA*)

By far the most common context (115 out of 294, or 39 per cent) for these statements of subjective right is that of the law of servitudes and the penumbra of the law of servitudes that Anglo-American lawyers call "nuisance."[9] The rights involved concern building or preventing building (30); rights of way and their expansion and negation (21); rights of *usus*, with or without *fructus* (18); getting, or getting to, water (16); various rights of *immittere*, letting or putting out something or letting in something (10); burial of the dead (7); and a miscellaneous collection (13), including some traditional servitudes and some non-traditional.

---

[8] See Donahue, "*Ius* in the Subjective Sense," 509, for how these and the following samples were drawn.

[9] *Ibid.*, Appendix I.

Most of these rights are subjective liberty rights ("privileges" in Hohfeld's terminology). They involve a state of legal affairs in which someone may choose to act, or not, and someone (normally the owner of the burdened property) has no right to compel or prevent the behavior. A few of these rights are claim rights ("rights" in Hohfeld's terminology), in which the holder of the right can require the performance of a duty (in all but one instance [D.8.5.6.2 (Ulp., Ed. 17); D.8.5.8pr (Ulp., Ed. 17)] a duty not to do something) by the holder of the burdened land. All of these rights involve human activity (sometimes in conjunction with beasts), or, in a few cases, stopping human activity. All of these rights are ascribed in these passages to a particular individual or, occasionally, a group. All of these passages will bear the translation into modern English of "A has a right to X" or "the right to X belongs to A." Most of them will not bear the translation "This is the objectively right thing in this situation," or "This is the law of this situation." Anyone who is seeking to argue that the Romans did not have a conception of subjective rights must come to grips with these passages.

The very number of these passages would suggest that this use of the word "ius" was part of the technical vocabulary of the law and not simply a popular usage that occasionally crept into juristic writing. We can rely, however, on more than statistics. The surviving fragments of the urban praetor's edict, the most technically worded of all Roman legal documents, contain no fewer than six instances of the phrase *ius alicui esse* in contexts where subjective right must be meant.[10] The late Max Kaser argued that this phrase was derived from the ancient formula of the "legis actio sacramento in rem."[11] It suffices to say here that the notion of subjective right was in the praetor's edict as it was consolidated by Julian.

More serious is a series of objections, raised especially by Villey, based on the Romans' conception of *iura* in general and *iura in re aliena* in particular: (1) that *iura in re aliena* adhered to the land, not to a given person; (2) that they were a narrow subclass of what we would call rights, never being applied, for example, to what we would call the right of ownership (*dominium*); (3) that *iura* in general were classified as a "thing" (*res*); and (4) that they were the product of an official decision of what was right in a particular situation (*ius dicere*) and hence could be used to speak of what we would call rights or of what we would call duties

---

[10] *Ibid.*, text and nn. 60, 173, 213, 214, 215, and 216.
[11] Kaser, "'Ius'-Begriff," 69–70.

or even penalties.[12] We deal with the first and portions of the fourth objection here. Consideration of the rest requires analysis of more of our passages.

The concept of *iura in re aliena* is certainly Roman, even if the phrase is not. A servitude (in the broad sense, including the so-called "personal servitudes") cannot exist without there being burdened property (normally land), the ownership of which is in another. One cannot have a servitude in one's own property (D.7.6.5pr [Ulp., Ed. 17]). Most servitudes (*usus* and *usus fructus* are notable exceptions) belong to a person in his or her capacity as owner of other land. Transfer of the burdened or benefited land carries the burden or the benefit of the servitude with it. Granted these facts it is not surprising that we occasionally find it said that land owes or is burdened with or is owed a servitude (D.8.3.23.3 [Paul., Sab. 15]; D.8.2.24 [Paul., Sab. 15]; D.8.5.4.7 [Ulp., Ed. 17]). Once it is said that a given river has a servitude-like *ius* (D.41.1.56pr [Proc., Ep. 8]).

These usages might lead one to think that when the Romans spoke of *iura in re aliena*, they were speaking of the objective legal situation with regard to the land and not of anyone's subjective rights. Such is not the case, however. If occasionally the land is said to have the benefit or the burden of a servitude, there are many more instances in which the person who holds the right is said to have it or the person who holds the burdened land is said to owe it. The right is a real one, in the sense that it is established by an *actio in rem*. This fact, however, does not make it any less of a subjective right for the one who holds it. If it is appurtenant to a given piece of land, the holder of the right will lose it if he parts with the land, but while he holds the benefited land, it is his subjective right, just as much as the rights that he has that are associated with his personal status.

Where the fact that the servitude is a real right does make a difference is not in the nature of the right but in the nature of the corresponding duties. The owner of the burdened land cannot be sued *in personam* for breach of these duties (though he may be subject to an interdict and/or be required to give a *cautio*, which would make him personally liable), and in the one case in which affirmative obligations are imposed on him, he may avoid them by abandoning the land (D.8.5.6.2 [Ulp., Ed. 17]).

Before proceeding to consider the objections to our argument more fully, let us consider once again the contents of the sample. If almost 40 per cent of the usages of *ius habere* and *ius esse alicui* are in the context of

---

[12] See Villey, "Droit subjectif," 224–6; Villey, "Sens de l'expression *jus in re*," *passim*; Villey, "Le 'Jus in re'," 192–5.

iura in re aliena, more than 60 per cent of them are not. Here categorization is more difficult, and there is some overlap, so that single categories may be somewhat arbitrary. Broadly speaking, however, the 180 remaining usages may be categorized as follows: 69 (23 per cent of the total) deal with property rights in a broader context than that of a specific *ius in re aliena* (sometimes, though not always, including the rights of owners); 55 (19 per cent) deal with rights of what modern, and perhaps ancient, authors call the law of persons; 28 (10 per cent) deal with public rights, normally of public officials; 14 (5 per cent) deal with rights associated with the law of actions and no substantive body of law, and 13 (4 per cent), with rights associated with the law of obligations. Each of these categories deserves further analysis.

PROPERTY RIGHTS IN BROADER CONTEXTS

As intimated above, standard Roman legal terminology gives priority to ownership (*dominium*) and describes lesser rights in a thing as, to use the modern term, *iura in re aliena*. This means that frequently the owner is said to have the thing (*rem/corpus habere*), while the holder of a lesser right is said to have a right (*ius habere*). One might argue from this undeniable fact that the Roman lawyers did not conceive of *dominium* as a right or, to use modern American terminology, "a bundle of rights." *Ius*, at least in the context of property, was, so we might suggest, properly confined to *iura in re aliena*, or, at least, to a *ius* less than ownership.[13]

There are texts in our sample that support this view.[14] The most notable support is provided by those texts that contrast a *ius* in the thing with the thing itself, or with property in the thing. In some cases, however, where this contrast seems to be being made, the passage turns out on closer examination to be more ambiguous. But we need not rely on these possibly ambiguous passages. No less than twenty-one of our seventy-two instances of "property rights in the broad" include the rights of owners within the term "ius." This includes most notably instances in which someone is said to have no right in a thing or to do something. It would make no sense in these passages if the negation were only of *iura in re aliena*; the negation must be of all rights, including those of owners. *Ius*, including rights of ownership, is also used quite frequently in a positive sense: "to have greater

---

[13] See Villey, "Sens de l'expression *jus in re*."
[14] Except where the text of a specific fragment is discussed, references for this section are to be found in Donahue, "*Ius* in the Subjective Sense," 513–14.

right [*plus iuris habere*]" (including rights of ownership) (D.41.3.15 [Paul., Plaut. 15]; D.50.17.160.2 [Ulp., Ed. 76]); "whether or not he had the right to do it [*utrum ius habuerit faciendi, an non*]" (owners must be included; see above on negation) (D.43.24.1.2 [Ulp., Ed. 71]); and "the right to give, sell, grant [*ius donandi, uendendi, concedendi*]" (preeminently rights of ownership) (D.50.17.163 [Ulp., Ed. 55]). Perhaps the most obvious instance is: "He who has either ownership or a servitude has the right to announce a new work [*ius habet opus nouum nuntiandi, qui aut dominium aut seruitutem habet*]" (D.43.25.1.3 [Ulp., Ed. 70]).[15]

RIGHTS IN THE LAW OF PERSONS

The fifty-five cases (19 per cent) of subjective rights in the law of persons are easier to classify.[16] There are nine examples of *ius testamenti faciendi* and its equivalents. Most of the others are also connected with inheritance. Eighteen examples deal with the rights of patrons, normally in the inheritance of their freedmen or emancipated sons. These rights – which range from the quite general, to the more specific, to the quite specific – are highly subjective, liberty rights. The only thing that even hints at objectivity is the fact that the word "*ius*" is used far more often than the word "*iura*," though the latter is not wanting. One phrase in this group (*ius liberti*) that could be taken as objective, from the context should not be so taken (D.26.5.13.1 [Pap., Qu. 11]). This is not the *ius* of the freedman (which, of course, is not a right in the modern sense but a duty or a liability), but rather the *ius* in the freedman (objective genitive).

The next largest group (nine) concerns the rights that accrue to kinship, normally in the context of inheritance, but sometimes more generally. One phrase in this group is worth particular note: "If natural children have been emancipated, adopted, and once again emancipated, they have the natural right of children [*si naturales* (sc. *liberi*) *emancipati et adoptati iterum emancipati sint, habent ius naturale liberorum*]" (D.38.6.4 [Paul., Sab. 2]). This is the only instance in the *Digest* where the phrase "ius naturale" is used in an unambiguously subjective sense (though, as we shall see, there are a few other possibly subjective uses). Notice that the text as we have it does not say "the *ius* of natural children [*ius naturalium liberorum*]," which would have been quite possible in the context. In all

---

[15] For a discussion confirming this general point with many examples, see Donahue, "*Ius* in the Subjective Sense," 515–19.

[16] Except where the text of a specific fragment is discussed, references for this section are to be found in Donahue, "*Ius* in the Subjective Sense," 517, 520–1.

cases the subjective nature of these rights is strengthened by the fact that when these texts were written most heirs could choose not to take up an inheritance, and praetorian grants of *bonorum possessio* had substantially increased the options available to the kin of the deceased.

Six instances in our group concern the rights that fathers and masters have over their children and slaves. These are all clear examples of subjective liberty rights. To these should be added the bald statement of the converse proposition: "A slave has no rights [*seruile caput nullum ius habet*]" (D.4.5.3 [Paul., Ed. 11]).

Eleven of our instances deal with rights under other aspects of the law of persons. One is closely related to inheritance. Two concern the right to kill (*ius occidendi*) an adulterer under the *l. Iulia de adulteriis*. One concerns the rights of a slave or son in his *peculium*. Three concern the *ius postliminii*. One concerns the right of *collegia* to meet (*ius coeuendi*); one, the *ius anulorum*, and two, the absence of rights of mothers who are managing the affairs of their fatherless children. Again, all the rights described here, with one possible exception (D.40.3.1 [Ulp., Sab. 5]), are subjective liberty rights.

RIGHTS IN PUBLIC LAW

The twenty-eight instances in our sample (10 per cent) of rights in public law are also relatively easy to classify.[17] Most of them concern public officials. Particularly notable are those which give to a public official the right to punish in a particular kind of way, or generally. Included among these is one concerning the right of delegation and one general etymological description. Another group concerns the right of a public official to appoint a tutor or curator. To this should be added the one *ius excusationis* (of *mensores frumentarios*). Six instances concern other rights of public officials, some quite specific, some more general. Two concern the rights of inhabitants of specific cities or of an *ordo* within a given city. One concerns the rights of individual members of the public in public places.

With the exception of this last (which is a normal subjective liberty right), the classification of these as subjective rights requires some explanation. When the jurists speak of the right of a public official to do something (or the absence of such a right), they are normally focusing, as do modern lawyers when they use the same phrase, on the question

---

[17] Except where the text of a specific fragment is discussed, references for this section are to be found in Donahue, "*Ius* in the Subjective Sense," 521–3.

of competence. If a public official has the *ius uerberandi*, no one can say to him: "You should not have whipped that man; that's not within your power." "Right" here means "power," not quite in the Hohfeldian sense, but in the sense of capacity. (We might say "jurisdiction," were it not for the fact that that word, in both Latin and English, tends to be confined to the question of competence in the judicial process.) The right in question is subjective; it inheres in the person of the official, so long as he has his office. The exercise of rights by public officials is, however, different from the usual exercise of rights by private persons. In the case of private persons, normally once we have determined that the person has a right to do something, that is the end of the matter. Law (as opposed to morality) normally has nothing more to say. In the case of the public official, however, there are normally two further legal questions that one must ask once one has determined that he has the capacity to act. First, is this factual situation one in which the law contemplates that he should exercise his undoubted power. "You should not whip that man; he has done nothing that deserves whipping." Second, in some, but not all, cases the official may have the discretion as to whether to act in a particular way. "You should not whip that man; for while he has done something for which you could whip him, in his case a lesser penalty is appropriate." If the official has no discretion, then his right is also a duty. It is interesting, and perhaps instructive, that most of the rights of public officials mentioned above were, at the time the texts were written, rights which not only gave them the power to act but also some discretion as to whether they should act or how they should act. It would seem that the word "ius" in the context of public officials came most easily to the Roman jurists in contexts in which it was most like a private, liberty right.

PROCEDURAL RIGHTS

There are fourteen instances in our sample (5 per cent) of purely procedural subjective rights.[18] On the civil side we have four examples of the right to have a case tried in one's domicile (*ius reuocandi domum* or *ius reuocandi forum*); on the criminal side we have two examples of *ius accusandi* generally and two that concern the *ius accusandi* in the case of *lex Iulia de adulteriis*. There are two examples of the *ius postulandi* being used as a criterion for whether someone can engage in another legal act. The other four examples are isolated. While the number of these cases of procedural

---

[18] References for this section are to be found in Donahue, "*Ius* in the Subjective Sense," 523.

rights is not large, there are enough of them to indicate that the jurists had no difficulty conceiving of a subjective liberty right in an area of law that we call procedure and for which they had no term.

OBLIGATION

There are only thirteen (4 per cent) examples in our sample of subjective rights in the area of obligations. The word "ius" seems to have come most easily to the jurists' minds in the context of the *ius nouandi* of which there are four examples (D.12.2.21 [Gai., Ed. prou. 5]; D.46.2.31.1 [Uen., Stip. 3]; D.46.2.34.pr [Gai., Uerb. obl. 3]; D.46.2.34.1 [Gai., Uerb. obl. 3]). One example, *ius uendendi* (e.g., D.38.5.1.12 [Ulp., Ed. 44]), could be classified with the broad property rights, though the verb "uendere" is more frequently found in the context of contracts than in that of the law of single things or inheritances.[19] Another instance of a capacity to alienate (*ius locandi*) (D.43.9.1pr [Ulp., Ed. 68]) must be classified as a right in the area of obligations, because of the well-known fact that Roman law did not give either possession or a *ius in re aliena* to the *conductor*. This example is particularly important because it comes from the praetor's edict. In a third example, priority among different creditors in a pledge is being discussed, but it is clear that the right in question is a right in the law of obligations, not in the property itself (D.20.4.12.9 [Marcian., Formula hyp. sing.]). In a fourth example, also involving *pignus* or *hypotheca*, one who *ex pacto conuento* is permitted (*licuit*) to sell a tenement house (*insula*) (presumably if the debt is not paid) is said to have the same right in the new *insula* if the *insula* burns down and the debtor rebuilds it with his own funds (D.20.1.35 [Lab., Pith. 1]). Again, this is clearly a right in the law of obligations, not in the property itself.[20]

There are two things to note about the employment of the terminology of subjective right in the context of the law of obligations. First, it was possible. Second, it was quite rare. In our sample of 294 fragments, there are only three from *Digest* 12.2.21 to 20.1.28, a gap of 220 pages in the Mommsen edition, and by far the largest gap in our sample. These pages contain many of the major titles on the law of obligations: *condictio, commodatum, depositum, mandatum, societas, emptio uenditio, locatio conductio*. In none of these titles, with the three exceptions (D.18.4.2pr [Ulp.,

---

[19] See *Vocabularium Iurisprudentiae Romanae*, 5 vols. in 7 (Berlin: G. Reimeri and W. de Gruyter, 1903–87), V:1271.4 to V:1279.12 (hereafter *VIR*).

[20] See Donahue, "*Ius* in the Subjective Sense," 524–5, for a discussion of the remaining passages from the law of obligations.

Sab. 49] [two instances]; D.18.4.13 [Paul., Plaut. 14]), all of which involve the sale of rights in an inheritance, is anyone said to have a subjective right, or is it said that a subjective right belongs to someone. We may argue, if we will, that the phrase "habere actionem," which is found many times on these pages,[21] was the functional equivalent of *ius habere* or *ius esse alicui*.[22] That possibility is one to which we shall return. For now, we simply note that *ius habere* and *ius esse alicui* were thinkable in the context of the law of obligations, but that the jurists did not use the phrases very often. Their focus in the law of obligations is on the obligation, the duty, and on the action. This means that they did not think, as modern jurists tend to think, of analyzing all legal situations, at least in private law, in terms of rights and duties. That much we must concede to the alternative view. We are reminded, however, of Hohfeld's fundamental insight that precision in analysis of rights frequently comes by looking to the correlative duty.

IUS NATURALE

The phrase "ius naturale" occurs twenty-five times in the *Digest*. In one instance, noted above, it is clearly to be taken in a subjective sense (D.38.6.4). In twenty instances, it is clearly to be taken in an objective sense.[23] We deal here with the four ambiguous cases, none of which is in our sample.

It is plain that those obligations that have a natural guarantee do not perish with a change of status [*capitis deminutio*], because civil reason cannot destroy natural rights [*naturalia iura*]. Therefore, an action for dowry, which is framed in the good and the just, survives *capitis deminutio*. (D.4.5.8 [Gai., Ed. prou. 4])

Prescinding from the question whether Gaius could possibly have written this, what the passage seems to say is that the *actio de dote* survives *capitis deminutio*. (The easiest context in which to think of this would be where the woman was emancipated by her father.) The reason offered is that the obligations of the *actio de dote* have a natural guarantee (*naturalis praestatio*). These obligations survive because "civil reason cannot destroy natural rights." The phrase is certainly obscure, but the underlying rights being referred to are subjective ones (the obligations enforced by the *actio de dote*). The passage does not say that natural law prevails over civil law.

---

[21] See *VIR*, I:110.23 to I:111.31.
[22] For a complicated argument that it is not, but that the idea of subjective right precedes that of action, see G. Pugliese, *Actio et diritto subiettivo* (Milan: Giuffrè, 1939).
[23] See Donahue, "*Ius* in the Subjective Sense," Appendix II.

Rather, it seems to contemplate that in certain actions, the *actio de dote* being one of them, a *naturalis obligatio* may be enforced, despite the fact that an obligation of the civil law only would have been destroyed by *capitis deminutio*. The more that we try to make sense of this passage in the context of a legal system that frequently did allow the civil law to prevail over the natural, the more it seems that we must understand *naturalia iura* here as subjective natural rights.

He who tears down another's house against the will of the owner and builds baths in its place, besides the natural *ius* that what is built on the surface [*superficies*] belongs to the owner of the land, is subject also to an action for the damage caused. (D.9.2.50 [Ulp., Op. 60])

The Watson group's translation takes this objectively ("quite apart from the rule of natural law that whatever is built on land belongs to the owner of the land"), and that certainly seems to be the easiest way to render this somewhat awkward phrase. If, however, we compare this statement with the statement of the same rule in Gaius's *Institutes* ("that which is built on our ground by another becomes ours by natural law, because what is built on the surface cedes to the ground [*superficies solo cedit*]") (GI.2.73), we see that Ulpian's statement of the rule is more subjective. The *superficies* does not cede to the soil but pertains to the owner of the soil. When we add this together with the fact that the owner of the soil has a right of action under the *lex Aquilia* (here stated in the passive because the subject of the sentence is the wrongdoer), we may suggest that the subjective natural right of the owner was not far from the author's mind.

If someone disinherits an emancipated son and afterwards adrogates [a form of adoption] him, Papinian in his twelfth book of *Questions* says that the *iura naturalia* take precedence in him; therefore the disinheritance is prejudicial. (D.37.4.8.7 [Ulp., Ed. 40])

The son is the natural child of his father whom the latter has disinherited. Civilly he is the adrogated child of his father, adrogated after the making of the testament, and not mentioned as such in it. If the civil status were allowed to be treated separately, the son might not only be entitled to *bonorum possessio* as one who had not been expressly disinherited, but he might also break the testament as a *praetermissus*. One can see how Papinian might have wanted to avoid that result, and the way he achieves it is by saying that the natural status takes precedence over the civil: *iura naturalia in eo praeualere*. The *iura* in question are highly subjective; the problem is that they are not, in this case, rights as we conceive of them, but liabilities, in particular the liability to being disinherited by the father's testament. The *ciuilia iura*, however, over which the *naturalia iura* impliedly prevail are, in this case, subjective rights as we understand them.

It is neither civil nor natural [*ius*] to anticipate the chance of ill fortune [falling on] a free man, for we properly deal with those things that can immediately be put to our use and ownership. (D.45.1.83.5 [Paul., Ed. 72])

It is not entirely clear that *ius* is to be supplied after *naturale*, though the editors of the *Vocabularium Jurisprudentiae Romanae* do so. If *ius* is to be supplied, we may take the phrase either in an objective or a subjective sense: "It is neither civil nor natural law to anticipate the chance of ill fortune [falling on] a free man." "It is neither a natural nor a civil right to anticipate the chance of ill fortune [falling on] a free man." The fact that the passage immediately precedes the matters about which "we rightly deal" (*negotium recte geremus*) suggests that a subjective understanding of *naturale* (*ius*) here is at least possible.

CONCLUSIONS

The use of the word "ius" in a subjective sense is so common in the texts of classical Roman law that one wonders how anyone could think otherwise. It is, however, possible to be misled by the insight that the word "ius" is frequently used in classical Roman legal texts in ways that cannot mean subjective legal right.

It is possible also to be misled by a linguistic fallacy that people who use the same word in two different senses are not aware of the two senses because they are using the same word.[24] That proposition is not true as a general matter, and is, I think, belied in this case by the rather careful way in which the Roman lawyers structured the words around the word "ius" when they were using the word in a subjective sense or when it was open to a subjective meaning. It is true, of course, that in many cases it does not make any difference whether a subjective or objective meaning of the word is intended, and it is also true that in almost all instances the subjective right in Roman law is dependent on an objective one.

This last observation should be scanned. We should not forget Holmes's aphorism: "[F]or legal purposes a right is only the hypostasis of a prophecy – the imagination of a substance supporting the fact that public force will be brought to bear on those who do things said to contravene it."[25]

---

[24] There are hints of this in Villey, "Droit subjectif," 225.
[25] Oliver Wendell Holmes, "Natural Law," *Harvard Law Review* 32 (1918): 40, 42.

Modern lawyers, particularly those trained in European civil law, tend to deal in legal categories shorn of their procedural context and hence of the enforcement mechanisms in which they are embedded. Classical Roman lawyers were not like that, particularly when they were not writing textbooks for first-year law students, like Gaius's *Institutes*. In the post-classical period this changed with the abandonment of the formulary system. The change, however, was not from objective right to subjective,[26] but from subjective right bounded by the formula to subjective right with a potentially less-well-defined import. In Hohfeldian terms, the discipline of the formula requires that one consider the correlative duties or no-rights of any subjective right, while the more open procedure of the *extraordinaria cognitio* may allow one to consider a subjective right without its defining correlatives.

There are, however, two areas in which we would expect to find subjective rights being discussed by the Roman jurists where we do not find them. Rarely, if ever, is the term used to describe the right of a citizen against the state. That absence may be the result of the fact that the *Digest* has relatively little to say about public law, but an unsystematic search in non-jurisitic authors did not find many instances of it in discussions of Roman "constitutional" law. We also find it only rarely (and we had to struggle to find it at all) in connection with natural law. If the jurists in the twelfth and thirteenth centuries were not particularly original in their use of the concept of subjective rights, they were original in their development of the idea of subjective natural right. How important this idea was before the debates about Franciscan poverty in the fourteenth century, I will not venture to say, but it clearly was there in a way in which it was not there in Roman law.[27]

This chapter has dealt with the classical Roman jurists, all of whom, so far as we know, were pagans.[28] The question then becomes whether the juristic conception of subjective right made its way into Christian thought prior to the revival of learning in Roman law in the twelfth century. It seems plausible that it did. Even Villey admitted that a subjective conception of right existed in non-juristic Roman thought, and it seems likely that at least some of the Church Fathers were familiar with juristic

---

[26] As Villey seems to argue in "Le 'jus in re'," 188–9.
[27] See further the chapter by R. H. Helmholz herein.
[28] The identification of the obscure second-century jurist Tertullian with the Church Father of the same name strikes me, as it has many historians, as implausible. See Timothy David Barnes, *Tertullian: A Historical and Literary Study* (Oxford: Oxford University Press, 1971), 22–9.

thought. Now that the entire contents of Migne's *Patrologia Latina* are available in digital form, it would be possible to study the use of the word "ius" in its various forms in the Latin Church Fathers in the same way in which it has been studied in the *Digest*, although it would be a large undertaking. Until that is done, the connection between the concept of *ius* in the Roman jurists and that in Christian thinkers prior to the twelfth century must remain an unproven possibility.

RECOMMENDED READING

Barnes, Timothy David. *Tertullian: A Historical and Literary Study.* Oxford: Oxford University Press, 1971.

Cortese, Ennio. *La norma giuridica: Spunti teorici nel diritto comune classico*, 2 vols. Milan: Giuffrè, 1962–4.

The Digest of Justinian, ed. Theodor Mommsen and Paul Krueger, trans. ed. Alan Watson, 4 vols. Philadelphia: University of Pennsylvania Press, 1985.

Donahue, Charles. "*Ius* in the Subjective Sense in Roman Law: Reflections on Villey and Tierney," in Domenico Maffei *et al.*, eds., *A Ennio Cortese*. Rome: Il Cigno, 2001, I:506–35.

Hohfeld, Wesley Newcomb. "Some Fundamental Legal Conceptions as Applied in Judicial Reasoning," *Yale Law Journal* 23 (1913): 16–59. Reprinted in Wesley Newcomb Hohfeld, *Fundamental Legal Conceptions*. New Haven: Yale University Press, 1919.

Holmes, Oliver Wendell, Jr., "Natural Law," *Harvard Law Review* 32 (1918): 40–5.

The Institutes of Gaius, ed. Francis De Zulueta, 2 vols. Oxford: Oxford University Press, 1946.

The Institutes of Justinian, ed. J. B. Moyle, 2 vols., 5th edn. Oxford: Oxford University Press, 1913.

Kaser, Max. *Das römische Privatrecht*, 2nd enl. edn, 2 vols. Munich: Beck, 1971–5.

"Zum 'Ius'-Begriff der Römer," in Wouter de Vos *et al.*, eds., *Essays in Honor of Ben Beinart*, 2 (= *Acta Juridica* [1977]): 63–81.

Pennington, Kenneth. *The Prince and the Law, 1200–1600: Sovereignty and Rights in the Western Legal Tradition*. Berkeley: University of California Press, 1993.

Schulz, Fritz. *Classical Roman Law*. Oxford: Oxford University Press, 1951.

Tierney, Brian. *The Idea of Natural Rights: Studies on Natural Rights, Natural Law and Church Law, 1150–1625*. Atlanta: Scholars Press, 1997.

Villey, Michel. "L'Idée du droit subjectif et les systèmes juridiques romains," *Revue historique de droit français et étranger*, 4e sér. 24–5 (1946–7): 201–28.

"Du sens de l'expression *jus in re* en droit romain classique," in Lucien Caes, René Dekkers, and Roger Henrion, eds., *Mélanges Fernand de Visscher*, 2 (= RIDA, 1er sér. 3) (1949): 417–36.

"Le 'jus in re' du droit romain classique au droit moderne," in *Conférences faites à l'Institut de droit romain en 1947*. Paris: Institut de droit romain de l'Université de Paris, 1950, 187–225.

"Suum jus cuique tribuens," in *Studi in onore di Pietro de Francisci*. Milan: Giuffrè, 1956, 361–71.

Vocabularium Iurisprudentiae Romanae, 5 vols. in 7. Berlin: G. Reimeri and W. de Gruyter, 1903–87.

CHAPTER 3

Human rights and early Christianity

David E. Aune

The ancient Mediterranean world was redolent with economic, national, racial, social and gender hierarchies, divisions, and inequalities – like many societies in the modern world. While the kinds of human rights that have developed in the West during the past two centuries, influenced by the Enlightenment, have roots in the ancient world, those rights were based not on *secular* conceptions of the human person that have flourished in modern liberal democratic regimes, but rather on the *religious* ideologies of various ancient ethnolinguistic groups. This chapter will focus on the evidence for the theoretical and practical conceptions of *equality* in early Christianity, with emphasis on equality in the three areas of nationality, social status, and gender, under the assumption that equality is a basic constituent of human rights everywhere.

Since ancient societies had an essentially religious orientation, conceptions of equality that have modern analogues were based on religious rather than secular or rational presuppositions. Monotheism (the belief that one God exists and no others), for example, appears to have functioned as a necessary though insufficient cause for the development of the conception of equality between major ethnolinguistic groups. In the post-exilic period, Judaism developed an ethnocentric form of ethical monotheism in which the God of Israel was identified with the one God of the cosmos with the implication that the gods worshiped by Gentiles were idols with no reality. While some Jews maintained that all people would eventually share the blessings attendant on recognizing the God of Israel as the one and only God (particularly in the latter days), other Jews were negative about the access that the Gentiles could have to God and expected that they would finally be excluded from his presence and annihilated.[1]

Another form of monotheism was developed in Stoicism, founded in the late fourth century. Stoics formulated a strikingly non-ethnocentric

[1] See E. P. Sanders, *Jesus and Judaism* (Philadelphia: Fortress Press, 1985), 212–18.

form of materialistic monism in which God and the material world were considered identical. God was also regarded as identical with Reason or Mind, which pervades the cosmos and is also present in gods and human beings. One social implication of this form of monotheism that helped to break down national and social barriers is that individual human natures are parts of universal nature. Stoics were famously cosmopolitans who held that all people are equal and should live in mutual love and understanding.

In addition to having an essentially religious orientation, ancient societies had conceptions of the human person that differed from notions of the autonomous self that developed in the West beginning with Augustine's *Confessions* through the Enlightenment to modern Western liberal democracies. The differences between ancient and modern Western conceptions of the person are often understood in terms of the dichotomous models of "individualism-collectivism" (describing cultures) or "idiocentrism-allocentrism" (describing individuals who are part of those cultures). Individualistic cultures and idiocentric persons emphasize values that serve the interests of the self (by making the self feel good, distinguished, independent), while collectivist cultures emphasize values that subordinate personal goals to the values of the group. The notion of *individual* rights is a modern Western conception centered on a post-Christian society made up of people who are largely of northern European ancestry living in modern liberal democracies.

Early Christianity began as a sectarian movement within Palestinian Judaism originally limited to Aramaic-speaking Palestinian Jews. Within ten to fifteen years after the death of Jesus (*c.* 29 CE), the Jesus movement had begun expanding outside of Palestine to Jewish communities in the Levantine diaspora, in cities such as Samaria, cities on the island of Cyprus, and Antioch on the Orontes in Syria (the third largest city of the Roman Empire). Paul was the central figure in the mission to the Gentiles and some time before he began writing letters to communities he had founded, the followers of Jesus adopted the innovative designation "church" (*ekklesia*) for individual local assemblies of believers. This conception, which included people of various nationalities, social statuses as well as both men and women, had no close analogy in the ancient world.

The earliest work in the New Testament, 1 Thessalonians (written *c.* 49 CE), is addressed "To the church of the Thessalonians in God the Father and the Lord Jesus Christ" (1:1). Later, Paul has occasion to refer to "the churches of God in Christ Jesus which are in Judea" (2:14) in the plural (see also 1 Cor. 11:16; 2 Thess. 1:4). Both uses of the term "church" suggest that it is already traditional and widespread usage. Even more striking is the fact that "church" is used in the singular to refer to the global community of believers (1 Cor. 10:32; 12:28; 15:9; Gal. 1:13; Phil. 3:6; Acts 20:28). In the ancient world, religious identity and ethnicity were virtually inseparable. After struggling for years with the particularity of its original Jewish identity, Christianity was somehow able to conceptualize itself on analogy to the ancient philosophical schools, as primarily a system of belief and practice unconnected in any essential way with ethnicity and nationality.

JESUS OF NAZARETH AND HUMAN RIGHTS

Raising the question of what Jesus said and did during his brief ministry in the early first century (*c.* 26–29 CE) is an historical problem with which generations of scholars have wrestled. Yet there are two very different ways of examining the influence that Jesus had on the socio-religious movement that he inspired.

First, it is possible to emphasize the importance of reconstructing the teachings and activities of the historical Jesus using the historical critical method.[2] While this is certainly a legitimate enterprise, one complication of this approach is the fact that there are major disagreements among critical scholars when it comes to deciding what the historical Jesus actually said and did. Currently there are two competing models of the historical Jesus. According to the older model, Jesus was an apocalyptic prophet, who proclaimed the imminent arrival of the Kingdom of God and taught an ethic (based in part on conventional Jewish moral teaching) appropriate for living under the reign of God.[3] Viewing Jesus as an apocalyptic prophet tends to emphasize the *distance* between Jesus and the modern world. The other model is that of Jesus as a prophet and teacher of subversive wisdom, a view that argues that apocalyptic features of the teaching of Jesus were a product of the early church (in the tradition of liberal Protestantism).[4] The view that understands Jesus primarily as a prophetic

---

[2] See John P. Meier, *A Marginal Jew: Rethinking the Historical Jesus*, Anchor Bible Reference Library, 4 vols. (New York: Doubleday, 1991–2009). A fifth volume is in preparation.

[3] See, for example, Sanders, *Jesus and Judaism*; Sanders, *The Historical Figure of Jesus* (London: Penguin Books, 1993); Dale C. Allison, *Jesus of Nazareth: Millenarian Prophet* (Minneapolis: Fortress Press, 1998); Bart D. Ehrman, *Jesus: Apocalyptic Prophet of the New Millennium* (Oxford and New York: Oxford University Press, 1999).

[4] See, for example, Marcus J. Borg, *Jesus, A New Vision: Spirit, Culture and the Life of Discipleship* (New York: HarperCollins, 1987); Borg, *Meeting Jesus Again for the First Time: The Historical Jesus and the Heart of Contemporary Faith* (New York: HarperCollins, 1994); John Dominic Crossan, *The Historical Jesus: The Life of a Mediterranean Jewish Peasant* (New York: HarperCollins, 1991);

David E. Aune

teacher of a this-worldly wisdom tends to lessen the historical distance between Jesus and the modern world. Those who have understood Jesus using this model have frequently exhibited a strong interest in the social relevance of Jesus's mission for the modern world. John Dominic Crossan, for example, presents Jesus as a revolutionary who preached social equality. Crossan regards the Jesus movement that developed after the death of Jesus as a social movement that emerged from the subjugated peoples of the Roman Empire, immersed in poverty and misery, that sought to transform a violent and predatory empire into an egalitarian society. Elisabeth Schüssler Fiorenza describes the movement in which Jesus and his companions participated as an egalitarian movement that formed an inclusive community of the downtrodden and powerless.[5]

Second, it is important to recognize the fact that the four Gospels *in their present written form* (admittedly combining history with legend and myth) have continued to exert influence on Christian belief and practice from the time of their origin and initial circulation (*c.* 70–100 CE) to the present. In other words, what the historical Jesus actually said and did (to the extent that can be reconstructed using various criteria of historicity) is not as important as what his followers *thought* that he said and did. In other words, the *Wirkungsgeschichte* ("history of influence") of the canonical Gospels has been more important and influential for the thinking of the church than the relatively recent attempts to reconstruct the historical Jesus or the "real" Jesus.

As the founder of a revitalization movement, Jesus was primarily interested in the restoration of all Israel in the end time. This program is symbolized by the fact that the twelve disciples were intentionally chosen by Jesus to represent the restoration of the twelve tribes of Israel. To that extent his proclamation of the imminent arrival of the Kingdom of God was an ethnocentric message, for Jesus did not regard either himself or his disciples as having a mission to the Gentiles. At the same time, his proclamation emphasized an eschatological social reversal, in which (for example) God accepted the poor and rejected the rich: "Then Jesus looked around and said to his disciples, 'How hard it will be for those who have wealth to enter the kingdom of God'" (Mark 10:23). This eschatological reversal had an important rhetorical function, for it signaled a subversion of the typical religious values and conceptions that characterized the

Crossan, *Jesus: A Revolutionary Biography* (New York: HarperCollins, 1994); Crossan, *The Essential Jesus: Original Sayings and Earliest Images* (New York: HarperCollins, 1994).
[5] Elisabeth Schüssler Fiorenza, *Jesus and the Politics of Interpretation* (London and New York: Continuum, 1997).

Jewish religious establishment. The conception of an eschatological social reversal is central to the Beatitudes, the first of which focuses on the plight of the poor (Luke 6:20; Matt. 5:3): "Blessed are you poor, for yours is the kingdom of God."

Another significant aspect of the eschatological reversal is God's rejection of Israel (doubtless because of its rejection of the message of Jesus) and acceptance of the Gentiles:

[Those Jews addressed will be thrown out of the kingdom and] There you will weep and gnash your teeth, when you see Abraham and Isaac and Jacob and all the prophets in the kingdom of God and you yourselves thrust out. And men will come from east and west, and from north and south, and sit at table in the kingdom of God. (Luke 13:28–9)

This kind of eschatological reversal, in which Israel, the traditional people of God, is rejected and replaced by Gentiles, is found in other sayings of Jesus including the allegorical parable of the wicked tenants (Mark 12:1–11), in which the tenants (Israel) will be destroyed by the owner (God), who will turn the vineyard over to others (Gentiles). While Jesus did not pursue a mission to the Gentiles, neither did he accept the ritual separation of Jews from Gentiles that was characteristic of Jewish religious practice.

Another striking characteristic of the ministry of Jesus is the fact that he rejected the "caste system" of official Judaism during the first century CE as well as the purity system on which it was based; he both accepted and associated with those whom official Judaism excluded. Matthew 21:31 is particularly provocative: "Truly I tell you, the tax collectors and the prostitutes are going into the kingdom of God ahead of you." Jesus consciously dramatized God's acceptance of social outcasts by having table fellowship with them, ignoring Jewish food and ritual purity laws, and thereby implicitly rejecting an unjust social structure. The kind of company Jesus kept is reflected in Matthew 11:18–19:

For John came neither eating nor drinking, and they say, "He has a demon"; the Son of man came eating and drinking, and they say, "Behold, a glutton and a drunkard, a friend of tax collectors and sinners!" Yet wisdom is justified by her deeds.

Finally, a story found in Mark 2:15–17 dramatizes Jesus's counter-cultural practice:

And as he sat at table in his house, many tax collectors and sinners were sitting with Jesus and his disciples, for there were many who followed him. And the scribes of the Pharisees, when they saw that he was eating with sinners and tax collectors, said to his disciples, "Why does he eat with tax collectors and sinners?" And when Jesus heard it, he said to them, "Those who are well have no need of a physician, but those who are sick; I came not to call the righteous, but sinners."

We have already mentioned the fact that the four Gospels agree that Jesus undertook no programmatic ministry directed toward the Gentiles as a group. When universalizing features are found in the Gospels, they are typically late and legendary additions reflecting developments in the Jesus movement from the late first century BCE, though only critical scholars have been aware of this fact. The absence of a Gentile mission is epitomized by the statement attributed to Jesus before sending his disciples out on a mission to the people of Israel (Matt. 10:5): "Go nowhere among the Gentiles, and enter no town of the Samaritans, but rather to the lost sheep of the house of Israel." Yet at the end of Matthew, the risen Lord tells the disciples (28:19–20):

Go therefore and make disciples of all nations, baptizing them in the name of the Father and of the Son and of the Holy Spirit, teaching them to observe all that I have commanded you; and lo, I am with you always, to the close of the age.

This passage reflects the fact that following the death of Jesus, his followers did inaugurate a mission to the Gentiles, which the author of Matthew wanted to trace back to Jesus.

Rather than reaching out to Gentiles as a group, there are three stories involving Jesus's outreach out to various distressed non-Jews: the Gerasene demoniac (Mark 5:1–20), the Syrophoenician woman (Mark 7:24–30; Matt. 15:21–8), and the Centurion's servant (Matt. 8:5–13; Luke 7:1–10). The story of the Syrophoenician woman, while probably not authentic, contains an emphasis on universality, but does not reflect very well on Jesus. Mark 7:24–30 contains the story of the healing of the demon-possessed daughter of a Gentile. Like many others, she had heard that a famous and effective healer was in the area, so she appealed directly to Jesus (v. 26): "Now the woman was a Greek, a Syrophoenician by birth. And she begged him to cast the demon out of her daughter." This gives way to a thrust-and-parry bit of dialogue (vv. 27–30):

And he said to her, "Let the children first be fed, for it is not right to take the children's bread and throw it to the dogs." But she answered him, "Yes, Lord; yet even the dogs under the table eat the children's crumbs." And he said to her, "For this saying you may go your way; the demon has left your daughter." And she went home, and found the child lying in bed, and the demon gone.

This story is striking for the harsh and insulting language used by Jesus, including characterizing Gentiles as "dogs" (using the so-called "criterion of embarrassment" one might argue for the authenticity of this story). The story also portrays Jesus's focus on Israel to the virtual exclusion of Gentiles, even those with pressing physical and emotional needs.

Jesus had a central concern for the equality of all Jewish people before God in his vision of the restoration of the twelve tribes of Israel, regardless of their social station, gender, occupations, and whether or not they maintained the requisite state of ritual purity demanded by traditional Judaism. Though Jesus did not pursue a mission to the Gentiles, neither did he argue that Jews keep separate from Gentiles because of the danger of ritual pollution. Jesus pursued an ethnocentric mission to Israel, but in so doing he disregarded the social rules that separated Jews from one another as well as from God. While the later mission to the Gentiles pursued by the followers of Jesus after his death was not part of a program envisaged by Jesus, it can be argued that such a universal mission is based on the inherent logic of the message of Jesus.

PAULINE CONCEPTIONS OF EQUALITY AND THEIR INFLUENCE

The earliest surviving Christian writings are the seven genuine letters of Paul, written from *c.* 49–58 CE – Romans, 1–2 Corinthians, Galatians, Philippians, 1 Thessalonians, and Philemon. One of Paul's central emphases, particularly in Romans and Galatians, is that the traditional God of Israel has now prepared a way of salvation not only for Jews but also for Gentiles. Taking a page from the ministry of Jesus, Paul ignored ethnic particularities, especially Jewish ritual regulations that made the close association of Jews with Gentiles virtually impossible. Paul understood faith in Jesus Christ to be the only requirement for salvation.

Perhaps the most radical statement of this idea is found in Galatians 3:26–8:

> For you are all sons of God through faith in Christ Jesus.
> For as many of you as were baptized into Christ have put on Christ.
> There is neither Jew nor Greek,
> There is neither slave nor free,
> There is neither male nor female;
> For you are all one in Christ Jesus.

This is a quite astonishing conception that seems to abolish in principle all inequities based on nationality, social status, and gender. Galatians 3:28 is not an isolated statement. 1 Corinthians 12:13, for example, mentions both nationality and social status in two parallel lines formulated antithetically as in Galatians 3:28:

> For it is by one Spirit we were all baptized into one body,
> Whether Jews or Greeks,
> Whether slaves or free,
> And all were made to drink of one Spirit.

The same two areas of equality are mentioned in Colossians 3:9–11 (a Deutero-Pauline letter written under the influence of Pauline thought):

Do not lie to one another, seeing that you have put off the old nature with its practices and have put on the new nature [a metaphor for baptism], which is being renewed in knowledge after the image of its creator. Here there is not Greek and Jew, circumcised and uncircumcised, barbarian, Scythian, slave, free man, but Christ is all, and in all.

Here the antithesis focusing on nationality, "Greek and Jew," is replicated with another common antithesis found in Pauline rhetoric: "circumcised [i.e., Jew] and uncircumcised [i.e., Greek]," expanded with "barbarian, Scythian [found nowhere else]." "Slave, free man" are also included, as in Galatians 3:28.

Most scholars agree that Galatians 3:28 is a traditional baptismal formula (baptism is explicitly mentioned in v. 27), but this actually makes little difference in how the passage is interpreted. The question is what did this passage and its parallels in 1 Corinthians and Colossians mean, regardless of whether they had a liturgical origin? Some understand these passages as theological, rather than social, statements; they refer, not to ethnicity, social status, and gender relationships *within the church between members*, but only to the fact that baptism into the body of Christ is available to all regardless of ethnicity, social status, and gender.[6] This reading does not go far enough. Paul is not only concerned with the irrelevance of nationality, social status, and gender for entry into the church through baptism, he is equally concerned to emphasize that after entry, they continue to be "one in Christ Jesus," i.e., brothers and sisters in the new family of God. According to Elisabeth Schüssler Fiorenza, "the Christian movement was based not on racial and national inheritance and kinship lines, but on a new kinship in Jesus Christ."[7] Further, in declaring the end of

---

[6] Pamela M. Eisenbaum, "Is Paul the Father of Misogyny and Antisemitism?" *Cross Currents* 50 (2000–01): 506–24, at 511; Troy W. Martin, "The Covenant of Circumcision (Genesis 17:9–14) and the Situational Antitheses in Galatians 3:28," *Journal of Biblical Literature* 122 (2003): 111–25, at 122.

[7] Elisabeth Schüssler Fiorenza, *In Memory of Her: A Feminist Theological Reconstruction of Christian Origins* (New York: Crossroad, 1983), 210.

ethnic, social, and gender polarities in the new creation (Gal. 6:15), Paul does not contemplate the abolition of ethnic, social, and gender differences in the real world, but rather the end of all social hierarchies. In Galatians 3:28, Paul rejects hierarchy but not difference as such.

For Paul, nationality, social status, and gender continue to be of no consequence in the church. *Spiritually*, all who have been baptized are "one in Christ Jesus" and are brothers and sisters in the family of God, a new spiritual reality, even though *physically* they remain what they were before baptism. There is an inevitable tension between physical reality and spiritual reality that Paul has not fully worked out as we shall see as we discuss each of the antithetical phrases in Galatians 3:28 (and parallels), particularly in our discussion of 1 Corinthians 7:21–4 and Philemon.

"There is neither Jew nor Greek." Paul often used the ethnic terms "Jew" and "Greek" in tandem, with the latter term meaning "Gentiles" (Rom. 1:16; 2:9, 10; 3:9; 10:12; 1 Cor. 1:22–4; 10:32; 12:13; Gal. 3:28; cf. Col. 3:11). "Jew and Greek" was an ethnocentric designation of everyone in the world, analogous to the equally ethnocentric Greek phrase "Hellenes and *barbaroi*," i.e., Greeks and non-Greeks. When Paul uses the phrase "neither Jew nor Greek," however, he is not simply referring to the eradication of ethnic differences generally, but rather to the abolition of Jewish ritual law as a primary means of eliminating the differences between Jew and Greek. In Romans 10:12–13, Paul expresses his view about ethnic divisions in very specific terms: "For there is no distinction between Jew and Greek; the same Lord is Lord of all and bestows his riches upon all who call upon him. For, 'every one who calls upon the name of the Lord will be saved.'" When Paul uses the phrase "Jew and Greek," and particularly in the form "the Jew first and also the Greek," he is referring to Jewish chronological priority in the history of salvation. The phrases "circumcised and uncircumcised" (Col. 3:11) and "circumcision and uncircumcision" (always in that order) are examples of synecdoche parallel to "Jew and Greek" that occur several times in the genuine Pauline letters.[8] A close parallel to Romans 10:12–13, cited above, is found in Galatians 6:15: "For neither circumcision counts for anything, nor uncircumcision, but a new creation." In the Old Testament and in early Judaism, circumcision was occasionally given a religious interpretation, i.e., "circumcision of the heart,"[9] a view

---

[8] Circumcised and uncircumcised: Rom. 3:30; 4:9; 1 Cor. 7:18; circumcision and uncircumcision: Rom. 2:25, 26; 1 Cor. 7:19; Gal. 5:6; 6:15; cf. Eph. 2:11.

[9] Deut. 10:16; 30:6; Jer. 4:4; 9:26; Ezek. 44:7, 9; 1QpHab. 11.13; cf. 1QS 5.5.

picked up by Paul and later Christian authors (Rom. 2:28–9) or baptism referred to as a "circumcision made without hands" (Col. 2:11–12).

In Galatians 3:28, then, when Paul says that there is neither Jew nor Greek, is he referring only to the fact that the initiatory rite of baptism is open to those of all ethnic groups, or does he mean in addition that equality among ethnic groups continues to characterize the behavior of all of those who are "one in Christ Jesus"? A clear answer to this question can be found earlier in Galatians, where Paul recounts his confrontation with Peter (Gal. 2:11–14). Paul tells us that Peter, along with other Jewish followers of Jesus, ate with Gentiles in Antioch. When a group of the "circumcision party" arrived from Jerusalem, however, Peter separated from the Gentiles following Jewish ritual laws. Paul opposed Peter for living like a Gentile, yet trying to compel the Gentiles to live like Jews. For Paul, the principle of "there is no Jew or Gentle" not only applies to those who enter the church through baptism, but also ought to be the attitude of those Jews and Gentiles who are members of the community of faith. Paul expresses this conviction differently in 1 Corinthians 10:17: "Because there is one loaf, we who are many are one body, for we all partake of the one loaf."

The expansion of the Jesus movement from a sect within Judaism to a socio-religious movement composed of both Jews and Gentiles was the cause of lasting conflict between these two ethnolinguistic entities. The central issue was the role played by Jewish ritual law (circumcision, food regulations, purity laws, Sabbath observance), i.e., symbolic markers of Jewish national identity. The Pauline affirmation that "there is neither Jew nor Greek" (Gal. 3:28) and the parallel expression "where there is no Greek and Jew, circumcised and uncircumcised" (Col. 3:11) is a concept of national or ethnic parity with which not all first-century Jewish followers of Jesus would have agreed. By the end of the first century the Jewish Christian groups in the eastern Mediterranean that insisted on combining ritually observant Judaism with belief in Jesus as the Messiah had effectively marginalized themselves and are now remembered only as isolated heretical sects that soon disappeared from the pages of history. Also by the end of the first century, Christianity had spread throughout the Mediterranean world as an unparalleled socio-religious movement that accepted people from all ethnic groups, the rich and the poor, men and women, slaves and free.

"There is neither slave nor free." Paul's declaration in various versions that "there is neither slave nor free" (Gal. 3:28; 1 Cor. 12:13; cf. Col. 3:11) was counter-cultural for his day. Aristotle, for example, had maintained that slavery is "natural," rather than conventional, and that slavery was both just and good for both the slave and the master.[10] The Roman law of Paul's day maintained that "all men are either free or slaves."[11] Paul discusses slavery at greater length in 1 Corinthians 7:21–4 and in Philemon. The relation of slaves to masters is mentioned in several of the Deutero-Pauline household codes (Col. 3:22–4; 4:1; Eph. 6:5–9; 1 Tim. 6:1–2; Titus 2:9–10). In 1 Corinthians 7:21–4, Paul argues that members of the church should remain in the same social station they had when they became part of the people of God (italics added):

Were you a slave when called? Never mind. But if you can gain your freedom, avail yourself of the opportunity. *For he who was called in the Lord as a slave is a freedman of the Lord. Likewise he who was free when called is a slave of Christ.* You were bought with a price; do not become slaves of men. So, brethren, in whatever state each was called, there let him remain with God.

Here the phrase "he who was called in the Lord as a slave is a freedman of the Lord" is clearly an example of freedom *coram Christo*; external circumstances are relatively unimportant compared with the new spiritual reality of being in Christ. As De Ste. Croix observes: "the equality exists 'in the sight of God' and has no relation whatever to temporal affairs."[12] In antiquity there was a widespread view, expressed by Epicureans, Stoics, and Christians, that slavery (like poverty and war, wealth and peace) is a matter of indifference affecting externals only (Lucretius, *De rerum natura* 1.455–8). The good and wise man is never really a slave even though he may actually be one; it is the bad man who is really a slave, since he lives in bondage to his own desires.[13] This ancient paradoxical commonplace is applied by Paul to followers of Jesus: those who are free are really slaves of Christ, while those who are slaves are really free in the Lord.

In 1 Corinthians 7, Paul also discusses the social situations of the married and the single (vv. 1–16, 25–8, 32–40), the circumcised and the uncircumcised (vv. 17–20), and slavery and freedom (vv. 21–4), all three of the

---

[10] Aristotle, *Politics* 1252a–1255b [1.1.1–2.23]. See G. E. M. de Ste. Croix, *The Class Struggle in the Ancient Greek World from the Archaic Age to the Arab Conquest* (Ithaca: Cornell University Press, 1981), 416–18.

[11] Gaius, *Institutes* 1.9; Justinian, *Institutes* 1.3.

[12] Ste. Croix, *The Class Struggle*, 419.

[13] Bion (Stobaeus, *Anthologium* 3.187.5): "Slaves who are morally good are free; masters who are morally evil are slaves of their desires." A later formulation of this principle is found in Augustine's *Civitate Dei* 4.3 (Loeb Classical Library trans.): "Hence even if a good man be a slave, he is free; whereas if a wicked man rules, he is a slave – and a slave not to one man but, what is worse, to as many masters as he has vices."

antitheses in Galatians 3:28. Paul's advice on all three issues is based on his expectation of the imminent end of the world, discussed in an explanatory digression in 1 Corinthians 7:29–31 (italics added), which applies directly to marriage and indirectly to slavery and circumcision:

I mean, brethren, *the appointed time has grown very short*; from now only, let those who have wives live as though they had none, and those who mourn as though they were not mourning, and those who rejoice as though they were not rejoicing, and those who buy as though they had no goods, and those who deal with the world as though they had no dealings with it. *For the form of this world is passing away.*

Therefore, Paul expects slaves as well as the married and single, the circumcised and the uncircumcised to consider their present situation in life within an *eschatological framework*, i.e., time is short and the form of this world is passing away. Slavery, like marriage or celibacy, circumcision or uncircumcision, belongs to the present scheme of things that is about to disappear. Moreover, in Christian reality, slaves are really the free masters, while the masters are really the slaves.

The situation behind Paul's Letter to Philemon is that Onesimus is a slave owned by Philemon (or Archippus), whom Paul had recently converted to Christianity. Onesimus has left or been sent from home in Colossae and has made contact with Paul. Onesimus is usually described as a runaway slave, but little in this short letter supports this. More probably, Onesimus had somehow wronged or injured Philemon (v. 18). Onesimus, who knew about Philemon's relationship with Paul, had come to Paul hoping that he would intercede for him with his master Philemon to heal whatever breach had arisen. Onesimus had clearly become one of Paul's valued coworkers, as verse 12 indicates:

I am sending him back to you, sending my very heart. I would have been glad to keep him with me, in order that he might serve me on your behalf during my imprisonment for the gospel.

Paul's Letter to Philemon provides a tantalizing snapshot of a master–slave relationship within the early church that has important implications for understanding the meaning of Galatians 3:28. Though the entire letter revolves about the issue of slavery, the term "slave" occurs just twice, both instances in v. 16. In vv. 15–16, Paul tells Philemon (italics added):

Perhaps this is why he was parted from you for a while, that you might have him back for ever, *no longer as a slave but more than a slave, as a beloved brother*, especially to me but how much more to you, both in the flesh and in the Lord.

The italicized portion indicates that though Paul is sending Onesimus back to Philemon "as a slave," since he has been converted to the faith after departing from his owner, he is now at the same time also a "beloved brother," i.e., using Galatians 3:28, they are now "one in Christ Jesus." While this passage has been construed in a variety of ways,[14] this reading coheres well with Paul's intentions in Galatians 3:28. For Philemon to have regarded Onesimus as both a physical slave and a spiritual brother would inevitably have involved a degree of tension and conflict between the two roles, a tension that Paul neither acknowledges nor explores. But this was a notable departure from most prevailing views in his day, though there were Roman Stoics and Essenes who also regarded slaves as brothers.[15]

Modern Christian readers often express disappointment that Paul does not forthrightly condemn slavery, advocate manumission, or propose a social program for abolishing slavery. On the other hand, Paul does not justify slavery or suggest that it is an institution ordained by God or sanctioned by nature. In the ancient world, slavery was concentrated primarily in Roman Italy and in mainland Greece and Greek settlements overseas; in these areas the idea of life without slavery would have been unthinkable. While a few fragments of debates on the subject among Greek thinkers have survived, no one, pagan or Christian, advocated the abolition of slavery. Both the Roman Stoics and Church Fathers argued for the humane treatment of slaves, but at the same time "preached obedience to the slaves."[16] This accords with the Deutero-Pauline household codes that briefly mention masters and slaves (Col. 3:22–4; 4:1; Eph. 6:5–9; 1 Tim. 6:1–2; Titus 2:9–10). These texts primarily emphasize the duties of slaves to their masters, but also enjoin the mistreatment of slaves.

"There is neither male nor female." The phrase "there is neither male nor female" in Galatians 3:28 (missing from 1 Cor. 12:13 and Col. 3:9–11), has attracted a great deal of interpretive interest, especially from feminists. Elisabeth Schüssler Fiorenza has referred to it aptly as "a focal point of feminist debate."[17] While the ancient Mediterranean world was a

[14] See John M. G. Barclay, "Paul, Philemon and the Dilemma of Christian Slave-Ownership," *New Testament Studies* 37 (1991): 170–5.

[15] According to Epictetus (*Dissertationes* 1.13.3–4), for example, all people are family, brothers and sisters by nature, and offspring of Zeus (cf. Seneca, *Epistulae morales* 40.1, 10). Philo also attributes the Stoic conception of universal brotherhood to the Essenes, whom he presents as a utopian community (*Quod omnis probus liber sit* 79; Loeb Classical Library trans. with modifications).

[16] Moses I. Finley, *Ancient Slavery and Modern Ideology* (New York: The Viking Press, 1980), 121.

[17] Elisabeth Schüssler Fiorenza, *Rhetoric and Ethic: The Politics of Biblical Studies* (Minneapolis: Fortress Press, 1999), 159 (see the discussion of Gal. 3:28 on pp. 159–73).

male-dominated hierarchical society,[18] some members of the Jesus movement evidently took counter-cultural stances on the public roles of women
in the church. This was facilitated in part by the sectarian nature of the
new movement, which needed to establish its own identity, norms, and
values over against those of pagan culture and society generally. Paul's
statement "there is neither male nor female" – unlike the companion
antithesis of "neither Jew nor Greek" and "neither slave nor free" – has
few parallels in the rest of Paul's letters. But in 1 Corinthians 11:11–12, Paul
relativizes the relationship between men and women, an insight expressed
more fully in Galatians 3:28:[19]

Nevertheless, in the Lord woman is not independent of man nor man of woman;
for as woman was made from man, so man is now born of woman. And all things
are of God.

It is important to observe that in this passage the hierarchical relationship
between men and women is relativized only *in the Lord*, a parallel to the
concluding phrase *all things are of God*. It is not only that men and women
are equal *coram deo*, but that the preceding injunction in 1 Corinthians
11:9–10 should not be read in a subordinationist way.[20]

The early church was ambivalent about gender roles. Some women held
significant leadership positions in the early churches, including the roles
of apostle (Rom. 16:7), deacon (Rom. 16:1–2),[21] leaders of house churches
(Acts 12:12; 16:14–15, 40; Col. 4:15) as well as teachers and prophets (1 Cor.
11:4–16). But there were frequent attempts to emphasize or reinstate traditional gender values by silencing women in public (1 Cor. 14:33–5)[22] and by
exhorting them to play a more conventional subordinate role in the family
(Eph. 5:22–6:4; Col. 3:18–4:1; 1 Tim. 2:11–15; Titus 2:1–10). However, since
Ephesians, Colossians, and the Pastoral Letters (1–2 Timothy and Titus)

---

[18] Dale B. Martin, *The Corinthian Body* (New Haven and London: Yale University Press, 1995),
3–135.
[19] Krister Stendahl, *The Bible and the Role of Women* (Philadelphia: Fortress Press, 1966), 35.
[20] Gordon D. Fee, *The First Epistle to the Corinthians*, The New International Commentary on the
New Testament (Grand Rapids, MI: Wm. B. Eerdmans, 1987), 522–4.
[21] In a letter written by Pliny the Younger, the Roman governor of Bithynia at the beginning of the
second century, to the emperor Trajan, we learn that two women slaves (*ancillis*) were "deacons"
(*ministrae*) in the church of Bithynia (Pliny, *Ep.* 10.96.8; see A. N. Sherwin-White, *The Letters of
Pliny: A Historical and Social Commentary* [Oxford: Clarendon Press, 1966], 708), indicating that
in this region and time, being a slave and being a woman were not obstacles to enjoying status in
the Christian communities (Schüssler Fiorenza, *In Memory of Her*, 209).
[22] This passage is widely, and I think correctly, understood as a reactionary interpolation into 1
Corinthians; a view held even by a conservative Evangelical scholar: see Gordon D. Fee, *The First
Epistle to the Corinthians*, 699–708.

are widely regarded as Deutero-Pauline, the subordinate role for women recommended by the unknown authors of these letters probably reflects post-Pauline developments during the late first and early second century CE. For whatever reason, the role of women in the church became increasing assimilated toward the hierarchical gender conception of the broader Graeco-Roman world during the early second century.

Let us look for a moment at two interesting important texts on the roles of women in the early church found in Romans 16. First, Paul mentions Phoebe the deaconess:

> I commend to you our sister Phoebe, a deacon [*diakonon*] of the church at Cenchreae [the seaport of Corinth], so that you may welcome her in the Lord as is fitting for the saints, and help her in whatever she may require from you, for she has been a benefactor [*prostatis*] of many and of myself as well. (Rom. 16:1–2, NRSV)

As with several other New Testament texts relating to women in ministry, the plain meaning of this passage has frequently been subverted, most easily by translating *diakonos* as "servant."[23] But although many earlier commentaries have tried to downplay Phoebe's role in the church in Cenchreaea, "it now seems more likely that she functioned as the leader of the congregation."[24] In addition, her role of "benefactor" or "patron" (commentators frequently fail to give *prostatis* its most natural and obvious sense of "patron"), suggests that she was a woman of wealth and a person of prominence in the ancient world,[25] one who personally sponsored projects of vital significance to Paul.

In Romans 16:7, two people are mentioned that Paul considers "prominent among the apostles." One of them is Andronicus (a masculine name). The name of the other has two different readings in the Greek manuscripts, one of which is Junia (a feminine name) while the other is Junias (a masculine name). Eldon Jay Epp has argued convincingly that the name originally written by Paul was "Junia."[26] While "Junia" was a

---

[23] For arguments against translating *diakonos* as "servant," see J. D. G. Dunn, *Romans 9–16*, Word Biblical Commentary 38b (Dallas: Word Books, 1988), 886–7.

[24] Robert Jewett, *Romans: A Commentary*, Hermeneia (Minneapolis: Fortress Press, 2007), 944; see the analysis of διάκονος (a word of common gender) by Bengt Holmberg, *Paul and Power: The Structure of Authority in the Primitive Church as Reflected in the Pauline Epistles* (Philadelphia: Fortress Press, 1978), 99–100 and esp. n. 30.

[25] Joseph A. Fitzmyer, S.J., *Romans: A New Translation and Commentary*. Anchor Bible 33. (New York: Doubleday, 1993), 731. For a more detailed discussion of the social and cultural significance of a *prostatis*, see R. A. Kearsley, "Women in Public Life in the Roman East: Iunia Theodora, Claudia Metrodora and Phoebe, Benefactress of Paul," *Tyndale Bulletin* 50 (1999): 189–211.

[26] Eldon Jay Epp, *Junia: The First Woman Apostle* (Minneapolis: Fortress Press, 2005). See also Schüssler Fiorenza, *In Memory of Her*, 47–8, 172.

common name that occurs hundreds of times in ancient sources, the masculine form "Junias" (possibly an abbreviation of "Junianus") is not attested in any Graeco-Roman sources. Moreover, Paul in Romans 16 is warmly commending several women, including Prisca, making Junia the natural name to include. The name "Junia" was the unanimous choice of interpreters during the first 1,300 years in the history of interpretation of Romans 16:7 and was chosen as the correct reading in all editions of the Greek New Testament until the Nestle edition of 1927. It was only English translations of the New Testament produced during the nineteenth and twentieth centuries that favored the masculine form "Junias." The choice of the masculine name in these instances appears to be the result of prejudice rather than reason. It was a woman, Junia, who was "prominent among the apostles."

CONCLUSIONS

While some nineteenth-century historians, like Adolf von Harnack, confidently reconstructed the teaching of Jesus in a way that was friendly to modern human rights, emphasizing the universal fatherhood of God, the brotherhood of man, and the infinite worth of the individual, that reconstruction was an anachronistic illusion. By the mid-twentieth century, New Testament scholars were making serious efforts to acknowledge and correct the problems of subjectivism inherent in reconstructing the life and teaching of Jesus. While it is legitimate to inquire whether particular sayings or deeds of Jesus are historical or not, the Gospels have been read as realistic narratives throughout the history of the church. It is primarily this commonsense reading that has influenced the church through the centuries.

Jesus is presented in the Gospels as one who proclaimed the coming of the Kingdom of God and the coincident restoration of the twelve tribes of Israel. While Jesus is not presented as engaging in a mission to Gentiles, he did emphasize a great eschatological social reversal in which the poor would not only be accepted by God and the rich rejected, but Israel as the people of God would be rejected, while the Gentiles would be accepted. Within Judaism itself, Jesus rejected the "caste system" that separated the non-observant from the observant Jews, those considered ritually unclean from those that were ritually pure. His proclamation of the Kingdom of God was in effect a democratizing of salvation in that he did not discriminate against the poor, the outcasts, Samaritans, Roman soldiers, prostitutes, and tax collectors. He dramatized the new conception of equality before God that he was proclaiming by sharing table fellowship with whoever accepted his message of the imminent Kingdom of God and its moral implications for daily living. In doing this he ignored the rigid system of purity laws that often functioned to exclude ordinary Jews from the Temple, where God was present and where salvation could be obtained through the sacrificial system.

In our discussion of the ideology and practice of equality advocated by Paul, we used the three consecutive phrases found in Galatians 3:28 as a springboard for examining various types of equality in the Pauline letters and other early Christian literature. While Paul's conception of aspects of human equality is not ethnocentric, neither is it universal in the sense advocated by the Roman Stoics. For Paul, human equality is limited to the church of God, though anyone who believes and is baptized can be a member. The phrase "there is neither Jew nor Greek" indicates that Paul thought that entry into the people of God by baptism was equally accessible to people of all nationalities, but particularly that Jews had no advantage over Gentiles. Yet it is clear that Paul did not consider equality as a reality only *coram Deo* ("before God"). He was convinced that Jewish believers and Gentile believers were obligated to share table fellowship (strongly reminiscent of the practice of Jesus) as part of their shared life "in Christ Jesus." The very fact that Paul thought that national differences were irrelevant for those who belonged to the new people of God suggests that the two other areas of equality – "neither slave nor free" and "neither male nor female" – not only reflect equal status before God, they also signal changed attitudes toward others that ought to prevail in the life of the church.

The statement "there is neither slave nor free" is somewhat more ambivalent. In Paul's relatively brief discussion of slavery in 1 Corinthians 7, he gives his version of the paradoxical saying widely found in antiquity (v. 22): "For he who was called in the Lord as a slave is a freedman of the Lord. Likewise he who was free when called is a slave of Christ." This is equality *coram Deo* ("before God") and has no relationship to actual social status. Elsewhere in 1 Corinthians 7, Paul advises slaves, like the unmarried, to keep the social status that they had when they became believers (based on the reason that the present world is about to pass away), but if they have the chance to become free they should take advantage of it (v. 21). In Paul's Letter to Philemon, he tells his friend to consider Onesimus as both a slave and a beloved brother. While Paul does not resolve the tension that would have existed between those two quite different roles, a transformation of social relationships is certainly in view.

When Paul maintains that "there is neither male nor female" in Galatians 3:28, he is not speaking of society in general, but only of the transformed relationship between men and women that characterized life "in Christ Jesus." Obviously, Paul is not claiming that the physical characteristics of females and males will be eliminated, or that the biological character of human beings will be nullified, but he is claiming that gender equality in the church is part of the new life in Christ. While Paul still shows the influence of the gender hierarchy that dominated Graeco-Roman society, it is nevertheless true, as Martin has observed, that "Paul assigns women a larger role and more respect in his churches and in his theology than they would have enjoyed in many other areas of Greco-Roman Society."[27] In the long history of Pauline interpretation in the church, it is remarkable how frequently in the last century and a half that the ideology of gender hierarchy has obscured and downplayed the role of Phoebe the deacon and patron of Paul (Rom. 16:1–2) or turned Junia the apostle into a male figure (Rom. 16:7). Now, perhaps more than ever before, it is possible to let Paul's views of the roles of men and women in the church be treated honestly and objectively.

RECOMMENDED READING

Barclay, John M. G. "Paul, Philemon and the Dilemma of Christian Slave-Ownership," *New Testament Studies* 37 (1991): 161–86.

Bassler, Jouette M. *Divine Impartiality: Paul and a Theological Axiom*. Chico, CA: Scholars Press, 1981.

Epp, Eldon Jay. *Junia: The First Woman Apostle*. Minneapolis: Fortress Press, 2005.

Finley, Moses I. *Ancient Slavery and Modern Ideology*. New York: The Viking Press, 1980.

Groothuis, Rebecca Merrill. *Good News for Women: A Biblical Picture of Gender Equality*. Grand Rapids, MI: Wm. B. Eerdmans, 1997.

Kahl, Brigette. "No Longer Male: Masculinity Struggles behind Galatians 3.28?" *Journal for the Study of the New Testament* 79 (2000): 37–49.

Meier, John P. *A Marginal Jew: Rethinking the Historical Jesus*, Anchor Bible Reference Library, 4 vols. New York: Doubleday, 1991–2009.

Rynne, Terrence J. *Gandhi and Jesus: The Saving Power of Nonviolence*. Maryknoll, NY: Orbis Books, 2008.

Sanders, E. P. *Jesus and Judaism*. Philadelphia: Fortress Press, 1985.

Schüssler Fiorenza, Elisabeth. *In Memory of Her: A Feminist Theological Reconstruction of Christian Origins*. New York: Crossroad, 1983.

Stendahl, Krister. *The Bible and the Role of Women*. Philadelphia: Fortress Press, 1966.

[27] Martin, *The Corinthian Body*, 199.

CHAPTER 4

Human rights in the canon law
R. H. Helmholz

To some observers, the search for human rights in the law of the medieval church has seemed a vain effort. Was not the canon law the source of the notorious Spanish Inquisition, granting inquisitors the power to condemn men and women to death because of their religious opinions? Did it not lodge all legitimate authority in an autocratic papacy, granting to the Roman pontiff a potentially unlimited power over church and clergy? Did it not perpetuate the Roman law's institution of slavery, allowing religious institutions to hold men and women in perpetual servitude? It did. And these are not idle questions or the product of an ignorant and reflexive anti-Catholicism. The historical record shows that in many areas of human life the medieval church fully deserves the censure of a more enlightened age. Only by selective reading or artificial invocation of the principle that the values of one place and time should not be imposed upon another can one celebrate the achievements of the medieval church's law in the creation of human rights. The implications of many attractive doctrines from the Scriptures, such as the notion that man was created in the image of God that is ably presented in this volume by Jeremy Waldron, were either distinguished away or ignored by most medieval and early modern jurists.

Why, then, does the law of the medieval church deserve any place at all in a work devoted to Christianity and human rights? Sound scholarship of recent years has argued that it does, indeed that the source of many modern rights is actually to be found in the evolution of the canon law. That scholarship invites readers to examine human rights as they were understood and worked out by learned jurists in the Middle Ages. This chapter summarizes the work that has been done so far, discussing the

The following abbreviations to the texts of the *ius commune* have been used:

D. 1.1.1   *Digestum Justiniani*, lib. 1, tit. 1, lex 1
Dist. 1 c. 1   *Decretum Gratiani*, Distinctio 1, canon 1
C. 1 q. 1 c. 1   *Decretum Gratiani*, Causa 1, quaestio 1, canon 1
X 1.1.1   *Decretales Gregorii IX*, Book 1, tit. 1, cap. 1

evidence that counts in favor of accepting its conclusions and assessing the extent to which the law of the medieval church in fact implemented human rights. The harsh treatment of some men and women that the canon law endorsed stands as a warning that the medieval law did not always recognize the *same* human rights we do today. No true right to freedom of religion or speech existed in the canon law, and granting anyone a right to follow whatever sexual desires he or she felt would have seemed perverse licentiousness to the medieval canonists. However, the canon law's recognition of the existence of human rights, including some that have remained vital to this day, should not be neglected in a study of the subject's history. True, it should not be exaggerated either. Too much should not be claimed for the work-product of lawyers. But there is something there all the same. The concept of a human right did not spring into existence *ex nihilo* with the Declaration of the Rights of Man and Citizen in France in 1789.

There are at least two basic ways of approaching the subject. The first begins by examining the language used by the jurists. The second begins by examining the content of particular rules found in the medieval law that were intended to ensure the observance of legal rights. The one asks whether the canon law knew the idea of a human right. The other asks whether that knowledge made any difference in the protection of ordinary men and women.

THE VOCABULARY OF RIGHTS

Charles Donahue's chapter on Roman law in this volume demonstrates that the classical heritage of the medieval church included the concept of a legally enforceable right that inhered in individual persons. Whether or not one concludes that these rights were human rights in the sense we mean today, his analysis of the term "ius" in the sixth-century *Digest* shows that the word served many purposes, and that some of them were very close to those now understood as subjective rights. This analysis is important for the subject of this chapter. The medieval church took over and used the Roman law, pruning it where necessary but accepting most of its vocabulary and many of its habits of thought. John McGuckin's chapter in this volume shows that in the East this inheritance had an impact on the thought of the Orthodox churches, and that influence was also felt in the West. From the earliest times, the clergy was said to "live according to the Roman law" – only a slight exaggeration of the reality. With the revival of Roman law that began in the eleventh century and with the formulation of a mature canon law in the twelfth, it was entirely natural that the men who framed the church's law (as well as the medieval civilians, the jurists who commented upon the Roman law's *Corpus iuris civilis*) should have followed this lead and built upon this classical foundation. That their habitual reference to the civil law had consequences is demonstrable in the texts of the canon law. One such consequence was that the term "ius" in the canon law embraced the idea that a lawful power could inhere in an individual, even a basic human right.

Yet the matter is not simple. The canonical texts cannot easily be read as a charter of individual rights. Compiled in the twelfth and thirteenth centuries, the *Corpus iuris canonici* shows the many and varied uses to which the term "ius" was put. Gratian's *Decretum* (c. 1140), the first great work of the classical canon law, contains an explicit discussion of the term. *Iure divino*, a foundational text in it states all earthly property was to be held in common (D. 8 c. 1). "The earth is the Lord's." Only out of God's good will was it committed to men, and they continued to hold it under limitations imposed by God's will. Rights so envisioned may seem at odds with the notion of strong human rights to property; indeed such a formulation might be subversive of any such right, since it could mean that all human claims to ownership of property were held subject to a stronger obligation to carry out God's purposes. Those purposes might, for example, require sharing the earth's bounty with others, as in times of special need. Or they might call for providing support for God's representatives on earth, the clergy. Indeed the term "ius" was used in this sense. In the hands of the canonists, Gratian's text thus required qualification of the right to hold property. It could not be absolute. At the same time, however, this same text in the *Decretum* went on to say that *iure humano*, individual property rights, could be established and that they would give lawful dominion to their possessors. They obviously had been in fact. At least without lawful justification, a man's property could not be seized by his lord, even the king. If seizure occurred, it was theft. Gratian thus attached the word "ius" to property rights granted by the positive law. For him, it was by virtue of a *ius*, one created by the emperor, that anyone could say, "This is my house" or "This is my land." Those words could be said by holders of property rights, and they did so with confidence and reason. Even if it was not absolute, Gratian conceived of *dominium*, of a *ius* in property, as a basic right held by an individual.

The texts found in the second half of the canon law, principally the *Decretales Gregorii IX* published in 1234 at the initiative of Pope Gregory IX, seem similar in the ways they made use of the term. Book 5 of the *Decretales* contains a definitional section; one of the words defined there is *ius* (X 5.40.12). The compiler chose to take his definition from the seventh-century encyclopedist, Isidore of Seville, and on one reading it fits the notion of a subjective right. Isidore put it in terms of a right to possess something, as when one can say "I have a *ius* to possess a thing." At the same time, however, the text goes on to say that the possession must be just if it is to deserve the law's full recognition. The quality of possession must be judged by the law, even the moral law. It may be (and this is an example given in the *glossa ordinaria*) that a miser or an overly greedy person could not make the claim that he holds the property rightly. In other words, this text seems to encompass something like a subjective right, but it is a right that is limited in scope by the use that is being made of it. It is not simply that the property may have to be surrendered to a more urgent purpose, the use being made of it must also conform to what is lawful and just.

In this understanding of the meaning of human rights, the canon law was in fact following and enlarging a path staked out by the medieval civilians. In this aspect of the law, the canonists and civilians kept to the same route. For instance, at the very beginning of the *Digest* comes a title that attempted to define the terms "ius" and "iusticia" (D. 1.1). As the civilians saw it, the two were linked. A right proceeds from justice as a child proceeds from its mother, opined the *glossa ordinaria* that was compiled in the thirteenth century to state the common understanding of this text.[1] Arriving at an exact understanding of what that relationship meant was clouded, it seems, by the scholastic love of disputation, the need to harmonize many divergent texts, and the desirability of conforming the law to the realities of human life. Sometimes the underlying human right almost disappeared from view in the process. Alternate readings of the texts were advanced, and limitations in the scope of rights were admitted. For instance, by the *ius naturale*, men were free. However, this recognition did not establish a human right to freedom that all men could exercise. The existence of human slavery was patent in the texts of the Roman law. It was equally recognized in many parts of medieval Europe. If *ius* descended from *iustitia*, as the jurists said it did, this did not guarantee that all human beings could actually claim a right to freedom from hereditary bondage. Wars and the human condition had established otherwise. Medieval commentators, canonists and civilians alike, read the texts as subject to practical limitations, nowhere with sadder consequences than in this subject. Their understanding of *ius* must be understood in that light.

---

[1] *gl. ord.* ad D. 1.1.1. v. *iustitia*.

Acceptance of limitations, large and small, did not mean that the medieval jurists could not envision the existence of human rights. Their understanding of the law of nature itself played a part in their thought. For instance, by the *ius naturale*, all persons held a right to defend themselves from attack or depredation. If they held no such right, all persons would have been subject to indiscriminate violence or worse. Their right to defend themselves was limited by the creation of an active government, one that would promote the peaceful settlement of quarrels and provide an adequate alternative to self-defense by an individual. However, the right could not be taken away altogether. In times of crisis or in cases of failure by the government, a right to self-defense would resurface as the only practical alternative. Indeed in some circumstances, that right must be recognized by the positive law itself. It would scarcely be just if a legal system did not permit a person being attacked and in fear of his life to defend himself. This same way of thinking about rights stood behind the widely recognized power to resist a tyrannical ruler during the Middle Ages. Even the famous defense of tyrannicide found in the *Policraticus* of John of Salisbury (d. 1180) found its justification under this understanding of the meaning of the term "ius". If all else failed, the natural right to defend oneself against a tyrant might be exercised by the human community.

The term "ius" thus meant more than one thing in the medieval law. Many commentators so stated, as for example the English canonist William Lyndwood (d. 1446): "The word *ius* is employed for various purposes" in the law.[2] It is even more apparent if one takes up one of the encyclopedic works compiled as a guide to the *ius commune*, the amalgam of the canon and the Roman laws that furnished the basic general law in continental Europe. The *Dictionarium iuris* compiled by Albericus de Rosate (d. 1354) provides an example. He recorded that "sometimes *ius* is taken to mean the civil law" and sometimes it is taken to mean "the art of the good and the equitable," and also sometimes it means something else. He went on to catalogue the possibilities. A love of multiple definitions was characteristic of many medieval jurists. Albericus was no exception. The seeming artificiality of some of those he hit upon should not, however, cause modern readers to lose sight of the fact that some of his definitions described subjective rights. To have a *ius*, for example, was to have a power

---

[2] *Provinciale (seu Constitutiones Angliae)* (Oxford, 1679), 162–3 v. *iuribus*: "Aliomodo et diversimodo sumitur ius."

of dominion over a thing.[3] What men and women enjoy as a *ius* should not be taken away by another.[4]

This was not just academic speculation. That the meaning of the term "ius" could include something very like a subjective right is also apparent in the working details of the medieval canon law. One of the most familiar and important at the time was the *ius patronatus*. This was a right that belonged to the patron of an ecclesiastical benefice to select a parson upon the death, resignation, or deprivation of the incumbent. Roughly speaking, it was equivalent to a right to choose the pastor of a parish church. The right could be held by a community, but more normally the *ius patronatus* belonged to an individual, often the successor of the person who had first built the church and endowed it. It was not an absolute right. The patron had to secure the consent of the bishop to his choice in the interests of protecting the well-being of the church as a whole, but it was a strong right in the sense that it could not be taken away without good cause. Subject to some limits, it belonged to a person, who held it as his right. The meaning of the term "ius" was not confined to describing a body of normative rules, a legal order, or an objective assessment of what was right.

Various areas of the medieval canon law made regular and similar use of the term. For example, the law drew a distinction between a *ius ad rem* and a *ius in re*. The right to be awarded an office or an inheritance was not equivalent to actually possessing the perquisites of office or the possession of inherited goods. Claiming a power is different from exercising it. That the medieval canonists discussed at length the practical consequences of the difference between them shows that their vocabulary embraced thought about the nature of personal rights. Similar usage appears elsewhere. For purposes of litigation, the canonists endorsed a *ius deliberandi*, the right to a delay to be given to each party so that they could adequately prepare an answer to a motion introduced by the other.[5] In the law of last wills and testaments, they shared with the civilians a concern to protect the *ius declarandi voluntatem suam* or the *testamenti faciendi ius*, that is the right freely to dispose of one's property at death.[6] The exact contours of testamentary freedom were open to debate; some canonists thought the right should be exercised in favor of the church; others allowed limitations

---

[3] *Dictionarium iuris tam civilis quam canonici* (Venice, 1573), 411: "Ius habere in re dicitur qui habet dominium tam utile quam directum."
[4] *Ibid.* "Ius suum cuiquam detrahi non debet."
[5] Domenicus Tuschus (d. 1620), *Practicarum conclusionum iuris* (Lyon, 1661), Lib. II, Lit. 'I', concl. 584.
[6] D. 28.1.16–18.

to be drawn in favor of the family. So this right remains, *mutatis mutandis*, in our own law.

Nevertheless, at many places where we should expect to hear "rights talk" in the canon law, we find little to justify that expectation. The right of appeal to the papal court provides a good example. Did all Christians have the right to invoke the protection of the Roman pontiff? Under King Henry II of England, this became a contentious question. The royal Constitutions of Clarendon (1164) denied that appeals could be taken to the Roman court without royal approval, even in ecclesiastical matters.[7] That proposition was resisted, and successfully resisted, by Archbishop Thomas Becket and his supporters. Becket's subsequent martyrdom established the principle that such appeals were to be allowed. The event was an important moment in establishing the *libertas ecclesiae*, the freedom of the church, in England. Yet to all appearances, the church's law books and the writings of the canonists did not regard this as establishing anything like a *ius appellationis*, a right of appeal, in a substantive sense. At least they seldom used the term. A long title in the Gregorian Decretals – seventy-three chapters in all – dealt with the problem of defining a workable law of appeals. The reasons given in it for allowing appeals were something of a mixed bag. Appeals respected the hierarchical nature of the church's jurisdiction, they provided a means of policing jurisdictional boundaries between secular and temporal matters, and they helped secure that that final sentence would be correctly decided and impartially declared. Even in minor matters, appeals must be permitted (X 2.28.11). These were good reasons. What is missing in them is any statement that all Christians held a fundamental right to make such an appeal. In the modern Catholic Code of Canon Law (1983),[8] the appeal is described as a *ius*, but that was not the normal terminology during the Middle Ages. Indeed many of the papal decretals in the title, building on a sentence by Ulpian in the *Digest* (D. 28.1.16–18), sought to curtail any such right, doing so in the interests of more effective administration of justice. Frivolous and repetitious appeals were to be discouraged. If Christians enjoyed a fundamental right to appeal to the Roman pontiff, as they did in most instances, it was a result of other goals in the canon law, not the goal itself.

Examples like these suggest caution. They also raise a legitimate question. Did any of these ways in which the term "ius" was used actually

---

[7] c. 8, in *Stubbs' Select Charters*, 9th edn, ed. H. W. C. Davis (Oxford: Oxford University Press, 1913), 165.
[8] See canon 1628, in *Codex iuris canonici* (Washington, DC: Canon Law Society of America, 1983), 582–3.

include human rights in the modern sense of the word? Modern controversy has shown that it is not easy to arrive at an agreed-upon definition of the concept of a human right, but ordinarily we think of it as a lawful power accorded to every person simply by virtue of his or her status as a human being. If the right is not adequately protected by the positive law, it should be. A human right is an interest of every person that should not be abridged without the strongest of reasons. Most of the examples just given do not seem to fit that definition. Are there others that do?

One of the early examples that does seem to fit the modern definition is the *ius sustentationis*, the right to subsistence. All people on earth have a claim to the necessities of life. According to the medieval understanding, the origins of this right lay in the law of nature, and it had potential consequences. In the canon law, a Christian duty of charity and almsgiving supported implementation of the claim to sustenance – it showed who had the duty to provide for the needy. As developed by the medieval canonists, the claim also went beyond a statement of pious and abstract principles. The *ius sustentationis* meant that in times of extreme dearth, the poor could take from the available stock of property. They had a right to take enough to sustain themselves without being guilty of theft. In a slightly different context, the principle meant that if a child was "exposed" by its father according to the Roman custom, that child was thenceforth freed from parental control (X 5.11.1). The same rule was applied to abandoned slaves. The master surrendered his control by his act of abandonment. Providing food and shelter was a precondition of the exercise of authority by parents and masters. By our lights, this movement toward recognition of a human right to subsistence seems halting. The canonists did not advocate the creation of a welfare state. They could not have envisioned such a development, and they might not have welcomed it. Nonetheless, they did recognize that "children and servants do have an integrity of their own that must be respected."[9] The vocabulary of the medieval canon law included this right as one all men and women held by virtue of their humanity.

THE CONTENT OF RIGHTS

Beyond the evidence provided by the canon law's vocabulary, a second reason exists for looking to the law of the church as part of a study of the origins of rights. It is that the canon law developed legal rules that in

---

[9] Scott G. Swanson, "Rights of Subsistence in the Twelfth and Thirteenth Centuries: The Case of Abandoned Children and Servants," in Kenneth Pennington *et al.*, eds., *Proceedings of the Tenth International Congress of Medieval Canon Law* (Vatican City, 2001), 675–91, at 685.

fact protected what would later be considered to be fundamental human rights. Many – perhaps most – of them were not normally described as *iura* in a subjective sense. However, in fact they provided protection for human liberty. The right of appeal discussed above is one example. Much of the recent historical scholarship on the origins of rights has dealt with the development of this kind of right, and it shows some striking connections between medieval and modern human rights. It also shows some clear differences. Three examples follow, one taken from procedural law, one from domestic relations law, and one from public law.

The first is the ancestor of the privilege against self-incrimination, the right to silence in the face of a criminal accusation. Widely regarded as a fundamental human right, it is enshrined in the Fifth Amendment to the United States Constitution and also held to be a salutary principle in European law. In fact, it was accepted and clearly stated by the medieval canonists and civilians. The Roman law provided only the sketchiest justification for the rule, but that no person could be compelled to incriminate himself was stated clearly in the most basic guide to the canon law, the *glossa ordinaria*: "No person is required to answer, because no one is bound to betray himself."[10] Of course, this was no guarantee that one would suffer no consequences from wrongful conduct. More centrally, all men were bound to confess their imperfections, including their crimes, to God. If all else failed, God would mete out appropriate punishment. But it was not so in the public courts of the church. If it were, all men and women would be subject to trial and public punishment. We are all guilty of having committed some criminal acts at one time or another in our lives, and it would upset the right order of society if we were all called to account for them, revealing the nature and extent of those crimes, in a public forum.

The scope of this privilege – the limitations attached to it and the extensions drawn from it – was worked out in learned commentaries, beginning in the later Middle Ages. Probably the most prominent examples of this literature were the treatises on civil and criminal procedure written during the sixteenth and seventeenth centuries. Julio Claro (d. 1575), the influential Italian jurist, is a representative figure. He repeated and endorsed the rule that no one could be obliged to reveal shameful facts about himself, but he also went on to qualify the rule. It admitted of exceptions. Like many of his fellow jurists, Claro confined it to situations where no lawful accuser had brought the charge or where no *fama publica* existed.[11] This was a serious check on anyone's ability to exercise the privilege of silence.

---

[10] *gl. ord.* ad X 2.20.37, v. *de causis.*
[11] Julius Clarus, *Sententiarum receptarum liber quintus* (Venice, 1595), Quaest. 45, no. 9.

It meant that, particularly if the crime were serious, widespread public fame that a particular individual had committed a crime could authorize a judge to question him or to put him to an oath in which he faced a choice between conviction or perjury. If he refused to answer or to take the oath, he could be punished for contumacy, perhaps even for the crime itself. The right to silence may not have vanished from Claro's pages, but it was confined within straitened limits. Under some readings, it applied only to truly secret crimes. Like many procedural rights even under modern law, this one was not absolute. Whether the limitations to it require that its medieval form does not count in the history of human rights is not an easy question to answer. Some would say yes; some would say no. At the least, however, one can see in the literature of the medieval canon law some of the same concern for the protection of ordinary men and women from aggressive criminal prosecution that lies behind the modern right.

A second example is the right to freedom of entry in marriage. Much has been written about this subject in recent years. The results have not been free from disagreement. It seems fair to say, nonetheless, that a consensus of opinion now holds that the medieval canon law sought to ensure that the decision to marry should be the product of free choice by the parties to the union. The wishes of the couple's parents or their feudal lords, the transfer or settlement of property, the publication of the banns of marriage and its public celebration, even sexual consummation of the union – all these fell to one side in the face of the consent of a couple to become man and wife. Where they had expressed their intention by words of present consent, as in "I take thee N. as my wife [husband]," and where that exchange of words could be proved in court, that was the end of the matter. They were validly married. Subsidiary rules also enlarged the scope of freedom. Coerced marriages were opened to invalidation by the party who had been coerced (X 4.1.14). Secular legislation restricting the ability of men and women to marry was invalidated, or at least subjected to the strictest sort of construction. The marriages of free and unfree were declared possible, even without the consent of the master of the unfree party, although it was open to dissolution if the condition of the parties had been unknown to the parties (X 4.9.1–2). "Marriages should be free" became a commonplace of the canon law, and it was a rule individual men and women could invoke. They did so in fact. Marriages like the one in Shakespeare's *Romeo and Juliet* were many times repeated in life.

Did the principle of freedom in marriage, then, rise to the level where we can speak of it as a human right? This has been the disputed question, and it is open to doubt. The medieval jurists did not normally speak of consent in marriage as a *ius*. The biblical marriage of Joseph and the Virgin Mary seems to have been more influential in establishing the principle that consent, not coitus, made a true and valid marriage than was a human right to freedom of contract. When the canonists were pressed for a reason for their insistence that freedom of consent exist in contracting marriage, their habitual answer was that "forced marriages have unhappy outcomes," not that it was the expression of a natural human right. They certainly did not say that anyone had a right to divorce. Moreover, the canonists were clear that a clandestine marriage, though valid and enforceable, was not itself lawful. It was not something of which the law approved. Indeed the couple who freely but secretly entered into a contract of marriage could actually be punished for disobedience of the church's law. If the canon law regarded marriage as a human right, therefore, it was a circumscribed right. The Council of Trent's 1563 decree *Tametsi*, requiring the presence of the parish priest for the validity of a marriage, further reduced the scope of marital freedom. Like many examples of human rights endorsed by the law of the church, this one existed, but in a form that seems unduly limited to modern observers. It may be only historians of the canon law who are impressed.

A third example is the right to participate in elections. Today a right to vote is commonly accorded to all adult men and women. It expresses a broadly agreed consensus among us: rulers require the consent of those they govern. If not respected in fact, the right is respected in form in most parts of the world. Where it is denied outright, something appears very wrong. Regimes where the right to vote is denied are classed as dictatorships. They are urged to reform themselves. Admittedly, this area of public law seems a strange place to hunt for the origins of human rights in the medieval canon law. The forests of Germany seem a more likely place to look. The canon law is said by some to have been characterized by a "descending theme" of government. It was a system in which all legitimate power flowed from God. It was exercised in practice by the popes and their delegates.[12] What part could elections play in such an institution? None, it would seem. But in fact, elections played a considerable role in the classical law of the church. The first book of the Gregorian Decretals contains a long title devoted to the subject (X 1.6.1–60). A *ius eligendi* was very much a part of the law of the church. The popes were themselves elected. Under the classical canon law, so were bishops and heads of

---

[12] This theme was repeatedly and forcefully stated by Walter Ullmann; see his *Law and Politics in the Middle Ages* (Ithaca: Cornell University Press, 1975), 31.

monastic houses. Even in parish churches, officers might be chosen by the election of parishioners. The question for the men who framed the medieval canon law was to establish how those elections were to be conducted, and (most important in the context of the history of rights) to decide who would be entitled to vote.

The system they worked out in practice was not free from ambiguity. In many ways it was very far from the "one person, one vote" ideal that is part of modern law. However, it did seek to guarantee that elections would be held and that every qualified elector would be able to cast an effective ballot. Gratian's *Decretum* sought to show that contrary customs, such as allowing a bishop to select his successor, were invalid (C. 8 q. 1 c. 4). The choice of a new bishop must be free, and it must be made by the proper persons. In episcopal elections, normally the electors were the members of the cathedral chapter, although this could be varied by local custom; for popes, it was the College of Cardinals (X 1.6.6). The Decretals established that all the qualified electors were entitled to be summoned to take their part, and in the absence of a valid summons, the election was to be declared invalid (X 1.6.35–6). Rules for voting – requiring time limits and proper forms for the ballots – were set forth in the texts and refined in the works of the commentators. The short of it was that the canon law sought to ensure that the *ius eligendi* would be exercised in fact and that elections would be the product of free and considered choice. It is true that the requirements did not meet the standards of a modern, democratic election. The laity was excluded on principle from most elections. The choice of the voters was subjected to review by their superiors, in part to guarantee the fairness of the procedures followed, in part to guarantee the suitability of the person elected. The principle that the majority of votes determined the outcome only gradually gained acceptance in law. Like many modern rights, the canonical *ius eligendi* seems a distant cousin of the modern democratic right. And, in fact, a large part of it was swept away in the course of later centuries by the rise of papal control in the Catholic Church. Still, the medieval church did at least have a sophisticated law of elections. The Roman law and most medieval customary laws did not. When it came time for European nations to adopt more democratic forms in the choice of rulers, one source to which they turned was the law of elections worked out by the medieval church. If that law fell short of treating the *ius eligendi* as a full human right, one available to all men and women, this did not mean that it was not a right at all.

Most of the other specific examples of human rights found in the medieval canon law were of a piece with these three examples. It was possible to speak of a right to select one's burial site, for example, but it was far from a right to be buried anywhere one liked. It was possible to speak of a right of children to inherit from their parents, but it was a right that could be abridged, and, in a case of filial disobedience, disregarded entirely. It was possible to speak of an individual right to take refuge in a consecrated place, as evidenced in the right of sanctuary, but the canon law itself curtailed this privilege as time went on and secular laws went even further down the same road. Probably the liberty interest most often mentioned in the legal records of the time was *libertas ecclesiastica*, but frequently, this turns out to have been an ample cloak that covered claims by churches to reclaim property allegedly wrongfully withheld from them. More often than not, freedom of religion meant the right of the church to advance its own interests. Although the Decretals contained a strong text holding that no unwilling person should be brought to the baptismal font (X 5.6.9), the practice of infant baptism (which could not be undone by later choice) rendered the rule of religious freedom a dead letter in most situations. Indeed, some of the rights asserted in the law of the church now seem quite perverse, a good example being the right of one spouse in marriage to require the other to pay the conjugal debt – no doubt the source of the much-derided historical rule that, in theory, married men have had a legal right to rape their wives.

Even with these qualifications, it does not follow that the human rights developed in the canon law and admitted in the courts of the church counted for nothing. Francisco de Vitoria, Bartholomeo de las Casas, and many of the other early modern Spanish thinkers who formed part of the learned tradition now known as the "Second Scholasticism" shared the view, drawn in part from the canon law, that the native peoples in the New World enjoyed a natural right to freedom. The Spanish *conquistadores* had no legitimate power to seize their property, much less to enslave them. At most, the Spaniards had the power to insist that the Christian Gospel be preached to the Indians. Native peoples must have the choice to accept the Gospel. To read through the history of what happened on the ground in Mexico and Peru is to come away discouraged about the effect of legal theory on human conduct. Vitoria and las Casas were themselves discouraged.

CONCLUSIONS

The standing of the law of the church in the recognition of human rights therefore requires an even-handed response. On the one hand, the canon law did state and promote some human rights. Its vocabulary built upon Roman foundations. Its practice expanded them to include recognition of fundamental human values. Many of them are still important. On the other hand, the canon law did not promote – indeed its practice denied – many human rights that are rightly regarded as fundamental to human liberty. This chapter has attempted to give examples of both. It concludes with an obvious but so far unstated point: the implementation of human rights cannot occur without a prior recognition of the existence of human rights. Showing that the medieval canon law was one vehicle by which their existence came to be recognized has been the accomplishment of recent historical scholarship. It is the reason the law of the medieval church requires a place in this volume.

RECOMMENDED READING

Berman, Harold J. *Law and Revolution: The Formation of the Western Legal Tradition.* Cambridge, MA: Harvard University Press, 1983.

Brett, Annabel. *Liberty, Right and Nature: Individual Rights in Later Scholastic Thought.* Cambridge: Cambridge University Press, 1997.

Helmholz, R. H., *The Spirit of Classical Canon Law.* Athens, GA: University of Georgia Press, 1996.

Hunt, Lynn. *Inventing Human Rights.* New York: W. W. Norton, 2007.

Mäkinen, Virpi and Petter Korkman, eds. *Transformations in Medieval and Early-Modern Rights Discourse.* Dordrecht: Springer, 2006.

Nederman, Cary J. "Property and Protest: Political Theory and Subjective Rights in Fourteenth-Century England," *Review of Politics* 58 (1996): 323–44.

Noonan, John T., Jr. "Power to Choose," *Viator* 4 (1973): 419–34.

Pennington, Kenneth. *The Prince and the Law, 1200–1600: Sovereignty and Rights in the Western Legal Tradition.* Berkeley: University of California Press, 1993.

Reid, Charles J., Jr. *Power over the Body, Equality in the Family: Rights and Domestic Relations in Medieval Canon Law.* Grand Rapids, MI: Wm. B. Eerdmans, 2004.

Sheehan, Michael M. *Marriage, Family and Law in Medieval Europe: Collected Studies,* ed. J. K. Farge. Toronto: University of Toronto Press, 1996.

Tierney, Brian. *The Idea of Natural Rights: Studies on Natural Rights, Natural Law and Church Law 1150–1625.* Atlanta, GA: Scholars Press, 1997.

CHAPTER 5

The modern Catholic Church and human rights: the impact of the Second Vatican Council

J. Bryan Hehir

The emergence of human rights as a central theme in world politics is a recent phenomenon. The basic catalyst has been the UN Declaration on Human Rights (1948), the document which established the political-legal recognition of human rights in world politics. But even this truly innovative text remained at the margin of international relations for the next twenty-five years. Its ideas were honored in principle, but there was little effort to relate them in specific terms to the policies of states. This step, the inclusion of human rights in the foreign policy of states and international institutions, was taken in the 1970s.[1] Since then both the study of world politics and its practice in political-strategic terms have been shaped – in part – by human rights. The literature on the topic has exploded into a cottage industry in the last forty years.[2] Among the themes examined in the literature is the relationship, or the lack of it, between religious traditions and institutions and human rights. There is a spectrum of opinions on the question. Some acknowledge and welcome religious traditions (particularly in the West) as sources of human rights ideas and agents of human rights advocacy. Others see the human rights narrative in purely secular terms, belonging uniquely to the post-Enlightenment era. Arthur Schlesinger, Jr., a major voice in foreign policy circles and a distinguished historian, represents the secularist argument with some intensity:

Human rights – roughly the idea that all individuals everywhere are entitled to life, liberty, and the pursuit of happiness on this earth – is a modern proposition. Orators like to trace this idea to religious sources, especially to the so-called

---

[1] For an introduction to the topic, see R. J. Vincent, *Human Rights and International Relations* (Cambridge: Cambridge University Press, 1986).

[2] For sources and commentary, see Walter Laquer and Barry Rubin, eds., *A Human Rights Reader*, rev. edn (New York: Penguin Books, 1990); Henry J. Steiner and Philip Alston, eds., *International Human Rights in Context: Law, Politics, Morals* (New York: Oxford University Press, 2000).

Judaeo-Christian tradition. In fact the great religious ages were notable for their indifference to human rights in the contemporary sense.[3]

While Schlesinger does not specify which religious traditions failed to support the modern conception of rights, it is a safe bet to presume that Roman Catholicism would be near or at the top of the list. Not only the role of the church from the Roman Empire through the seventeenth-century ("the great religious ages"), but also specific declarations of the church about "modern civil liberties" reflect Schlesinger's critique. Professor Charles E. Curran in his comprehensive volume on Catholic Social Teaching opens his treatment of human rights this way:

Nineteenth-century Roman Catholicism strongly opposed the concept of human rights. Human rights were identified with the Enlightenment in the philosophical realm and with the call for democracy in the political realm.[4]

In the nineteenth century, when democracy, nationalism, and liberalism were major forces on the European scene, both Pope Gregory XVI (1831–46) and Pope Pius IX (1846–78) were resolutely opposed to the idea of "modern liberties." Professor David Hollenbach, S.J., reminds us that, "Pope Gregory XVI had declared that the right to freedom of conscience is an 'insanity' [*deliramentum*]."[5] Similarly, Leo XIII (1878–1903), the pope committed to reestablishing relationships between the church and the diplomatic and intellectual worlds of his time, was resolutely opposed to classical liberalism, even as he began to invoke the concept of human rights.

This background highlights the major transition which occurred in the twentieth century. Catholicism moved from a position of skepticism and opposition to the concept of human rights to an endorsement and appropriation of the concept in its teaching and ministry in the last fifty years of the century. The transition was driven: (1) by changing historical circumstances; (2) by intellectual work in history and philosophy; and (3) by key figures in the academy and the hierarchy. The transition is not accurately described as a "conversion," i.e., Catholicism and liberalism did not come to agreement. It is more accurately described as Catholicism embracing human rights in spite of its opposition to liberalism as a philosophy.

---

[3] Arthur M. Schlesinger, Jr., "Human Rights and the American Tradition," in *The Cycles of American History* (Boston: Houghton Mifflin Co., 1986), 87.

[4] Charles E. Curran, *Catholic Social Teaching 1891 – Present: A Historical, Theological and Ethical Analysis* (Washington, DC: Georgetown University Press, 2002), 215.

[5] David Hollenbach, "A Communitarian Reconstruction of Human Rights: Contributions from Catholic Tradition," in R. Bruce Douglass and David Hollenbach, eds., *Catholicism and Liberalism: Contributions to American Public Philosophy* (Cambridge: Cambridge University Press, 1994), 127.

Theologians in the Catholic tradition would describe the transition on human rights as a "development of doctrine," a change in teaching carried out by a critique of previously held positions and a recognition of truths previously unacknowledged or at least understood from a new perspective. John Courtney Murray, S.J., a uniquely influential source in the transition on human rights, once described the theologian's role in any development of doctrine in the following way:

> He must so present the faith that that which was formerly believed but obscurely understood is now believed and understood more clearly so that posterity may understand and venerate what antiquity had venerated but not understood.[6]

Murray's works are not a perfect fit to explain what occurred within Catholicism concerning human rights. His quote referred in the first instance to doctrinal issues; while human rights and particularly the right of religious freedom are part of the church's social teaching, they are not quite of the doctrinal order.[7] In addition, Murray depicts development as a move from implicit to explicit understanding. Development on human rights had some of that character, but it also involved a move away from some specific judgments of the teaching authority in the nineteenth century. The church of that century saw human rights and democratic freedom as much more of a threat than a promise.[8] The same church over time saw a way of grounding, defining, and specifying human rights as a central element of its social vision. While the transition took over a century, the focus of this chapter will be on Catholicism since the Second Vatican Council (1962–5). More specifically, I shall examine Catholic teaching in four stages: (1) pre-conciliar preparation in Pius XII (1939–58); (2) conciliar era texts: *Pacem In Terris* (1963) along with *Dignitatis Humanae* (1965) and *Gaudium et Spes* (1965); (3) the papacy of John Paul II (1978–2005); and (4) an assessment of the impact of human rights ministry. Throughout the narrative, I shall identify key political and theological themes which influenced developments in Catholic thought and social teaching.

---

[6] Quoted in Francis P. Fiorenza, "Theologian: Witness to Growth," *The Voice* (Winter, 1964): 6.

[7] In making his substantial contribution to a reframing of Catholic teaching on religious freedom, Murray did show how the argument touched on doctrinal issues, particularly issues of ecclesiology, but the dominant concerns were moral, legal, and political. See his historical and theological narrative "The Problem of Religious Freedom," in J. Leon Hooper, ed., *Religious Liberty: Catholic Struggles with Pluralism* (Louisville, KY: Westminster/John Knox Press, 1993), 127–97.

[8] Eamon Duffy, *Saints and Sinners: A History of the Popes* (New Haven: Yale University Press, 1997), 215–35; Peter Steinfels, "The Failed Encounter: The Catholic Church and Liberalism in the Nineteenth-Century," in Douglass and Hollenbach, eds., *Catholicism and Liberalism*, 19–44.

A TRANSITIONAL PAPACY: PIUS XII

It may seem counterintuitive to describe a papacy spanning two decades, a world war and the Cold War as transitional, but in terms of his role in Catholic theology, Pius XII played a critical transitional role in the life of the church. The papacy taken as a whole was a conservative era; Pius XII brought the style of a centralized papacy to the pinnacle of its development. In part this was due to new technology, which allowed him to reach out to Catholics around the world without ever leaving the Vatican; in part it was due to the critical period in which he governed the church; and in part it was due to his conception of leadership which required direct papal influence on all aspects of the church's life. His leadership was transitional in the sense that he provided a bridge between his predecessors and the teaching of the Second Vatican Council. His careful but substantial changes, which he introduced in Catholic biblical studies, in the worship of the church, and in its self-understanding, all provided a foundation for much deeper and broader change in the era of the council.[9]

For the purposes of this essay Pius XII's impact on Catholic moral theology and social teaching is the key question. The papacy from Leo XIII through Pius XI (1922–39) had turned to human rights language in the social encyclicals. They did so in a way that highlighted the differences between the liberal doctrine on rights and Catholic teaching. Liberal theory's focus – rooted in Locke and modern philosophy – stressed rights as immunities. Rights were protectors against interference by the state or other actors in society. In contemporary terms, the liberal tradition was the source of political-civil rights. The social encyclicals, focused primarily as they were prior to Pius XII on the social and moral consequences of the Industrial Revolution, stressed rights as empowerments, as social and economic claims made in the name of workers and their families. Again, in modern terms the church was concerned with social justice and rights claims as a way to achieve justice in a new economic era. The late Ernest Fortin, a philosopher who was less than enthusiastic about the turn to rights language in the social teaching, still recognized the significance of the papal teaching on social justice when he characterized Leo XIII's *Rerum Novarum* (1891) in the following way:

---

[9] For an assessment of Pius XII, see Carlo Falconi, *The Popes in the Twentieth Century: From Pius X to John XXIII* (Boston: Little Brown and Co., 1967), 234–303; see also Duffy, *Saints and Sinners*, 262–8.

One thing is certain: its publication marks the spectacular reentry of the Church in an arena from which it had been excluded as a major player by the great intellectual and political events of the Enlightenment and its aftermath.[10]

Pius XII inherited, therefore, a strain of human rights teaching almost wholly concentrated on the socio-economic order. It addressed the role of the state in terms of its duties toward the poor and marginalized in industrial society. The distinctive step taken by Pius XII was to engage the "other side" of human rights concepts in terms of the role of freedom in civil society. The nineteenth-century papacy saw freedom and democracy as threats to societal order with potentially revolutionary consequences. The social encyclicals saw liberal appeals to freedom as part of the problem of unjust economic relations as the owners of capital oppressed workers.

Left out of these considerations was one of the key issues that political-civil rights were designed to address: protection of the citizen and civil society from the power of the state. Pius XII took the first steps to bring the church's teaching on political-civil rights in line with the socio-economic teaching of the encyclicals. His chosen venue was the traditional Christmas Address which the pope delivers to the College of Cardinals. During the early 1940s, Pius XII developed a body of teaching on political rights and democracy. In doing so he was engaging the liberal tradition, opening space in the Catholic social teaching for the value of freedom and providing the foundation for human rights upon which John XXIII and Vatican II would build.[11]

What moved Pius XII to step significantly beyond his predecessors? Three reasons were certain contributions to this move. First, the encounter with the multiple forms of twentieth-century totalitarian/authoritarian regimes made him sympathetic to human rights and limited government. While Pius XII clearly saw the greatest threat in communism, he had been Secretary of State in the 1930s, when his predecessor, Pius XI, had struggled against both Nazism and fascism. These regimes, the threat they posed to the person and to the church itself, brought home to Pius XII the value of moral restraint on state power. As John Courtney Murray has argued, it led Pius XII to affirm a range of political and civil human rights, and to endorse the notion of a limited (constitutional) state.[12]

---

[10] Ernest A. Fortin, "'Sacred and Inviolable': Rerum Novarum and Natural Rights," *Theological Studies* 53 (1992): 209.

[11] For the evolution of teaching on rights under Pius XII, see David Hollenbach, *Claims in Conflict: Retrieving and Renewing the Catholic Human Rights Tradition* (New York: Paulist Press, 1979).

[12] John Courtney Murray, "The Problem of Religious Freedom," in Hooper, ed., *Religious Liberty*, 165–7.

Second, the devastation of the second global conflict in thirty years led Pius XII to focus his Christmas Addresses and his post-war teaching on the concept of the political and legal order. Pius XII spent his life in the Vatican diplomatic service; in many ways he had the mind of an international lawyer. His Christmas Addresses stressed the need of order within states and among states. The concept of human rights provided building blocks for a new order.

Third, in his moral and social teaching Pius XII relied extensively on the tradition of natural law. He invoked it when addressing politics, war and peace, and medical ethics. To bring together his espousal of a strong legal order and the need to protect the citizen from state power, Pius XII used a version of natural law.

Recognizing the role of this ancient philosophy in Pius XII's invocation of human rights and in that of his successor John XXIII, it is necessary here to comment briefly on a standard theme in political philosophy: the relationship of the natural law and natural rights traditions of discourse.[13] The former traces its lineage to the classical philosophy of Greece and Rome; the latter is rooted in the rise of modern political philosophy in the sixteenth and seventeenth centuries. All commentators affirm the different character of the two traditions: they cannot simply be collapsed. Charles Curran and David Hollenbach, strong supporters of the papal turn to human rights, both stress that such a move could never be the church simply taking over the modern conception of rights. As Curran puts the case:

Catholic social teaching cannot accept an approach that absolutizes human freedom and autonomy. Again, the question of human rights goes to the foundational issues of anthropology. Catholic social teaching denies human autonomy, refuses to absolutize freedom, and sees the human person in relationship with God, other human beings and the world itself.[14]

The differences of the two traditions are not simply linguistic. While it is possible at a practical political level to find some overlap of ideas, the traditions are rooted in different origins. The deeper one goes in comparing the traditions the starker the contrast becomes.[15] Three points of comparison will illustrate how the traditions differ. First, the conception of

---

[13] For a treatment which seeks limited continuity, see Brian Tierney, "Natural Law and Natural Rights," in John Witte, Jr. and Frank S. Alexander, eds., *Christianity and Law: An Introduction* (Cambridge: Cambridge University Press, 2008), 89–103.

[14] Curran, *Catholic Social Teaching*, 220.

[15] For a synthetic historical account of continuity and change in the human rights narrative, see Kenneth Minogue, "The History of the Idea of Human Rights," in Laquer and Rubin, eds., *The Human Rights Reader*, 3–17.

the person or philosophical anthropology; as the Curran quote highlights, the natural law tradition stresses two characteristics about the human person: sacredness (dignity) and social nature. Each person has a unique dignity and every person is social by nature. The latter characteristic means that the person is destined for relationship with others and for life in community. Community in turn cuts across family, civil society, and the human community. Human rights are rooted in human dignity and they are to be exercised in community. The natural rights tradition began with the pre-political individual in possession of a corpus of rights understood as immunities. At least in principle there is far less stress on the social character of existence.

Second, the differing conceptions of the person yield differing accounts of the origin and role of civil society and the state. The natural law conception understands both society and state to be rooted in the social nature of the person. Both arise from the requirement of sociality which seeks a multi-level community within which human dignity can flourish. The tradition reflects Aristotle's observation that angels and animals do not need community but humans do. The natural rights tradition is rooted in a contractual conception of civil society and state. Neither is necessary for the person, but both can be created for protection or convenience by human choice.

Third, the traditions differ in their conception of the relationship of rights and duties. The natural law traditionally gives priority to human duties understood in light of a larger moral order; rights then are affirmed as the means necessary to fulfill duties. More recent statements of the tradition correlate rights and duties and lay less stress on the priority of duty. Natural rights traditions lay primary if not exclusive stress on rights; duties are not a prominent category in this statement of social order.

A final note: the transitional nature of Pius XII's teaching on human rights is that he affirmed an order of political-civil rights, but he never included in it the right of religious freedom. In failing to acknowledge this right – a traditional category in modern human rights discourse – Pius XII aligned his teaching with his predecessors, but he had opened the door for his successors to fill this gap in the church's teaching on human rights. That would be the task of Vatican II.

THE CONCILIAR ERA: JOHN XXIII AND VATICAN II

When Pius XII died in 1958, the Cold War was at its height. World politics was dominated by superpower competition from space to science to ballistic missiles. Europe was caught in the vise of the superpower face-off, and decolonization was moving rapidly but often at great cost to the countries and peoples seeking independence. There was little room on the agenda of global affairs for human rights advocacy. Pius XII had undeniably moved Catholic teaching forward on human rights, but his broader diplomatic role of strong opposition to communism as a theory and in practice at the global and European levels made it difficult for him to advance beyond these large and important struggles. His successor in the Chair of Peter, John XXIII, brought both diplomatic and pastoral experience to the papacy along with a conviction that an open moment existed for the church in both spiritual and temporal affairs. He sought to grasp the moment by convoking an ecumenical council, the most broadly representative council in the history of the church.[16] The Second Vatican Council opened on October 11, 1962, one week before the Cuban Missile Crisis launched the world into thirteen days of supreme danger. While John XXIII's greatest accomplishment was the calling of Vatican II, he was moved by the Missile Crisis to plan another initiative, an encyclical letter addressing the nuclear age and the idea of human rights. These were two distinct themes, but he combined reflection on them in his text entitled *Pacem In Terris* (1963).

John XXIII's encyclical is the most systematic statement of Catholic teaching on human rights we have from the papacy. In a sense John XXIII stands between Pius XII and John Paul II. Pius XII opened the door for Catholic advocacy on human rights and democracy, but the human rights language was not expansive. *Pacem In Terris* is a broadly conceived and systematically argued statement of the church's commitment to human rights.[17] As we shall see below, John Paul II brings his own distinctive philosophical style and, uniquely, his global advocacy to the human rights ministry of the church. There is continuity of substance between the two popes, but also some interesting differences. John XXIII's encyclical is a natural law case from beginning to end. All the popes of the twentieth century were defenders of it, but John XXIII's letter presented a sweeping, systematic statement of natural law, engaging issues from interpersonal relations to international relations.

---

[16] For the texts of the Council, see Austin Flannery, O.P., *Vatican Council II: The Conciliar and Post Conciliar Documents*, rev. edn (Northport, NY: Costello Publishing Company, 2004), vol. I; for commentary on key texts and themes, see John Miller, ed., *Vatican II: An Interfaith Appraisal* (Notre Dame, IN: University of Notre Dame Press, 1966).

[17] The text is found in David J. O'Brien and Thomas Shannon, eds., *Catholic Social Thought: The Documentary Heritage* (Maryknoll, NY: Orbis Books, 1992), 131–62.

As Charles Curran has shown, John Paul II does not cast his human rights teaching in natural law terms.

The case made in *Pacem In Terris* is thematically built around the concept of order in human relationships. The letter opens with this theme:

Peace on Earth, which all men of every era have most eagerly yearned for, can be firmly established only if the order laid down by God be dutifully observed.[18]

The "order" in question is the moral order found, John XXIII believes, in the natural law which can be understood by all through the use of reason and dialogue. Its order is the basic theme of *Pacem In Terris*; the structure of the moral order is explicated in the language of human rights and duties. The integrating idea of the encyclical is set forth early in the text:

Any human society, if it is to be well-ordered and productive, must lay down as a foundation this principle, namely that every human being is a person; that his nature is endowed with intelligence and free will. Indeed, precisely because he is a person, he has rights and obligations flowing directly and simultaneously from his very nature. And these rights and obligations are universal and inviolable, so they cannot in any way be surrendered.[19]

From this baseline, *Pacem In Terris* unfolds in architectonic style over four chapters. The framework of natural law and the concepts of rights and duties are used to evaluate (1) relationships among individuals; (2) the relationship of citizen and state; (3) the relationships among states in the international arena; and (4) the relationship of each person and their state to the international community.

Its statement of natural law (generally regarded as more personalist and less static than earlier uses of the doctrine in Catholic teaching); its casting of right and duties (in a fashion seeking common ground with other theories of rights); and its support for institutions of both democracy (within states) and international order (among states), brought John XXIII's encyclical universal attention and established a foundation from which later Catholic teaching would be articulated. The fact that the letter appeared in the midst of Vatican II (as his personal initiative) and that it was published less than a few weeks before his death gave it a kind of iconic quality in Catholic teaching.

The encyclical in fact provided the baseline for the two documents of Vatican II which addressed human rights. The first, *Dignitatis Humanae* (The Declaration of Religious Freedom), flowed directly from *Pacem In Terris*. Its significance went well beyond the specific words of the text.

[18] *Ibid.*, 131 (para. 1).   [19] *Ibid.*, 132 (para. 9).

Religious freedom had been for centuries a neuralgic issue for Catholicism. Partly because of an understanding of its teaching mission, partly because of historic circumstances (the post-Reformation division of European states along religious lines), Catholicism had long resisted any statement in principle about religious freedom. Leo XIII's statements on rights and democracy stopped short of declaring a human and civil right to religious freedom. *Pacem In Terris* crossed the threshold on the issue stating a conclusion without arguing how or why the teaching had changed. It simply said: "This too must be listed among the rights of a human being, to honor God according to the dictates of his own conscience, and therefore the right to practice his religion privately and publicly."[20] Previous teachings reaching back centuries had affirmed "the freedom of faith," that no one should be coerced to believe, but the sticking point had always been the right to express one's faith publicly. John XXIII, as he did on many things, had opened a new vista for Catholic teaching, but he did not provide the argument for this conclusion.

This is the role which *Dignitatis Humanae* fulfilled.[21] The relationship with *Pacem In Terris* was direct and complementary. Both texts flowed from and exemplified the natural law tradition at work in Catholic teaching. Professor Leslie Griffin has pointed out that the two principal authors of the conciliar text, John Courtney Murray and Pietro Pavan, both tied *Dignitatis Humanae* to *Pacem In Terris*.[22] The conciliar document faced a double challenge. First, in the religious community and in the secular world there were significant doubts about the willingness of the Catholic Church to state clearly its belief in the right of religious freedom. John XXIII's encyclical had been widely welcomed, but a single sentence on this topic did not satisfy deeply rooted doubts. Second, the church itself needed a fully developed argument as it presented to the world a significant change of its teaching. Building on *Pacem In Terris*, the conciliar document needed to provide an integrated moral-legal-political rationale for asserting the right of religious freedom as a universal right. Principal elements of the argument follow.

First, the conciliar text grounds the right of religious freedom in the dignity of the person, the same foundation which *Pacem In Terris* used for all human rights. Second, the right is an immunity – a protection

---

[20] *Ibid.*, 133 (para. 14).
[21] The text of *Dignitatis Humanae* is found Flannery, ed., *Vatican Council II*, 799–812.
[22] Leslie Griffin, "Dignitatis Humanae," in Kenneth R. Hines *et al.*, eds., *Modern Catholic Social Teaching: Commentaries and Interpretation* (Washington, DC: Georgetown University Press, 2005), 253.

from state action or other groups in society. Third, the content of the right involves a double protection: no one is to be forced to believe, and no one is to be prevented from expressing their religious convictions privately or publicly (this was the major advance beyond previous teaching). Fourth, the right is thoroughly social: it belongs to individuals and to religious communities. Fifth, the limiting condition on the exercise of the right lies in the state's responsibility to protect "public order." Murray drew this category from the Anglo-American legal tradition and defined its content as the protection of public peace, the rights of others, and public morality.[23]

As part of the broader narrative of the Catholic position on human rights, *Dignitatis Humanae* has a double significance. First, as a tightly honed statement of principle – with universal scope – it went a long way in clarifying a fundamental ambiguity in traditional Catholic teaching. Second, it illustrated how a human right could be asserted, defined, justified, and limited in its exercise in the natural law tradition. The precedent established by the conciliar text was that the broader range of human rights found in *Pacem In Terris* could be set forth in similar fashion.

In an extensive article a year after Vatican II, Murray analyzed *Dignitatis Humanae* and *Gaudium et Spes* (The Pastoral Constitution on the Church in the Modern World) in tandem, arguing that together they established a distinctly different position for the church's ministry in the world than had prevailed for much of the previous century.[24] Unlike the two texts analyzed thus far, *Gaudium et Spes* is not focused primarily on human rights as such, but in terms of its influence on the church's role in human rights advocacy after Vatican II, its contribution is essential.[25] As the last and longest document of the council, *Gaudium et Spes* had emerged from the conciliar debate itself – there had been no plan for such a document when the council began. Moreover, it had a distinctive style and content which set it off from other texts of the social tradition. Unlike *Pacem In Terris* or *Dignitatis Humanae*, it was not a document in the natural law tradition. The content and concepts of the text were primarily theological not philosophical. Indeed its theological content was its contribution to Catholic social teaching.

[23] Murray, "The Problem of Religious Freedom," in Hooper, ed., *Religious Liberty*, 153.
[24] Murray, "The Issue of Church and State at Vatican Council II," in Hooper, ed., *Religious Liberty*, 201–5.
[25] The text of *Gaudium et Spes* is found in O'Brien and Shannon, eds., *Catholic Social Thought*, 166–237.

The primary focus of *Gaudium et Spes* is a theological reflection on the church's relationship to the world. In that sense it lies directly in the tradition of Augustine's *Civitate Dei*, not in the moral analysis of specific social issues which one finds in the encyclical tradition. I have argued in other places that the contrast between the encyclical tradition and the conciliar text, however, opens the way to understanding their relationship.[26] Indeed, the thoroughly philosophical tone and content of *Pacem In Terris* provides the best example of how *Gaudium et Spes* fulfills a unique role in the church's social ministry and human rights advocacy.

Because the social encyclicals were meant to address the church and the world, they were appropriately philosophical. The natural law style had been used in Catholic teaching to address two challenges: empirical complexity and social pluralism. Natural law provided a body of concepts and distinctions which offered a bridge between religious convictions and the factual complexity of social problems. The use of Aristotle's theory of justice exemplified this method. The secular cast of natural law also provided a bridge between a religious community and secular, pluralistic societies. But the limits of social philosophy lay in the lack of connection between it and the inner life of the church. In brief, the social tradition seemed like an extension of the church's life but not something central to it. *Gaudium et Spes* provided the way to join social analysis and social advocacy with the center of the church's life. It provided theological legitimation for an activist ministry in the world in support of the human rights set forth in *Pacem In Terris*.

As Murray illustrated in his essay, the heart of the document's analysis about the church–world relationship asserted two basic propositions. First, the church had no specific political role or mission – its mission was religious in origin, purpose, and content. Second, as it carried out its religious ministry, however, it should do so in a way which fostered four significant secular objectives: the defense of human dignity, the advancement of human rights, the fostering of the unity of the human family, and the provision of meaning to human activity.[27] This quite expansive "indirect" role in the world set a broad agenda for ministry and secular engagement but not direct political action.

---

[26] J. Bryan Hehir, "The Church in the World: Responding to the Call of the Council," *Marianist Award Lecture 1995* (Dayton, OH: University of Dayton, 1995), 18–23.

[27] Murray, "The Issue of Church and State," 218–19.

THE PAPACY OF JOHN PAUL II (1978–2005)

The post-conciliar life of Catholicism – not least in its human rights advocacy – has seen an often intense debate about the meaning, limits, and content of this directive from Vatican II. The locus of the debate has cut across Latin America, South Africa, South Korea, the Philippines, and the United States. At the heart of the council's deliberations and at the center of the post-conciliar debate about the distinction between social ministry for human rights and political activity (beyond the church's mission) was the mind, the voice, and the activity of Karol Wojtyła, Pope John Paul II. To his role in the human rights narrative I now turn.

The role and its influence are not easily captured. To assess them one needs to attend to John Paul's words and deeds. I shall use three principal texts as reference points for his teaching: his UN Addresses of 1979 and 1995 and his encyclical *Centesimus Annus* (1991).

John Paul II's signature moral theme of his pontificate was his teaching on the human dignity of the person. This, of course, connected him to the social teaching tradition and quite directly to *Pacem In Terris*. He also had been a major voice at Vatican II in support of *Dignitatis Humanae* – a text resisted by a small but influential group of conservative bishops. For John Paul II the theme of human dignity was grounded in his philosophical writing and in his pastoral ministry. As an academic throughout his priestly and episcopal ministry, John Paul combined themes drawn from phenomenology and personalism with Catholic thought.[28] As a professor of ethics, he used this combination of ideas to shape his intellectual legacy across a wide spectrum of human activity. As a priest and bishop ministering in a communist country with an overwhelming Catholic population, he was in a constant struggle – of ideas and power – about whom people should trust: the government or the church. He brought this combination of intellectual and practical experience to the papacy, and it shaped his unique leadership on human rights.[29]

The significance of the election of a pope from "The Second World" of the communist orbit was immediately recognized by those who analyzed world politics in secular terms. The veteran journalist Tad Szulc set the stage in *The New Republic*: "By electing Poland's Cardinal Karol Wojtyła

---

[28] For background on the thought of John Paul II, see George H. Williams, *The Mind of John Paul II: Origins of His Thought and Action* (New York: The Seabury Press, 1981), xi–xvi, 5–18, 261–341.

[29] George Weigel, *Witness to Hope: The Biography of John Paul II* (New York: HarperCollins, 1999). Weigel describes a wide variety of papal visits to and interaction with local churches in *ibid.*, 259–90, 363–95.

to the papacy, the Roman Catholic Church has thrust world politics into a wholly new dimension with extraordinary and far-reaching consequences that can be measured only with the passage of time."[30]

It did not take long for Szulc's prediction to take shape. Barely into the ministry of successor to St. Peter, John Paul decided to participate in the crucial "Puebla Meeting" of Latin American Bishops. Here, on the continent representing much of the future of Catholicism, major themes of politics and religion, Marxism and Catholicism, human rights and economic oppression came together. There were two broad sets of issues: internal church theology and discipline in the continent which had produced the widely influential "Theology of Liberation," together with the external struggles analogous to but still very different from the question John Paul had faced in Poland: who stood for the person, who would speak with and defend the poor? In a series of dense theological lectures, John Paul carved out a role for himself and the church which was focused on a ministry of human rights and social justice. But it was a ministry distinctly separate from Marxist social themes and one demanding internal church unity. The ripples of this encounter continued over the next decade from South America to the struggles in El Salvador and Nicaragua where bishops, priests, nuns, and laity paid the price of social witness with their lives. John Paul called the church to a ministry of human rights and social justice using the language of *Gaudium et Spes*, engaging the church with the world, but within a strict vertically directed definition of Catholicism.

Latin America was and remains a high-stakes arena for the church. But it was only one arena for the human rights ministry of John Paul II. In October 1979 he brought his conception of human rights to the United Nations. Here he encountered the international system as a whole and the solemn way he addressed the assembly showed that he fully appreciated the significance of the opportunity. In many ways the UN Address to the General Assembly set the direction for his ministry and the way he wished the Catholic Church to be understood by the world at large.

The address from beginning to end was structured around human rights. He described the UN Declaration as "a milestone on the long and difficult path of the human race."[31] Following *Pacem In Terris* he affirmed the church's support for the two broad categories of human rights. He then assumed the role of the professor as he invited the diplomatic assembly to think about the foundation of rights and how the two sides of the

---

[30] Tad Szulc, "Politics and the Polish Pope," *The New Republic* (October 28, 1978): 19.
[31] John Paul II, *Address to the UN General Assembly* (October 2, 1979), para. 6.

UN debate, political vs. economic rights, should be understood. The key concept, of course, was not rights but the dignity of the person: rights exist to guarantee the protection and promotion of human dignity.

Staying with the structure of the UN categories – political-civil and economic-social rights – he moved to define them differently. His contrast was rights to spiritual goods and rights to material goods.[32] The move was not designed to replace the normal terms of analysis and discussion, but to open up both traditional categories to their inner meaning. The person required both spiritual and material resources to flourish fully. Neither was dispensable; both must be protected and provided. He then argued for the primacy of the spiritual goods – rights of conscience, speech, thought and, crucially, religious freedom.[33] These goods – being spiritual – are not diminished when they are guaranteed for all. Material goods – food, housing, health care – are equally fundamental, but they pose a different problem. As they are provided they also become scarce. The focus of the address as a whole was to align the church with the United Nations on rights, but also to use the unique opportunity he had as a religious leader in the assembly to highlight the inner complexity and significance of what the United Nations and its member states were committed to by their own Declaration.

John Paul returned to the United Nations during its fiftieth anniversary year (1995), once again choosing human rights as his basic theme. In an address which garnered much less attention at the time and since then, he focused on "the rights of nations." Two ideas stand out from this address. First, looked at in light of the 1979 address which located the person and rights as the key issue, the 1995 address stands as a correlative theme. The pope cast his discussion of national rights as an aspect of how the universal community of nations must provide space for particular communities.[34] While his purpose seemed again to lay stress on the philosophical issues underlying international relations, he was speaking in the midst of a decade when internal conflicts among ethnic, religious, and national communities had outnumbered interstate wars. This was the decade of Bosnia, Somalia, Kosovo, and Rwanda. The persistent themes of self-determination, nationalism, and post-Cold War realignment of borders were the background for an address which defended the "rights of nations" without necessarily arguing that such rights should produce new states. Second, not lost on the audience was the significance of a Pole, who

---

[32] *Ibid.*, para. 13.   [33] *Ibid.*, para. 14.
[34] John Paul II, *Address to the UN General Assembly* (October 1995).

had lived through both world wars and occupation of his nation by Nazi and communist regimes, addressing the world on the importance of maintaining the "rights of nations" in a world of states.

The capstone of John Paul II's social teaching was the encyclical *Centesimus Annus*, written to commemorate the hundredth anniversary of Leo XIII's *Rerum Novarum* and appearing two years after the end of the Cold War and the collapse of communism in Central and Eastern Europe.[35] The very public role the pope had played in delegitimizing communist rule, often with a human rights critique as his principal weapon, attracted global attention to this encyclical.

Unlike *Pacem In Terris*, this encyclical of 1991 was not wholly devoted to explicating the Catholic position on human rights. It is clear from the outset of *Centesimus Annus* that John Paul II is presupposing the content of Catholic teaching and intending both to apply it and expand it in light of the "new things" of the final decade of the twentieth century. From this design flow three contributions to Catholic teaching on human rights all made by *Centesimus Annus*. First, the pope reflects upon "The Year 1989" offering his analysis of what brought about the total collapse of communist rule in the Soviet bloc. A principal feature of his reflections is the way he draws connections between the events in Europe and the rest of the world. Noting that authoritarian regimes had fallen in the southern hemisphere in the 1980s, prior to what occurred in Europe, he specifies the church's role in these events in the 1980s:

> An important, even decisive, contribution was made by the church's commitment to defend and promote human rights. In situations strongly influenced by ideology … the church affirmed clearly and forcefully that every individual – whatever his or her personal convictions – bears the image of God and therefore deserves respect.[36]

John Paul II clearly believed that the events of 1989 created a global "teachable moment" which he sought to highlight by offering a commentary on the momentous events of 1989–91. His analyses went beyond – or at least stood apart from – the torrent of words and commentary which dominated the media, the academy, and the diplomatic arena concerning what caused the collapse of an empire.

For most, the focus had been on the decisions made by Mikhail Gorbachev, the leadership of Lech Wałęsa, Václav Havel *et al.* and the

---

[35] John Paul II, *Centesimus Annus* (1991); text in O'Brien and Shannon, eds., *Catholic Social Thought*, 439–88.
[36] *Ibid.*, 455 (para. 22).

failure of the command economy. John Paul's analysis began with "the violation of the rights of workers" by the very ideological system which proposed to speak in their name. He then continued his human rights critique with a comment on "the inefficiency of the economic system, which is not to be considered simply as a technical problem, but rather a consequence of the violation of human rights to private initiative, to ownership of property, and to freedom in the economic sector."[37] Finally he argued that "the true cause of the new developments was the spiritual void brought about by atheism" which ultimately led many of the young "to rediscover the religious roots of their national cultures."[38] While many analysts of the events of 1989 framed these arguments in less universal terms, John Paul II, in fact, believed that lessons from Europe potentially had worldwide implications. Among these in his mind was the potential for his own church to play a human rights role in other political systems.

As a guide and catalyst for such engagement, he then turned to the work of expanding and extending his own tradition in the two broad areas of human rights: the economy and civil society. John Paul had addressed the moral dimension of the economy at length in encyclicals of 1981 and 1987.[39] *Centesimus Annus* draws on the earlier texts, but approaches the question of the economy in the context of a post-Cold War world. For most of the last century, Catholic social teaching had a standard template: it would, for different reasons, critique the two dominant models of political economy. The critique would be made in terms of the premises of each system and in terms of their capacity to meet human needs. With the virtual collapse of Marxist Socialism as a theory and a functioning economy, John Paul II brings a different lens to the problem of the domestic and global economy.

He reiterates his philosophical critique of why the Marxist program failed. But that is retrospective; his principal focus is to address the meaning, potential, and limits of the market economy, within states and globally. To some degree this is simply a recognition that it is the dominant framework which now touches the life of most of the world. But he also brings to the assessment a more positive view of the potential of the market economy than his predecessors. He recognizes and affirms the market's role in contributing to a rational allocation of resources, in protecting freedom from state control of an economy, and in fostering

---

[37] *Ibid.*, 456 (para. 24).   [38] *Ibid.*
[39] *Laborem Exercens* (1981); *Sollicitudo Rei Socialis* (1987); texts in O'Brien and Shannon, eds., *Catholic Social Thought*, 352–92, 395–436.

innovation.⁴⁰ He is not prepared, however, to espouse the idea that market efficiency is sufficient to meet the moral requirements of a just society. Here his human rights concerns are evident. The limits of the market reside first in the fact that without financial resources some can never enter the market to meet basic human needs. Second, the market mechanism of supply and demand is inherently incapable of recognizing the intrinsic worth of certain goods; health care, for example, is so directly related to basic human welfare that access to it cannot be left ultimately to market forces. John Paul's proposal is that the market should be surrounded by a "juridical framework" which should complement its role in society.⁴¹ In secular terms, such a framework would be called public policy. The purpose of the policy is to allow the market to play its appropriate role, but to complement the logic of the market (supply and demand) with stable guarantees which meet basic human rights for all citizens of society. In John Paul's words: "there are many human needs which find no place in the market. It is a strict duty of justice not to allow fundamental human needs to remain unsatisfied, and not to allow those burdened by such needs to perish."⁴² To interpret this statement, "fundamental human needs" constitute a human rights claim; and "strict duties of justice" involve the obligations of both civil society and the state for its citizens.⁴³

When John Paul II addresses the role of the state in *Centesimus Annus*, three ideas shape his vision. First, he distinguishes between "direct and indirect" state intervention in the economic order. Direct intervention is based on the principle of solidarity (a favorite theme of the pope, expressing a basic obligation for individuals and societies to be responsible for others); direct intervention includes protecting the vulnerable in terms of working conditions and social insurance. Indirect intervention, based on the principle of subsidiarity, includes the responsibility of the state to create "favorable conditions for the free exercise of economic activity," enhancing opportunities for employment and economic stability.⁴⁴

Second, while the pope can be described as supporting an activist state to meet basic needs, he is careful to set limits on this role. When he advocates state intervention to substitute for economic failures he argues such activity "be as brief as possible"⁴⁵ so other agencies in society can assume their rightful role in the economy. A "limited but activist" state

---

⁴⁰ John Paul II, *Centesimus Annus* (1991); text in O'Brien and Shannon, eds., *Catholic Social Thought*, 463 (para. 32).

⁴¹ *Ibid.*, 450 (para. 15); *ibid.*, 471 (para. 42).   ⁴² *Ibid.*, 464 (para. 34).

⁴³ *Ibid.*, 465 (para. 35).   ⁴⁴ *Ibid.*, 450 (para. 15).   ⁴⁵ *Ibid.*, 476 (para. 48).

may best capture his view of the relationship of human rights, the state, and the economy.

Third, John Paul II applies these broad themes of solidarity, justice, and the role of public authorities to the international arena: "Just as within individual societies it is possible and right to organize a solid economy which will direct the functioning of the market to the common good, so too there is a similar need for adequate interventions on the international level."[46] This brief statement is another expression of the meaning of the principle of solidarity at work, now globally; it has embedded in it the human rights theme of the universality of basic rights and the need, as *Pacem In Terris* held, for greater international collaboration in support of the universal common good.

THE PAST AND THE FUTURE: 1965–2010

The objective of this chapter, to present the record of Catholicism and human rights since Vatican II, has concentrated on what has been taught about the topic. This final section seeks to present in very synthetic fashion some of the impact of the teaching and to locate the role of the church in the contemporary international system.

In retrospect one can argue that in the period 1960–90 secular and religious themes converged to catalyze the Catholic Church into the human rights arena. A church which had long been suspicious of human rights claims entered the period after Vatican II comfortable with the language of human rights. This had taken twenty years of internal developments within Catholicism, but *Pacem In Terris* and *Dignitatis Humanae* had made clear that human rights – including religious freedom – corresponded to the church's role in the world. By the 1970s secular developments in world politics, including the rise of rights language, the role of non-governmental organizations, increasing interdependence and growing transnational activity, all had created a context for human rights advocacy to be seen as legitimate and necessary policy for state and non-state actors.

The Catholic Church was both a long-recognized non-governmental actor and (by nature and definition) a transnational actor. In describing how this potential became a concrete reality, it is tempting to focus only on John Paul II's combination of teaching and travel to some of the world's most conflicted settings. To do so would be to miss the critical role of

---

[46] *Ibid.*, 478 (para. 52).

local churches which preceded the pontificate of John Paul and then was expanded by his leadership.

The late Samuel P. Huntington's essay on "Democracy's Third Wave" places the church's role in context. Huntington begins the essay with a statement of fact: "Between 1974 and 1990, at least 30 countries made transitions to democracy, just about doubling the number of democratic governments in the world."[47] Huntington's concern is the spread of democracy, a distinct theme from human rights but not entirely separate from it. In describing the factors causing this shift to democratic governance, he identifies Catholicism's role: "A striking shift in the doctrines and activities of the Catholic Church, manifested in the Second Vatican Council of 1963–65 and the transformation of national Catholic churches from defenders of the status quo to opponents of authoritarianism."[48]

Those "national churches" to which he refers included Latin America (Brazil and Chile), Central America (El Salvador and Nicaragua), the Philippines, South Korea, and Poland, among others. They also included complementary advocacy on human rights in Canada, Western Europe, and the United States, responding to requests for influence on their governments from churches directly engaged in the struggle for democracy and human rights. The pattern of human rights advocacy varied in each country and cannot be described here in any detail. At its most effective it involved leadership in the hierarchy, combined with grassroots advocacy and the engagement of well-organized support of priests and nuns. But the pattern varied, up to and including tensions and divisions in the local church about how far and how fast to move and with whom to join in advocacy.

John Paul II's election to the papacy had a profound human rights impact throughout the church. Having established the theme in his UN Address of 1979, he pursued it through scores of "pastoral visits" across the globe. His influence and impact in Poland was unique – providing direct advice to the hierarchy, urging non-violence always, and strategically visiting his homeland for high profile face-offs with the government. No one doubted the profound personal effect he had; in other cases his role was not as dramatic, but it was always significant. At times he would prod the local church into action (Haiti); at other times he would argue for redirection of theory, strategy, or tactics (Nicaragua). His basic conviction, drawn from his Polish experiences, was that the church should act in unison. The

---

[47] Samuel P. Huntington, "Democracy's Third Wave," *Journal of Democracy* 2 (Spring 1991): 12.
[48] *Ibid.*, 13.

applicability of this method was not always evident; at times the divisions in society spilled over into the church. All parts of the church depended upon his human rights teaching; the application in diverse situations was neither simple nor always successful.

Five years after John Paul's death, the church faces a world strikingly different from the one he faced when elected in 1979. His successor Benedict XVI comes from a different background and possesses different skills. He has less direct pastoral experience, has less inclination to play a direct public role, and by inclination and accomplishment is primarily a theologian focused on the internal life of the church. Having observed these features, it still must be recognized that in his first five years as pope he has issued three encyclicals all of which address the church and world themes, and he gave an important role to human rights in his address to the United Nations in 2008.[49] To be sure, he has recognized that the modern papacy must be a voice for social justice, human rights, and peace in the world.

The world he must address does not have the stark character of Cold War bipolarity; it continues to have multiple examples of authoritarian rule and crushing poverty. Its conflicts are primarily within states, rooted in ethnic, class, and cultural divisions. In global terms, transnational terrorism poses a threat of unique complexity, particularly since it is associated with religious themes, even if those are a distortion of authentic religious traditions. If anything, religion as a category has a higher international profile and receives more secular attention than during the years of the Cold War.

The potential for Catholicism to exert a positive and effective influence on human rights will not be confined to the papacy. While Benedict XVI's priorities and policies will profoundly shape the church, the local churches now influenced for almost a half-century by the human rights era launched by *Pacem In Terris* will be expected to fulfill their own role in a continuing defense of human dignity and human rights.

RECOMMENDED READING

Curran, Charles E. *Catholic Social Teaching 1891 – Present: A Historical, Theological and Ethical Analysis.* Washington, DC: Georgetown University Press, 2002.
Douglass, Bruce and David Hollenbach, eds. *Catholicism and Liberalism: Contributions to American Public Philosophy.* Cambridge: Cambridge University Press, 1994.

---

[49] Benedict XVI, *Deus Caritas Est* (2007); *Spe Salvi* (2008); *Caritas In Veritate* (2009). All are published in the United States by Pauline Books and Media (Boston).

Duffy, Eamon. *Saints and Sinners: A History of the Popes.* New Haven: Yale University Press, 1997.

Falconi, Carlo. *The Popes in the Twentieth Century: From Pius X to John XXIII.* Boston: Little Brown and Co., 1967.

Flannery, Austin, O.P. *Vatican Council II: The Conciliar and Post Conciliar Documents*, rev. edn. Northport, NY: Costello Publishing Company, 2004.

Fortin, Ernest A. "'Sacred and Inviolable': Rerum Novarum and Natural Rights," *Theological Studies* 53 (1992): 203–33.

Hehir, J. Bryan. "The Church in the World: Responding to the Call of the Council," *Marianist Award Lecture 1995.* Dayton, OH: University of Dayton, 1995.

Himes, Kenneth R. *et al.*, eds. *Modern Catholic Social Teaching: Commentaries and Interpretation.* Washington, DC: Georgetown University Press, 2005.

Hollenbach, David. *Claims in Conflict: Retrieving and Renewing the Catholic Human Rights Tradition.* New York: Paulist Press, 1979.

Hooper, J. Leon, ed. *Religious Liberty: Catholic Struggles with Pluralism.* Louisville, KY: Westminster/John Knox Press, 1993.

Huntington, Samuel P. "Democracy's Third Wave," *Journal of Democracy* 2 (Spring 1991): 12–34.

Laquer, Walter and Barry Rubin, eds. *A Human Rights Reader*, rev. edn. New York: Penguin Books, 1990.

Miller, John, ed. *Vatican II: An Interfaith Appraisal.* Notre Dame, IN: University of Notre Dame Press, 1966.

O'Brien David J. and Thomas Shannon, eds. *Catholic Social Thought: The Documentary Heritage.* Maryknoll, NY: Orbis Books, 1992.

Tierney, Brian. "Natural Law and Natural Rights," in John Witte, Jr. and Frank S. Alexander, eds., *Christianity and Law: An Introduction.* Cambridge: Cambridge University Press, 2008, 89–103.

Vincent, R. J. *Human Rights and International Relations.* Cambridge: Cambridge University Press, 1986.

Weigel, George. *Witness to Hope: The Biography of John Paul II.* New York: HarperCollins, 1999.

Williams, George H. *The Mind of John Paul II: Origins of his Thought and Action.* New York: The Seabury Press, 1981.

CHAPTER 6

Rights and liberties in early modern Protestantism: the example of Calvinism

John Witte, Jr.

In the Introduction to this volume, I summarized some of the main Protestant contributions to the development of rights in the Western tradition. Each of the four main branches of the Reformation – Lutheran, Anglican, Calvinist, and Anabaptist – offered distinct teachings on rights in the sixteenth century. Over the next three centuries, their views, separately and together, helped shape the law of Protestant lands in northern Europe and North America. Nicholas Wolterstorff's chapter in this volume analyzes crisply and critically the main schools of Protestant rights talk in the twentieth century before defending his own brilliant new Protestant theory of human rights based on human dignity and moral worth.

In this chapter, I trace one line of Protestant rights development, namely that of the Reformed tradition, and more particularly the Reformed movements influenced by John Calvin. Building in part on classical and Christian prototypes, Calvin developed arresting new teachings on authority and liberty, duties and rights, and church and state that have had an enduring influence on Protestant lands. Calvin's original teachings were periodically challenged by major crises in the West – the French Wars of Religion, the Dutch Revolt, the English Revolution, and the American Revolution. In each such crisis moment, Calvinists modernized Calvin's original teachings and converted them into dramatic new legal and political reforms. This rendered early modern Calvinism one of the driving engines of Western constitutional laws of rights and liberties.[1]

JOHN CALVIN AND GENEVA

Calvin learned a lot about rights (*iura*) and liberties (*libertates*) from the Roman civil law and the Catholic canon law that he studied as a French

---

[1] This is the main thesis of my *The Reformation of Rights: Law, Religion, and Human Rights in Early Modern Calvinism* (Cambridge: Cambridge University Press, 2007) (hereafter RR).

law student in the 1520s. He learned more from the many Lutheran reformation ordinances and legal textbooks that he read as a new convert to the Protestant cause in the early 1530s. It is thus no surprise that Calvin opened his first major theological publication, the 1536 edition of the *Institutes of the Christian Religion*, with a loud Luther-like call for freedom: freedom of conscience, freedom of exercise, freedom of assembly, freedom of worship, freedom of the church, and attendant public, penal, and procedural rights for church members. Calvin's opening dedication of his *Institutes* to King Francis I was, in reality, a cleverly drafted lawyer's brief on behalf of Protestants who were being persecuted by church and state authorities alike.

Only one paragraph after his glowing tribute to this "most mighty, illustrious and glorious" monarch of France, Calvin launched into his legal argument. He cleverly singled out those abuses of Protestants that defied widely recognized rights and freedoms of his day, particularly criminal procedural rights.[2] Calvin protested the widespread and unchecked instances of "perjury," "lying slanders," "wicked accusations," and the "fury of evil men" that conspired to incite "public hatred" and "open violence" against believers. He protested that "the case" of the Protestants "has been handled with no order of law and with violent heat rather than judicial gravity." He protested various forms of false imprisonment and abuses of prisoners. "Some of us are shackled with irons, some beaten with rods, some led about as laughing stocks, some proscribed, some most savagely tortured, some forced to flee." He protested the many procedural inequities. Protestants are "fraudulently and undeservedly charged with treason and villainy." They are convicted for capital offenses, "without confession or sure testimony." "[B]loody sentences are meted out against this doctrine without a hearing." He protested the bias of judges and the partiality of judicial proceedings. "Those who sit in judgment … pronounce as sentences the prejudices which they have brought from home." He protested the intrusions on the church's freedoms of assembly and speech. "The poor little church has either been wasted with cruel slaughter or banished into exile, or so overwhelmed by threats and fears that it dare not even open its mouth." All these offenses stood diametrically opposed to basic political freedoms recognized at the time both in the Empire and in France. "[A] very great question is at stake," Calvin declared to King Francis: "how

---

[2] See John H. Langbein, *Prosecuting Crime in the Renaissance: England, Germany, France* (Cambridge, MA: Harvard University Press, 1974); Adhemar Esmein, *A History of Continental Criminal Procedure with Special Reference to France*, repr. edn. (South Hackensack, NJ: Rothman Reprints, 1968).

God's glory may be kept safe on earth, how God's truth may retain its place of honor, how Christ's kingdom may be kept in good repair among us."[3]

Later on in his same 1536 *Institutes*, Calvin called for the freedom not just of Protestants, but of all peaceable believers, including Catholics, Jews, and Muslims. He denounced the forced baptisms, inquisitions, crusades, and other forms of religious persecution practiced by the medieval church and state:

[W]e ought to strive by whatever means we can, whether by exhortation and teaching or by mercy and gentleness, or by our own prayers to God, that they may turn to a more virtuous life and may return to the society and unity of the church. And not only are excommunicants to be so treated, but also Turks and Saracens, and other enemies of religion. Far be it from us to approve those methods by which many until now have tried to force them to our faith, when they forbid them the use of fire and water and the common elements, when they deny them to all offices of humanity, when they pursue them with sword and arms.[4]

Over the next twenty-three years, Calvin continued to build his case for freedom. His touchstone was the Bible, especially those many passages on freedom in the letters of St. Paul. "There is nothing more desirable than liberty," he wrote. Liberty is "an inestimable good," "a singular benefit and treasure that cannot be prized enough," something that is worth "more than half of life." "There is nothing more desirable than liberty." Liberty is "an inestimable good," "a singular benefit and treasure that cannot be prized enough," something that is worth "more than half of life." "How great a benefit liberty is, when God has bestowed it on someone." Calvin emphasized the importance of political suffrage and the franchise in the political community. The "right to vote," he once said, is the "best way to preserve liberty." "Let those whom God has given liberty and the franchise use it." "[T]he reason why tyrannies have come into the world, why people everywhere have lost their liberty ... is that people who had elections abused the privilege." "[T]here is no kind of government more salutary than one in which liberty is properly exercised with becoming moderation and properly constituted on a durable basis."[5]

[3] John Calvin, *Institutes of the Christian Religion*, trans. Ford Lewis Battles (Atlanta, 1975), dedicatory epistle (hereafter *Institutes* [1536]).

[4] *Ibid.*, 2.28.

[5] John Calvin, *Institutes of the Christian Religion*, ed. John T. McNeill, trans. Ford Lewis Battles (Philadelphia: Westminster Press, 1960, 3.19.1–8, 14 (hereafter *Institutes* [1559]); Serm. Gen. 39:11; Serm. 1 Sam. 8, 17; Comm. Harm. Law Deut. 15:1–11; 17:14–18; 24:7; Serm. Deut. 16:18–19; 18:14–18; *Institutes* (1543), 20.7, all included in *Calvini opera quae supersunt omnia*, ed. G. Baum *et al.*, 59 vols. Corpus Reformatorum Series, vols. 29–87 (Brunswick: C. A. Schwetschke et filium, 1863–1900) (hereafter CO).

In his later years, Calvin also began to speak at times about the subjective "rights" (*iura, droits*) of individuals, in addition to their "liberties" or "freedoms" (*libertates, libertés*). Sometimes, he used such general phrases as "the common rights of mankind" (*iura commune hominum*), the "natural rights" (*iura naturali*) of persons, the "rights of a common nature" (*communis naturae iura*), or the "equal rights and liberties" (*pari iura et libertates*) of all.[6] Usually, he referenced more specific subjective rights. He spoke, for example, about the "rights of Christian liberty," the "rights of citizenship" in the Kingdom of God or in heavenly Jerusalem, and, one of his favorite expressions, the "right of adoption" that Christians enjoy as new sons and daughters of God and brothers and sisters in Christ. He referenced "the right to inhabit," "the right to dwell in," and "the right and privilege to claim the territory" that Yahweh gave to the chosen people of Israel. He mentioned "Paul's rights of Roman citizenship." He spoke frequently, as a student of Roman law would, about property rights: "the right to land," and other property, "the right to enjoy and use what one possesses," the "right to recover" and the "right to have restored" lost or stolen property; the "right to compensation" for work; the right "to sell," "to bequeath," and to "inherit" property, particularly in accordance with the "natural rights of primogeniture." He spoke of the "right to bury" one's parents or relatives. He also spoke frequently of the "marital" or "conjugal" rights of husband and wife, and the "sacred," "natural," and "common" "rights" of parents over their children – in particular, the "right" and "authority" of a father to "name his child," "to raise the child," and to set the child up in marriage. He spoke in passing about the "sacred right of hospitality" of the sojourner, the "right of asylum" or of "sanctuary" for those in flight, the "right of redemption" during the year of Jubilee, and the "natural rights" and "just rights" of the poor, the needy, the orphans, and the widows.[7] Rights talk became increasingly common currency in Calvin's writings, providing a treasure trove on which his later followers would call.

Church and state. Calvin called for a basic separation of church and state, even quoting Ephesians 2:14 to call for a "wall of separation" between the two. "There is a great difference and unlikeness between the ecclesiastical and civil power" of the church and state, said Calvin. "A distinction should always be observed between these two clearly distinct areas of

---

[6] Comm. Gen. 4:13; Comm. Harm. Law Num. 3:5–10, 18–22, Deut. 5:19; Comm. Ps. 7:6–8; Lect. Jer. 22:1–3, 22:13–14; Lect. Ezek. 8:17; Comm. 1 Cor. 7:37.
[7] See detailed citations in RR, 57–8.

responsibility, the civil and the ecclesiastical." The church has no authority to punish crime, to remedy civil wrongs, to collect taxes, to make war, or to meddle in the internal affairs of the state. The state, in turn, has no authority to preach the Word, to administer the sacraments, to enforce spiritual discipline, to collect tithes, to interfere with church property, to appoint or remove clergy, to obstruct bans or excommunications, or to meddle in the internal affairs of a congregation. When church officials operate as members of civil society, they must submit to the civil and criminal law of the state; they cannot claim civil immunities, tax exemptions, or privileges of forum. When state officials operate as members of the church, they must submit to the constitution and discipline of the church: they cannot insist on royal prerogatives or sovereign immunities. To permit any such interference or immunity between church and state, said Calvin, would "unwisely mingle these two [institutions] which have a completely different nature."[8]

Both the church and the state are separate legal entities, Calvin argued. Each institution has its own forms of organization and order, its own norms of discipline and rule. Each must issue positive human laws on the basis of God's natural law and in extension and application of these enduring moral norms. Each must play a distinctive role in the enforcement of Godly government and discipline in the community, and in the achievement of the "uses" of God's law. Each provides "external means or aids through which God invites us into communion with Christ, and keeps us there."[9]

Calvin described state rulers in largely general and homiletic terms following Protestant conventions of his day. God has appointed political rulers to be his "vice-regents," "vicars," and "ministers" in the earthly kingdom. Indeed, wrote Calvin citing Psalm 82:6, "those who serve as magistrates are called 'gods'." They are vested with God's authority and majesty. They are "called" to an office that is "not only holy and lawful before God, but also the most sacred and by far the most honorable of all callings in the whole life of mortal men." They are commanded to embrace and exemplify clemency, integrity, honesty, mercy, humanity, humility, grace, innocence, continence, and a host of other Godly virtues. Political rulers must govern the earthly kingdom by written positive laws, not by personal fiat. Their laws must encompass the biblical principles of love of God and neighbor, but they must not embrace biblical laws per se. Instead, "equity

---

[8] *Institutes* (1559), 3.19.15; 4.11.3–16; 4.20.1–4; CO 10/1:15–30, 215–17, 223–4.
[9] *Institutes* (1559), subtitle of book 4.

alone must be the goal and rule and limit of all laws," a term which Calvin used both in the classic Aristotelian sense of correcting defects in individual rules if they work injustice in a particular case, and in his own sense of adjusting each legal system to the changing circumstances and needs of the local community. Through such written, equitable laws, political rulers must serve to promote peace and order in the earthly kingdom, to punish crime and civil wrongdoing, to protect persons in their lives and properties, "to ensure that men may carry on blameless intercourse among themselves" in the spirit of "civil righteousness."[10]

Calvin was more innovative in arguing that the structure of political governments must be "self-limiting" so that "rulers are check-mated by their own officers" and offices. Such inherent political restraints rarely exist in a monarchy, Calvin believed, for monarchs, too, often lack self-discipline and self-control, and betray too little appetite for justice, prudence, and Christian virtue. "If one could uncover the hearts of monarchs," Calvin wrote late in his life, "he would hardly find one in a hundred who does not likewise despise everything divine." Thus, "it is safer and more tolerable that government be in the hands of a number of persons who help each other," such as prevails in an aristocracy, or even better in "a [mixed] system comprised of aristocracy, tempered by democracy." What Calvin had in mind was rule by the "best characters," by the spiritual and moral elite, who were elected to their offices by the people. Mere division of political authority, however, was an insufficient safeguard against political tyranny. Calvin thus encouraged all magistrates to govern through local agencies, to adhere to precedent and written rules, to divide their power among various self-checking branches and officials, to stand periodically for elections, to hold regular popular meetings in order to give account of themselves and to give air to popular concerns.[11] These views would be axiomatic in later Calvinist communities, particularly among New England Puritans who developed them into a theory of political democracy, as we saw in the Introduction.

While the state holds the legal power of the sword, the church holds the spiritual power of the Word. Ministers are to preach the Word and administer the sacraments. Doctors are to catechize the young and to educate the parishioners. Elders are to maintain discipline and order and adjudicate disputes. Deacons are to control the church's finances and to

---

[10] *Institutes* (1536), 1.33; 6.36–9; 6.48–9; *Institutes* (1559), 4.20.
[11] Serm. 2 Sam. 1–4; Serm. Job 10:16–17; 19:26–9; 34:138; Serm. Deut. 17:16–20; 18:14–18; *Institutes* (1559), 4.20.9–11, 31; Comm. Rom. 13:1–10.

coordinate its care for the poor and needy. The church polity, comprised of these officers, holds three forms of power (*potestas*), Calvin argued in his 1559 *Institutes*. The church holds "doctrinal power," the power to set forth its own confessions, creeds, catechisms, and other authoritative distillations of the Christian faith, and to expound them freely from the pulpit and the lectern. The church holds "legislative power," the power to promulgate for itself "a well-ordered constitution" that ensures "proper order and organization," "safety and security" in the church's administration of its affairs and "proper decency" and "becoming dignity" in the church's worship, liturgy, and ritual. And, the church holds "jurisdictional power," the power to enforce positive ecclesiastical laws that help to maintain discipline and to prevent scandal among its members.[12]

The church's jurisdictional power remains "wholly spiritual" in character, Calvin insisted. Its disciplinary rules must be "founded upon God's authority, drawn from Scripture, and, therefore, wholly divine." Its sanctions must be limited to admonition, instruction, and, in severe cases, the ban and excommunication – with civil and criminal penalties left for the magistrate to consider and deliver. Its administration must always be "moderate and mild," and left "not to the decision of one man" but to a consistory, with proper procedures and proper deference to the rule of law.[13] But the Genevan consistory in Calvin's day had vast subject matter jurisdiction – over cases of sex, marriage and family life, charity and poor relief, education and child care, and "public morality," which included "idolatry and other kinds of superstition, disrespect toward God, heresy, defiance of father and mother, or of the magistrate, sedition, mutiny, assault, adultery, fornication, larceny, avarice, abduction, rape, fraud, perjury, false witness, tavern-going, gambling, disorderly feasting, gambling, and other scandalous vices."[14]

Obedience and disobedience. Calvin insisted that private individuals have a Godly duty to obey tyrannical church or state officials up to the limits of Christian conscience. "The powers that be are ordained by God," Calvin reminded his readers, and the Bible repeatedly enjoins our obedience to them (Rom. 13:1–7; Titus 3:1; 1 Pet. 2:13). These obligations of obedience continue even when these authorities become abusive and arbitrary, Calvin insisted. This is particularly true in the political sphere, which provides order and stability for individual persons as well as for

---

[12] *Institutes* (1559), 4.1.5; 4.8.1; 4.10.27–8; 4.11.1, CO 2:749–51, 846–7, 887–8, 891–3.
[13] *Institutes* (1559), 4.10.5, 30; 4.11.1–6; 4.12.1–4, 8–11, CO 2:870–1, 890, 891–7, 905–7, 910–12.
[14] *Les sources du droit du canton de Genève*, ed. Emile Rivoire and Victor van Berchem, 4 vols. (Aarau: H. R. Sauerlände, 1927–35), vol. III, item no. 992.

families, churches, businesses, and other social structures to flourish. Some political order is better than no order at all, and private disobedience usually brings greater disorder. Some justice and equity prevails even in the worst tyrannies, and even that is jeopardized when individuals take the law into their own hands. Sometimes tyrannies are God's test of our faith or punishment for our sin, and we insult God further by resisting his instruments. Individuals must thus obey and endure patiently and prayerfully, and leave vengeance and retribution to God.

But to honor earthly authorities cannot be to dishonor God, Calvin continued. When earthly authorities command their individual subjects to disobey God, to disregard Scripture, or to violate conscience, their political citizens and subjects not only may disobey – they must disobey. Our "obedience is never to lead us away from obedience to Him, to whose will the desires of all kings ought to be subject, to whose decrees their commands ought to yield," Calvin wrote. "If they command anything against Him, let it go unesteemed." For to love and honor God is the first and greatest commandment. All authorities who betray their office to the detriment or defamation of God forfeit their office and are reduced to private persons. They are no longer authorities but mere "brigands" and "criminals." "Dictatorships and unjust authorities are not governments ordained by God." "Those who practice blasphemous tyranny" are no longer "God's ministers" of law.[15]

The question that remained for Calvin was how such abusive or tyrannical authorities should be disobeyed. Calvin urged a "moderate and equitable" solution. He knew enough about the insurrection and rioting triggered by the Anabaptist radicals of his day and had read enough in classical history about the dangers of simply unleashing the crowd against tyrants. So, he sought a more structured and constructive response both by the state and church authorities – even while calling individual persons quietly to disobey laws that violated Christian conscience and commands. No political regime is governed by "one person alone," Calvin argued. Even monarchs have a whole coterie of lower officials – counselors, judges, chancellors, and others – charged with implementation of the law. Moreover, many communities have "magistrates of the people, appointed to restrain the willfulness of kings," whether the ephors of ancient Greece or the elected parliamentarians of our day. These lower magistrates, especially elected officials, must protect the people through active resistance,

---

[15] *Institutes* (1536), 6.56, CO 1:248; Comm. Rom. 13:1–7, CO 4:248–52; Comm. Acts 5:29, 7:17, CO 48:109, 138–9.

even revolt, if higher magistrates become abusive or tyrannical in violation of God's authority and law.[16]

Church leaders, in turn, must preach and prophesy loudly against the injustice of tyranny and petition tyrannical magistrates to repent of their abuse, to return to their political duties, and to restore the political freedom of religious believers. Calvin's petition to King Francis I in his 1536 *Institutes* was just the kind of advocacy he thought appropriate, and he left that opening petition in every new edition over the next twenty-five years. Against "overbearing tyranny," Calvin later put it, a Christian must "venture boldly to groan for freedom."[17]

THEODORE BEZA AND FRENCH CALVINISM

Shortly after Calvin's death in 1564, his teachings on law and liberty, and church and state faced their first major crisis. The crisis was the St. Bartholomew's Day Massacre of 1572, where up to 100,000 French Calvinists were slaughtered in a month of barbarism instigated by French Catholic authorities. A mere decade before, Calvinism had seemed ready to contest Catholicism for the heart and soul of France. By 1562, some two million French souls had converted to Calvinism gathered in more than two thousand new churches throughout France. The number of Calvinist converts and churches was growing rapidly in all ranks of French society, but especially among the aristocracy. This growth was due in no small part to the disciplined campaigns of missionary work, book publication, church planting, school building, and charity work offered by the Calvinists. It was also due in part to the ready exportation of Geneva's sturdy system of local city-state rule and spiritual discipline that was ideally suited for many of the small French cities and towns that converted to Calvinism.

After 1560, the spread of French Calvinism was also due to the growing military prowess of French Calvinists. That year, despite strong protests from Geneva, a group of Calvinists attempted a *coup d'état* against the young French king Henry II. This brought harsh reprisals on various Calvinist communities and the establishment of a French inquisitorial court targeting Calvinists. In 1562, French Catholic forces slaughtered a Calvinist congregation gathered for worship in the town of Vassy. That triggered a decade of massive feuds between Catholic and Calvinist forces in many parts of France. The St. Bartholomew's Day Massacre of

---

[16] *Institutes* (1536), 6.55, CO 1:246–7.   [17] CO 12:98–100.

1572, which exploded after a lull in hostilities, placed French Calvinism in grave crisis.

Calvin's teachings on point provided too little guidance to respond to a crisis of this magnitude. Calvin assumed that each local community would have a single faith. How could Calvinists countenance religious pluralism and demand toleration as a religious minority in a majority Catholic community? Calvin assumed that church and state would cooperate in the governance of a Godly polity. What if church and state came into collision, or even worse into collusion against Calvinists? Calvin assumed that Christian subjects should obey political authorities up to the limits of Christian conscience, and bear persecution with penitence, patience, and prayer in hopes that a better magistrate would come. But what if the persecution escalated to outright pogrom? Were prayer, flight, and martyrdom the only options for conscientious Christians? Was there no place for resistance and revolt, even regicide and revolution in extreme cases? These challenges had faced Calvinists in various places throughout the 1540s to 1560s. They became stark life-and-death issues for French Calvinists after 1572.

It was Calvin's hand-picked successor in Geneva, Theodore Beza, who responded most decisively to this crisis. His most important work was the 1574 tract, *The Rights of Rulers Over Their Subjects and the Duty of Subjects Toward Their Rulers*, whose themes echo in several of his other writings.[18] Every political government, Beza argued, is formed by a covenant or contract sworn between the rulers and their subjects before God who serves as both third party and judge. In this covenant, God agrees to protect and bless the community in return for their proper obedience of the laws of God and nature, particularly as set out in the Decalogue. The rulers agree to exercise God's political authority in the community, and to honor these higher laws and protect the people's rights. The people agree to exercise God's political will for the community by electing and petitioning their rulers and by honoring and obeying them so long as they remain faithful to the political covenant. If the people violate the terms of this political covenant and become criminals, Beza argued, God empowers rulers to prosecute and punish them – and sentence them to death in extreme cases. But if the rulers violate the terms of the political covenant and become tyrants, God empowers the people to resist and to remove them from office – and sentence them to death in extreme cases. The power to

---

[18] See Théodore de Bèze, *Du Droit des Magistrats*, ed. Robert M. Kingdon (Geneva: Droz, 1970), and further materials in Bèze, *Tractationum Theologicarum*, 3 vols., 2nd edn (Geneva, 1582).

remove tyrants, however, lies not directly with the people, but with their representatives, the lower magistrates, who are constitutionally called to organize and direct the people in orderly resistance – in all-out warfare and revolution if needed.

For Beza, tyrants were rulers who violated the terms of the political covenant – particularly its foundational requirement that all must honor the rights of God to be worshipped and the rights of God's people to discharge the duties of the faith in conformity with God's law. Beza made the rights of the people the foundation and condition of good government. "The people are not made for rulers, but rulers for the people," he wrote. If the magistrate rules properly, the people must obey him. But if the magistrate abuses his authority in violation of the political covenant, the people, through their representatives, have the right and the duty to resist him as a tyrant.

The issue that remained for Beza was how to ground his doctrine of rights and to determine which rights were so fundamental that, if breached by a tyrant, triggered the right to organized resistance. Here Beza cleverly reworked Calvin's main arguments, taking his cues from Calvin's own late-life statements about the "natural rights" or "common rights of mankind," and the "the equal rights and liberties" of all persons. The first and most important rights, Beza reasoned, had to be religious rights – "liberty of conscience" and "free exercise of religion." Persons are, after all, first and foremost God's subjects and called to honor and worship God. If the magistrate breaches these religious rights, then nothing can be sacred and secure any longer. What is essential to the protection of the liberty of conscience and free exercise of religion, Beza continued catechetically: the ability to live in full conformity with the law of God. What is the law of God: first and foremost the Decalogue which sets out the core duties of right Christian living. What do these Ten Commandments entail: the rights to worship God, to obey the Sabbath, to avoid foreign idols and false oaths in accordance with the First Table of the Decalogue, and the rights to marriage, parentage, and a household, and to life, property, and reputation protected by the Second Table. Is the Decalogue the only law of God: no, the natural law that God has written on the hearts of all people teaches other rights that are essential to the protection of a person and a people. Beza touched on several of these broader natural rights: freedom of religious mission and education, freedom of church government and emigration, freedoms of speech, assembly, and petition, and freedom of marriage, divorce, and private contract. Beza did not do much to ground and systematize these natural rights, nor did he make clear which of them were so fundamental that their breach could trigger organized resistance. But he put in place much of the logic of a fundamental rights calculus that later Calvinists would refine and expand.

These types of arguments had immediate application in the revolt of Dutch Calvinists against the tyranny of their distant sovereign, Spanish emperor Philip II. In the 1560s, Philip imposed a series of increasingly onerous restrictions on the Netherlands – heavy taxes, commercial regulations, military conscriptions, forced quartering of soldiers, and more – in breach of centuries-old charters of the rights and liberties of the Dutch provinces, cities, and orders. Even worse, Philip set up the terrifying Spanish Inquisition in the Netherlands, slaughtering Calvinists and others by the thousands and confiscating massive amounts of private property in a determined effort to root out Protestantism and to impose on the Netherlands the sweeping new decrees of the Catholic Council of Trent. In the later 1560s and 1570s, under the inspired leadership of William of Orange and others, the Dutch put into action Calvinist principles of resistance and revolution. Whipped up by thunderous preaching and thousands of pamphlets, Calvinists and other Dutchmen eventually threw off their Spanish oppressors. They issued a declaration of independence in 1581, justifying their revolt from Spain on the strength of "clear truths" about "the laws and liberties of nature." They established a confederate government featuring seven sovereign provinces and a national government, each with its own constitution and its own bill of rights. Some of these provincial constitutions embraced the most advanced rights protections of the day, rendering the Netherlands a haven for many, though not all, cultural and religious dissenters from throughout Europe.[19]

The Dutch Revolt and the founding of the Dutch Republic drew to itself a number of powerful Calvinist jurists and political theorists. The most original work came from the prolific pen of the German-born Calvinist jurist, Johannes Althusius, who served as both a city counselor and consistory member in the city of Emden in the early seventeenth century. Drawing on a vast array of biblical, classical, Catholic, and Protestant sources, Althusius systematized and greatly expanded many of the core political and legal teachings of Calvin, Beza, and other co-religionists – that

---

[19] E. H. Kossman and A. Mellink, eds., *Texts Concerning the Revolt of the Netherlands* (Cambridge: Cambridge University Press, 1974).

the republic is formed by a covenant between the rulers and the people before God, that the foundation of this covenant is the law of God and nature, that the Decalogue is the best expression of this higher law, that church and state are separate in form but conjoined in function, that families, churches, and states alike must protect the rights and liberties of the people, and that violations of these rights and liberties, or of the divine and natural laws that inform and empower them, are instances of tyranny that must trigger organized constitutional resistance.

Althusius added a number of other core ideas to this Calvinist inheritance in his two masterworks: *Politics* (1603/14) and *A Theory of Justice* (1617/18).[20] Althusius developed a natural law theory that still treated the Decalogue as the best source and summary of natural law but layered its Commandments with all manner of new biblical, classical, and Christian teachings. He developed a theory of positive law that judged the contemporary validity and utility of any human law, including the positive laws of Moses and the canon laws of the church, against both the natural law of Scripture and tradition and the fundamental law of the state. He called for a detailed written constitution as the fundamental law of the community and called for perennial protection of the "rule of law" and "rule of rights" within church and state alike. He developed an expansive theory of popular sovereignty as an expression of the divine sovereignty that each person reflects as an image bearer of God. He developed a detailed and refined theory of natural rights – religious and social, public and private, substantive and procedural, contractual and proprietary rights. He demonstrated at great length how each of these rights was predicated on the Decalogue and other forms of natural law, and how each was to be protected by public, private, and criminal laws and procedures promulgated by the state. Particularly striking was his call for religious toleration and absolute liberty of conscience for all as a natural corollary and consequence of the Calvinist teaching of the absolute sovereignty of God whose relationship with any of his creatures could not be trespassed.

More striking still was Althusius's "symbiotic theory" of human nature and "covenantal theory" of society and politics. While acknowledging the traditional Calvinist teaching of the total depravity of persons, Althusius emphasized that God has created all persons as moral, loving, communicative, and social beings, whose lives are most completely fulfilled through

---

[20] *Politica Methodice Digesta of Johannes Althusius (Althaus)*, ed. Carl J. Friedrich (Cambridge, MA: Harvard University Press, 1932); Althusius, *Dicaeologicae libri tres, totum et universum Jus, quo utimur, methodice complectentes* (Herborn, 1617; Frankfurt, 1618).

symbiotic relationships with others in which they can appropriately share their bodies and souls, their lives and spirits, their belongings and rights. Thus, while persons are born free, equal, and individual, they are by nature and necessity inclined to form associations – marriages and families, clubs and corporations, cities and provinces, nation-states and empires. Each of these associations, from the tiniest household to the vastest empire, is formed by a mutually consensual covenant or contract sworn by all members of that association before each other and God. Each association is a locus of authority and liberty that binds both rulers and subjects to the terms of their founding contract and to the commands of the foundational laws of God and nature. Each association confirms and protects the sovereignty and identity of its constituent members as well as their natural rights and liberties.

Althusius applied this Christian social contract theory most fully in his description of the state. Using the political history of ancient Israel as his best example, he showed historically and philosophically how nation-states develop gradually from families to tribes to cities to provinces to nations to empires. Each new layer of political sovereignty is formed by covenants sworn before God by representatives of the smaller units, and these covenants eventually become the written constitutions of the polity. The constitutions define and divide the executive, legislative, and judicial offices within that polity, and govern the relations of its rulers and subjects, clerics and magistrates, associations and individuals. They determine the relations between and among nations, provinces, and cities, and between and among private and public associations – all of which Althusius called a form of "federalism" (from "foedus," Latin for covenant). The constitutions also make clear the political acts and omissions that constitute tyranny and the procedures and remedies available to those who are abused. Althusius produced the most comprehensive Calvinist theory of law and politics in the early modern period, and many of his insights anticipated teachings that would become axiomatic for Western constitutionalism.

JOHN MILTON AND PURITANISM

Such ideas found immediate application a generation later in England, and became part of what John Milton called "a new reformation of the Reformation" of law, authority, and liberty. The catalyst for this new English reformation was, again, tyranny – this time, by the English monarchy against the people of England, not least the swelling population of English Calvinists descended from the first Puritans who had settled in

England a century before. In 1640, these Calvinists joined many others in armed rebellion against the excesses of the English Crown – the oppressive royal taxes and fees, the harsh new Anglican establishment laws, the abuses of the royal and ecclesiastical courts, and more. When Parliament was finally called into session in 1640, after an eleven-year hiatus, its leaders seized power by force of arms. Civil war erupted between the supporters of Parliament and the supporters of the king. The parliamentary party, dominated by Calvinists, eventually prevailed and passed an act in 1649 "declaring and constituting the People of England to be a Commonwealth and Free State." Parliament abolished the kingship, and, remarkably, King Charles was tried by a special tribunal, convicted for treason, and beheaded in public. Parliament also abolished the aristocratic House of Lords and declared that "supreme authority" resided in the people and their representatives. Anglicanism was formally disestablished, and episcopal structures were replaced with Calvinist church forms. "Equal and proportional representation" was guaranteed in the election of local representatives to Parliament. England was now to be under "the democratic rule" of Parliament and the Protectorate of the Calvinist military leader, Oliver Cromwell.

After Cromwell died in 1658, however, the Commonwealth government collapsed. King Charles II, son of Charles I, returned to England, reclaimed the throne in 1660, and restored traditional monarchical government, Anglican establishment, and pre-revolutionary law. This Restoration era was short lived, however. When his successor King James II, the other son of Charles I, began to abuse his royal prerogatives as his father had done, Parliament forced him to abdicate the throne in 1688 in favor of the new dynasty of William and Mary. This was the Glorious Revolution. It established permanently government by the king in Parliament and introduced a host of new guarantees to English subjects, notably those set out in the Bill of Rights and the Toleration Act of 1689.

The English Revolution unleashed a massive torrent of writings and legislation calling for the reformation of English law and the enforcement of the rights and liberties of Englishmen. Part of the effort was to extend the traditional rights of life, liberty, and property in the Magna Carta (1215) to apply to all churches and citizens, not just Anglicans and aristocratic freemen. Part of the effort was to build on the Petition of Right (1628), a parliamentary document that had set out several public, private, and procedural rights for the people and their representatives in Parliament. But the most radical and memorable efforts of the English Revolution were the many petitions and platforms issued in the 1640s and 1650s calling for the establishment of a democratic government dedicated to protection of a full panoply of rights and liberties of the people. These included freedoms of religion, speech, press, and assembly, the right to conscientious objection to oaths, tithes, and military service, freedom from forced quartering of soldiers and sailors, freedom of private property and from unjust takings, freedom from excessive taxation and regulation, freedom of private contract, inheritance, marriage, and divorce, the right to civil and criminal jury trial, and all manner of criminal procedural protections – no ex post facto legislation and bills of attainder, no warrantless arrests, no illegal searches and seizures, the right to bail, the right to a fair and speedy trial, the right to face one's accusers, the right to representation in court, the privilege against self-incrimination, freedom from cruel investigation and punishment, the right to appeal. While most of these rights proposals were quashed – partly by Cromwell's Protectorate and altogether by the Restoration government of 1660 – they provided a normative totem for the later common law to make real. Already in the Glorious Revolution of 1688, freedoms of religion, speech, and assembly were partly realized, as were several criminal procedure protections. And, many more of these rights proposals came to vivid expression and experimentation in the English colonists in North America.

Scores of sturdy English and Scottish Calvinists emerged to lead this "reformation of the Reformation." It was the great poet and political philosopher John Milton who provided the most interesting integrative political theory. While some of Milton's ideas strayed beyond Calvinist conventions, most of his political ideas remained within the Calvinist tradition and indeed extended it.[21] Drawing on Calvin and an array of continental Calvinists, Milton argued that each person is created in the image of God with "a perennial craving" to love God, neighbor, and self. Each person has the law of God written on his and her heart, mind, and conscience, and rewritten in Scripture, most notably in the Decalogue. Each person is a fallen and fallible creature in perpetual need of divine grace and forgiveness which is given freely to all who ask for it. Each person is a communal creature, naturally inclined to form private, domestic, ecclesiastical, and political associations. Each such association is created by a consensual covenant or contract that defines its form and function and the rights and powers of its members, all subject to the limits of natural law. Each association is headed by an authority who rules for the

---

[21] See *Complete Prose Works of John Milton*, 7 vols., gen. ed. Don M. Wolfe (New Haven: Yale University Press, 1953–80).

sake of his subjects and who must be resisted if he becomes abusive or tyrannical. All such resistance must be as moderate, orderly, and peaceable as possible, but it may rise to revolt and regicide if necessary in the political sphere.

In devising his own reformation of rights, Milton seized on what he thought to be the Calvinist reformers' most important lesson – namely, that the Reformation must always go on, *semper reformanda*. England must not idolize or idealize any Protestant teachings, Milton insisted, even those of Calvin and the Genevan fathers. England must rather develop and deepen, apply and amend these teachings in a continuous effort to reform church, state, and society anew. Milton further seized on what he took as a cardinal teaching of Calvinism – that God calls each and every person to be a prophet, priest, and king, and vests each person with natural rights and duties to speak, worship, and rule in church and state, family and society at once. For Milton, the driving forces of England's perpetual reformation, therefore, were not only clerics or magistrates, scholars or aristocrats. The true reformers were just as much the commoners and householders, craftsmen and farmers of every peaceable type. Every person was created by God with the freedom of conscience, reason, and will. Every person was called by God to discharge both their private Christian vocations and their public social responsibilities in expression of their love of God, neighbor, and self. This was a form of Christian populism and popular sovereignty that the Calvinist tradition had not put quite so strongly before.

Milton went even further beyond traditional Calvinist teachings in defining the religious, domestic, and civil rights and liberties that each person must enjoy in discharging these offices of prophet, priest, and king. Among religious liberties, he defended liberty of conscience, freedom of religious exercise, worship, association, and publication, equality of multiple biblical faiths before the law, separation of church and state, and disestablishment of a national religion. Among domestic liberties, he stressed urgently the right to marry and divorce in accordance with the explicit teachings of Scripture alone as well as attendant rights to nurture, discipline, and educate one's children and to have one's private home free from unwanted searches and seizures of papers and possessions. Among civil liberties, he offered a brilliant defense of the freedoms of speech and press, and also defended earnestly the rights to democratic election, representation, petition, and dissent, as well as the rights to private contract and association and to jury trial. All these rights arguments were echoed in hundreds of Calvinist pamphlets, sermons, and learned treatises on both sides of the Atlantic, and would become commonplaces among Calvinist constitutional reformers in the eighteenth and nineteenth centuries.

Some of the most vivid amplifications and applications of these English legal and political ideas in action came in Puritan Massachusetts and other New England colonies after their first settlement in 1620. The Puritan colonists were given freedom in their founding charters to experiment locally with many of the most radical proposals and ideals that the English Calvinist revolutionaries had propounded. While adapting Geneva's congregational polity and consistorial government within the church, the colonists adopted English proposals for a democratic state government. In his famous *Body of Liberties* (1641), Calvinist jurist and theologian Nathaniel Ward set forth a twenty-five-page bill of rights for the colony of Massachusetts Bay, which captured every one of the rights and liberties proposed by Calvin, Beza, Althusius, Milton, and the Puritan pamphleteers, and added many more rights and liberties besides, particularly in protection of women, children, and animals. The *Body of Liberties* was an anchor text for New England colonial constitutionalism and anticipated many of the rights provisions of the later American state constitutions. While these legal instruments were often breached and ignored by autocratic and theocratic colonial leaders, they provided an essential legal substratum of rights that has proved enduring. Many of these early rights provisions found their way into the laws of other American colonies and figured prominently in the new American state constitutions forged after 1776, alongside more overtly Enlightenment views.[22]

The famous Virginia Declaration of Rights (1776), for example, provided in Article 1: "That all men are by nature equally free and independent, and have certain inherent rights, of which, when they enter into a state of society, they cannot, by any compact, deprive or divest their posterity; namely, the enjoyment of life and liberty, with the means of acquiring and possessing property, and pursuing and obtaining happiness and safety." The Declaration went on to specify the rights of the people to vote and to run for office, their "indubitable, unalienable, and indefeasible right to reform, alter or abolish" their government if necessary, various traditional criminal procedural protections, the right to jury trial in civil and criminal cases, freedom of press, and various freedoms of religion. But the Declaration also reflected traditional Christian sentiments in providing in Articles 15 and 16 that "no free government, or the blessings of liberty,

---

[22] Reprinted in Francis N. Thorpe, ed., *The Federal and State Constitutions, Colonial Charters, and Other Organic Laws*, 7 vols. (Washington, DC: Government Printing Office, 1909), VII:3813.

can be preserved to any people but by a firm adherence to justice, moderation, temperance, frugality, and virtue and by frequent recurrence to fundamental principles," and further by insisting that it was "the mutual duty of all to practice Christian forbearance, love, and charity toward each other."

Even stronger such traditional Christian formulations stood alongside the new Enlightenment views in the 1780 Massachusetts Constitution. This state constitution, which amply amended remains in place, sought to balance the freedom of all private religions with "a mild and equitable establishment" of a public religion, as its principal author John Adams described it. Article II provided: "It is the right as well as the duty of all men in society, publickly, and at stated seasons to worship the SUPREME BEING, the great Creator and preserver of the Universe." Article III stated the reason for this: "[T]he public worship of GOD and instructions in piety, religion, and morality ... promote their happiness, and secure ... the good order and preservation of their government."[23] The same constitution also insisted that all persons, particularly political leaders, maintain rigorous moral and religious standards, which they must confirm publicly when taking their oaths of office. It also rendered these same moral qualities essential ingredients of education within the state, since "the encouragement of arts and sciences, and all good literature, tends to the honor of GOD, the advantage of the Christian religion, and the great benefit of this and the other United States of America."

CONCLUSIONS

In his *Social Contract* of 1762, Jean-Jacques Rousseau offered this charitable assessment of his compatriot, John Calvin: "Those who consider Calvin only as a theologian fail to recognize the breadth of his genius. The editing of our wise laws, in which he had a large share, does him as much credit as his *Institutes* ... [S]o long as the love of country and liberty is not extinct among us, the memory of this great man will be held in reverence."[24] A similar assessment might be offered about much of early modern Calvinism. Calvinism was both a theological and a legal movement, a reformation both of church and state. Beginning with Calvin and Beza who were trained in both fields, theologians and jurists together

---

[23] Massachusetts Constitution (1780), Pt. I, Arts. II and III; this language is retained in Amendment, Art. XI (1833), which replaced Pt. I, Art. III.

[24] *Du contrat social* (1762), 2, 7n., in Jean Jacques Rousseau, *The Social Contract and the Discourse on the Origin of Inequality*, ed. Lester G. Crocker (New York: Pocket Books, 1967), 44n.

formed the leadership of the Reformed churches, and they made ample use of pulpits and printers alike. For every new Calvinist catechism in the early modern era there was a new Calvinist ordinance, for every fresh confession of faith an elaborate new bill of rights. Early modern Calvinists believed in natural and positive law – as a deterrent against sin, an inducement to grace, a teacher of Christian virtue. They also believed in the rule of law – structuring their churches and states alike to minimize the sinful excesses of their rulers and to maximize the liberties of their subjects to live their lives more promptly and more readily in loving obedience of God and service of his church.

RECOMMENDED READING

Althusius, Johannes. *Politica Methodice Digesta of Johannes Althusius (Althaus)*, ed. Carl J. Friedrich. Cambridge, MA: Harvard University Press, 1932.

Beza, Theodore. *Concerning the Rights of Rulers Over Their Subjects and the Duties of Subjects Toward Their Rulers*, trans. Henri-Louis Gonin. Cape Town and Pretoria: Juta Publishers, 1956.

Bohatec, Josef. *Calvins Lehre von Staat und Kirche mit besonderer Berücksichtigung des Organismusgedankens*. Breslau: M. & H. Marcus, 1937.

Calvin, John. *Institutes of the Christian Religion*, ed. John T. McNeill, trans. Ford Lewis Battles. Philadelphia: Westminster Press, 1960.

Doumergue, Emile. *Jean Calvin. Les hommes et les choses de son temps*, 7 vols. Lausanne: G. Bridel, 1899–1927.

Kingdon, Robert M. *Myths About the St. Bartholomew's Day Massacres, 1572–1576*. Cambridge, MA: Harvard University Press, 1988.

Kossman, E. H. and A. Mellink, eds. *Texts Concerning the Revolt of the Netherlands*. Cambridge: Cambridge University Press, 1974.

Milton, John. *Complete Prose Works of John Milton*, 7 vols., gen. ed. Don M. Wolfe. New Haven: Yale University Press, 1953–80.

Morgan, Edmund S., ed. *Puritan Political Ideas 1558–1794*, repr. edn. Indianapolis and Cambridge: Hackett Publishers, 2003.

Strohm, Christoph. *Calvinismus und Recht*. Tübingen: Mohr Siebeck, 2008.

Witte, John, Jr., *The Reformation of Rights: Law, Religion and Human Rights in Early Modern Calvinism*. Cambridge: Cambridge University Press, 2007.

CHAPTER 7

Modern Protestant developments in human rights

Nicholas P. Wolterstorff

A new narrative of the origin of the idea of natural human rights has been emerging in recent years. Three books stand out. Brian Tierney, in his 1997 publication *The Idea of Natural Rights: Studies on Natural Rights, Natural Law and Church Law: 1150–1625*,[1] shows that the idea of natural human rights was explicitly formulated and often employed by the canon lawyers of the 1100s. John Witte, in his 2007 publication *The Reformation of Rights: Law, Religion, and Human Rights in Early Modern Calvinism*,[2] shows that the idea was employed almost incessantly by the early Calvinists. And the earlier 1979 publication by Richard Tuck, *Natural Rights Theories: Their Origin and Development*,[3] goes some way toward filling in the gap between the medieval and early modern periods that Tierney and Witte focus on.

The old and still-popular narrative holds that the idea of natural human rights was created by the individualistic political philosophers of the Enlightenment, notably Thomas Hobbes and John Locke. Those who espouse this narrative customarily add that the Enlightenment was a secular, anti-Christian movement. What the new counter-narrative shows beyond doubt is that the idea was given birth some six centuries earlier by medieval Christian thinkers, and that it continued to be used through the centuries by Catholic writers and, once Protestantism arose, by Protestant writers as well. Hobbes and Locke inherited the idea from their Christian forebears.

Should a young scholar become acquainted with this new narrative and then later read around in Protestant writings of the twentieth century, he will be surprised to discover that the idea of natural human rights is seldom employed in these writings, and, when it is, it is usually in an off-hand manner. Opposition to the idea is far more common than systematic employment. The word "rights" does not occur in the index to

---

[1] Atlanta, GA: Scholars Press, 1997.   [2] Cambridge: Cambridge University Press, 2007.
[3] Cambridge: Cambridge University Press, 1979.

Dietrich Bonhoeffer's *Ethics*,[4] nor does it occur in the index to Reinhold
Niebuhr's two-volume work, *The Nature and Destiny of Man*.[5] In the index
to the book on Christian ethics that Karl Barth wrote late in his career,
The Christian Life,[6] one does find the entry, "right of man." But when one
looks up the two passages cited, one discovers that it was not human rights
that Barth had in mind.

I mean to speak here only about Protestant *writing*, not about Protestant
writers. It may well be that a good many of the twentieth-century writers
who have systematically employed the idea of natural human rights and
defended their doing so were in fact Protestants. I mean to speak about
those writings that are clearly identifiable as located within the Protestant
tradition of Christianity.

The story of what happened between early Calvinist Protestantism and
the Protestantism of the twentieth century, to account for this truly start-
ling difference, remains to be told. Did the twentieth-century Protestant
writers reject their Catholic and Protestant heritage knowing full well
what they were rejecting? Or had historical amnesia set in? Clearly the
latter. The twentieth-century Protestant writers betray no knowledge of
the history that Tierney, Tuck, Witte, *et al.* have unearthed. When they
refer or allude to a narrative of origins, that narrative is always the common secular-origins narrative. There is irony in this. Protestant writings
of the twentieth century are full of attacks on secularism; ironic, then,
that those same writings should buy into a central plank in the platform
of modern secularism, namely, the secularist's telling of the story of the
origins of the idea of natural human rights. Of course, typically there is
a difference in how the story is told. When Protestant writers explicitly
refer to the narrative, they almost always frame it as a story of decline;
secular writers usually, though by no means always, frame it as a story of
progress.

I am not sufficiently learned to be able to offer a survey of twentieth-
century Protestant writings so as to determine when they had something
significant to say about human rights, and when they did, what that was;
but neither do I think that a survey would be of much use. Instead, I
propose to offer a typology of how the idea is treated by those who do
mention it. Useful though typologies often are, they have the defect of
ignoring individual nuances and of concealing from view how particular thinkers found themselves led to one or another of the typologized

---

[4] New York: The Macmillan Company, 1955.   [5] New York: Charles Scribner's Sons, 1949.
[6] Grand Rapids, MI: Wm. B. Eerdmans, 1981.

positions. The person who constructed the typology will have been aware of these particularities, but the typology itself abstracts from them. To compensate for this defect, I will in each case present the thought of a paradigmatic representative of the position. Of course, this in turn courts the distinct danger of annoying all those who have articulated one of the positions in my typology but whom I do not select as my example; to them, my apologies.

THE AGAPIST REJECTION OF HUMAN RIGHTS

In a good deal of twentieth-century Protestant writing one finds a flat-out rejection of the idea of natural human rights. Sometimes this rejection takes the form of rejecting the idea of natural rights while affirming the importance of justice; in other cases it takes the more radical form of insisting that Christians should discard from their moral culture all considerations of justice and injustice. Let me begin with this latter, more radical, position.

The rejectionist position was most vividly presented, and most rigorously developed, by the Swedish Lutheran bishop, Anders Nygren, in his now-classic *Agape and Eros*, published in installments in the early 1930s.[7] Whereas the Old Testament, according to Nygren, is all about justice, agapic love has displaced justice in the life and teaching of Jesus. Jesus "enters into fellowship with those who are not worthy of it." His doing so is directed "against every attempt to regulate fellowship with God by the principle of justice" (86). "That Jesus should take lost sinners to Himself was bound to appear, not only to the Pharisees, but to anyone brought up and rooted in Jewish legal righteousness, as a violation of the order established by God Himself and guaranteed by His justice" (83). For them it was "a violation not merely of the human, but above all of the Divine, order of justice, and therefore of God's majesty" (70).

The point is unmistakable: the agapic love displayed and enjoined by Jesus does not supplement justice but supersedes it. "'Motivated' justice must give place ... to 'unmotivated' love" (74). We are not to love the neighbor agapically *in addition to* treating her as justice requires; we are to love her *instead of* treating her as justice requires.

Part of what led Nygren to this conclusion was his conviction that in the second love command, "Love your neighbor as yourself," Jesus

---

[7] Translated by Philip S. Watson (London: SPCK, 1953). Further citations to Nygren occur in the text within parentheses.

was not just enjoining us to love everyone who is one's neighbor but to love the neighbor with that special form of love that came to be called *neighbor love* by the members of the twentieth-century agapist movement that Nygren was instrumental in inspiring. Nygren's great forebear on this point, that Jesus was enjoining us to love the neighbor with a special kind of love, was the Danish theologian, Søren Kierkegaard, in his *Works of Love*.

What is that special form of love that Jesus enjoined us to have for every neighbor? It is love that takes God's loving forgiveness of the sinner as its model. Justice does not require forgiveness; one is not treating the person who wronged one unjustly if one finds it impossible to forgive him, or if one refuses to do so. Forgiveness is an act of gratuitous love. Agapic love in general is like forgiveness in this regard. Nygren often speaks of agapic love as *spontaneous*; the contrast he wants us to hear is: spontaneous rather than *required*. Agapic love is pure generosity, pure benevolence. Here is how Emil Brunner puts the point in *Justice and the Social Order*: love "does not render to the other what is his due, what belongs to him 'by right,' but gives of its own, gives precisely that to which the other has no right."[8] Agapic love is justice-blind.

Many members of the twentieth-century agapist movement took for granted that agapic love, though blind to what justice requires, would nonetheless not perpetrate injustice; Brunner, in *Justice and the Social Order*, is an example. Not so Nygren; he interpreted the landowner in Jesus's parable of the laborers in the vineyard (Matt. 20:1–16) as conceding the charge by those who had worked all day that he was treating them unjustly by paying them no more than the late-comers. "No matter," says the landowner in Nygren's interpretation: "Am I not allowed to distribute my generosity as I wish?"

Very few Protestants, whether scholars or laypeople, have shared Nygren's clarity and rigor and been willing to follow him all the way to this conclusion. But the sense that Jesus enjoined us to love our neighbor with a form of love that pays no attention to justice – the sense that in the life and teaching of Jesus, love superseded justice – is common among twentieth-century Protestants. Nygren both articulated and reinforced this intuition. But if justice is superseded, then perforce natural human rights are superseded.

---

[8] New York and London: Harper & Brothers, 1945, 17. Further citations to Brunner occur in the text within parentheses.

THE REJECTION OF NATURAL HUMAN RIGHTS
AS A LAMENTABLE MODERN INVENTION

A less-radical position than the one just considered affirms the importance of justice but rejects the idea of natural human rights. Justice has nothing to do with natural rights. The idea of natural rights is a lamentable invention of the individualist political philosophers of the Enlightenment – or perhaps of the late medieval nominalist, William of Ockham.

Those who espouse this position commonly credit Leo Strauss, *Natural Right and History*,[9] with introducing the crucial idea. Strauss distinguished between *natural law or right* and *natural rights* – in the plural. A right is something that someone *has*, something that he or she *possesses*. Strauss contrasts rights with *the obligatory* or *the right* – as in the phrase, "doing the right thing."

Having drawn this distinction, Strauss's central thesis was that whereas for most of Western history, thinkers have thought in terms of the right or the obligatory, in the Enlightenment the idea of the right was transmuted into the idea of rights, with Thomas Hobbes being the principal proponent. Whereas thinkers had once believed that there was a natural right order, or, if one prefers, a natural order of the right, this order determining the right or obligatory thing for a person of a certain sort to do in a certain situation, now they thought in terms of members of the social order bearing natural rights. "The fundamental change [was] from an orientation by natural duties to an orientation by natural rights," says Strauss (182). Whereas it was once thought that a society is just insofar as it measures up to the natural order of the right, now it was thought that a society is just insofar as the natural and other rights of its members are honored.

Strauss saw this change as an important mark of the transition to modernity. And he left no doubt as to his judgment on the change. The idea of natural rights is an inextricable component in the atomistic and agonistic political philosophies that emerged in the Enlightenment; it cannot be extracted from such a context. The idea of natural rights carries possessive individualism in its DNA. The language of rights is for each of us asserting his claims, his entitlements, his rights, each against the other.

A decade or so after Strauss's 1953 publication, the French legal historian Michel Villey, in a long series of publications, located the shift in conceptuality that Strauss had ascribed to the Enlightenment several centuries

---

[9] Chicago: University of Chicago Press, 1953. Further citations to Strauss occur in the text within parentheses.

earlier, in fourteenth-century nominalism, with William of Ockham rather than Hobbes now being the principal culprit. Villey identified himself as part of the nineteenth- and twentieth-century neo-Thomist movement which sees Western philosophy as having reached its apogee in Thomas Aquinas and as having been in decline ever since.

In my presentation of this movement, I have said nothing thus far about Protestantism. The narrative and the moral drawn from it were neither originated by Protestants nor has their subsequent espousal been monopolized by Protestants. Both the narrative and the moral have, however, been taken up by Protestant thinkers, so much so that I judge that this line of rejection of natural rights is now at least as common among Protestant scholars, if not laypeople, as the previous. Let me cite some passages from Joan Lockwood O'Donovan who is, in my judgment, along with Oliver O'Donovan among the best Protestant proponents of the position.[10] "The modern liberal concept of rights belongs," she says, "to the socially atomistic and disintegrative philosophy of 'possessive individualism.'"[11]

A close analysis of the history of the concept of subjective rights in the light of earlier theological-political conceptualization reveals a progressive antagonism between the older Christian tradition of political right and the newer voluntarist, individualist, and subjectivist orientation. The contrasting logic of the two orientations may be conveyed quite simply: where in the older patristic and medieval tradition, God's right established a matrix of divine, natural, and human laws or objective obligations that constituted the ordering justice of political community, in the newer tradition God's right established discrete rights, possessed by individuals originally and by communities derivatively, that determined civil order and justice.[12]

She then describes what she calls "the older traditions":

In the older traditions, the central moral-political act on the part of ruler and ruled alike was to consent to the demands of justice, to the obligations inhering in communal life according to divine intention and rationally conceived as laws. The ruler commanded, legislated, and issued binding judgments, but these acts were to embody his consent to an order of right and obligations binding his own will. The subject was obligated to obey the ruler's commands, statutes, and

---

[10] Oliver O'Donovan's statements of the position tend to be scattered, occurring in the context of his treatment of other topics. His most sustained statement of the position is "The Language of Rights and Conceptual History," *Journal of Religious Ethics* 37(2) (June 2009): 193–207.

[11] "Natural Law and Perfect Community: Contributions of Christian Platonism to Political Theory," *Modern Theology* 14(1) (January 1998): 20.

[12] "The Concept of Rights in Christian Moral Discourse," in Michael Cromartie, ed., *A Preserving Grace: Protestants, Catholics, and Natural Law* (Grand Rapids, MI: Wm. B. Eerdmans, 1997), 145.

judgments, not only because of his rightful authority, but also because these acts conformed to the requirements of justice.[13]

Given what she sees as the patent incompatibility between the idea of natural human rights and sound Christian theology, an obvious question for O'Donovan is "why Christian thinkers have been and are willing" to buy into the idea. Why have they been "willing to adopt a child of such questionable parentage as the concept of human rights?" It is, she adds, a "question that has yet to be satisfactorily answered."[14]

It is important to add an explanatory qualification. The right-order theorists are not opposed to all rights talk. They are opposed to all talk of *natural* rights; they hold that there are no such rights. But as for talk about so-called *positive* rights, they are wary but not dismissive. Oliver O'Donovan puts the point well:

The language of subjective rights (i.e., rights which adhere to a particular subject) has, of course, a perfectly appropriate and necessary place within a discourse founded on law. One's "right" is the claim on which the law entitles one to demand performance ... What is distinctive about the modern conception of rights, however, is that subjective rights are taken to be original, not derived ... The right is a primitive endowment of power with which the subject first engages in society, not an enhancement which accrues to the subject from an ordered and politically formed society.[15]

RIGHTS TALK: USEFUL BUT DISPENSABLE

A third position that one finds in Protestant writings of the twentieth century is that talk of natural human rights is sometimes useful, but always dispensable; one could make the same point with other concepts. Let me take the book of Emil Brunner already referred to, *Justice and the Social Order*, as an example of the position. Brunner was second only to Barth in his prominence as a German theologian of the first six or so decades of the twentieth century.

"From time immemorial," stated Brunner, "the principle of justice has been defined as the *suum cuique* – the rendering to each man of his due ... Who or whatever renders to every man his due, that person or thing is just" (17). Brunner takes for granted that what can be said with the term "due" can also be said with the term "a right." "The sphere of justice embraces all that 'belongs,' all that is a man's due, all that he has a 'right to'" (17).

---

[13] *Ibid.*   [14] *Ibid.*, 155.
[15] *The Desire of the Nations* (Cambridge: Cambridge University Press, 1996), 262.

Immediately after connecting justice with what is due a person, Brunner adds that what is due a person is not exhaustively determined by "the positive law of the state, firstly because it is precisely the idea of justice which enables us to distinguish between a just and an unjust law, secondly because we also speak of justice in cases where there could be no recourse to a legal settlement by the state" (17). Justice is grounded in "an underived, primal order of things established by no human lawgiver" (17). "An action or an attitude of mind, a law or an institution, can only claim to be called 'just' if it corresponds to that primal order" (18–19). As one would expect, Brunner relates this primal transcendent order to God. We shall see later what he takes the relationship to be.

Justice, what is due a person, is intimately related to equality. There is, for one thing, the formal relationship to equality of our all being equally subject to the primal order of justice. As to the substantive relationship, Brunner thinks that Aristotle got it right when he said that to distribute goods justly is to distribute them equally:

Aristotle was the first to enquire into the nature of justice and to recognize both the close connection of justice with equality and the dual nature of justice. The first, simple justice, which gives the same to each, he called arithmetical or contractual, the second, which gives the same to each according to a scale of actual inequality, he calls proportional, geometrical, or distributive. In this way he established a fundamental rule for all time, and we can understand why the theory of justice has at all times taken its stand on these Aristotelian definitions. We can even say that the theory of justice has never gone beyond Aristotle, but has always harked back to him. (27–8)

What neither Aristotle nor anyone else in pagan antiquity discerned, however, is the presence of a fundamental and ineradicable equality among human beings. "That conception of justice by which all human beings, old or young, man or woman, bond or free, have equal rights in the sense that they *ought* to be treated alike, is in essence derived from the revelation of Scripture, according to which God created man 'in his image'" (34). "The doctrine of the *imago Dei* … is the fundamental principle of the Protestant doctrine of justice" (36).

Christianity does not only affirm the dignity that we share equally as image bearers of God. It adds that God "calls [each] person into being and thereby endows him with responsibility … [E]very human being has his own personal dignity which resides in his predestination to personal being and is identical with the dignity of every other human being" (40). We are alike in being responsible to God.

To this we must add that "it is the will of the Creator that the individual human being should not be self-sufficient … It is His will that human beings should be dependent on each other … Creation has so disposed human beings that they must seek and have each other … The uniqueness of each individual human being is the limitation of that individual, and from that limitation there arises mutual dependence" (42).

Let us pull these last two points together. "The cardinal factor is the direct responsibility of the individual to God implied in God's call, and the dignity and equality which result from it. The secondary … factor is the mutual dependence resulting from man's predestination to fellowship and its substratum in nature, individual limitation, and idiosyncrasy. Hence, in the Christian idea of justice, equality and the equal right of all are primary, while the difference of what is due to each in the fellowship is, though not inessential, secondary" (43).

The fact that we are equal in the dignity we have on account of bearing the image of God, and likewise equal in the dignity we have on account of being called by God to responsible service, implies that, in fundamental ways, we are to be treated alike; justice requires equal treatment. The additional fact that we are created by God as unique persons each with a unique contour of social responsibilities implies that, once the requirements of equal treatment have been satisfied, we are to treat each person in a way that is due that unique person with her unique contour of responsibilities. One would like Brunner to develop this last point; but he does not. He remarks that "the child has a sacred right to be treated as a child and not as an adult. Its specific nature as a child implies *ipso facto* the right to be *treated* as a child" (51). In another passage he says that "what is due to the man is not the same as what is due to the woman, although what is due to both as human beings is equal" (50). He contents himself with these quick examples.

We can now take up the topic of the relation of God to the primal order of justice. "The law of justice is also the law of a divine will," stated Brunner. "Underlying the *suum cuique* there is the order of creation, the will of the Creator which determines which is each man's due" (48). But just how is the will of the Creator related to what is each person's due? Does God create human beings as equal in the dignity of each bearing the image of God but unique in the way that he or she is human and related to others? Does God then call each to serve in accord with his or her particularity so that all alike have the dignity of being called by God while at the same time each has a unique contour of responsibility? And does God then *in addition* to these acts of creation and call *determine* what is each person's due? Or do the equalities and inequalities of creation and call already determine what is due each person, so that no additional declaration of what is due people is required? Suppose those equalities and inequalities do already determine what is due each person. Does God then *in addition command* us to treat each other in accord with what is due us? Is it that additional command which is the primal order of justice of which Brunner speaks? Or was no such additional command required for there to be a primal order of justice? Is the primal order of justice simply that whole complex of equalities and inequalities which make things due us? If Brunner's view was the first of these three possibilities, there would be no significant difference between his view on this point and that of Joan and Oliver O'Donovan.

Though Brunner is less clear on the point than one would wish, I think the evidence points toward the last of the three possibilities mentioned. That seems to me clearly the most plausible interpretation of the following passage:

To every creature, there is given at its creation, with the mode of being manifested in it, its law of life. Its right is given, its scope delimited, what is due and what is not due to it is determined ... The fact that every human being, without prejudice to his specific mode of being, is, like every other, a creature who must give an account of himself ... – therein every human being has his dignity as a human being, which is identical with that of every other human being ... That is the equality of men founded in creation, the source of the eternal inalienable rights of man ... At the same time, however, every human being is endowed by the Creator with a specific mode of being ... Both their equality of dignity as human beings, as persons, and their inequality in kind and function are established by creation. Both must, as it were, be acknowledged, both are due and must be taken into account in the allocation of rights and duties. (49–51)

The picture here is clearly not that of God first creating and calling and then, in addition, doing something else to establish the primal order of justice. The creating and calling establish the order.

In presenting Brunner's view, I have several times spoken of the *dignity* we share equally on account of all bearing the image of God and on account of all being called by God to responsible service. Rather often Brunner speaks of dignity in this connection. But dignity is not what is most fundamental in his theory. What is most fundamental is the idea of something being due a person, plus the Aristotelian thesis that what is due a person is equal treatment of the relevant sort. What is important about the *imago Dei* is not that every human being possesses a certain dignity on account of bearing the *imago* – though every human being does possess that dignity; what is important is that human beings are all *alike* in bearing the *imago Dei*. Likewise, what is important about being called by God to responsible service is not that every human being possesses a certain dignity on account of being called – though every human being does possess that dignity; what is important is that human beings are all *alike* in being called by God. Brunner's theory of justice is an Aristotelian equality-based theory, not a dignity-based theory.

Aristotle did not speak of rights. He *could* have spoken of rights; he could have said that we all have a right to equal treatment. But he did not. He defines justice as equal treatment, assumes that we should treat people justly, and lets it go at that. So, too, for what Brunner appropriates from the Roman jurists, namely, the idea of something being due a person. One could speak of a right at this point.[16] One could say that if something is due a person, then that person has a right to it. Now and then Brunner does say this. But it is entirely incidental. He can say everything he wants to say without ever using the concept of *a right*, using only the concept of something being *due* a person.

Brunner never stands back to reflect on the role of the concept of *a right* in his thought; he never says that the concept is useful but dispensable. But that is how the concept does in fact function in his thought.

HUMAN RIGHTS AS INDISPENSABLE BUT NOT FUNDAMENTAL

Another position that one finds in Protestant writings of the twentieth century is that talk of natural rights is indispensable, but that natural rights themselves are not fundamental in the moral order. More fundamental are duties; rights are grounded in duties. If you are obligated to do something, then you have a right to do that, along with a right to do whatever else is necessary as a means. And if your obligation to do the thing in question is a natural obligation, an obligation not generated by any act on the part of human beings, then the correlative rights must also be natural.

Those Christians who sense that talk about human rights is getting at something of deep importance but who, at the same time, feel uneasy with giving natural rights a fundamental place in the moral order, are often inclined toward this view. Thus it is that one finds this account of human rights being employed every now and then in official

---

[16] See the chapter by Charles Donahue herein which shows that a few Roman jurists did speak of rights in this connection.

ecclesiastical declarations. Here is an example taken from "The United Church Pronouncement on Human Rights":[17]

Because of God's claim upon all God's creatures human rights have to do with the basic answerability or responsibility of being a human creature ... The fundamental human right is the right to be responsible to God. Human rights and human duties are two sides of the same coin ... In view of God's claim upon God's human creatures, rights are given by God as the means for all human beings to fulfill their duties before God's righteousness. Thus human rights are what people need in order to fulfill their fundamental task of becoming a human person, that is, fulfilling their calling as the image of God.

Paul Ramsey, who taught Christian ethics for many years at Princeton University, is as articulate a defender of this position as any. Here is what he says in his essay, "The Created Destination of Property Rights":[18]

If human rights are the rights of fellow humanity, "inalienably" connected with this human nature in us and with our life with fellow man and with our duties to other men, then rights must be whatever it is necessary for me to have in order to be with and for fellow man. If I have an inalienable natural right to life simply by my being a man, this is because life is the single most basic precondition to human existence in covenant. (37)

It is of natural human rights that Ramsey is explicitly speaking in this passage. But that he means his thesis concerning the connection between rights and duties to be understood more generally is clear from an earlier passage in the essay:

The state and its law as an ordinance of creation, natural justice, human and legal rights and social institutions generally, so far as these have a positive purpose under the creative, governing, and preserving purposes of God – all are the external basis making possible the actualization of the promise of covenant; while covenant or fellow humanity is the internal basis and meaning of every right, true justice, or law. (25–6)

Ramsey's use in this passage of the distinction between "external basis" and "internal basis" is an allusion to Karl Barth's apothegm that covenant is the internal basis of creation and creation, the external basis of covenant. God's covenant dealings with humankind is the purpose of creation; God's creation of humankind makes those covenant dealings possible.

---

[17] The full text of the Pronouncement is to be found in Appendix IV of Max L. Stackhouse, *Creeds, Society, and Human Rights: A Study in Three Cultures* (Grand Rapids, MI: Wm. B. Eerdmans, 1964). The passage quoted is found on *ibid.*, 298.

[18] The essay is the first chapter in Ramsey's book, *Christian Ethics and the Sit-In* (New York: Association Press, 1961). Further citations to Ramsey occur in the text within parentheses.

God's covenant dealings with humankind have the overarching character, according to Ramsey, of God's being *for* humankind; and as a component of God's being *for* humankind, God asks of us that we be *for* our fellow
human beings. God's being for humankind is God's mercy, God's "steadfast
covenant-love"; our being for each other is correspondingly our mercy, our
charity, our neighbor-love (26). It follows that "the requirements of charity,
or of steadfast covenant-love, and the requirements of justice, or of natural
right, are ultimately inseverable" (26). "[I]n being *for* fellow man is revealed
the internal basis of any sort of justice, or the meaning and intentionality
there were present all along in that life of man *with* man which God directs
in creating, preserving, and governing the world by means of the social
order. His rights are a man's capability to covenant" (30).

Ramsey observes that if one looks at love through the lens of justice,
rather than looking at justice through the lens of love, then one has to
acknowledge that "justice bears only the external marks of man's destiny
for steadfast covenant-love. It provides only the external possibility of covenant, or a minimum sign and promise of this." Accordingly, "the fellow
humanity of man that shows forth in the order of justice" can perhaps
best be described "as the life of man *with* fellow man (not *for* him)" (26).
Nonetheless,

To be *for* fellow man (charity) and to be *with* fellow man (justice) indicates the
permeability of justice to charity. Charity (*for* fellow man) is the internal basis
and meaning of natural justice (*with* fellow man), as justice in turn is the promise and possibility of close meeting and steadfast covenant. This has to be said of
every human right … Human rights all bear the marks of the primal justice of
man's creation for fellow humanity. (26–7)

WHY THE PRECEDING VIEWS ARE UNTENABLE

The last position in our typology is that the discourse of natural human
rights is indispensable, and that natural rights themselves are as fundamental in the moral order as duties. Since this is the position that I have myself
developed in *Justice: Rights and Wrongs*,[19] and that I develop somewhat
further in my forthcoming *Justice in Love*, let me take my own account
as our example of this position. Before I present my account, however, I
must briefly indicate why I find each of the preceding views unsatisfac-
tory. Everything I say here by way of critique is developed more fully in
Justice: Rights and Wrongs.

---

[19] Princeton: Princeton University Press, 2008.

To the best of my knowledge, all those twentieth-century writers who shared Nygren's conviction that Jesus, in the second love command, enjoined a special kind of love for all those who are one's neighbors, also shared his conviction that such love pays no attention to what justice requires. Neighbor-love is purely gratuitous benevolence. Nygren was one of the relatively few in the movement who seriously addressed the question whether such love might sometimes do what justice forbids. (Reinhold Niebuhr was another.) He answered the question as I think it must be answered. Such love does sometimes do what justice forbids. Nygren's view was that, in such a case, Christianity calls us to remain faithful to love and say farewell to justice. That position seems to me incoherent.

Take the parable of Jesus that Nygren himself used as an example: that of the laborers in the vineyard. Nygren interprets the landowner as conceding that he had treated the early workers unjustly but insisting that he was permitted to dispense his generosity as he wished. But if the landowner did indeed wrong the early workers by treating them as he did, then they had a right with respect to him that he not treat them that way. And if they had a right with respect to him that he not treat them that way, then he, conversely, had an obligation toward them not to treat them thus. But if he had an obligation not to treat them thus, then it cannot be the case that he was permitted to do that. If one is obligated not to do something, then one is not morally permitted to do it. The standard agapist understanding of neighbor-love cannot be correct; love must be understood in such a way as to incorporate seeing to it that one does what justice requires.[20]

My difficulties with the second position in our typology will already have been evident to the reader. An essential part of this position is the embrace of one or another version of the narrative which claims that the idea of natural rights had its origins in atomistic and agonistic political philosophies; those who espouse the position then add that these origins cannot be left behind. There are two ways of responding to these claims: one can develop a theory of natural rights which is clearly not agonistic and atomistic, or one can challenge the historical claims. Let me here confine myself to the latter. We know now that the canon lawyers of the twelfth century employed the idea of natural human rights; they were not possessive individualists. We also know now that the idea was employed by the early Calvinists; they too were not possessive individualists. My own view, which I do not have the space here to defend, is that the

[20] In my forthcoming *Justice in Love*, I develop such an alternative account of love.

existence of natural rights, both ours and God's, was assumed though not conceptualized by the writers of the Old and New Testaments.

Brunner is correct in observing that Aristotle's equality-account of just-ice has been taken as "gospel truth" for millennia. To me it seems, however, not only not to be gospel truth but to be clearly false. Is it at all plausible to say that what is wrong with rape is that the rapist is not distributing ben-efits and burdens equally? Or suppose that a teacher sets up an extremely onerous system of grading, so onerous that there is no chance of anyone getting an A no matter how gifted and informed he may be. The teacher, in applying the system, may be equitable to a fault; everybody is graded in proportion to how well he or she did. But most of the students have been wronged, treated unjustly.

Lastly, the Ramsey position. Ramsey holds that if one ought to do something, then one has a right to do it; and conversely, if one has a right to do something, then one has an obligation to do it. Distinguish between permission-rights and claim-rights. If one ought to do something, then one is morally permitted to do it; one has a permission-right to do it. But natural human rights are claim-rights, not permission-rights. The relevant claim-right here would be the claim-right to be *free* to do what one ought to do. It is less obviously true that if one is obligated to do something, then one has the claim-right to be free to do it, than it is that one has the per-mission-right to do it. But rather than pondering the truth or falsehood of that thesis, let us consider the other side of Ramsey's thesis, that all rights are implications of duties. The Alzheimer's patient has no duties; yet she has rights. And the person who pruriently spies on me but does nothing with what he learns, other than enjoy it privately, in no way impairs my ability to carry out my responsibilities; nonetheless he has deprived me of my right to privacy.

INDISPENSABLE AND FUNDAMENTAL

My account of rights is a dignity-based account. A right is a legitimate claim to the good of being treated a certain way by one's fellows – or in the limiting case, by oneself. But there are many ways of being treated by one's fellows to which one does not have a right even though it would be a good in one's life to be so treated. The goods to which we have rights are a sub-division of goods in general. One of the most daunting challenges facing anyone who wishes to give an account of rights is to explain what it is that accounts for the fact that one has a right to some of the ways of being treated that would be a good in one's life but not to others.

My view is that one has a right to be treated a certain way by another just in case, were the other not to treat one that way, the other would be treating one with under-respect. He would not be treating one in a way that befits one's worth; he would be treating one in a way that would only befit someone or something of less worth. Rights are what respect for worth requires. We each have worth on account of one or another feature, accomplishment, or relationship in which we stand. And many of our actions have what one might call respect/disrespect import. One is wronged, deprived of what one has a right to, when the respect/disrespect import of how one is treated does not befit one's worth, when it would only befit someone of less worth.

The other comes into my midst bearing worth. By virtue of bearing that worth she has rights with respect to me; she is susceptible of being wronged by me. But I also have worth; thereby I have rights with respect to her and am susceptible of being wronged by her. The situation is entirely symmetrical. The language of rights and of being wronged is for bringing these realities to speech. The language is often abused; the possessive individualist insistently calls attention to his own rights while brushing aside those of the other. That is what those who want to get rid of rights talk, on the ground that it expresses and abets possessive individualism, call attention to. But it is not the rights talk that is at fault; it is the possessive individualism. Every component of our moral vocabulary suffers from abuse; if abuse of some component was a good ground for discarding it, we would have no moral vocabulary left.

Ramsey was right to contend that there is an intimate connection between rights and duties. The connection is not that which he suggested, however, but that which is expressed in the following "Principle of Correlatives": if R is the sort of being that can have rights, then R has a right against S to S's doing X if and only if S has an obligation toward R to do X. Mary has a right against John to John's not insulting her if and only if John has an obligation toward Mary not to insult her.

It is tempting to conclude from the Principle of Correlatives that rights talk is, after all, dispensable in favor of duty-talk – though if that were true, it would be equally true that duty-talk is dispensable in favor of rights talk. Neither inference is correct. The Principle of Correlatives is what philosophers call a *synthetic necessary* truth; though necessarily true, it is not true by virtue of the meanings of the words plus the law of non-contradiction. When one says that Mary has a right with respect to John to John's not insulting her, one is not saying the same thing in different words as when one says that John has an obligation toward Mary not to insult her.

The language of duty brings to speech (one aspect of) the moral significance of *what we do*; the language of rights brings to speech the moral significance of *how we are done unto*. If John insults Mary, then the moral significance for himself of what he has done is that he is guilty; the moral significance for Mary of what he has done is that she has been wronged. The moral order has two fundamental dimensions, interlocking but distinct: the agent-dimension and the recipient- or patient-dimension. The language of duty, responsibility, and the like is for bringing to speech the agent-dimension; the language of rights is for bringing to speech the recipient-dimension.

And what, lastly, about natural human rights? These are rights that one has by virtue of the worth one has just *qua* human being. What accounts for such worth? Far and away the most common view among Christian writers has been that it is bearing the *imago Dei* that gives each of us the worth that grounds human rights; we saw that to be Brunner's view. I think the claim has been made far too quickly; too little attention has been paid to those who are severely impaired – Alzheimer's patients, those who are cognitively impaired from birth, and so forth. Brunner connects the *imago Dei* to being a creature called by God to responsible service; the Alzheimer's patient cannot engage in responsible service. We need an understanding of the *imago Dei* such that those who are severely impaired nonetheless bear the *imago Dei*. But then it becomes a question whether bearing the *imago Dei* gives a creature sufficient worth to ground human rights. My own view is that we have to bring into the picture a worth-bestowing relation to God that even the most impaired human beings possess. God loves redemptively all who bear the *imago Dei* – loves them equally and loves them perpetually. It is the worth we have on account of being so honored by God that grounds natural human rights.

RECOMMENDED READING

Brunner, Emil. *Justice and the Social Order*. New York and London: Harper & Brothers, 1945.

Nygren, Anders. *Agape and Eros*, trans. Philip S. Watson. London: SPCK, 1953.

O'Donovan, Oliver. *The Desire of the Nations*. Cambridge: Cambridge University Press, 1996.

"The Language of Rights and Conceptual History," *Journal of Religious Ethics* 37(2) (June 2009): 193–207.

O'Donovan, Joan Lockwood. "The Concept of Rights in Christian Moral Discourse," in Michael Cromartie, ed., *A Preserving Grace: Protestants, Catholics, and Natural Law*. Grand Rapids, MI: Wm. B. Eerdmans, 1997, 145–56.

"Natural Law and Perfect Community: Contributions of Christian Platonism to Political Theory," *Modern Theology* 14(1) (January 1998): 20–38.

Ramsey, Paul. *Christian Ethics and the Sit-In* (New York: Association Press, 1961).

Stackhouse, Max L. *Creeds, Society, and Human Rights: A Study in Three Cultures.* Grand Rapids, MI: Wm. B. Eerdmans, 1984.

Tierney, Brian. *The Idea of Natural Rights: Studies on Natural Rights, Natural Law and Church Law: 1150–1625.* Atlanta, GA: Scholars Press, 1997.

Tuck, Richard. *Natural Rights Theories: Their Origin and Development.* Cambridge: Cambridge University Press, 1979.

Witte, John, Jr. *The Reformation of Rights: Law, Religion, and Human Rights in Early Modern Calvinism.* Cambridge: Cambridge University Press, 2007.

Wolterstorff, Nicholas P. *Justice: Rights and Wrongs.* Princeton: Princeton University Press, 2008.

Justice in Love. Grand Rapids, MI: Wm. B. Eerdmans, 2010.

CHAPTER 8

The issue of human rights in Byzantium and the Orthodox Christian tradition

John A. McGuckin

ORTHODOXY AND RIGHTS: SOME BASIC TERMS OF ARGUMENT AND REFERENCE

In many recent fora, the Orthodox Church has been depicted as fundamentally an "Eastern" tradition that has not been squarely represented in the counsels that constituted the formation of Western Christendom. Given that this is an opinion often aired, in explanatory ways, in relation to why the Orthodox Church sometimes takes angular, not parallel, positions in relation to European human rights discourse, it is important to remember that this is fundamentally a late modern view, highly contentious in character, and one that raises as many problems for its inherently *orientaliste* agenda than it resolves. Insofar as world Orthodoxy still represents a common intellectual allegiance to foundational biblical prescripts, determinative patristic doctrinal and conciliar formulations, and enduringly influential Byzantine social, philosophical, political, and cultural influences then, simply put, it is necessary to insist that the Byzantine Orthodox Christian mentality is quintessentially European. It is, indeed, the seedbed of European Christian civilization; not some debased "oriental" variation on it. The Byzantines (first called such by eighteenth-century English historians) always called themselves *Romaioi*, the Romans. Greece is not (by any stretch of a non-colonial imagination) the Orient. And would anyone (*pace* Huntington) still care to argue that Russia's "distinctive difference" lies in its "orientalizing" margins? These old and worn-out slippers have to be laid aside. If there are reasons why many contemporary Orthodox church leaders seem to have problems with modern human rights philosophy, they need to be exegeted from other bases.

The Greek Christian foundations of European civilization were forged, in the classical patristic age, from a major synthesis of biblical and Hellenic philosophical axioms. Such a synthesis was the glory of the early Christian centuries in which times the Gospels were transmitted to a wider society in Greek; the creeds in Greek; the earliest Christian law codes in Greek; the early liturgies in Greek; and the first Christian philosophy in Greek. In short, the Orthodox Christian world, which before the great fractures of second-millennium Christendom was a world that was already multi-lingual and religiously pluralist, was consciously involved in the care and craft of constituting a socio-political theology. This was so even before the first Christian members of the imperial household had been arrested and purged from the corridors of power by pagan emperors such as Nero, Diocletian, Galerius, Licinius, and Julian. We note, albeit in passing, the tremors of shock that ran through the emperors of the third century when they found the extent to which Christianity had permeated the imperial courts. If it is true, as it may well be, that Emperor Philip the Arab (r. 244–9) was a Christian, then the supreme power had already been attained by a Christian in the mid-third century. Such things do not happen accidentally. Eastern Christians had an active and energetic social policy from earliest times, with an eye on the throne from the early third century at the latest. With Constantine, the Orthodox Church did come into a new era, but one that never lost its caution with regard to problems of church–state balances. The Eastern Church has always existed in the tension between establishment and dissidence.

Constantine, for all he is vaunted as the "Thirteenth Apostle," advocated and policed a state policy of Arianism. It was passionately resisted, and finally overturned, in the name of Nicene Orthodoxy. This was a victory that foreshadowed many other (often violent) reversals of state religious policy the "God-Loving Emperors" tried at various times to force upon a far from supine Christian people – Monothelitism, Iconoclasm, Mono-Energism, and Unionism, being some of the other instances. Many have caricatured "Constantinianism" as a church–state relationship in which the Gospel lay prone under imperial tyranny; but they can do so today only by ignoring the increasingly excavated historical realities. Throughout its long and continuing history, Orthodox monasticism clearly played a perennially resistant role to imperial claims. Innovative Orthodox Patriarchs offset the absolutisms of rulers whose ambitions pushed monarchism to unacceptable limits. And the ordinary Orthodox populace even expressed its own disenfranchised "vote" for its leaders (who were named "Autokrats of the Romans") by assassinating or overthrowing as many of them as ever died in their beds, and by consistently refusing at any stage to accept or validate a dynastically based imperial theology.

The Byzantine ruler was always the one who could hold the throne and master the armies which would defend the state: and not the one possessed, otherwise, of any divine right to rule. The Byzantine theory of political *symphonia* has been much vaunted in modern post-communist times. It is necessary, however, to note that most of those who have raised this theory to new light, have not understood it: preferring instead to imagine that Byzantine theory of *symphonia* was a kind of return to Romanov-era attitudes of state–church synergy. It is quite clear, however, from the real study of Byzantium that *symphonia* meant a harmony of powers whose very juxtaposition delineated precise limits of power: to each their own, and from each their proper sphere of accountability. This is as near an evocation of later subsidiarity theory as we might hope to find in antiquity.

The close exegesis of what Byzantine *symphonia* of church and state powers meant in various iterations of this across the ages suggests to the realist historian that the Orthodox Church never really had a clear church–state policy that was in any generation more than a set of very practical and "testable" principles of operation. The Orthodox Church has lived under tyrants and benefactors, under strong and weak govern-ance, under establishment and disestablishment, across many centuries. In recent centuries its experience of government has been a sobering one. Even under the Orthodox czars it had much to lament, and its free lead-ers did lament it, as much as its sycophantic leaders lauded it. *Symphonia*, that much vaunted term in recent discussions of Byzantine political the-ology, meant exactly what it stated: two differently sounding agendas, a political and a religious-ecclesiastic, constantly seeking to broker bal-ance. *Symphonia* does not, and never did, mean the church went hand-in-hand with the state. Byzantine polity elevated the ruler as God-fearing Augustus, precisely as a new David set over a new Israel. But exactly in accord with biblical kingship theology (and we note that the emperor was expressly called "*Basileus*-King" for the first time by the *Romaioi*), the king was given authority by God only to the extent that he upheld the values of God's covenant with his people. These strictures not only meant he presided over the purity of worship. They also expressly meant that he had to do justice to the poor and not lord it over Israel like a pagan king whose authority was claimed to be "god-like," or like one of the unjust kings (such as an Ahab) whose tyranny *de facto* invalidated any Godly authority he might claim to have.

If we elevate strong biblical paradigms for sacred kingship in Byzantium, it is just as important to remember Saul alongside David. The one is rejected while the other is blessed, but both stood under the judgment of a much higher authority. When Justinian, in his *Novellae*, set out the terms of Byzantine kingship, the psalms are extensively alluded to,[1] signifying how much this biblical theology of the limits of God's blessing over kingship was consciously invoked. It is, therefore, fundamentally erroneous to conclude that the historical weight of Byzantine polity will inevitably tend to commit the Orthodox to a supine position vis-à-vis the state. It is equally wrong to conclude that Orthodoxy cannot reposition itself in relation to modern politics in the aftermath of such major social changes as the Enlightenment, the fall of Turkokratia, the end of twentieth-century totalitarianism, the renascence of Islam, or the decline of Christendom in Western Europe. Subtle and energetic reactions to all of these things are within its capacity, within its wide range of imagination, within its vital and ceaseless spiritual vision.

Why, then, does Orthodoxy so often present itself to the Western world as reactionary, hostile to dialogues on rights, repressive (if not oppressive) in times when religious liberty or humanistic values are discussed? One reason may well be that in the relatively short aftermath of times of appalling tyranny, *traumata* among the *mentalité* of the leadership are still more the order of the day than common sense. Pathology does not dissipate as soon as the tyrant's statue has fallen. Many wounds remain to be healed. Another reason may be the wider, long-term view, that the Orthodox Church system has so profoundly lost through Islamic and then communist overlordship two of its major classical pillars – its universities and its lay aristocracy – which were once the envy of the Western nations. It will take more time to resume "business as normal" than the West needed with its more coherent and undamaged linear intellectual history.

The idea of Orthodoxy's marginal status, however, certainly can open up a revealing perspective on why Orthodoxy was not so affected by issues of post-medieval philosophy (one thinks of the importance of natural law theory in establishing a theological basis for human rights), or by post-Enlightenment humanistic thought in which cradle the philosophy of universal human and inalienable human rights was born in post-revolutionary France and America as a decided reaction to the vagaries of those religious orthodoxies that had caused so much conflict and human suffering in recent European history. But, in both cases, it is not sufficient even to say that the Orthodox Church remains marginalized because it missed out on high medieval philosophical revivals or on early modern Enlightenment rationalism. For the Orthodox Church had its Aristotle,

---

[1] See John A. McGuckin, "The Legacy of the Thirteenth Apostle: Origins of the East-Christian Conceptions of Church–State Relation," *St. Vladimir's Theological Quarterly* 47 (2003): 251–88.

Pythagoras, Plato, Zeno, and Democritus from the very beginning, and in its own languages. It did not need to rediscover them in the Middle Ages insofar as they had already been profoundly synthesized into the Patristic sources from the early fourth century, and established as the basis of its higher educational curriculum from the ninth century onward.

More than this, perhaps, the Byzantine Orthodox world was built out of the raw fabric of Roman polity. What this meant in practice was that the church adopted a substructure in all its thinking of Roman legal philosophy of *ius* and *iustitia*. This developed in manifold ways: (1) the *ius gentium*, the common law of what was appropriate for the governance of widely variegated societies;[2] (2) the *ius naturale*, the ethical notion of how to speak in common language to the Christians as well as the Jews and pagans of the Christian Empire[3] and still of immense significance for the charting of common religious and moral discourse between Christians and non-Christians in pluralist societies;[4] (3) the *ius civile*, particularly the right of the emperor to speak for the civil society and legislate for its good order with the assistance of the senate; and, lastly, (4) the *ius ecclesiae*, the extensive set of legislation that governed all affairs relating to the church. The law of the church was held binding on the emperor himself (when all other laws were not, since he was technically the *fons et origo* of Roman law), for this was a universal code that recognized precedence of divine law.

Ecclesiastical law was given into the administration of the bishops, in synodical process. The bishop in his own diocese, and the synod of the larger province,[5] ensured that the church's law grew as a protective wall around the Gospel charter. Its application was strictly observed: "without reference to person." It applied as much to the bishop as to the humblest of the laity. This church law legislated for the rights of the Christian within the wider society where their civil rights would be policed and represented

---

[2] In Byzantium's case: from the sparse hills of Iraq and Ethiopia, to the great cities of Constantinople, Alexandria, Rome, and Antioch; from the borders of China, to the Balkan and Slavic tribes.

[3] Constantine employed the services of a Christian bishop and a pagan priest-soothsayer to grace his dedication of the new Christian capital of Constantinople in 337. Lithuania had Christian rulers of mass pagan populations even into the thirteenth century. We deal in fictive romances when we think the Byzantine Empire was a universally "Christian establishment."

[4] It is erroneous to imagine natural law theory is a *proprium* of Latin Christian thought. It is extensively alluded to in the early Fathers, especially Justin Martyr, Irenaeus, Tertullian, Lactantius, Origen, Athanasius, and others, and used to mark how God has established in the hearts of all men and women an "innate" understanding of moral goodness. It is, of course, regarded as a common substrate for a moral societal discourse that is inferior to the evangelical illumination, but nevertheless one that is a good basis for dialogue between the church and the wider world.

[5] Ultimately the worldwide Ecumenical Council for major international disputes.

by the civil law. The extensive collections of Orthodox church law decree that those blatantly disregarding the rights of others will be censured in accordance with the severity of the offense. Many cases exist in which bishops were deposed for inappropriate physical violence against, or excessive taxation of, their people. One famous case in point was the holding of an ecclesiastic trial for Nestorius, Patriarch of Constantinople (the Ecumenical Council of Ephesus, 431), on the grounds that he had offered violence to a monk (he had instructed his cathedral police to beat up a heckler in 430) even before the decision to advance complaints against his theology at that council. If an individual could not sustain justice from the local episcopal court, he had the capacity to refer the claim to the higher ecclesiastic court of the same province. If not satisfied there, he was able to refer the case to the patriarchal court. The basic system of referral to higher tribunals still remains in place in the manner the Orthodox world affords levels of seniority to synodical adjudication of the canons applicable to clergy and laity.

These canons of the Orthodox Church are extensive,[6] dating back to the Council of Nicaea in 325 – earlier, if one accepts the apostolic authorship of other ancient collations. Although they have not been revised with anything like the regularity and consistency of the Roman Church's canon law, they manifest on every page a code of governance that protects, defends, and orders the Orthodox Christian community. These canons are, it has to be asserted, regarded by all the Orthodox as a fundamental part of what is called the "Holy Tradition" of the church. They are, therefore, inarguable, basic, central. In them at every instance shines the concept of just order, defense of good process. This development and flourishing of canon law in the East, understood not as the extending hand of "repression" on the individual, but rather the principled protection of common good order, is a major rebuttal of the idea that Orthodoxy is not concerned with the rights of the individual, or that Orthodoxy can hardly conceive of the concept of the individual as such, only of the collective.[7] It is equally a defense of the fundamental

---

[6] See Nicodemus the Hagiorite and Macarius of Corinth, *Pedalion* (Athens, 1908), trans. D. Cummings as *Pedalion: Or The Rudder* (Chicago: Orthodox Christian Educational Society, 1957).

[7] A suggestion in the conclusions of A. Pollis, "Eastern Orthodoxy and Human Rights," *Human Rights Quarterly* 15(2) (May, 1993): 339–56. Her analysis of Orthodox theology, which leads to somewhat pessimistic conclusions about resources available for Orthodox leaders to grapple with rights issues, leaves a lot to be desired; and it gives her conclusions, which she presents as systemically indicative of flaws in Orthodoxy's base axioms, merely the status of present sociological criticism of the Greek and the Russian hierarchies (the one for support for the Junta as paradigmatic of its politics, and the other for addiction to nationalistic ideologies).

Orthodox understanding that rights of persons cannot be separated from duties and responsibilities.

Indeed, it was the Orthodox philosophical debates on the personhood of Christ in the fifth century that brought to the European world the very vocabulary for human personhood. Before that monumental philosophical shift, Hellenism (following Aristotle) regarded the individual (*to idion*) as a peripheral and idiosyncratic term in approaching anthropology. After the Christological councils, Orthodoxy[8] brought to the European mind the understanding that personhood was vested with divine potency. This applied directly in the case of the divine personhood of Christ (now incarnate among humanity). But it also referred to the human person, as a potentiality of grace (what the Orthodox tradition described as deification by grace). It was, therefore, Orthodox philosophical theology[9] that historically brought the very terms of "person" and "individual" from the margins of irrelevance to the central stage of anthropological philosophy. They made them key terms in the definition of the human *telos*, but also radically reoriented Aristotle's apprehension of what that *telos* of the *humanum* was, by depicting a transcendentalist end for it. It is this theological stance underpinning all Orthodox theology, the deification of the human race by the grace of divine incarnation within it, which is the root of how Christian-inspired philosophers of a later age could declare, "We hold these truths to be self-evident," and go on to cite the inalienable dignity of the human person as one of the "self-evident" things they took as axiomatic.

Both the civil and ecclesiastical law of the Orthodox Church, therefore, recognized the principle of human rights long before the deists of the Enlightenment era. Built into the very ancient fabric of the Byzantine ideas of *symphonia* is this deep-rooted sense that civil law and ecclesiastical law, in closely related ways, protect the freedom of the individual in society to strive to the fulfillment of a much higher law that cannot be commanded, but can be held out as a spiritual vision which can demand respect and inspire emulation. But even if these higher transcendental values (take the widely held idea of divinization as a goal for the life of the Christian commonwealth) or "higher biblical ethics" (take the evangelical counsels as

---

[8] Latin terminology of personhood (*persona*) remained externalist (it derived from the "actor's mask") and vested in a concept of possession. The Greek Christian neologism of *hypostasis* (subsistent) gave to the idea of person an ontologically significant semantic.

[9] The historical moment can be traced to the Christological writings of Cyril of Alexandria. Further see John A McGuckin, *St. Cyril of Alexandria and the Christological Controversy* (Leiden: Brill, 1994; repr. edn, New York: SVS Press, 2004).

an example of moral code) were not sufficient to establish a common allegiance in a wider society, Orthodoxy in ancient times knew that the law code at least guaranteed a safe hedge around those loftier values that were a presupposition of any secure society. Life in ancient Byzantium was not what we today in the liberal West would regard as a "free society." But it had solid and serious commitment to the rule of law under the principle of justice, especially as that idea had been extensively exegeted by Christian values derived from the Gospel of mercy.

It is thus wholly disingenuous to speak of human rights issues as if somehow they are not part of the fundamental fabric of Orthodoxy's ancient constitution. Why, then, do many Orthodox do just that in contemporary arguments about human rights? I suspect that it is because there is a set of miscommunications about what one is actually speaking of. My diagnosis is that it is the Orthodox who need to clarify their language most, and, more than that, clarify their true historical and philosophical tradition and recognize that it is profound. Indeed, it is a force that civilized Europe and gave a model of rule by Christian law that was once the envy of tribes that still made up the violent fringes of Western Europe

These preliminary remarks can serve to set the tone of a major premise of this chapter: that those who represent the Orthodox tradition as fundamentally mystical, as opposed to rational; as deeply liturgical as opposed to socially active; as reactionary as opposed to pro-active; as anti-humanistic as opposed to inclusive – need to examine their discourse. They need to ask themselves if they have not unconsciously adopted an *orientaliste* prejudice of evidence about a church that is slowly emerging from a long winter, albeit with resources of great antiquity and profound richness that should allow a rapid recovery, given the right conditions. *Orientalisme*, of course, can be equally matched by the supine *Subalternism* of those Orthodox themselves who wish (for lack of deeper intelligence, lack of profounder perspectives on history) to play this role of the passive mystical East, waving its handkerchief in horror at the ravisher lustily come from the West. There are many today who play the Orientalist game from both sides, imposing and colluding. But the time has surely come to move beyond this intellectual decadence.

PATRISTIC AND BYZANTINE RESOURCES FOR ORTHODOX REFLECTION ON HUMAN RIGHTS

What then could be the resources the Orthodox Church looks to for its foundational thinking on human rights? Some of the basic concepts have already been sketched above. Let me restate the foundations here. First, insofar as the Orthodox Church exists in, and through, and by virtue of, its discipleship of its Lord and Saviour, then the charter of its existence and fundamental attitude within society is determined to be that of Christ himself as laid out in the Gospel and the Apostolic exegeses of the Gospel. This is the root meaning of what Orthodoxy is. Its primary tradition and orientation in all subordinate aspects of its polity, including its attitudes to the earthly society which it believes it is passing through as its medium, its testing ground, toward the heavenly kingdom. Orthodoxy does not generally adopt the post-Augustinian solution[10] of the "two cities" sketched out in the *Civitate Dei* as a suitable Christian polity, and even less that of the "two swords."[11] Rather, it accepts the more synthetic model of the Lord's parable of the wheat and the tares (Matt. 13:24–30). The church cannot stand apart from a so-called "secular" society. Instead it views all humanity and all humanity's activities as God-graced in such a profound, constitutive way (just as the human being is a creature capable of divinization) that all the extensions of humanity (its social constructs among them) are unable to be demeaned as "merely secular" but share in the destiny of human beings themselves. They stand either as forces progressive to God's presence, or regressive from God's presence. In short, all things human are luminous with the potential of divine grace. There is no secular realm or dimension of human life, no secular city, no secular sword.

Following from this, as St. Gregory the Theologian said,[12] the church must adopt the mind of its law-giver (*phronema*), if it is to understand the commandments he gave to it.[13] What he meant by this was to adopt the fundamentally compassionate attitude that Gregory saw at every instance applied in Christ's negotiations with men and women of his time.[14]

---

[10] I say this because Augustine's historical point was not to draw a strong dichotomy between ecclesiastical culture and secular culture, but to point to two overarching principles in the world: "forces toward obedience to God, and forces against obedience to God. He himself saw the position of the Church as directly comparable to that of the field of wheat and tares." His later commentators, especially the medieval papacy, did develop this sketch into a polity theory of the "two swords" and built this on the back of the "two cities" imagery.

[11] The interpretation of Luke 22:38, that the secular arm has a domain of power in society and the ecclesiastical arm has a corresponding domain of power. It led directly to the concept of papal monarchy. Orthodoxy, following a Byzantine polity, regards this as an illegitimate usurpation by clergy of the civil dominion, and still regards it as grounds for a theological, not merely political divergence with Western Catholicism.

[12] Oration, 37 in J. P. Migne, ed., *Patrologia Graeca* (Paris, 1859), vol. XXXVI, col. 283ff.

[13] See Phil. 2:5; Rom. 8:5–6.

[14] Gregory, the greatest rhetorician of his age and Archbishop of Constantinople in 380, was specifically addressing the question of allowing second marriages; but he rolled back his legal judgment so that he could start from base axioms: Christ, the Law-Giver, always determining the spirit in which the Church ought to approach all questions of legal hermeneutic.

According to St. Gregory, in the discussion of any law that affects men and women, the tendency of the church ought to be to support leniency and compassion, because men and women "are like fishes swimming in a sea of sorrows." It is not in accordance with the mind of the law-giver to add to their burdens, but rather to take their troubles away. Throughout the Gospel we see the kenotic Christ, one who demands much, not by force, but by free consent, always along the path of humility, never of constraint. It is this spirit of kenosis, strongly maintained as a fundamental tradition within Orthodox spirituality and culture, that (in my opinion) will be the primary and strongest of all "lights" to guide contemporary Orthodoxy toward a considered view of what human rights would look like if they were reconfigured in theological vocabulary (and even what they mean for Christians when presented in apparently secular discourse).

It cannot be admitted that human rights are not the concern of the church when they so obviously represent a nexus of concerns so close to the heart of the Saviour who was willing to leave all behind, to search and find out even the least that had been lost, and ready to spend himself in the compassionate service of others. This kenosis leads, therefore, to humility, and to an attitude (as Gregory the Theologian expresses it) of habitually leaning toward compassionate freedom. Such a "basic starting-point" seems to me to derive in Orthodoxy from its fundamental reception of the Gospel as its Charter for a New Society. This is what, theologically, the Orthodox would express as the dawning of the Kingdom of God in the society of the sanctified elect, and the dawning of that vision of the good (even despite humanity's resistance to the good and the true), in a compassionate "bearing with" difference, dissociation, and dissent – "since no-one," as the church's funeral prayer expresses it, "is without sin; only you, O Lord, are without sin."

Social difference, therefore, is not something that the Orthodox Church must fight on every front, as if to allow or acknowledge it would betray the Gospel values it has to stand for. On the contrary, the recognition that many in a pluralist society will not find even the base terminology of the church to be persuasive, let alone the great ideas and moral values it represents, is something that is not an abnegation of the church's duty to preach *metanoia* (repentance) but part of its duty of *philanthropia* (educative compassion) so as to continue to engage patiently in a dialogue of love until free persons can see the values it points to and lives out. This ongoing learning process about values is part of the basic apostolic doctrine of Christian *paideia*.[15] It can never be presumed (even in the great

---

[15] Rom. 7:22–4.

so-called "ages of faith") that societies at large would share a common mind about high values that ought to be defended by law. Even today, many societies accept human rights rhetoric in public and blatantly show their disregard for it whenever they think they can get away with it. This is a fault that cannot only be attributed to "rogue states," as recent scandals over torture and state-sanctioned violence in democratic nations can serve to remind us. The church can never foist salvation on anyone, not even on its baptized members. Iconically it has to demonstrate the grace of the Lord to society – not least in presenting to contemporary society the icon of the compassionate, humble, and kenotic Savior who dialogued with his enemies as well as his friends, and who forgave his murderers as readily as his apostles. Orthodoxy, perhaps in its anxiety to "stave off" a putative modern collapse of values, too often appears authoritarian, grumpy, and repressive. Christ took a different road: as an educator of *mores*, the Lord's own approach has much to commend it.

The Orthodox Church can find its doctrine of human rights and glories and duties not only in the Gospel and the Prophets but also in the deep systems of law and protection of the rights of individuals that are enshrined in the ancient canons of the church. These canons can model for Orthodoxy a corresponding sense to ensure that civil laws are renewed and adopted in the community's heart just as "spiritually" the church's canons have been taken to its collective heart over many centuries so as to become a palpable Orthodox ethos. Orthodoxy in many Slavic countries has very recently emerged from deep sufferings (and extensive murders) in the name of unjust laws that it must now be ready to speak for the notion of law as the protector of the individual *qua* sacred reality in the body politic. It is falling to the church especially today to be a continuing voice for the defense of individual rights as ever explicated in the context of a theology of loving communion, precisely because so many other *loci* of political reflection have forgotten the deep truth that the individual can only be properly exegeted in terms of the communion that constitutes it as a noble (not pathological) ideal.[16] To abandon even a single one for the sake of the people's collective, is a principle the Gospel does not endorse, though it wryly notes it.[17]

The Orthodox Church, given its bitter experiences in totalitarian and communist regimes, ought to be in the very forefront of social groups serving as watchdogs on civil rulers who administer (and make) civil laws

---

[16] Further, see C. Yannaras, *The Freedom of Morality* (New York: SVS Press, 1984), 22–3.
[17] See John 11:50.

that sacrifice the individual and his rights for the sake of some collective agenda. The Orthodox Church's role in this regard ought to be constantly on the watch that civil laws, while not reproducing the content of ecclesiastical canons (designed for the believers), will not be dissonant in the face of the notion of the sacred dignity of persons and their rights to freedom of conscience.

MODERN ORTHODOX REFLECTIONS ON ISSUES OF
HUMAN RIGHTS: AN EMERGING DIALOGUE

In recent decades, several Orthodox thinkers have turned their attention to the issue of human rights in the context,[18] largely, of the expansion of the European Convention of Human Rights (1950) as it was being progressively inserted into the laws of traditionally Orthodox countries. This process began in Greece, and extended in due course to Romania, Poland, Bulgaria, Serbia, and beyond. This human rights reform also resonated in Russia, which, though it remains outside the ambit of the European Community organization, has nevertheless taken close notice of the European process because of its considerable ecclesiastical footprint in European Community states. Moreover, in the days of glasnost and perestroika, Russia ratified several international human rights instruments and incorporated several of their human rights norms into the 1993 Russian Constitution. Both the political and religious leadership of Russia has retreated from some of these norms since and have been involved with many comments on the philosophical and moral values inherent in human rights.

The leading hierarchs of the Russian Orthodox Church have recently composed a significant and wide-ranging policy statement about Orthodoxy and social thought, which was originated by Metropolitan Kirill, now the Patriarch of Moscow.[19] In this and other statements, however, it appears that human rights issues are regarded as very much a "curate's egg." That old joke (for those who may not know it) works on the

---

[18] See notably the writings of Vigen Guroian, S. E. Rogobete, Christos Yannaras, A. Yannoulatos, and Stanley Harakas, as well as other learned Orthophile observers such as Paul Valliere, all cited in Recommended Reading.

[19] "The Basis of the Social Concept," which can be read on the patriarchate website: www.mospat.ru/index.php?mid=90. For commentary, see H. Alfeyev, "The Socio-Political Relevance of Orthodox Christianity in Russia," in Alfeyev, *Orthodox Witness Today* (Geneva: WCC Publications, 2006), 112–24. The document itself is a synopsis of the Russian Orthodox hierarchy's teaching on human dignity, freedom, and rights, which can be found at: www.mospat.ru/index.php?mid=463.

basis of the stern canon's wife asking the timid young curate how he liked the breakfast egg he had just consumed; to which he felt obliged to present a positive face and reply: "It was good in parts, Ma'am." The joke being, of course, that a breakfast egg, which is only good in parts, is a synonym for one which is totally bad. Reading Orthodox assessments of human rights philosophy one superficially gets the impression (something echoed in the writings of Yannaras, Guroian, Pollis, and others) that this is not something Orthodoxy wishes to chime in with. How many parts of the egg have to be bad before it is pronounced uneatable? This is certainly a problem demanding a much wider and deeper consideration of the theme of human rights from world Orthodoxy than has so far appeared. It is a problem of magnitude in terms of the church's missionary *paideia*, because, frankly, when Orthodox voices utter sharp dissension from human rights language,[20] the many (admittedly the many who may not be Orthodox or even Christian) are scandalized that the Eastern Church's leaders apparently do not share a passionate belief that so many of them nurture: that human rights talk represents a high moment in the spiritual development of mankind, and perhaps even a set of values that some see as a directly extrapolated philosophy, for a wider society, out of the raw material of base Christian moral principles.

What is often at stake in many Orthodox dissensions from human rights language can be traced directly to the European Community's process of inserting its human rights norms into the law codes of the "joining members." Two operative issues have been highly prevalent in that process. The first is that a context of a secular separation of church and state is presumed. As we have seen that is not the self-evident status quo in Orthodox conceptions of society. It goes further than this. In most European thought it is equally presumed that secularism ought to replace religion as a basis for societal organization on the alleged grounds that religious discourse (be it moral or metaphysical) cannot command the assent of the majority. It might be added as a subtext that there is also often a deep suspicion of religious power bases in the minds of self-styled secularist politicians in Europe, facing the realities of religious community life in Europe (now multi-faith and disparate). It was, after all, something similar for the Deists of the nascent American state, who were propelled toward a secularized basis for human rights affirmations (so influential in the modern iteration of all human rights philosophy) out of the jaundiced

[20] Yannaras's book title is a simple example: *The Inhuman Character of Human Rights.*

view of just how much religion had proved to be a force pulling Europe to pieces, and not helping its coherence.

Often today, much fear is expressed that a religious mindset will spell the end of a philosophy of freedom. Although Islam is often scapegoated, Christianity does not escape criticism. Orthodox official affirmations that, despite severe criticism of human rights philosophy, the church nevertheless cherishes essential human rights as a part of its view of humanity and each human person, especially the poor and downtrodden, as a sacred and inviolable reality, can meet with many raised eyebrows when social commentators look at other aspects of the relation of church leaders and state officials: aspects such as the rights of non-Orthodox missionaries in Orthodox lands (widely resisted as "proselytism"), or the attitude to the societal rights of individuals whose positions on ethical matters the church objects to (such as gay rights or abortion legislation). Behind much of the Orthodox hierarchs' objections to human rights language is what appears to them to be a determined "pushing" of a secularist, non-Christian moral agenda, at the heart of which is the axiom that social politics must now be governed on non-religious principles or at least religiously neutral principles.

In the face of this it is necessary for the Orthodox Church to more clearly distinguish, in its own language, the root causes of its objections. Its own philosophy of the human person will always resist the presupposition of secularist existentialism that there can be such a thing as a religiously neutral social contract. Yannaras, Yannoulatos, and Guroian have been among the leading voices in contrasting the transcendental-personalist philosophy of personhood against the de-personalization inherent in rights language as separated from the culture of social communion. Yannaras, for example, maintains a central insight of Orthodoxy that the presumption that human rights are "self-evident" is not sustainable, and the basis for rights has to be asserted on the fundament of a preexisting philosophy. For Guroian, rights language derives simply from law: moral values are categorically different. For Orthodoxy in general, the key issue is the successful bringing of this nexus of values to the fore in social discourse. For the church, this amounts to the axiom of the creation of mankind by a philanthropic God, who leaves the Icon of his own merciful presence in the ontological fabric of the race, and sets the terms of the "social agenda" as the kenotic serving of one another in mutually sacrificing love. Theologically, Orthodox would express this in terms of a positive creation theology, and a compassionate soteriology that calls men and women onwards to the ascent to divine communion, while always being

realistic about the ever-present need for *metanoia* (repentance and reconciliation). It is largely because of the secularist banishment of divine tran-
scendence from many human rights fora, and also because of the equally
hubristic exiling of the language of kenotic repentance, that Orthodoxy
today finds secularist rights language so suspicious. Yannaras would go so
far as to say that Orthodoxy finds it de-personalizing because it establishes
in place of transcendental personalism, a philosophy of utility that leads
to the barrenness of individualistically oriented consumerism. He finds
in the unarguable achievements of the "triumph of individual rights and
liberties" the sobering evidence that: "these positive triumphs are undermined by their same keystone and foundation: the fortification of the priority of the individual's autonomy."[21]

Nevertheless, it is not enough simply to denounce human rights language as faulty because it appears, so often, to rest on such a defective ped-
estal. It is necessary to take the argument several stages further, because to
do so recognizes the basic facts of contemporary politics that a majority in
society (even in old Orthodox lands) may no longer be motivated, even in
their memories, by Christian principles and Christian moral foundations.
The Orthodox Church needs to be able to represent its own philosophy in
all its purity, and argue for its positions as energetically as it can, yet to be
willing to dialogue with those who are "not far away from the Kingdom"
(Mark 21:34). The church needs to know how to recognize those who may
dissent from a complete harmony with pure Christian doctrine and yet
might be among those who are "for us" insofar as they are not wholly
"against us" (Mark 9:40).

Perhaps I say this because I work in a school where Reinhold Niebuhr
used to teach and advance his notion of Christian realism. But it seems
to me that this has been political common sense in Orthodoxy even from
ancient patristic times, when the church already inhabited a religiously
pluralist, morally indeterminate, philosophically eclectic society, and
espoused the attitude that it would serve as the leaven in the midst, rather
than the policeman. It is an insight that has been immeasurably strengthened by decades of uncomfortably close association, in the Orthodox lands,
with totalitarian collectivist (and murderous) governments who have permanently tempered any dreams Orthodox leaders might seem to voice for
the marriage of church and government in the modern technological age.

[21] Yannaras as re-presenting a digest English version of his 1998 book, *The Orthodox Church,* on
October 4th, 2002 at Holy Cross Greek Orthodox school, Boston, Massachusetts. The English
text of this talk ("Human Rights and the Orthodox Church") is available on the website of the
Greek Orthodox Archdiocese of America. www.goarch.org.

CONCLUSIONS

Rogobete in his excellent analysis sums up the chief insight that Orthodox theology can bring to bear on the modern human rights debate: "A complementary teaching to the one resulting from western individualist and secular culture, which can sometimes run into the danger of ignoring the value of community, tradition, and commonly shared values."[22] This communitarian *Grundschrift* of Orthodox thought about human personhood, rights, and obligations ultimately derives from the overarching key of the Orthodox theology of deification and Trinitarian theology.[23] This definition of "Being as Communion," as Metropolitan John Zizioulas so memorably expressed it, underlies the incessant message of Orthodoxy: that human rights cannot be discussed solely in individual terms, only in personalist terms as conceived in communion. The church itself tries to model the kenotic communion of love, but it also knows that society is wider than the body of believers. Accordingly, it attempts to re-seat human rights language in the nurturing context of social care and communality. This is why many of its objections to "lead elements" in modern secularist human rights discourse (points of legislative friction in terms of their secularist presuppositions or their moral quality) have been vociferous – arguing, as is the church's social right and obligation, that such things are not advances in terms of human rights, but (as presented) are rather seeds of dissociation in terms of wider social cohesion, and traditional moral formation underlying shared human values. But this, too, is not the last word.

The extremely pressing agenda is for the Orthodox world, and especially its most visible leaders, to reflect much more on the profundities of the deep Orthodox tradition of human rights philosophy, and not to dismiss the language simply as an alien concept from the West. There is a great need for Orthodoxy to clarify and repristinate its ancient deep traditions. It will find there beautiful things: things that put it squarely on the side of the liberation of humanity from oppressive forces. For the church is the servant of the kenotic Christ who came to set the world free, not to enslave it. Only then can it hope to dialogue on equal terms with the raucous voices of Western secularism that now (temporarily) command the

---

[22] See S. E. Rogobete, "Morality and Tradition in Post-Communist Orthodox Lands: On the Universality of Human Rights, with Special Reference to Romania," *Religion, State and Society* 32 (September 2004): 275–98, at 283.

[23] See further John McGuckin, *The Orthodox Church: An Introduction to its History, Doctrine, and Spiritual Culture* (Oxford: Blackwell-Wiley, 2008), 120–276.

stage. Among the gifts it can bring to the dialogue will be the notion of law as protection of the innocent, the notion of why the sacredness of the person is "self-evident," the concept of communion as society's freedom, and the deep instinct that beauty and grace educate far more effectively than loud voices and stout sticks. Only when it can articulate its deep and complex resources, however, will it be able to command the hearing of those political critics with which it needs so urgently to engage. Until this happens we shall be in the position of the sad parody of two protagonists, shouting loudly, each with their fingers in their ears.

RECOMMENDED READING

Alfeyev, H. "The Socio-Political Relevance of Orthodox Christianity in Russia," in Alfeyev, *Orthodox Witness Today*. Geneva: WCC Publications, 2006, 112–24.

Guroian, Vigen. "Human Rights and Modern Western Faith: An Orthodox Christian Assessment," *Journal of Religious Ethics* 26(2) (Fall 1998): 241–7.

Harakas, Stanley. *Let Mercy Abound: Social Concern in the Greek Orthodox Church*. Brookline, MA: Holy Cross Press, 1983.

"Human Rights: An Eastern Orthodox Perspective," *Journal of Ecumenical Studies* 19(3) (Summer 1982): 13–24.

Juviler, Peter. "Political Community and Human Rights in Post-Communist Russia," in A. Pollis and P. Schwab, eds., *Human Rights: New Perspectives, New Realities*. Boulder, CO: Lynne Rienner Publishers, 2000, 115–38.

McGuckin, John A. "The Legacy of the Thirteenth Apostle: Origins of the East-Christian Conceptions of Church–State Relation," *St. Vladimir's Theological Quarterly* 47 (2003): 251–88.

The Orthodox Church: An Introduction to its History, Doctrine, and Spiritual Culture. Oxford: Blackwell-Wiley, 2008.

Pollis, A. "Eastern Orthodoxy and Human Rights," *Human Rights Quarterly* 15(2) (May 1993): 339–56.

Rogobete, S. E. "Morality and Tradition in Post-Communist Orthodox Lands: On the Universality of Human Rights, with Special Reference to Romania," *Religion, State and Society* 32 (September 2004): 275–98.

Foundations for the Practice of Human Rights. Timisoara: Editura Universitatii de Vest., 2005.

Rosenbaum, A. S. *The Philosophy of Human Rights*. Westport, CT: Greenwood Press, 1980.

Runciman, Steven. *The Orthodox Churches and the Secular State*. Oxford: Oxford University Press, 1971.

Valliere, Paul. "Russian Orthodoxy and Human Rights," in Irene Bloom, J. Paul Martin, and Wayne Proudfoot, eds., *Religious Diversity and Human Rights*. New York: Columbia University Press, 1996, 278–312.

Yannaras, Christos. *The Freedom of Morality*. New York: SVS Press, 1984.

The Inhuman Character of Human Rights (Greek text). Athens: Domos Press, 1998.

"Human Rights and the Orthodox Church," in Emmanuel Clapsis, ed., *The Orthodox Churches in a Pluralistic World: An Ecumenical Conversation.* Brookline, MA: Holy Cross Press, 2004, 83–9.

Yannoulatos, A. "Eastern Orthodoxy and Human Rights," *International Review of Mission* 73 (1984): 454–66.

Facing the World: Orthodox Christian Essays on Global Concerns. New York: St. Vladimir's Seminary Press, 2003.

Christianity and the modern human rights framework

CHAPTER 9

The human rights system

T. Jeremy Gunn

The preceding chapters have explored concepts of human rights in the history of the West – both in biblical and classical sources as well as in various Christian theological traditions. These chapters demonstrate, in part, "that there was ample 'liberty before liberalism,' and that there were many human rights in place before there were modern democratic revolutions fought in their name."[1] They further illustrate that Christianity produced several important human rights ideals, even when it often defied those ideals in practice.

The following chapters take up several modern human rights issues that ought to be of deep concern not only to modern-day Christians, but to all people who share an interest in the rights of human beings. These issues include freedom of conscience and freedom from religious discrimination, freedom of expression and religious association, religious autonomy and the right to religious self-determination, the rights of women, children, and parents, and issues involving social, economic, cultural, and environmental rights. These topics and others are now the subject of an immense body of international and regional human rights instruments as well as domestic constitutional laws and their judicial interpretation. This chapter provides a brief overview of the main forms and norms of human rights law that obtain today. Subsequent chapters will consider how Christianity has influenced and might further engage some of these human rights norms.

The modern human rights system came into existence only after the Second World War. The two principal components of this new system have been (1) the articulation of internationally accepted human rights standards protecting the rights of individuals and communities to civil, political, economic, and social rights, and (2) the creation of mechanisms to implement those rights. The four forces that created the modern

---

[1] See the Introduction by John Witte, Jr.

framework have been (1) the United Nations; (2) regional organizations (such as the Council of Europe and the Organization of American States); (3) civil society and non-governmental organizations (NGOs); and (4) individual states (some of which have been particularly influential in promoting international standards and some of which have implemented human rights standards domestically).

Prior to the Second World War, the international community as a whole limited its human rights concerns principally to two issues: rules governing the conduct of armed conflict known as "humanitarian law," and the protection of religious and ethnic minorities in certain specified countries. With regard to armed conflict, several states entered into a series of international agreements known as The Hague Conventions of 1899 and 1907, that pertained to the settlement of disputes among countries and that restricted the types of weapon and ammunition that could be used in times of war. An entirely separate series of agreements known as the Geneva Conventions (1864, 1906, 1929), negotiated under the leadership of the International Red Cross, were designed to protect the wounded and prisoners during times of armed conflict. After the Second World War, again under the leadership of the International Red Cross, the earlier Geneva and Hague Conventions were revised in 1949 into three new Geneva Conventions (containing common articles) along with a new fourth Geneva Convention designed to protect the rights of civilians in times of war. The four Geneva Conventions, along with subsequently adopted protocols, have been widely ratified since 1949 and now constitute the core basis of modern humanitarian law.[2]

The second major human rights concern was the protection of certain ethnic and religious minorities immediately following the First World War. With the final collapse of the Ottoman and Habsburg empires, several nation-states fell under international supervision, including most notably Poland, Czechoslovakia, and Greece, as well as others in the Balkans and the Baltic. For a variety of reasons, several states became concerned about the possibility that these states would mistreat or even persecute national minority communities within their midst. Largely under the rubric of the new League of Nations, a series of bilateral and multilateral

---

[2] Geneva Convention for the Amelioration of the Condition of the Wounded and Sick in Armed Forces in the Field, 75 UNTS 31, *entered into force* Oct. 21, 1950; Geneva Convention for the Amelioration of the Condition of Wounded, Sick and Shipwrecked Members of Armed Forces at Sea, 75 UNTS 85, *entered into force* Oct. 21, 1950; Geneva Convention Relative to the Treatment of Prisoners of War, 75 UNTS 135, *entered into force* Oct. 21, 1950; and Geneva Convention Relative to the Protection of Civilian Persons in Time of War, 75 UNTS 287, *entered into force* Oct. 21, 1950.

treaties was imposed upon these states by outside powers. These treaties were not covenants to protect rights freely recognized by the states themselves, but were part of the spoils of victory of the relatively powerful over those less so. Although scholars continue to debate whether the League of Nations "minority treaty" system was a failure, a success, or even counterproductive, the new United Nations in the 1940s did not attempt to revise or duplicate the system.

THE UNITED NATIONS AND THE CREATION OF A NEW INTERNATIONAL HUMAN RIGHTS FRAMEWORK

Beginning in 1946, the United Nations, whose Charter went into effect in late 1945, played the decisive role in drafting the Universal Declaration of Human Rights (UDHR, 1948), which articulated what are now recognized as the core human rights standards.[3] The United Nations also has played a vital role in the preparation and implementation of the subsequent major international human rights treaties. The UN Charter contained dramatically new language for an international, intergovernmental organization: it created a permanent body that was assigned the responsibility for making "recommendations for the purpose of promoting respect for, and observance of, human rights and fundamental freedoms for all."[4] The permanent institution within the UN system with responsibility for human rights was the Economic and Social Council (ECOSOC). According to the Charter, ECOSOC was authorized not only to make recommendations on human rights, but also to "prepare draft conventions for submission to the General Assembly" and to "set up commissions … for the promotion of human rights."[5] With the International Red Cross having taken the lead in revising the Geneva Conventions and with the disrepute of the pre-war minorities treaties, ECOSOC began to create the new international human rights framework. Pursuant to the authority granted by the Charter, ECOSOC, at its first meetings in December 1947, made arrangements for the drafting of what would become known as the Convention on the Prevention of the Crime of Genocide (adopted 1948, ratified 1951) and created the Human Rights Council.

The Universal Declaration of Human Rights. During the 1940s, several prominent individuals and organizations had urged that the

---

[3] Charter of the United Nations, June 26, 1945, 59 Stat. 1031, T.S. 993, 3 Bevans 1153, *entered into force* Oct. 24, 1945; Universal Declaration of Human Rights, G.A. res. 217A (III), UN Doc A/810 at 71 (1948).

[4] UN Charter, art. 62(2).   [5] UN Charter, art. 62(3), 68.

international community adopt a declaration of rights. H. G. Wells, the famous British writer, drafted and published his own idea for a Declaration of Rights in 1940 and sent a copy of it to President Franklin D. Roosevelt, urging that such a statement be prepared to show "what we are fighting for." After the war, draft human rights proposals were prepared by the American Jewish Committee, the American Law Institute, a leading international jurist, Hersch Lauterpacht, the International Labour Organization, the *Institut de droit international*, and other organizations and activists. After the creation of the Commission on Human Rights in 1946, chaired by Eleanor Roosevelt, efforts to draft a human rights charter began.[6] A "Nuclear Committee" for preparing a human rights charter was established in 1946, and its work began in earnest by early 1947. The drafting committee was subsequently expanded and ultimately included Mrs. Roosevelt, John Peters Humphrey (a Canadian jurist who was then part of the UN Secretariat), Charles Malik (a Maronite Christian from the Lebanon), Peng-chun Chang (a scholar of Confucianism from China), René Cassin (a secular Jewish jurist from France who later would receive the Nobel Peace Prize and become the President of the European Court of Human Rights), Jacques Maritain (a prominent French Catholic theologian), and others.

In preparing what became the first draft of the UDHR, completed by June 1947, Humphrey and his staff collected examples of draft proposals, constitutions, and bills of rights from around the world. The first draft was designed to identify the widest possible scope of potential rights, going far beyond not only those rights traditionally relating to political liberties and freedom of expression that were familiar to Americans in their Bill of Rights, but to include the "economic and social rights" of medical care, employment, leisure, and housing. Although the US State Department expressed objections to including economic and social rights in the Declaration, it was persuaded – in part through the prestige of and role played by Eleanor Roosevelt – not to object formally because the document was destined to be only a declaration of principles rather than a legally binding document that states would be required to implement.[7] The

---

[6] Johannes Morsink, *The Universal Declaration of Human Rights: Origins, Drafting & Intent* (Philadelphia: University of Pennsylvania Press, 1999); Mary Ann Glendon, *A World Made New: Eleanor Roosevelt and the Universal Declaration of Human Rights* (New York: Random House, 2001).

[7] During the course of revisions, Charles Malik made important changes to the article concerning freedom of religion (ultimately number Article 18), including the right to change religion, that were included in the final document but proved to be controversial with several majority-Muslim states who opposed it in committee.

Human Rights Commission's draft was submitted to the Third Committee of the General Assembly (Social, Cultural, and Humanitarian), which conducted several dozen review sessions in the fall of 1948. The final vote on Article 18 was forty-eight countries voting in favor and eight abstaining. The UDHR was adopted by the General Assembly the day after the Genocide Convention (drafted by the UN Secretariat) was adopted. The UDHR is the centerpiece of the modern human rights movement and has been the single most influential document in shaping the language of human rights instruments both internationally and within states. The United Nations has declared each "December 10" to be "Human Rights Day" in memory of the date in 1948 that the UDHR was adopted by the General Assembly, and the day is celebrated around the world.

Consisting of a preamble and thirty articles, the UDHR begins with language that signals a dramatic departure from the pre-war international order: "the inherent dignity and the equal and inalienable rights of all members of the human family is the foundation of freedom, justice and peace in the world." The document declares that the cause of human strife and suffering, whether at times of war or peace, occurs as a consequence of a failure to recognize the rights and dignity of human beings. The document creates a "common standard of achievement" that is universally recognized, and that is designed to set parameters for the actions of all signatory states. The articulated rights include the equal treatment of human beings, life, liberty, security, protection from torture, freedom of association, religion, expression, and of effective remedies for the violation of rights. In addition to these "civil and political rights," the UDHR also acknowledges the rights to work, to leisure, and to education.

The UDHR ultimately is a secular document. Despite the important role played by Jacques Maritain, one of the leading theologians of the twentieth century, the document does not claim to derive any authority from any religious teaching, nor does it assert that a religious belief of any type is a prerequisite for exercising a right, nor does it presuppose that God or a divine reality underlies the statement of rights. While it may be observed that Christians played a disproportionate role in drafting the text – even the Lebanese and Saudi Arabian delegates were Christians – the text does not place Christianity or any other religion in a privileged position. René Cassin and P. C. Chang, two of the most influential members of the drafting committee, were neither Christian nor "religious" in the sense of believing that God or any divine power was necessary either to presume or include in the text.

The 1966 covenants. When the UN Human Rights Commission under the leadership of Eleanor Roosevelt began its preparatory work on a human rights charter in 1946, it was assumed that the Commission would prepare only one human rights instrument that would be ratified and become part of international law. Very quickly thereafter, however, it became clear that there were sufficiently strong disagreements among UN member states regarding the content of the document that the decision was made to begin by drafting a declaration – which ultimately became the UDHR – and at the same time separately prepare legally binding international conventions that would require state ratification. The two principal conventions that emerged were (1) the International Covenant on Civil and Political Rights (ICCPR), and (2) the International Convention on Economic, Social, and Cultural Rights (ICESCR).[8] From the time of the first negotiations on the ICCPR, it was planned that a separate document would be drafted to create an optional, quasi-judicial enforcement mechanism to oversee implementation of the ICCPR. This separate treaty became the Optional Protocol to the International Covenant on Civil and Political Rights.[9] The three treaties were negotiated concurrently, were approved by the General Assembly in 1966, were ratified separately, and came into force in 1976. These three conventions, along with the 1948 UDHR, are collectively known as "the International Bill of Human Rights."[10]

---

[8] International Covenant on Civil and Political Rights, G.A. res. 2200A (XXI), 21 UN GAOR Supp. (No. 16) at 52, UN Doc. A/6316 (1966), 999 UNTS 171, *entered into force* Mar. 23, 1976 (ICCPR) and International Covenant on Economic, Social and Cultural Rights, G.A. res. 2200A (XXI), 21 UNGAOR Supp. (No. 16) at 49, UN Doc. A/6316 (1966), 993 UNTS 3, *entered into force* Jan. 3, 1976 (ICESCR). Each state has its own procedure for ratifying (or acceding to) an international treaty in order to make it legally binding. In the United States, for example, the President submits a proposed treaty to the Senate that provides its "advice and consent" (by a two-thirds vote in the affirmative), after which the treaty is ratified by presidential signature. It has become part of international practice, although widely criticized, for states to ratify subject to certain "reservations," "understandings," and "declarations" (collectively "RUDs"). RUDS provide a unilateral interpretation of one or more provisions of a treaty that allows a state-party, and often are understood to suggest that a state will not adhere to a treaty unless its own interpretation is recognized. For a list of RUDs to the ICCPR, for example, United Nations Treaty Collection, Status of Treaties, ICCPR (http://treaties.un.org/doc/Publication/MTDSG/Volume%20I/Chapter%20IV/IV-4.en.pdf). The 1969 Vienna Convention on the Law of Treaties, UN Doc. A/Conf.39/27; 1155 UNTS 331, *entered into force* May 23, 1969, was designed, in part, to circumscribe unilateral interpretations that undermine treaties and conventions.

[9] Optional Protocol to the International Covenant on Civil and Political Rights, G.A. res. 2200A (XXI), 21 UN GAOR Supp. (No. 16) at 59, UN Doc. A/6316 (1966), 999 UNTS 302, *entered into force* March 23, 1976.

[10] See, for example, the Fact Sheet prepared by the UN's Office of the High Commissioner for Human Rights. www.unhchr.ch/html/menu6/2/fs2.htm. A second optional protocol to the ICCPR, prohibiting the death penalty, was adopted by the General Assembly in 1989 and went into effect in 1991. Second Optional Protocol to the International Covenant on Civil and Political

The ICCPR, which adopted numerous revisions from the original UDHR, consists of a preamble and fifty-three articles. The first half identifies the core rights belonging to individuals and communities, as well as establishes the responsibilities of states to protect those rights. Among the rights that are identified are political rights to participate in government; rights of equality; the right not to be subjected to discriminatory treatment on the basis of race, color, sex, language, religion, or opinion; rights of fair treatment with respect to criminal arrest and prosecution; prohibitions against slavery and involuntary servitude; rights of travel and movement; rights to freedom of thought, conscience, and religion, as well as the rights to choose a religion, to express views, to associate with others, and to marry and form a family.

The identification of the scope of rights typically is presented in two parts: first, the "granting clause" that identifies the right, followed by a second "limitations clause" that identifies the specific circumstances under which a state may limit the scope of the right. For example, ICCPR Article 18, pertaining to religion, provides:

1. Everyone shall have the right to freedom of thought, conscience and religion. This right shall include freedom to have or to adopt a religion or belief of his choice, and freedom, either individually or in community with others and in public or private, to manifest his religion or belief in worship, observance, practice and teaching.
2. No one shall be subject to coercion which would impair his freedom to have or to adopt a religion or belief of his choice.
3. Freedom to manifest one's religion or beliefs may be subject only to such limitations as are prescribed by law and are necessary to protect public safety, order, health, or morals or the fundamental rights and freedoms of others.

The granting clauses of paragraphs 1 and 2 describe "everyone's" right to freedom of thought, conscience, and religion, including the rights to associate with others when enjoying that right and to manifest beliefs through a variety of activities. Paragraph 3, however, authorizes the state to limit

Rights, aiming at the abolition of the death penalty, G.A. res. 44/128, annex, 44 UN GAOR Supp. (No. 49) at 207, UN Doc. A/44/49 (1989), *entered into force* July 11, 1991. The United States neither signed nor ratified the second optional protocol to the ICCPR. The second optional protocol is often included as one of the elements of the International Bill of Human Rights. The United States signed and ratified the ICCPR, but neither signed nor ratified the optional protocol. The United States signed the ICESCR during the administration of Jimmy Carter, but never ratified it.

the *manifestation* of religion or beliefs if such actions would otherwise harm public safety and order, health, morals, or would interfere with the freedoms of others. Notably, the state is not empowered to interfere with beliefs themselves – only the manifestation of beliefs. This formulation of a right, a granting clause followed by a limitations clause, has become the standard approach to drafting rights both in international instruments and in domestic constitutions.[11]

Article 4 of the ICCPR provides that in some extreme cases, and with a declared national emergency, a state may temporarily "derogate" some of the rights included in the ICCPR for the duration of that emergency. Nevertheless, there are strict limits and procedures that must be followed in these cases of national emergency. The state must notify the Secretary-General of the United Nations that such an emergency is taking place as well as when the emergency is over. The emergency does not in any case permit a state to discriminate among people on the basis of race, sex, language, or religion. In addition, the state is not permitted to derogate some of the rights guaranteed in the covenant, including the rights of religion, conscience, and belief that are presented in Article 18 as well as several others.[12]

The second half of the ICCPR, Articles 28–45, created the Human Rights Committee (known within the UN as the CCPR)[13] and provided the framework for its responsibilities and activities. The CCPR and comparable entities in other UN human rights conventions are commonly referred to as "treaty bodies" in order to differentiate them from other UN entities that were created by the UN Charter (such as ECOSOC) or that were created by other UN institutions (such as ECOSOC's creation of the Human Rights Commission in 1946). Countries that ratify the ICCPR are required, under Article 40, to submit reports to the CCPR on their compliance with the convention. The CCPR reviews country reports and issues its own follow-up reports to the United Nations General Assembly. Although the ICCPR does not specifically authorize the CCPR

---

11 For a collection of leading articles on limitations clauses as interpreted internationally and in the context of particular states, see Emory International Law Review, "The Permissible Scope of Legal Limitations on the Freedom of Religion or Belief," *Emory International Law Review* 19(2) (2005).

12 Limits are established on derogating rights under Articles 6, 7, 8 (paragraphs 1 and 2), 11, 15, 16, and 18.

13 This is a UN designator that essentially is an abbreviation for the Committee on Civil and Political Rights and differentiates the CCPR from the original Human Rights Commission (subsequently Human Rights Council), which has the same initials. The ICCPR and the optional protocol, however, refer to the CCPR as the "Committee."

to issue guidelines for interpretation of the convention, it has issued a series of "General Comments" that are now widely understood to be authoritative. For example, in 1993, the CCPR issued General Comment 22 on interpretation of Article 18 on freedom of religion.[14]

The first optional protocol to the ICCPR, described above, also gives the CCPR the additional authority to adjudicate complaints brought by individuals who assert that their rights under the ICCPR were violated by states that ratified the optional protocol. The CCPR has now heard and decided hundreds of applications. The CCPR, pursuant to its responsibilities as a treaty body under both the ICCPR and the first optional protocol, has played a highly visible and important role and is generally regarded as one of the most influential mechanisms in the modern international human rights system.

The ICESCR reaffirms some of the rights articulated in the ICCPR, but identifies additional rights, including those pertaining to working people (including safe working conditions, fair compensation, leisure, the ability to form unions, and the right to strike), and to all people to have social security, health care, food, housing, clothing, education, and to participate in cultural life. Like the ICCPR, countries prepare reports on their compliance with the convention, but unlike the ICCPR the reports are submitted to the Secretary General of the United Nations who in turn forwards them to the UN's Economic and Social Council for review. Unlike the ICCPR, the ICESCR did not create a monitoring committee to review compliance with the convention. To fill this gap, ECOSOC created, by resolution, just such an entity that is known as the Committee on Economic, Social, and Cultural Rights. Also unlike the ICCPR, no separate protocol was drafted in the 1960s to create an optional enforcement mechanism. That difference was mitigated on December 10, 2008, Human Rights Day, when the UN General Assembly adopted an optional protocol for the ICESCR that gives the committee jurisdiction to hear complaints in the same manner as the CCPR. The protocol would enter into force three months after being ratified by ten states.

Other international instruments and tools in the UN human rights system. In addition to the core components of the UN human rights mechanisms identified above, it is useful to divide the system into four parts: (1) human rights mechanisms with criminal sanctions;

---

[14] Human Rights Committee, General Comment 22, Article 18 (Forty-eighth session, 1993). Compilation of General Comments and General Recommendations Adopted by Human Rights Treaty Bodies, UN Doc. HRI/GEN/1/Rev.1 at 35 (1994), CCPR/C/21/Rev.1/Add.4.

(2) legally binding treaties and implementation mechanisms; (3) declarations and other non-legally binding instruments; and (4) other UN human rights institutions and offices that play a role in promoting human rights.

Human rights mechanisms with criminal components and crimes against humanity. On December 11, 1946, the UN General Assembly adopted Resolution 95(II) declaring "genocide" to be "a crime under international law" and directed ECOSOC to prepare a draft convention on the topic. ECOSOC, as it had in the past, turned to the UN Secretariat to prepare a draft, which was done with the expert assistance of Raphael Lemkin, a Polish Jew who fought against the invading Nazi army and who managed to escape to the United States thereafter. (It was Lemkin who first coined the term "genocide.") The first binding human rights treaty adopted and ratified under the auspices of the United Nations was the Convention on the Prevention and Punishment of the Crime of Genocide, which was adopted by the General Assembly the day before it adopted the UDHR in 1948, and went into force in 1951. The Genocide Convention has been invoked far more in rhetoric than in practice, in part because of the extremely high threshold necessary to trigger its application. In order to be guilty of the crime of "genocide," the perpetrator must do more than engage in massive killings, but must have the added "intent to destroy, in whole or in part, a national, ethnical, racial or religious group, as such."[15]

Although it was the first UN human rights convention, the Genocide Convention was not the UN's first foray into crimes against humanity. On February 13, 1946, the General Assembly, acting on a resolution proposed by the Byelorussian Soviet Socialist Republic, adopted Resolution 3(1) that urged both UN member states and other states to locate, arrest, and send accused war criminals to trial in the places where they had committed their crimes. On December 11, 1946 (the same day that it recommended the preparation of a genocide convention), the General Assembly adopted Resolution 95(1) supporting the allied powers' war crimes trials in Nuremberg. More recently, the UN Security Council has taken a lead role in punishing crimes against humanity by establishing specialized tribunals to punish genocide and crimes against humanity (as identified in the Geneva Conventions) in the ad hoc International Criminal Tribunal for the former Yugoslavia (1993) and the International Criminal Tribunal for Rwanda (1994). However effective (or ineffective) these courts might

---

[15] Convention on the Prevention and Punishment of the Crime of Genocide, 78 UNTS 277, *entered into force* Jan. 12, 1951, art. 2.

be perceived, they, like the Nuremberg and Tokyo tribunals, were ad hoc, temporary, and lacked a solid and continuing international mandate.

The most significant step in the criminalization of violations of human rights during the last fifty years was the United Nations' promotion of the creation of an international criminal court to try those who have been accused of crimes against humanity. The effort led to the adoption of the Rome Statute of the International Criminal Court (Rome Treaty) in 1998 (in force as of 2002).[16] The Rome Statute created a new International Criminal Court (ICC) in The Hague, Netherlands, and granted it jurisdiction as a "court of last resort" over the crime of genocide, crimes against humanity, war crimes, and (tentatively) "the crime of aggression." The ICC is the first internationally recognized treaty body with responsibility over criminal human rights violations, though it prosecutes cases solely when other tribunals are unable or unwilling to do so. While the ICC was created as a result of UN efforts, unlike the International Court of Justice, its operations are not a part of the United Nations system.

Treaties, conventions, and "treaty bodies." In addition to the UDHR, the ICCPR, and the ICESCR, the United Nations has been responsible for drafting and overseeing several other major international human rights treaties.[17] They include (followed by their dates of adoption and of entering into force): the International Convention to Eliminate All Forms of Racial Discrimination (CERD) (1965, 1969); the Convention on the Elimination of All Forms of Discrimination against Women (CEDAW) (1979, 1981); the Convention against Torture and Other Cruel, Inhumane or Degrading Treatment or Punishment (CAT) (1984, 1987); the Convention on the Rights of the Child (CRC) (1989, 1990); and the International Convention on the Protection of the Rights of All Migrant Workers and Members of Their Families (MWC) (1990, 2003). Most of these treaties, like the ICCPR (and of late the protocol to the ICESCR), establish monitoring bodies that examine ratifying states' compliance with the treaties and

---

[16] Rome Statute of the International Criminal Court, 2187 UNTS 90, *entered into force* July 1, 2002. Three of the five permanent members of the Security Council have *not* ratified the ICC: the United States, Russia, and China.

[17] The United Nations itself refers to the three instruments, combined with the two optional protocols of the ICCPR, as the "International Bill of Rights." See, for example, the Fact Sheet prepared by the UN's Office of the High Commissioner for Human Rights. www.unhchr.ch/html/menu6/2/fs2.htm. The first optional protocol grants individuals the right to bring claims before the Human Rights Committee against states that have ratified it. The optional protocol to the ICCPR also entered into force in 1976, albeit without the ratification by the United States. The second optional protocol pertains to the elimination of the death penalty. It was approved by the General Assembly in 1989 and went into force in 1991.

issue comments on interpreting the treaties and reports on the substantive issues within their domains.

Declarations and other non-binding instruments. As mentioned above, it has become standard practice at the UN to prepare non-binding "declarations" as a preliminary step before drafting a legally binding treaty. Such declarations have been prepared on a variety of topics that have subsequently become conventions, including all of those listed in the previous section. In addition to the dozen binding treaties and ratified optional protocols, the United Nations has been responsible for sponsoring dozens of other international human rights instruments that although lacking in legal authority have contributed to establishing international standards. Among the more than one hundred such instruments, particularly important documents include the 1993 Vienna World Conference on Human Rights Declaration and Programme of Action (which recommended, ultimately successfully, the establishment of the position of UN High Commissioner for Human Rights), the 1981 Declaration on the Elimination of All Forms of Intolerance and of Discrimination Based on Religion or Belief, and the General Assembly's September 8, 2000, Resolution 55/2 "United Nations Millennium Declaration."[18]

Other UN human rights institutions and offices. In addition to the so-called "treaty bodies," such as the Human Rights Committee and the Committee on the Rights of the Child, several other institutions within the United Nations play important roles in the international human rights system. The original institution, and long the most famous and influential, was the Human Rights Commission first headed by Eleanor Roosevelt. States were elected to be members of the Human Rights Commission on a rotating basis, and it would conduct hearings typically in Geneva and New York in conjunction with its work. Challenges to the legitimacy of the Commission grew over time, as some of the world's worst abusers of human rights ultimately became members and then used their positions to prevent the Commission from receiving criticisms of them and their allies. Rather than being a serious and respected body that would investigate human rights abuses, it became an institution that became perceived as cynically protecting human rights abusers. The increasingly politicized

---

[18] Vienna Declaration, World Conference on Human Rights, Vienna, 14–25 June 1993, UN Doc. A/CONF.157/24 (Part I) at 20 (1993); Declaration on the Elimination of All Forms of Intolerance and of Discrimination Based on Religion or Belief, G.A. res. 36/55, 36 UN GAOR Supp. (No. 51) at 171, UN Doc. A/36/684 (1981); and United Nations Millennium Declaration, G.A. Res. 55/2, UN GAOR, 55th Sess., Supp. No. 49, at 4, UN Doc. A/55/49 (2000). For a lengthy list, see www2.ohchr.org/english/law/.

and self-serving actions of the Commission finally led to its abolition, followed by General Assembly's creation of a new replacement Human Rights Council in 2006. Critical observers of the new Council find that it has simply replicated the problems and controversies that led to the abolishment of its predecessor.

Although one of the newest members of the United Nations community, the entity that now has the broadest mandate to deal with human rights issues is the Office of the High Commissioner for Human Rights (OHCHR), based in Geneva, Switzerland.[19] The OHCHR has little actual authority to deal with human rights abuses beyond the powers specifically granted by member states. It nevertheless coordinates the administrative apparatus for many of the UN human rights bodies and possesses a moral authority that can be effective in particular circumstances. There are other institutions within the UN that have mandates to deal with other specific human rights issues, such as the Office of the High Commissioner for Refugees. The General Assembly has also appointed dozens of "Special Rapporteurs" who have the assignment of collecting information on particular areas prone to human rights abuses (such as torture, freedom of religion or belief, migrant workers, etc.) and issuing regular reports to the General Assembly and other bodies (such as the Human Rights Council). More broadly, it may be said that *all* United Nations institutions have at least some responsibilities for human rights issues, including the principal institutions created in the United Nations Charter itself: the General Assembly (UNGA), the Security Council, the Economic and Social Council (ECOSOC), and the International Court of Justice.

REGIONAL HUMAN RIGHTS INSTRUMENTS AND ORGANIZATIONS

While the United Nations and its components are the predominant players in the international human rights system, regional human rights groups are playing an increasingly important role.

The Council of Europe. The most effective and important regional human rights organization is the Council of Europe, an organization consisting of more than forty-five states including Iceland, the Scandinavian region, Central, Eastern, and Western Europe, Turkey, Armenia, and Azerbaijan.[20] In many ways, the institutions of the Council of Europe,

---

[19] www.ohchr.org.
[20] As of 2009, the only "European" country not included was Belarus. The five former Soviet Republics of Central Asia also were not members.

most of which are based in Strasbourg, France, resemble, albeit on a smaller scale, those of the United Nations. The European human rights instrument that plays a role similar to that of the ICCPR is the [European] Convention for the Protection of Human Rights and Fundamental Freedoms (signed 1950, entered into force in 1953), a document that drew largely on the UDHR but that preceded the ICCPR by more than a decade and a half.

Without question, the major contribution that the Council of Europe system has offered to the international human rights framework is the European Court of Human Rights (ECHR), which has the responsibility of adjudicating claims brought against member states under the European Convention. Individuals who have been unsuccessful in their pursuit of remedies in the courts of member states may file applications to be heard before the European Court, which has now decided hundreds of cases on a very broad range of human rights issues coming under the European Convention. Unlike either the UN's ICCPR (or the system of the Organization of American States described below), the European Convention is effectively the centerpiece of the Council of Europe, and member states are expected to ratify the convention and subject themselves to the jurisdiction of its court. During the first thirty years of the existence of the ECHR, when cases were first screened for admissibility by the European Commission for Human Rights, the Court's impact was relatively limited. It has now, however, become a serious, active, and prolific interpreter and judge of the European Convention and offers the world's most effective model of an international human rights tribunal that has the power, prestige, and influence to make judgments against member states and to have those judgments respected in practice. To the extent that the international human rights system continues to progress and to provide effective remedies for the violation of human rights, we can expect that the European Court will provide the most compelling model to be followed.

The Council of Europe operates many institutions in addition to the Court that promote human rights. There is an office of the "Commissioner for Human Rights" and a "Directorate General of Human Rights and Legal Affairs" which, together, play a role parallel to that of the UN High Commissioner for Human Rights. The Council of Europe also has promulgated conventions on social rights, torture, the protection of national minorities, and race. One semi-autonomous organ of the Council of Europe is the "Venice Commission," an institution that includes distinguished jurists from the European region who provide legal analyses of state laws that implicate human rights.

The Organization of American States. Probably the second most influential regional organization that promotes human rights is the Organization of American States, which also has institutions and instruments that resemble both the United Nations and the Council of Europe. Its main headquarters has long been in Washington, DC. The OAS system has both a human rights declaration, the American Declaration of the Rights and Duties of Man (1948), as well a human rights treaty, the American Convention on Human Rights (signed 1969, entered into force 1978). The OAS human rights system operates the Inter-American Commission on Human Rights (Washington, DC) and the Inter-American Court of Human Rights (San Juan, Costa Rica). The largest and most powerful member of the OAS, the United States, signed but never ratified the American Convention and is not subject to the jurisdiction of the Inter-American Court. Nonetheless, this court has issued important statements on human rights violations in other participating states, particularly in politically turbulent Central American nations.

The Organization for Security and Cooperation in Europe. There are several other regional systems that play important roles, though relatively less significant than those played by the Council of Europe and the Organization of American States. Probably the third most important on an international basis is the Organization for Security and Cooperation in Europe (OSCE), which includes more than fifty "participating states." Unlike the Council of Europe and the OAS, the OSCE is not founded on legally binding treaties but on a series of political "commitments" made by the participating states. Its forerunner, the 1975 Conference on Security and Cooperation in Europe (CSCE), essentially obtained its charter from the Helsinki Final Act of 1975. The CSCE had grown out of the Cold War and included as participating states the members of the North Atlantic Treaty Organization (NATO) and the Warsaw Pact, as well as some ostensibly neutral jurisdictions such as Switzerland, the Holy See, and Monaco. Notably, the OSCE now includes not only the countries that comprise the Council of Europe, but also the United States, Canada, and all of the former republics of the Soviet Union. The OSCE is unique among regional organizations not only in the fact that it is not built on treaty arrangements, but it has from the beginning consciously attempted to link human rights commitments to other interests such as national security, economics, and the environment. Human rights concerns of the OSCE are coordinated institutionally by the Office for Democratic Institutions and Human Rights (ODIHR), located in Warsaw, Poland. ODIHR is best known internationally for its election-monitoring activities, though it also sponsors other innovative human rights procedures including its multi-national Advisory Panel of Experts on Freedom of Religion or Belief.

The Organization of African Unity. There are other regional organizations that play similar though less prominent and effective roles than those mentioned above. The member states of the Organization of African Unity (OAU, created in 1963), which now includes more than fifty countries, adopted in 1981 the African [Banjul] Charter on Human and Peoples' Rights, which entered into force in 1986. The Banjul Charter itself established the African Commission on Human and Peoples' Rights, which has played a modest role in interpreting the Banjul Charter. A subsequent protocol was adopted that created an African Court on Human and Peoples' Rights, but its ultimate effectiveness has yet to be seen.[21] The OAU system has, in the pattern of the United Nations and other regional organizations, adopted additional legal instruments, including the African Charter on the Rights and Welfare of the Child (entered into force 1999) and an optional protocol on the Rights of Women in Africa (entered into force in 2005).

The Arab League and the Organization of the Islamic Conference. Other "regional" organizations include the League of Arab States (Arab League) and the Organization of the Islamic Conference (OIC). The Arab League, formed in Cairo in 1945, now includes more than twenty states in North Africa and the Middle East (whose populations are more than 50 per cent Arab). Its Arab Charter on Human Rights, which entered into force only in 2008, stirred some controversy. The UN's High Commissioner for Human Rights, Louise Arbour, issued a diplomatically worded statement noting that not all of the new charter's provisions comply with the standards of the International Bill of Human Rights. She specifically drew attention to provisions that would permit states to allow the death penalty for children, that would undermine rights of women, as well as its having equated "Zionism" with "racism." The Arab Charter provided for the creation of an Arab Human Rights Committee that would operate roughly in the manner of the UN Human Rights Committee albeit without the equivalent of the ICCPR's optional protocol.

The Organization of the Islamic Conference, which consists of more than fifty-five Muslim-majority countries, began in Rabat, Morocco, in 1969. A condition of membership in the OIC is having a Muslim-majority population (OIC Charter, art. 3[2]). Although the majority of states that

---

[21] Efforts have taken place to merge the new human rights court and the African Court of Justice into a single court.

belong to the OIC are headed by ostensibly secular leaders (rather than religious scholars), the OIC nevertheless describes itself as speaking for the world's Muslim community and as being guided by "the noble Islamic values of unity and fraternity" and defending "the universality of Islamic religion" (OIC Charter, preamble). It also sees its role as to "protect and defend the true image of Islam" (OIC Charter, art. 1[12]). The majority-secular heads of state of the OIC are identified collectively as the "Islamic Summit," which is given the role to "deliberate, take policy decisions and provide guidance on all issues pertaining to the realization of the objectives as provided for in the Charter and consider other issues of concern to the Member States and the Ummah" (OIC Charter, art. 7). Most of the subsidiary organs of the OIC are located in Jeddah, Saudi Arabia, though some institutions are located elsewhere, such as the Islamic Social, Economic, Scientific, and Cultural Organization (ISESCO), in Rabat, Morocco. Although the OIC does not have a legally binding general document, its conference of foreign ministers adopted the "Cairo Declaration on Human Rights in Islam" in 1990. The text includes the statement: "The preservation of human life throughout the term of time willed by Allah is a duty prescribed by Shari'ah" (Cairo Declaration, art. 2[c]). It provides that women are equal to men, but that husbands are "responsible for the maintenance and welfare of the family" (Cairo Declaration, art. 6). Islam is declared to be "the religion of true unspoiled nature" (Cairo Declaration, art. 10). Several provisions require consistency with the Islamic law or Shari'ah, though no definitive statement of where Shari'ah can be found is provided. The Declaration's two concluding articles, 24 and 25, provide that: "All the rights and freedoms stipulated in this Declaration are subject to the Islamic Shari'ah" and "The Islamic Shari'ah is the only source of reference for the explanation or clarification of any of the articles of this Declaration." The OIC has proposed a legally binding treaty entitled the Covenant on the Rights of the Child in Islam, the draft of which provides that "Every child has a right to free compulsory basic education by learning the principles of Islamic education (as well as belief and Shari'ah according to the situation) …" (Covenant on the Rights of the Child in Islam, art. 12[1]).

The Arab League and the OIC are the only two major intergovernmental organizations that explicitly declare themselves to be either ethnically or religiously based (rather than geographically or ideologically based). There is, of course, an obvious concern in having international human rights systems use identifying terms such as "Arab" (a racial or ethnic group) as well as "Islamic" (identifying a religion). There are, of course, many citizens of these "Arab" and "Islamic" countries who are neither Arabs nor Muslims. It can well be imagined the appropriate criticism that would levied if the Council of Europe renamed itself "Caucasian" or "Christian" (or refused to include as member states Turkey, Albania, or Azerbaijan on the grounds that they were not "majority Christian"). The irony in having such names as qualifiers is even more troubling when such an organization declares that "Zionism" is a form of racism, as if its own name were somehow exempt from the aspersion that it casts elsewhere.

CIVIL SOCIETY AND THE HUMAN RIGHTS FRAMEWORK

The most active and vocal participants in the international human rights movement typically are not governments (who are often the leading abusers of human rights) nor intergovernmental organizations (which often downplay and sometimes justify human rights abuses by their member states), but the activists outside of government who draw attention to human rights abuses. There are many prominent international "nongovernmental organizations" (NGOs) that have for years mobilized activists, issued reports and rankings of human rights abuses, and otherwise drawn attention to violations of human rights. Among the two largest and most prominent are Amnesty International (AI), which received the Nobel Peace Prize in 1977 for its work that focused particularly on prisoners of conscience, and Human Rights Watch (HRW). Both organizations have offices throughout the world, with their principal headquarters in London and New York City respectively. AI has a large membership base that is encouraged to participate actively not only in making financial contributions, but "adopting" prisoners of conscience in whom they take a personalized interest by sending letters not only to the prisoner, but also to governments and prison officials seeking release and better treatment. HRW relatively emphasizes fact-finding, detailed reporting, and lobbying government officials. Both publish an annual report that are among the most closely read surveys of developments and emerging problems in the human rights world.

While AI and HRW are among the most prominent and largest, they work in the company of hundreds of other NGOs that may focus either on particular substantive issues (e.g., the International Religious Liberty

Association, Privacy International, the Association for the Prevention of Torture), or particularly vulnerable groups (e.g., Human Rights Council for Bangladesh Minorities, Refugee Law Project), or regions (e.g., Asian Legal Resource Center, South Asian Human Rights Documentation Center), or particular countries (e.g., the Kyrgyz Committee for Human Rights, Sudan Human Rights Organization, the American Civil Liberties Union), or whose members bring a particular expertise (e.g., Doctors Without Borders or the International Commission of Jurists). NGOs range in size from Amnesty International, which claims to have 1.8 million members, to tiny NGOs that may be nothing more than single individuals working from their homes. Among them are Nobel Peace Prize laureates, including not only AI, but Doctors Without Borders (*Médecins sans Frontières*) (1999), the International Campaign to Ban Landmines (1997), the Friends Service Committee (1947), and the International Committee for the Red Cross (1944).

A second part of civil society that plays a particularly prominent role in the human rights system includes prominent individuals who draw attention to human rights violations by virtue of their fame and prestige – or who become famous *because of* their involvement in human rights issues. Several of the most prominent also are Nobel Peace Prize laureates, including Shirin Ebadi (2003), Jimmy Carter (2002), Nelson Mandela (1993), Rigoberta Menchu Tum (1992), Aung San Suu Kyi (1991), the Dalai Lama (1989), Martin Luther King, Jr. (1964), and many others. But these are only a few of hundreds of major figures who have devoted great efforts to promoting human rights.

Jurists and attorneys constitute a third prominent group that is involved in the human rights arena. Legal scholars have published detailed analyses and commentaries of the wide range of human rights issues, treaties, and documents. Although hundreds of scholars have published in the field, some of the most important have been René Cassin (mentioned elsewhere), Manfred Nowak, Philip Alston, Thomas Buergenthal (later a judge on the International Court of Justice), Asbjorn Eide, Richard Falk, Louis Henkin, Theodor Meron, and Louis Sohn. Jurists and attorneys also have played an important role in bringing human rights cases before both international tribunals (such as the UN Human Rights Committee and the European Court of Human Rights), but also before domestic tribunals alleging violation of either constitutions or human rights obligations. Since the mid-1980s there has been an explosion of academic interest in the field of human rights, with universities and faculties of law developing programs and diplomas in the field.

INDIVIDUAL STATES

Other significant actors in the modern human rights framework – and in many ways the ultimate actors – are the individual states that play three important roles in promoting human rights: (1) as implementers of human rights standards within their own legal systems; (2) as proponents of human rights standards within international organizations; and (3) as influential voices of conscience (or political pressure) on behalf of those whose rights have been under attack.

The introduction to this chapter suggested that the modern human rights framework, which particularly emphasizes the rights of individuals and communities and provides for enforcement mechanisms to guarantee those rights, is largely a phenomenon that emerged following the Second World War. It has been shown above that this is particularly true in the international arena, where all of the major human rights declarations, treaties, conventions, and mechanisms largely emerged beginning in the late 1940s.

The notion of rights of individuals and communities began, of course, long before the 1940s, as several earlier chapters in this volume have already shown. Arguments can even be made that even if not explicit in Hammurabi's code (and its presumption of innocence for the criminally accused) or in the edicts of the Emperor Ashoka, they were implicit. These rights became more explicit in the West in the medieval *ius commune*, and in charters like the English Magna Carta (1215), although even there it may well be argued that the rights belonged merely to certain noblemen with respect to limiting some royal prerogatives. Some of the most famous later examples, that come closer and closer to resembling modern human rights declarations that preceded the Second World War include the (English) Bill of Rights (1689), the Virginia Declaration of Rights (1776), the French Declaration of the Rights of Man and Citizen (1789), the American Bill of Rights (1789), the (Spanish) Cadiz Constitution of 1812, the Belgian Constitution of 1831, and the (German) Weimar Constitution of 1919.

Even with these declarations that increasingly resemble modern human rights instruments, the states that promulgated them were often slow and reluctant to implement them. An interesting case in point is that of the United States which – in spite of its poor record in ratifying international human rights instruments and reluctance to accept the jurisdiction of non-American courts – has one of the most robust domestic systems for the protection of what Americans more typically call "civil rights" and "civil liberties." The point of interest is that courts in the United States, led by the Supreme Court, largely did not begin to apply constitutional rights seriously and systematically before the 1940s, coinciding with the drafting and ratifying of international human rights instruments. For example, Americans often think of religious liberty as the "first freedom," and point with pride to the protections for that right granted in the United States Constitution. Yet the US Supreme Court did not hand down its first modern decisions that enshrined freedom of religion as a fundamental right until the 1940s in the cases of *Cantwell* v. *Connecticut*, 310 US 296 (1940) and *West Virginia State Board of Education* v. *Barnette*, 319 US 624, and in *Barnette* the Court did not hinge its decision on the Constitution's religion clauses.[22] While there were some important pre-Second World War decisions on freedom of speech, the major cases ensuring citizens' rights against government intrusions begin in the 1950s and 1960s. While perhaps the coincidence of the post-war adoption of international human rights instruments and the beginning of recognition of human rights by national courts and parliaments is most salient in the United States, other countries have followed similar patterns. The first full Canadian articulation of rights was in the Canadian Charter of Rights and Freedoms, which came into effect only in 1982. Despite its illustrious history of identifying rights, England (and now the United Kingdom) did not adopt its first full modern standards until 1998 in the Human Rights Act.

A development that has occurred in some countries is their willingness to implement *international* human rights standards in domestic law. While the countries that take that obligation seriously are still in a minority, there is something of a trend in that direction. Here again, the most important and influential example of this comes from the countries that have ratified the European Convention on Human Rights and that are legally and morally obligated to provide relief when a judgment is rendered against them. While some states have been reluctant even to provide the required redress, and others do little more than institute the remedy required by the European Court, other countries, such as the Netherlands and Norway, have traditionally taken seriously reviews of their own laws to ensure their compliance with the standards outlined by the European Court.

---

[22] In a decision from the 1920s that struck a state law requiring parents to send their children to public schools, the US Supreme Court based its decision not on freedom of religion grounds, but on the "due process" right of parents to make decisions about their children's education. Notably, the case was not brought by parents, but by two private schools – one of which was a *military* academy – that alleged the state law infringed on the *schools'* right of due process. *Pierce* v. *the Society of Sisters*, 268 US 510 (1925).

States, of course, have been the principal engines behind the adoption and shaping of international human rights conventions. The United
States, for example, played a leading role in promoting some of the early
human rights instruments and in shaping the language ultimately adopted
in many other conventions, including those that it ultimately did not
ratify. The United States also has played a vastly disproportionate role,
particularly since the mid-1970s, in placing human rights on its foreign
policy agenda and calling other nations to account for their violations
of international human rights standards. Since the 1970s, the US State
Department has issued an annual *Country Reports on Human Rights* that,
despite many weaknesses and inconsistencies in its coverage, is the leading
and most authoritative annual report on the status of human rights in the
world. Since the late 1990s it has issued a similar report on the recognition
of religious freedom by countries in the world. The United States, more
than any other country, raises issues of human rights in international fora
while vocally and materially assisting NGOs in gaining access to such
events. This very high profile on criticizing other countries and advocating
human rights opens it to the repeated accusation of hypocrisy in calling
other countries to account at the same time that it refuses to allow its own
practices to be evaluated by international tribunals.

CONCLUSIONS

The international human rights framework that emerged following the
Second World War was a sharp break from the past. It has become commonplace to believe, and for states to accept at least in principle, that individuals are entitled to certain rights that governments should not violate,
and that it is the responsibility of the state to help guarantee those rights.
The core rights in this new order are freedom of expression, freedom of
association with others, freedom of religion or belief, the right to fair judicial procedures (particularly in criminal matters), and freedom against
discrimination based on religion, race, gender, and ethnicity. While there
are fewer legal guarantees for social and economic rights, they, too, are
now fully a part of the international human rights discourse, even if often
politically unacceptable in some countries. Although individuals, organizations, and some governments had advocated each of these elements
prior to the Second World War, no international ratified treaty or broadly
accepted declaration embodied them. Beginning in 1948, with the adoption of the UDHR by the UN General Assembly, these modern human

rights have infused not only the international system, but the domestic legal structures of countries throughout the world.

RECOMMENDED READING

De Jong, Cornelius D. *The Freedom of Thought, Conscience and Religion or Belief in The United Nations (1946–1992)*. Antwerp: Intersentia, 2000.

Evans, Carolyn. *Religious Freedom under the European Court of Human Rights*. Oxford: Oxford University Press, 2001.

Evans, Malcolm D. *Religious Liberty and International Law in Europe*. Cambridge: Cambridge University Press, 1997.

Glendon, Mary Ann. *A World Made New: Eleanor Roosevelt and the Universal Declaration of Human Rights*. New York: Random House, 2001.

Gunn, T. Jeremy. "Symposium: The Permissible Scope of Legal Limitations on the Freedom of Religion or Belief," *Emory International Law Review* 19(2) (2005): 465–1320.

Morsink, Johannes. *The Universal Declaration of Human Rights: Origins, Drafting & Intent*. Philadelphia: University of Pennsylvania Press, 1999.

Robbers, Gerhard, ed. *State and Church in the European Union*. 2nd edn. Baden-Baden: Nomos Verlagsgesellschaft, 2005.

Stahnke, Tad and J. Paul Martin, eds. *Religion and Human Rights: Basic Documents*. New York: Columbia University Center for Human Rights, 1998.

Tahzib, Bahiyyih G. *Freedom of Religion or Belief: Ensuring Effective International Legal Protection*. The Hague: Martinus-Nijhoff, 1995.

Taylor, Paul M. *Freedom of Religion: UN and European Human Rights Law and Practice*. Cambridge: Cambridge University Press, 2005.

Witte, John, Jr. and Johan D. van der Vyver, eds. *Religious Human Rights in Global Perspective*, 2 vols. The Hague: Martinus-Nijhoff, 1996.

CHAPTER 10

The image of God: rights, reason, and order

Jeremy Waldron

> And God said, "Let us make man in our image, after our likeness." So God
> created man in his own image, in the image of God created he him; male
> and female created he them.   (Gen. 1:26–7)

Imago Dei – the doctrine that men and women are created in the image of
God – is enormously attractive for those of us who are open to the idea of
religious foundations for human rights. It offers a powerful account of the
sanctity of the human person, and it seems to give theological substance to
a conviction that informs all foundational thinking about human rights –
that there is something about our sheer humanity that commands respect
and is to be treated as inviolable, irrespective of or prior to any positive law
or social convention.

In this chapter I want to do three things. First, I want to survey some of
the difficulties that might stand in the way of treating *imago Dei* as a foundation for human rights. Some of these have to do with the specifically
religious character of the doctrine; the fact that this might disqualify the
doctrine in the eyes of secular political liberals. But I shall argue that this
objection is perhaps less telling than objections that might arise *within* the
tradition of Judeo-Christian thought. We must not assume that a doctrine
that seems, at first glance, attractive as a foundation for human rights is
actually capable (in light of its specific theological character and the controversies that surround it) of doing the work that a given human rights
theorist wants it to do. It may not be appropriate as a ground for rights at
all, or if it is looked to as a ground, it may make a considerable difference
to the character of the rights theory we erect on its foundation.

Second, assuming that we think it is appropriate to persevere with
imago Dei in this context, there is the further question of what work it
can do in human rights theory. Is it just an abstract all-purpose premise,
a general religious foundation on which rights of all sorts may be erected?
Or is it congenial in spirit to some rights rather than others? I shall argue

that human rights theory can avail itself of deep insights generated by the idea of *imago Dei* in a number of different ways, and I shall set out what these are.

The third part pursues one possibility in particular. If *imago Dei* is relevant to rights at all, it may be thought especially relevant to our assessment of *political* rights – the right to participate in various ways as a citizen in the governance of one's society. Humans may be regarded as bearing the image of their Creator in their ability to apprehend and participate in an intelligible order. Such a conception puts front and center the rational and moral capacities of the human being and their role in personal, social, and political life. The conclusion of the first part of my inquiry is that the choice of a specific religious foundation cannot be expected to leave everything as it is so far as the rights theory that is built on the foundation is concerned. At the end of the chapter, I shall make good on this point, by tracing some differences that *imago Dei* may make in our conception of participatory rights.

IMAGO DEI AS A PROBLEMATIC FOUNDATION

The importance of *imago Dei* for religious, social, and political thought is best known from Roman Catholic teaching. But it is not peculiarly Catholic. American evangelical Protestants, white and black, invoke the doctrine, and of course because of its scriptural provenance it extends beyond Christianity. The doctrine that man is created in the image of God and that this makes a difference to how it is permissible to treat us is first stated in the Torah, and it is a mainstay of Jewish as well as Christian social thought.

Though it is attractive to those who are open to religious foundations of human rights, the doctrine excites considerable anxiety among those who reject a religious worldview or who are, for other reasons, committed to an approach to rights that can sustain itself in a multi-faith society. The idea of grounding the dignity and the rights of man on *imago Dei* may have broad appeal among followers of the Abrahamic religions. But its appeal is far from universal. While its adherents will say that it provides exactly the foundation that a universalist approach to rights requires, others will object that the requisite universalism is not just a matter of the logic of a particular set of foundations. It is a matter of the broad appeal of such foundations, so that the reasons the foundation provides can plausibly be regarded as reasons *for* everyone whose conduct is supposed to be affected. We know that those who formulated some of the most important human rights documents took this view: a proposal to include a reference to man's creation in the image of God in the Universal Declaration of Human Rights was considered and rejected on the ground that this would undermine the Declaration's broader appeal.[1]

Many object to the political use of any deep doctrine of this kind. For some, this is a special case of a Rawlsian commitment to standards of public reason generally: "In discussing constitutional essentials and matters of basic justice we are not to appeal to comprehensive religious or philosophical doctrines – to what we as individuals or members of associations see as the whole truth." According to John Rawls, any such appeal would problematize the legitimacy of individual rights in the eyes of many citizens: their legitimacy is much better secured if it rests on "plain truths now widely accepted, and available, to citizens generally."[2] Not all liberals share Rawls's general view, however, and the grounds he has adduced for his "political liberalism" have attracted some criticism.[3] But even those who embrace some form of foundationalism are likely to be uneasy about using foundations that seem bewildering or worse to atheists or followers of other traditions. After all, *imago Dei* is a highly specific and recondite theological doctrine. It is not just a vague expression of respect and concern, and it is not at all clear that it can be given anything remotely resembling a secular translation.

For others the misgivings about *imago Dei* reflect a pragmatic confidence in a shared aversion to human rights abuses that has nothing to do with deep philosophical foundations. Anthony Appiah says that "[w]e do not need to agree that we are all created in the image of God … to agree that we do not want to be tortured by government officials."[4] But should this be a reason for *denying* the relevance of *imago Dei* (as opposed to not obsessing about it)? Appiah acknowledges "the reason why we do not need to ground human rights in any particular metaphysics is that they are

[1] This is based on the Summary Records of Meetings of the Third Committee Sept. 21–Dec. 8, 1948, Official Records of the Third Session of the General Assembly, Part I, at 55, UN Doc. (A/C.3/SR.) 84–180 (1948), cited in Courtney W. Howland, "The Challenge of Religious Fundamentalism to the Liberty and Equality Rights of Women: An Analysis under the United Nations Charter," *Columbia Journal of Transnational Law* 35 (1997): 271, 341.

[2] John Rawls, *Political Liberalism* (New York: Columbia University Press, 1993), 224–5.

[3] See, for example, Ronald Dworkin, "Rawls and the Law," *Fordham Law Review* 72 (2004): 1387, 1396–9; Joseph Raz, "Facing Diversity: The Case of Epistemic Abstinence," *Philosophy and Public Affairs* 19 (1990): 3–46; Jeremy Waldron, "Public Reason and 'Justification' in the Courtroom," *Journal of Law, Philosophy and Culture* 1 (2007): 107–34.

[4] K. Anthony Appiah, "Grounding Human Rights," in Michael Ignatieff, Anthony Appiah, and Amy Gutmann, eds., *Human Rights as Politics and Idolatry* (Princeton: Princeton University Press, 2003), 101, 106.

already grounded in many metaphysics." One might infer from this that in the context of overlapping consensus, there is nothing wrong with some people holding fiercely to this deeper idea or even in their believing (for their part) that this is a more satisfactory foundation than the shallow commitments of their more pragmatic fellow-travelers.

Another set of misgivings about the use of this idea might arise from within the Jewish and Christian traditions themselves. *Imago Dei* is far from a straightforward or uncontroversial theological doctrine. Scripturally, it is presented first in the form of a doctrine of creation, and there we find a variety of possible meanings. Humans are said to have been created in the likeness of God and created in the image of God. Also some Jewish rabbinical sources suggest that there might have been two phases of the creation of human being, with the image of God playing a different role in each.[5] Do human rights theorists have to take sides in these exegetical debates?

Second, there are questions about what *imago Dei* means in the light of doctrine of the fall into sin. What is the relation between *imago Dei* and our fallen sinful nature? What can human rights theory do with Calvin's doctrine that the image of God in us is now but a "relic" or Martin Luther's teaching that since the Fall we are more "like" the devil than "like" or "in the image of" God?[6] When we use this doctrine in the context of human rights, are we committing ourselves to saying that Luther and Calvin were wrong?

Third, there are specifically Christian questions about the meaning of *imago Dei* in light of the Incarnation. Is the sense in which Christ is the image of the Father (John 14: 8–9; 2 Cor. 4:4; Col. 1:15; and Heb. 1:3) the same as or different from the sense in which mere mortals are created in the image of God?[7]

I have neither space nor wit to address these questions. But it is surely worth pausing to ask whether we should be associating human rights with this degree of theological controversy. And this is to say nothing about whether we should expect the theologians to be happy about having the waters of controversy which lap around the doctrine of *imago Dei* muddied by the opportunistic enthusiasm of human rights advocates, casting

[5] See also George P. Fletcher, "In God's Image: The Religious Imperative of Equality Under Law," *Columbia Law Review* 99 (1999): 1608, 1615–17.
[6] See the discussions of the image of God in fallen man in David Cairns, *The Image of God in Man* (London: SCM Press, 1953), 131–2 (on Luther) and 137–41 (on Calvin).
[7] There is useful discussion of this in Claus Westermann, *Genesis 1–11: A Continental Commentary* (Minneapolis: Fortress Press, 1994), 155.

around for something that can serve as a religious foundation (to substantiate their claim that they have the resources to do what their secular brothers and sisters cannot do).

I put these forward as genuine questions about the relation between the theological agenda and the human rights agenda. It is not my intention to refute the interest of *imago Dei* for human rights theory. But I want to insist on due caution and counsel against just grabbing at the doctrine because it seems like an impressive bauble to produce as a distinctive religious foundation.

We should remember, too, that this is far from the only theological doctrine that might ground human rights. There are many ways in which "theology plumbs the depths of what it means to be human as a basis for supporting and providing a continuing critique of existing human rights declarations and debates."[8] One is the idea – less formal and abstruse than *imago Dei* – that we are all God's children, and we are required to mirror in our dealings with each other the same concern that He has in His love for us. Or consider John Locke's theory of natural rights. The doctrine of *imago Dei* was not unknown to Locke; he used it in some parts of his political philosophy.[9] But he did not cite it as a foundation for his doctrine of natural rights. He based that, instead, on the premise that we are God's workmanship and created by Him for a purpose:

> Men being all the Workmanship of one Omnipotent, and infinitely wise Maker; All the Servants of one Sovereign Master, sent into the World by his order, and about his business; they are his Property, whose Workmanship they are, made to last during his, not one another's Pleasure. And being furnished with like Faculties, sharing all in one Community of Nature, there cannot be supposed any such *Subordination* among us, that may Authorize us to destroy one another, as if we were made for one another's uses, as the inferior ranks of Creatures are for ours.[10]

On this account, what distinguishes us from other creatures, which are also God's workmanship, is not that we bear the image of God but that it is plausible to suppose that we have been sent into the world on God's business and are entitled to protection and respect on that account. I am not saying that this is a better foundation for a rights theory than the doctrine of *imago Dei*. But it is important to be aware of the alternatives.

---

[8] Charles Villa-Vicencio, "Christianity and Human Rights," *Journal of Law and Religion* 14 (1999–2000): 579, 594.

[9] John Locke, *Two Treatises of Government*, ed. Peter Laslett (Cambridge: Cambridge University Press, 1988), I, §30.

[10] *Ibid.*, II, §6

Another possible foundational idea, this one specifically Christian, is the premise that there is something of Christ in every needy person with a claim on us:

For I was an hungered, and ye gave me no meat: I was thirsty, and ye gave me no drink: I was a stranger, and ye took me not in: naked, and ye clothed me not: sick, and in prison, and ye visited me not. Then shall they also answer him, saying, Lord, when saw we thee an hungered, or athirst, or a stranger, or naked, or sick, or in prison, and did not minister unto thee? Then shall he answer them, saying, Verily I say unto you, Inasmuch as ye did it not to one of the least of these, ye did it not to me. (Matt. 25:42–5)

This imagery is commonly associated with *imago Dei*, but the relation is by no means straightforward. It is capable at any rate of being grasped independently. Certainly it is more directly normative in its tendency than *imago Dei*, for it can be seen as a direct presentation of the sort of moral duties that human rights are supposed to involve.

As we sound these various notes of caution, we should also observe that *imago Dei* may play a role in Christian social thought which is not necessarily associated with human rights (as human rights lawyers understand them). In Roman Catholic social thought, there is a very strong link between *imago Dei* and the idea of human dignity.[11] Now it is true that many human rights advocates – and many Catholics, too – regard dignity as having foundational importance for human rights. But, as I understand it, not all Catholic thinkers who associate *imago Dei* with dignity are happy about this next step. Conservative Catholics are suspicious of contemporary human rights rhetoric.[12] They prefer to give dignity its own normative significance – a significance that (to their mind) points in a rather different direction. So, for example, they will use the idea of human dignity, associated as it is with *imago Dei*, to oppose stem-cell research or abortion. They might express this in terms of the "rights" of fetuses and embryos or they might not; but they will have considerable difficulty with the idea that dignity, so understood, might also lie at the basis of demands for women's autonomy or their reproductive freedom. Though the papacy has committed itself to the human rights idea in recent years,[13] still human

---

[11] Cf. John Paul II, *Original Unity of Man and Woman: Catechesis on the Book of Genesis* (1981), cited in John J. Coughlin, "Pope John Paul II and the Dignity of the Human Being," *Harvard Journal of Law & Public Policy* 27 (2003): 65, 72–4.

[12] See the discussion in Roger Ruston, *Human Rights and the Image of God* (London: SCM Press, 2004), 10–12.

[13] For example, John XXIII, *Pacem in Terris*, §11, and John Paul II, *Redemptor Hominis*, §17. See further the chapter by J. Bryan Hehir herein.

rights doctrine and theory often move in directions that are incompatible with Catholic religious thought: in their insistence on radical individualism, for example, or in the dogma that rights can be identified without any objective doctrine of the human good or any form of tradition and authority (save perhaps the authority of recent positive law). There might also be some more generalized discomfort at the association of something as deep and distinctive as *imago Dei* (or human dignity founded on *imago Dei*) with what many regard as the grab-bag of items – due process, freedom of the press, language rights, holidays with pay – that one finds in modern human rights conventions.

I say again that awareness of these various objections and these various alternative possibilities is not fatal to regarding *imago Dei* as a foundation for human rights. My arguments at this point are intended just to slow us down, in a way that is consonant with what we all acknowledge is the seriousness with which the foundational question should be approached.

If we do decide to explore further the possibility that *imago Dei* provides a grounding for rights, we have to consider the exact shape of its normativity. One idea behind human rights is an emphasis on the value to be accorded each person. This seems straightforward enough in the light of *imago Dei*. That doctrine seems to imply that there is something precious, even sacred, in each human being – something which commands respect of the kind that is commanded by the very being of God. I hope it is not pedantic, however, to point out that even this may move too quickly. It is not entirely clear that *imago Dei* is a conception of worth or value at all. And certainly the idea that the image of God commands anything like the same respect that *God* commands is not self-evident; on the contrary, it sounds idolatrous at first hearing (though of course that impression may be dispelled in various ways).

Once one moves beyond the idea that each human is precious, there are further questions about the deontic structure and the specific normativity of rights. Rights are supposed to be correlative to duties incumbent on persons other than the right-bearer. But I can imagine a strongly pietistic conception of *imago Dei* that holds that respect for the divine image in each person is a matter primarily for that person, as he or she endeavors (with God's grace) to live a life more faithful to that image. The one use of the image idea in the Gospels (an indirect but an unmistakable use, as David Cairns points out)[14] emphasizes wholly its use in generating duties of man to God, to render oneself unto God just as one renders coins stamped with

---

[14] Cairns, *The Image of God in Man*, 38. See Matt. 22:21, Mark 12:17, and Luke 20:25.

the image of Caesar unto Caesar. Admittedly, this may show only that *imago Dei* cannot generate rights against God. One could say that, while still insisting "that human dignity … makes every man an object of reverence to other men, and gives him right over against them."[15]

Here is another difficulty. It might be thought that *imago Dei* is incapable of supporting the sort of radical individualization of moral demands that human rights theory presupposes. In liberal political philosophy, an emphasis on individual rights is at odds with community or at least with communit*arian* concerns; but is the same true of *imago Dei*? Some theologians place great emphasis on the plural formulations used in the biblical texts: "Then God said: 'Let us make human beings in our image, after our likeness'."[16] On this account, the image of God may inhere not in every individual as such but in the love between or other relationality among individuals. Now it is true that human rights, too, are conceived in relational terms – in the correlativity and reciprocity of rights and duties, for example. It is true, too, that rights can be attributed to collectivities not just to individuals. Even so, the question of parsing the relation between the normativity of *imago Dei* and the normativity of human rights will be a delicate one. We know that one of the distinctive things about rights-discourse is the endeavor to identify for each right a specific right-bearer (mostly individual, sometimes a group) and distinguish it both from a specific duty-bearer (sometimes individuals, sometimes entities like governments, sometimes both) and from other members of the same moral community (whose interests may have to be subordinated from time to time to a trumping right). Will this answer to the relationality associated with *imago Dei* by the sort of theological accounts I mentioned at the beginning of this paragraph? I am not sure. We might try to force some sort of fit, but it is not clear that it can be done without doing violence to human rights or *imago Dei* or both.

A further feature of human rights which may not sit comfortably with *imago Dei* is the litigiousness that human rights involve. We are told in the Sermon on the Mount that "if any man will sue thee at the law, and take away thy coat, let him have thy cloak also … Give to him that asketh thee, and from him that would borrow of thee turn not thou away" (Matt. 5:38–42). The image of the right-bearer is more self-assertive than this. But when we contrast the self-assertiveness of the right-bearer with the self-abnegation recommended by Jesus, to which side should we assign

---

[15] Cairns, *The Image of God in Man*, 283.
[16] See the discussion of Barth's *Dogmatik* in Cairns, *The Image of God in Man*, 24 and 167ff.

the doctrine of *imago Dei*? Or think of Jesus's response to the abuse, perjury, violence, and injustice in his own trial and execution: "Father, forgive them for they know not what they do" (Luke 23:34). Again: if there is a contrast between sticking up for one's rights and forgiving one's enemies, to which side should we assign *imago Dei*?

These questions are not supposed to settle anything, just to make us a little less comfortable than we might be with *imago Dei* as a ground of rights. On the other hand, there may be resonances of the doctrine that do accord with some aspects of liberal rights ideology. *Imago Dei* is associated in the original Genesis passage with dominion (Gen. 1:26) – God's giving those created in his image dominion over the earth – and of course dominion is an active juridical idea strongly connected with rights in later jurisprudence.[17] More generally, that *imago Dei* is not altogether out of place in a legalistic context is indicated by its use later in Genesis to expound the Noahide laws regarding homicide: "Whoso sheddeth man's blood, by man shall his blood be shed: for in the image of God made he man" (Gen. 9:8).

CONTRIBUTIONS TO HUMAN RIGHTS THEORY

Having considered all these difficulties, if we are still convinced that *imago Dei* has something to offer human rights theory, how should we think about its contribution?

Imago Dei is a doctrine pertaining to our ontological status (our relation to God and the particular nature of our creation and redemption). As such it presents many aspects – as an image can relate to what it is an image *of* in a variety of ways.[18] And of course human rights is also a multifaceted idea: it embraces moral and legal claims of various kinds (e.g. rights differentiated by subject-matter as liberty rights, protective rights, legal process rights, political rights, socio-economic rights, etc.) as well as moral and legal claims made at various levels (fundamental claims about dignity or autonomy versus quite specific claims about particular freedoms or protections). And human rights are surrounded by almost as much controversy as *imago Dei*; so there is a further question about the ways in which its association with human rights will bear upon those controversies.

---

[17] See Richard Tuck, *Natural Rights Theories: Their Origin and Development* (Cambridge: Cambridge University Press, 1979), 86ff.

[18] See Ruston, *Human Rights and the Image of God*, 283. Also Fletcher, "In God's Image," 1619–20 (reminding us that the idea of an image is not the idea of a single-property similarity; it is more holistic than that, more of a *gestalt*).

If *imago Dei* does relate to human rights, it probably does so at a foundational rather than at a derivative level. It might be seen as the basis of our dignity, in the sense that "dignity" means the rank that we hold in creation. We are of higher rank than the animals, "for God created man for incorruption, and made him in the image of his own eternity" (Wisd. 2:23). We are "like" God in our capacity for immortality. And it also contributes to a sense of our equality as the bearers of rights. Now, the proposition that we are each of us created in the image of God is, not strictly speaking, an egalitarian idea. It expresses something momentous about each of us. Still, it has an equalizing tendency, particularly when it is asserted of those who historically have been treated as inferiors. So, for example, in the momentous case of *Dred Scott* v. *Sanford* (1856), dissenting Justice McLean thought it necessary to remind his colleagues on the United States Supreme Court that "[a] slave is not a mere chattel. He bears the impress of his Maker, and ... he is destined to an endless existence."[19]

More recently, in a 2005 decision of the Supreme Court of Israel, which considered the Israeli government's policy of preventive strikes aimed at killing members of terrorist organizations in the West Bank and the Gaza Strip even when they were not immediately engaged in terrorist activities, President (Emeritus) Aaron Barak prefaced his opinion with this observation:

Needless to say, unlawful combatants are not beyond the law. They are not "outlaws." God created them as well in his image; their human dignity as well is to be honored; they as well enjoy and are entitled to protection ... by customary international law.[20]

The reference here to the image of God is intended to pull us up short and remind us that, although we are dealing with someone who will kill and maim scores of innocent people given the opportunity and one who is justly liable through his actions and intentions to deadly force, still we are not just talking about a wild beast or something that may be killed as though its life did not matter. The unlawful combatant is also *man-created-in-the-image-of-God* and the status associated with that characterization imposes radical limits on how we must treat the question of what is to be done with him.

---

[19] McLean J., dissenting in *Dred Scott* v. *Sanford*, 60 US 393, at 550 (1856). Also citation to Frederick Douglass in Ruston, *Human Rights and the Image of God*, 269.

[20] *The Public Committee against Torture in Israel and Palestinian Society for the Protection of Human Rights and the Environment* v. *The Government of Israel and others* (HCJ 769/02), Dec. 11, 2005, §25.

The foundational work that *imago Dei* does for dignity is, in my opinion, indispensable for generating the sort of strong moral constraint associated with rights – and for overriding the temptation to demonize or bestialize "the worst of the worst." This temptation is so natural that it can only be answered by something that goes beyond our attitudes, even beyond "our" morality, something commanded from the depths of the pre-political and pre-social foundation of the being of those we are tempted to treat in this way. *Imago Dei* presents the respect that humans as such are entitled to as something grounded, not in what we happen to care about or in what we happen to have committed ourselves to, but in facts about what humans are actually like, or, more accurately, what they have been made by the Creator to be like – like unto Himself and by virtue of that likeness sacred and inviolable. We are not just clever animals, and the evil-doers among us are not just good animals gone bad: our dignity is associated with a specifically high rank in creation accorded to us by our Creator and reflecting our likeness to the Creator. Our status even as wrong-doers is to be understood in relation to this.

Besides this vital work in regard to human dignity in general, *imago Dei* may also be used in connection with certain particular rights or particular kinds of rights. I want to briefly summarize three such uses, before turning at greater length in my final section to a fourth.

The first and most obvious relation between *imago Dei* and particular human rights derives from the doctrine's use in the Noahide law to express the basic right to life – the sacredness of human life – and the seriousness with which the taboo on killing must be taken. (No doubt, modern human rights advocates will be uneasy with the connection intimated in this passage to capital punishment. Maybe this can be explained away by various interpretive contortions.[21] But I guess it indicates a further reason for saying that when we go looking for a rights-foundation, we should be careful what we wish for.)

Second, *imago Dei* may be used to bolster the case that is made with regard to welfare rights – the most elementary requirements of concern for one another's subsistence. I said earlier that the Gospel account of the presence of Christ in every needy or vulnerable person can, in theory, be understood independently of *imago Dei*. But the two doctrines can also be used together, with the account in Matthew's Gospel moving us from the

---

[21] For an interpretation of *imago Dei* that is severely restrictive of capital punishment, see Yair Lorberbaum, "Blood and the Image of God: On the Sanctity of Life in Biblical and Early Rabbinic Law, Myth and Ritual," in Kretzmer and Klein, eds., *The Concept of Human Dignity in Human Rights Discourse*, 55, 58, 82.

rather abstract idea of the image of God in Genesis to the awfully concrete sense of the incarnate presence of Christ in the Gospel, and in Christ's insistence that in responding in various ways to humanity as it presents itself, it is as though we are responding to Him.

Third, the doctrine has a use in regard to rights not to be subject to degrading treatment. There is an old Talmudic story, known as "The Parable of the Twins," used to illuminate Deuteronomy 21:23:

> Two twin brothers dwelt in one city. One was appointed king and the other took to banditry. The king gave an order and they hanged the bandit. But all who saw the bandit said: "The king is hanged!" So the king gave an order and they took his twin down.[22]

The implication of the parable – indeed the implication of *imago Dei* – is that when we treat humans in certain ways, for example when we torture them or mutilate their bodies, we present the image of God within us in a certain ugly light. We do so not only in our own self-presentation of how we think it is appropriate for beings like us to behave, but also in the presentation of the tortured body of our victim. Like the mutilation of a valued painting, our actions not only degrade the art object but mock the person whom it portrays.

All these resonances are important. Still, there may be more to the implications of *imago Dei* for human rights even than this.

RIGHTS AND REASON

Consistently, for almost the whole of the Christian era, *imago Dei* has been associated with man's capacity for practical reason, using God-given powers of reason and understanding to apprehend something of God Himself and His order and purpose in the world. According to Augustine, the human soul "is made after the image of God in respect to this, that it is able to use reason and intellect in order to understand and behold God."[23] And Thomas Aquinas says something similar when he observes that "man is united to God by his reason or mind, in which is God's image."[24] Christian thinkers who take this view associate it also with our freedom of will: our reason, in respect of which we resemble God, is not just theoretical but practical reason. It is not only the capacity for rational

---

[22] Babylonian Talmud, Sanhedrin 46b. I am grateful to Moshe Halbertal for this reference.
[23] Augustine, *De Trinitate*, XIV, 4 (cited by Cairns, *The Image of God in Man*, 117).
[24] Aquinas, *Summa Theologica*, 2a, Q100, 2.

apprehension of God's order in the world; it involves also the ability to shape our lives and actions in according with that apprehension.

Associating this conception of *imago Dei* with human rights gives a particular cast to our understanding of what our rights amount to. Certainly the idea that we have rights in virtue of our reason and our normative agency is a familiar one.[25] But *imago Dei* seems to privilege not reason as such, but a particular form and orientation of reason. Roger Ruston warns that "[w]hat is not intended is … 'reason' in the modern sense of the dry, calculative activity of our minds abstracted from everything else that makes life worth living." Instead, he says, "[i]t is a passionate reason, ordered to our ultimate end in the presence of God."[26] The idea that we resemble God in the sheer ability to reason and understand – with or without regard to ethical good – is rejected by most theorists of *imago Dei*. So this conception is going to sit uncomfortably with any understanding of human rights that privileges the free decision of the subject simply on account of that decision's representing an exercise of will. It consorts more comfortably with a conception of rights that understands them partially as responsibilities, so that P's right to do X or receive Y is connected with some responsibility in relation to God's order that it is incumbent on P to discharge. It will, in other words, tend to favor an objective rather than a subjective conception of rights.

It is sometimes thought that human rights ideas could not have emerged from the discourse of natural rights, if the objective understanding of rights as responsibilities had not been superseded by a more subjective conception. But actually that may be a mistake.[27] Early modern ideas of inalienable rights and the Lockean understanding of natural rights as individualized responsibilities for our own flourishing according to God's purpose, a responsibility with which others are not entitled to interfere, represented a resurgence of something like an objective theory of rights. And this is reflected in the content of many modern human rights claims, which are oriented not just to individual freedom but to responsibilities – like rights of family – in which individuals must be assisted and protected. These responsibilities are not just duties, in the sense of specific actions that we must or must not do. They call upon resources of thought and practical reason as they require continual exercises of intelligence to discern what is necessary for ordering the area of human life committed to one's care.

---

[25] Cf. James Griffin, *On Human Rights* (Oxford: Oxford University Press, 2008).
[26] Ruston, *Human Rights and the Image of God*, 56. See also *ibid.*, 112 and 279.
[27] There is an excellent discussion in Tuck, *Natural Rights Theories*, 143ff.

Much the same can be said about those conceptions that use Genesis 1:26 to identify *imago Dei* with man's being given dominion over the earth. It is true that subjective rights have, historically, been associated with rights as *dominium*. But it is evident that man's dominion is given for a purpose and conditioned by that purpose. Again, however, the fact that our dominion over the earth is understood as a responsibility does not imply that it is purely a matter of submission to an order that one apprehends only well enough to fall into line with it. There is a political aspect to *imago Dei* which amounts, as Hoekema has indicated, to something active, something approaching the exercise of rulership. The award of dominion gives man "an exalted position on the earth," making him in effect "God's viceregent, who rules over nature as God's representative."[28]

The theme of rulership seems inseparable from *imago Dei*. Even apart from our lording it over the animals, there is a political aspect to the powers that *imago Dei* suggests for ourselves. *Imago Dei* connotes powers of self-mastery and autonomy (in the literal sense: our ability to give law to ourselves). The dominion over nature which is given to us includes dominion over our animal natures, if only we will exercise it.

What are the implications for rights of taking this power seriously? One immediate consequence is a connection between *imago Dei* and rights of religious freedom. Our lives need to be ruled in respect of faith and worship; our natural impulse to neglect our Creator in favor of mundane concerns needs to be mastered and suppressed. But *imago Dei* implies that we are actually the sort of beings that can master themselves in this way. We can be trusted in these matters. We are capable of the appropriate kind of self-regarding dominion in respect of these momentous matters. We do not need rule imposed from the outside.

There may also be a broader implication for how we think about rights more generally. The attribution of rights to individuals is an act of faith in the capacity for moral thinking of each individual right-bearer. Rights involve choices; and their exercise requires the agent to select which of a number of options he would like to realize in his life and in his dealings with others. Of course, rights may be abused; indeed a right may be exercised wrongly. But we are the sort of beings who can exercise rights responsibly, and who can discern the moral order in whose context particular exercises of rights count as responsible.

Self-mastery includes an ability to discern a moral relation between what can be claimed for oneself and what is claimed for others. This is an

---

[28] Anthony A. Hoekema, *Created in God's Image* (Grand Rapids, MI: Wm. B. Eerdmans, 1994), 78–9, 85. See also Westermann, *Genesis 1–11*, 151.

old natural rights idea. In the hands of John Locke and others, the idea of natural rights connoted not just the objective existence of certain entitlements that people held and certain constraints on the actions of others, but also an ability in all the persons concerned to figure this out responsibly for themselves. Yet again it was a point about trust: individuals have what it takes to figure out a system of rights in the state of nature. Indeed Lockean natural rights theory holds that it is safer to entrust such decisions to ordinary individuals, safer than trusting to statesmen or philosophers or those whose powers of moral reasoning have been corrupted by the "artificial Ignorance, and learned Gibberish" of legal scholasticism.[29] This tends to be downplayed a little in modern notions of human rights, which are given as positive law rather than as products of reasoning available to every man. But positive law does not come out of the air; bills and charters of rights are typically founded (even if indirectly) upon popular sovereignty, so that there is a theoretical commitment to the proposition that those who are to have the rights in question are also in principle capable of thinking them properly through.

This brings us to the question of politics and government and the implications of *imago Dei* for our understanding of political rights. Here there seems to be a divide in modern understandings of *imago Dei* – a division in the canon of theology between those who pursue the intellectual conception of *imago Dei* in a political direction and those who do not. Aquinas does not see any wider political consequences; and Catholic reasoning tends to follow him in this regard.[30] But in modern Protestant thought, *imago Dei* has been associated with participation in politics. The National Association of Evangelicals affirms, in its statement on civic responsibility, that

We engage in public life because God created our first parents in his image and gave them dominion over the earth (Gen. 1:27–8) … The responsibilities that emerge from that mandate are many, and in a modern society those responsibilities rightly flow to many different institutions, including governments, families, churches, schools, businesses, and labor unions. Just governance is part of our calling in creation.[31]

---

[29] See Locke, *An Essay Concerning Human Understanding*, Bk. III, Ch. x, para. 9, p. 495. See also the discussion in Jeremy Waldron, *God, Locke and Equality: Christian Foundations in Locke's Political Thought* (Cambridge: Cambridge University Press, 2002), 83ff.

[30] See Ruston, *Human Rights and the Image of God*, 54.

[31] National Association of Evangelicals (NAE), *For the Health of the Nation: An Evangelical Call to Civic Responsibility* (available at www.nae.net/images/civic_responsibility.pdf), 2. See also David P. Gushee, "Evangelicals and Politics: A Rethinking," *Journal of Law and Religion* 23 (2007–8): 101–14.

The variety of institutions and organizations cited here connects pretty clearly the implications of *imago Dei* for governance of our own lives and its implications for governance in general. The immediate consequence is a connection between our accounts of what humans are like (in light of *imago Dei*) and human rights of conscience and association:

Because God created human beings in his image, we are endowed with rights and responsibilities. In order to carry out these responsibilities, human beings need the freedom to form associations, formulate and express beliefs, and act on conscientiously held commitments.[32]

Beyond that, however, we look also to specifically political rights: the rights associated with democratic participation and enfranchisement – the right to take part in the government of one's country, directly or through freely chosen representatives – and the broader rights-based conviction that the will of the people (the will of those created in the image of God) shall be the basis of government. Seen in this light, *imago Dei* sponsors a healthy correction of perspective on the nature and function of human rights. Rights are not just rights against government, born of what Judith Shklar called a "liberalism of fear," a panic about the worst that governments can do.[33] They make government possible by empowering the governed to participate in forging the very order they will live by.

We noted in the first section of this chapter that some theologians attribute significance to the fact that the image of God is associated biblically with human plurality. One can imagine a tension between the claim that each human is created in the image of God and the claim that humans are collectively (or in their relationship with one another) created in the image of God. Equally, we know that political philosophers have sometimes discerned a tension between rights that are attributable to isolated individuals and those whose attribution makes sense only in respect of people acting together. Karl Marx, for example, said that the rights of man (in the 1789 *Declaration of the Rights of Man and the Citizen*) emphasize "egoistic man … an individual withdrawn behind his private interests and whims and separated from the community," whereas the rights of the citizen, which are "rights that are only exercised in community with other men," value man "as a communal being" and "as a moral person."[34] Now, we

---

[32] NAE, *For the Health of the Nation*, 10.
[33] Judith Shklar, "The Liberalism of Fear," in Nancy Rosenblum, ed., *Liberalism and the Moral Life* (Cambridge, MA: Harvard University Press, 1989), 21.
[34] Karl Marx, "On the Jewish Question," in Jeremy Waldron, ed., *Nonsense Upon Stilts: Bentham, Burke and Marx on the Rights of Man* (London: Methuen, 1987), 137, 140, 144, 147, and 150.

might not want to accept that a human can be counted as a moral person only when he is exercising rights "in community with other men." There are important moral dimensions to the exercise of solitary conscience in religious and other matters; and we have already seen that, in the natural rights tradition, even the individual right-bearer is conceived as one who is morally conscious not only of his own entitlements but of others' rights and the limits on what he is entitled to demand from others. Still, when we are talking about something as momentous as *imago Dei*, we have to maintain a careful balance between the privileges of individual judgment and conscience and the modes of action – some morally assertive, some morally deferential to the judgments of others – that are required for responsible political participation.

Some may understand the individualistic attribution of *imago Dei* as licensing something like an unqualified right of conscience, even in matters political. Elisha Williams, a New England Protestant minister and legislator, wrote this in 1744:

To submit our Consciences to the Guidance of any Man, or Order of Men is not to reason and act according to our own Understanding … And in every Instance wherein we thus submit ourselves to the Direction of any humane Authority, so far we set aside and renounce all other Authority, our own Light and Reason, and even the Word of God and Christ … And therefore if our Consciences are under the Direction of any humane Authority as to religious Matters; they cease to be under the Direction of Christ.[35]

But *imago Dei* is not a doctrine of special revelation, by conscience or otherwise. There is no reason to suppose that persons created in the image of God are incapable of succumbing to mistaken or wicked convictions (through the agency of "conscience") when they cut themselves off from the sort of reasoned interactions with others that have always characterized the proper use of our moral capabilities. Reasoning is something we do mostly together – in the context of organized and disciplined inquiry – and it is not clear at all that *imago Dei* privileges individual reasoning when it is deliberately cut loose from these moorings. Not that there is any guarantee that collective or consensual conclusions are wise or good: the point is that we are all fallible, collectively and individually.

---

[35] Elisha Williams, *A Seasonable Plea for the Liberty of Conscience and the Right of Private Judgment in Matters of Religion, Without any Controul from Human Authority* (Boston: S. Kneeland and T. Green, 1744), 12–13, cited in Steven D. Smith, "The Promise and Perils of Conscience," *Brigham Young University Law Review* 3 (2003): 1057, 1063–4.

In any case, when we are talking about the doctrine's implications so far as civic participation is concerned, there is no question of individual hegemony. Some biblical scholars note that the Genesis account of *imago Dei* turned its back deliberately on the ancient Babylonian proposition that the king alone was created in the image of God and that this status underwrote his exercise of regal power.[36] We now see this regal image in every man. So, to the extent that it is exercised politically, the image of God is necessarily represented by the participation of *millions* in a polity not just one person. This means it has to associate itself with the logic of political action: (1) the need in some circumstances for a common line of action, even when there is disagreement as to what it should be;[37] (2) the need for decision-procedures which respect everyone in their inputs, but which nevertheless yield determinate decisions, even in circumstances of controversy; and (3) the importance of our accepting that the order we discern individually or together is also an order for us to live by and, in some sense, submit to. (One way of thinking about this is through the Aristotelian conception of citizenship: "The citizen … is the person who has a share in ruling and being ruled; in the best system of government a citizen is both able and willing to rule and be ruled in accordance with a life lived with excellence as its aim."[38]) Playing one's part politically is not just a matter of voicing one's opinion; it is also a matter of responsible submission to, participation in, and self-application of the norms that emerge from collective involvement in government. Philippians 2:5–8 teaches us that there is nothing incompatible with *imago Dei* in such submission and that humility as well as the confident exercise of one's moral capabilities are bound up together in the doctrine.

CONCLUSIONS

Foundations matter; they are not just nailed on to the underside of a theory or a body of law as an after-thought. If we are looking for foundations for our convictions about human rights, we are looking for something that may well make a difference to what it is that we believe about rights. This is particularly true if we say we are looking for religious foundations. It is not their function simply to reassure us or strengthen us in our preexisting

---

[36] See, for example, Westermann, *Genesis 1–11*, 151–4. I am grateful to Nigel Biggar for this reference. For the "democratization" of this idea, see Lorberbaum, "Blood and the Image of God," 55.

[37] See Jeremy Waldron, *Law and Disagreement* (Oxford: Oxford University Press, 1999), 114–17, on "the circumstances of politics."

[38] Aristotle, *Politics* 1283b42–1284a4.

convictions. As I said at the outset, we cannot assume that a religious foundation – let alone a difficult and controversial doctrine such as *imago Dei* – will leave everything as it is. I believe that if we build a conception of human rights on the basis that humans are created in the image of God, we must expect to find some differences between our conception and conceptions erected on other foundations or conceptions arrived at pragmatically with no foundations at all. Some of these changes we may find congenial: I think, for example, it is much easier to defend certain rights (like the right not to be tortured) as moral absolutes in the light of the doctrine we have been considering;[39] and I also argued that *imago Dei* will license a more insistent emphasis on the humanity and rights of those we have good reasons (good *moral* reasons) to fear and despise than secular conceptions of rights which answer only to our considered judgments in reflective equilibrium. Other changes we may find disconcerting: a greater emphasis on those rights that can be seen also as responsibilities and a greater emphasis on the responsible rather than the willful or disordered exercise of our rights.

I hope I have shown, finally, that *imago Dei* is above all an empowering idea, validating and affirming our powers of reason when they are oriented not just to discerning God's order in the world, but participating with others in its realization, both in the modest tasks of ordinary politics and in the broader anticipation of Christ's kingdom. True, as I have emphasized, political rights should not be conceived in this light as a triumph of conscience or as an anarchy of individual conviction. But they are an empowerment, an empowerment of those, created in His image, to whom Jesus can say: "Henceforth I call you not servants; for the servant knoweth not what his lord doeth: but I have called you friends; for all things that I have heard of my Father I have made known unto you" (John 15:15).

RECOMMENDED READING

Altmann, Alexander. "Homo Imago Dei in Jewish and Christian Theology," *Journal of Religion* 48 (1968): 235–59.

Cairns, David. *The Image of God in Man*. London: SCM Press, 1953.

Fletcher, George P. "In God's Image: The Religious Imperative of Equality Under Law," *Columbia Law Review* 99 (1999): 1608–29.

Griffin, James. *On Human Rights*. Oxford: Oxford University Press, 2008.

---

[39] See Jeremy Waldron, "What Can Christian Teaching Add to the Debate about Torture?" *Theology Today* 63 (2006): 330.

Gushee, David P. "Evangelicals and Politics: A Rethinking," *Journal of Law and Religion* 23 (2007–8): 101–14.

Hoekema, Anthony A. *Created in God's Image*. Grand Rapids, MI: Wm. B. Eerdmans, 1994.

Ignatieff, Michael *et al*. *Human Rights as Politics and Idolatry*. Princeton: Princeton University Press, 2003.

Kretzmer, David and Eckart Klein, eds. *The Concept of Human Dignity in Human Rights Discourse*. The Hague: Martinus Nijhoff, 2002.

Ruston, Roger. *Human Rights and the Image of God*. London: SCM Press, 2004.

Shestack, Jerome J. 1998. "The Philosophic Foundations of Human Rights," *Human Rights Quarterly* 20 (1998): 201–34.

Tuck, Richard. *Natural Rights Theories: Their Origin and Development*. Cambridge: Cambridge University Press, 1979.

Waldron, Jeremy. "Dignity and Rank," *Archives Européennes de Sociologie* 48 (2007): 201–37.

  "What Can Christian Teaching Add to the Debate about Torture?" *Theology Today* 63 (2006): 330–43.

Westermann, Claus. *Genesis 1–11: A Continental Commentary*. Minneapolis: Fortress Press, 1994.

Wolff, Hans Walter. *Anthropology of the Old Testament*. Philadelphia: Fortress Press, 1974.

Religion and equality

Kent Greenawalt

The movement toward equality of persons is centuries old, and, despite occasional setbacks, it will continue. It is typically impossible to determine the exact weight of various influences on moral, political, and cultural ideas, but within the Western tradition, movements within Christianity have contributed significantly, in ways that the Introduction to this volume outlines, to our concepts of equality. Perhaps the most fundamental insight is that human beings are equal in the sight of God. As Paul wrote in his Letter to the Galatians: "there are no more distinctions between Jew and Greek, slave and free, male and female, but all of you are one in Christ Jesus."[1] Of course, in its origins, this understanding was spiritual, not implying that social and legal distinctions, such as that between master and slaves, should disappear.[2] In the history of the Christian church, this basic sense of equality did affect the internal life of some small religious communities; on the other hand, the strong sense of hierarchy in the Roman Catholic Church and the deep convictions that Christianity was true and other religions were false both helped to sustain social and legal distinctions at odds with modern ideals of equality.

The Protestant emphasis on the "priesthood of all believers" and its strong individualism, as well as the powerful equalitarian premises of discrete groups such as the Levellers, helped to lay the foundation for broader notions of political and legal equality that emerged from the Enlightenment.[3] The Enlightenment is often conceived of as predominantly secular, but some of its most influential thinkers, including in England John Locke, and in the United States James Madison, relied partly on religious premises. In terms of actual social struggles for equality within the United States, religious individuals and groups were crucial

---

[1] Gal. 3:28 (Jerusalem Bible).   [2] See the chapter by David Aune herein.
[3] See chapters by Jeremy Waldron and John Witte, Jr. herein.

in movements to abolish slavery in the nineteenth century and to combat racial discrimination from the 1960s forward.

Developments toward equality during the last hundred years have been remarkable in many countries, including the United States. The equality with which this chapter concerns itself is the notion that treatment by the law, basic opportunities in society, and respect for persons should not depend on one's gender, race, national origin, ethnic background, sexual orientation, and, most important for our purposes, religion.

Three initial cautions are in order. First, this kind of equality has been regarded so far as perfectly consistent with vast disparities in wealth. In the United States, and many other countries, the gap between rich and poor has grown in the last half-century, and the most radical social philosophy supporting rough equality of welfare, Marxist communism, has suffered setbacks that appear to be irreversible. Second, in its general political manifestation, this notion of equality tends to be significantly negative – that certain characteristics should not be taken into account – rather than strongly affirmative: along the lines that all people count equally because of God's equal love for each human being. Third, a society's formal commitment to equality hardly means its members have freed themselves of the prejudices that accompanied older notions of unequal status. Still, even in respect to personal attitudes, we have come a long way.

Although the idea of equal respect for persons regardless of certain characteristics has owed a good deal to Christian and other religious understandings, it is complicated in a particular way in regard to religion. Many modern citizens are fully comfortable with religious pluralism, believing either that religion is basically a personal matter or that most religions, if not all, have profound insights into a complex and elusive spiritual truth, and that it is pointless to think that one religion alone has got it right. But other people in the United States, mainly Christians, continue to believe that their religion alone is true. In the eighteenth century, many American Protestant religious leaders thought the pope was the antichrist, and Catholic views about Protestants were hardly more positive. Jews, Muslims, Buddhists, and Hindus were well outside the circle of true religious understanding. Some Christians still feel that way about non-Christians. They can accept non-Christians as political and social equals, and they can respect them as human beings, but they think they are fundamentally unenlightened, in the manner of someone who is ignorant about fundamental facts or who embraces moral views that are understandable but perverse. Such Christians can sincerely say they *respect* people of all religions equally; but non-Christians on the receiving end of messages that they are lost unless they recognize Jesus as their Savior often do not *feel* that they are being regarded as equals.

Whatever individuals may believe about the unique truth or insight of their particular religion, it is widely understood that government, whether federal, state, or local, should not take a stand in favor of the truth of any one religion. This is in sharp contrast with much of the nineteenth century in which most public schools were unabashedly Protestant and the Supreme Court occasionally announced that Christianity was part of the common law.

Until the mid-1960s, immigration policy in the United States was powerfully favorable to Europeans. With that approach, the country could remain primarily a haven for people who were from Christian traditions, if not themselves practicing Christians. Reform of immigration laws has changed that.[4] With a large percentage of immigrants now arriving from Asia, the already substantial number of Muslims, Hindus, and Buddhists will continue to rise. The movement toward equality among religions and among citizens of diverse religious origins fits this pluralism well.

EQUALITY AND THE LAW OF RELIGIOUS FREEDOM

The focus of this chapter is some conundrums about how the movement toward equality may, and should, affect the law's treatment of religion. I concentrate on the United States, in which the twin concepts of free exercise of religion and non-establishment of religion are embodied in the Constitution and guide understanding of how equality should be realized. Although major international documents do not include a preclusion of established religions, which still exist in weaker or stronger forms in many countries, they do include protection of religious liberty and broader bans on discrimination. For example, the United Nations Declaration on the Elimination of All Forms of Intolerance and Discrimination Based on Religious Belief (1981) provides that no one shall be subject to discrimination "on the grounds of religion or other beliefs."[5] And the Declaration of the Rights of Persons Belonging to National or Ethnic, Religious and Linguistic Minorities (1992) includes the right to "profess and practice" one's religions without discrimination.[6] Christian churches, among other

---

[4] 79 Stat. 911 (1965).
[5] See Declaration, Art. 2, §1(1981), reprinted in Tad Stahnke and J. Paul Martin, eds., *Religion and Human Rights: Basic Documents* (New York: Columbia University Press, 1988), 102–4.
[6] Declaration of UN General Assembly, Dec. 18, 1992, art. 2, §1, reprinted in Stahnke and Martin, eds., *Religion and Human Rights*, 162–4. See further the chapter by T. Jeremy Gunn herein.

religious groups, have supported the movements toward religious liberty and non-discrimination.[7] For the Catholic Church, the Second Vatican Council in 1962–5 was a watershed, with its approval of individual religious liberty and institutions of liberal democracy.

In what follows, I do not pay primary attention to what have been two of the dominant issues about America's religion clauses: whether legal concessions should be made to religious practices and whether religious groups should get public aid to run soup kitchens, adoption agencies, drug rehabilitation programs, and schools. Rather, I ask whether, and when, religious claims should be treated as special, an issue that is bound to arise under any document that explicitly or implicitly bars discrimination based on religion.

During the last fifty years, questions about equality of ideas and equality of personal convictions have become important.[8] One central question is this: if people want to behave in a certain way, or believe they should behave in a certain way, should it matter whether their reasons are religious or not? In other words, should non-religious convictions be treated like religious convictions if they lead to the same consequences? This issue is posed most starkly in the case of conscientious objection. The scope of an exemption from combatant duty, or from military service altogether, is most pressing during a draft; but it still retains some importance as a basis for military personnel, committed to a term of service, who then become conscientious objectors. From the end of the Second World War, the statute setting the conditions for conscientious objection required opposition to war in any form, based on a religious ground that was understood as involving belief in relation to a Supreme Being. During the Vietnam War, the Supreme Court made short work of the Supreme Being clause and the requirement of religion. In 1965 it said that any belief that occupies a place in someone's life parallel to that filled by an orthodox belief in God satisfies the Supreme Being standard.[9] In other words, someone who

---

[7] For an account of efforts of the World Council of Churches contributing toward the 1948 Universal Declaration of Human Rights, see John Nurser, *For All Peoples and All Nations: Christian Churches and Human Rights* (Geneva: World Council of Churches Publications, 2005). See further the chapter by J. Bryan Hehir herein.

[8] Within the United States, issues about equality of opinions concerning religion are one facet of a broader concern about the government treating ideas equally. A crucial aspect of the modern law of free speech is that when a government establishes a public forum, it cannot discriminate on the basis of viewpoint; it cannot welcome support of keeping troops in Afghanistan and reject speech urging their withdrawal. See *Rosenberger* v. *Rector and Visitors of the University of Virginia*, 515 US 819 (1995). I explore the difficult question of what precisely separates viewpoint discrimination from other content distinctions in Kent Greenawalt, "Viewpoints from Olympus," *Columbia Law Review* 96 (1996): 697.

[9] *United States* v. *Seeger*, 380 US 163 (1965).

does not believe in a Supreme Being can count as believing in a Supreme Being. Five years later, a plurality of justices said that the strong ethical convictions of someone who initially described his beliefs as non-religious qualified as religious.[10] In other words, someone who was not religious in any standard sense could count as religious for this purpose. The Court managed to strain the statute beyond recognition in these two cases, but I believe the practical result was right. Whether young men and women count as conscientious objectors should not depend on whether they are religious.

This conclusion raises a yet broader question. Should it *ever* matter for how individuals are treated by the state whether their reasons are religious ones? In terms of treatment by the law, should it *ever* matter whether organizations are religious? And there is a parallel question about messages the state conveys: should there be any sharp distinction between religious messages and other kinds of messages, or should whatever lines between what the state can and cannot say be drawn in other terms?

At first glance one might think that a sweeping version of equality, one that precludes not only distinctions among religions but also legal distinctions between religion and other categories of connections, ideas, and organizations, best fits the conditions of religious pluralism, including non-belief. And some scholars have urged such equality.[11] But one doubts whether the most healthy regime for religious pluralism is to cease treating religion itself as distinctive. I explore these questions briefly in terms of some particular aspects of the law's treatment of religion.

Government speech and religion. Let me start with ideas the government itself propagates. When they speak for themselves, governments are free to express all sorts of ideas, including, of course, the idea that people are entitled to equal respect regardless of race, religion, etc. Within a wide domain, American governments can make claims about both factual and normative matters. They do so not only in public schools but also in publications aimed at adults. But the government as government cannot make claims about religious truth. (I am putting aside here complex questions about when officials actually speak for their government. I am also putting aside whether certain very general, vague forms of endorsement, such as "under God" in the Pledge of Allegiance, are acceptable.[12]) What would

[10] *Welsh* v. *United States*, 398 US 333 (1970).
[11] Christopher Eisgruber and Lawrence G. Sager, *Religious Freedom and the Constitution* (Cambridge, MA: Harvard University Press, 2007).
[12] I discuss this question at some length in Kent Greenawalt, *Religion and the Constitution*, vol. II: *Establishment and Fairness* (Princeton: Princeton University Press, 2008), 69–121.

it mean to say that, for government expression, religion should be treated equally with other ideas in this context?

There are two general possibilities. The first is that the power of government to address religious ideas would greatly increase. Localities and states, as well as the federal government, would be able to opine on religious questions, as they now do on many historical, moral, and political questions. This form of equality would amount to a throwback to a much earlier era and, given Christian dominance, would not likely benefit minority religions. This form of equality of ideas would impede equality among religions.

The other possibility is that many other areas would be marked off, along with religion, from assertions of truth by government agencies. We can identify one obvious candidate for such treatment. The government as such should not praise the merits of one political party to the detriment of another. Perhaps one can find in our constitutional scheme an implicit basis for such a restriction. But that would be a very limited restriction, not dealing with a broad range of ideas. Presumably the government should still be able to teach as true factual claims supported by techniques of science and social science. Should it refrain from broad suggestions about what is a good life, or about moral right and wrong?

Some scholars have suggested that government should be agnostic about what is a good life,[13] limiting itself to what are just relations among citizens. Separating questions about the good life from ones of justice is not so simple. For example, discussions of justice toward gays typically involve some moral evaluation of homosexual relations. More to the point, it is misguided in the extreme to suppose that public schools should stop teaching that healthy activity is preferable to indolence, that excessive use of drugs and alcohol is destructive, that advanced education not only opens opportunities but can be enriching, that art and literature have value. Those are messages that government appropriately expresses not only in schools but in other fora. In short, there is *no* broader class of ideas in which ideas about religion fall that should be out of bounds for government in the manner of religious ideas. Governments are incompetent in respect to religion and government support of one set of religious ideas is at odds with an ideal and reality of religious pluralism. In this respect at least, religion warrants the special treatment it has under the Constitution's free exercise and establishment clauses,

---

[13] See, for example, Bruce Ackermann, *Social Justice in the Liberal State* (New Haven: Yale University Press, 1980), 10–11.

however hard it may be to say where and how religion differs from other social phenomena.

The government's relation to religious ideas goes beyond whether it can promote a particular religious point of view. By its actions, such as fighting wars or integrating its schools, it indirectly implies the falsity of religious ideas that condemn those actions as against God's will. By teaching the truth of scientific theories such as evolution, it implies the inaccuracy of religious ideas that oppose those theories. No movement toward equality can eliminate these inevitable conflicts.

Government aid to religion. A related question concerns conditions the government sets on what the recipients of its aid can teach. In 2002, the Supreme Court upheld an Ohio program to give vouchers to parents whose children were in private schools, mainly private religious schools.[14] A condition of aid was that the schools not "advocate … unlawful behavior or teach the hatred of any person or group on the basis of race, ethnicity, national origin, or religion." The state reasonably does not want to fund education that is directly opposed in its teaching to basic values of its liberal democracy. But what amounts to teaching of hatred on the basis of religion is hard to say. As I have mentioned, many American Protestants in the eighteenth century asserted that the pope was the antichrist. Was this a teaching of hatred of Catholics? Perhaps it was. Governments need to be careful not to impinge more than is really necessary on the messages of religious groups, and concern about overreaching in this respect is one reason to worry about extensive state aid to religious education.

Intrachurch disputes. Closely related to the principle that government should not involve itself in the truth or falsity of religious claims is an approach American courts have developed in disputes between factions of churches, typically over which faction is entitled to the church property.[15] The dispute may be between a national or regional organization and one of its local churches or between two factions of a local church. According to a rule that I believe still prevails in England and Canada, a court can determine that the officials of a religious organization, or a majority of members, have departed so far from the basic doctrines of the religion that disputed property should go to the segment that has remained faithful. Building on a nineteenth-century decision,[16] the United States Supreme Court has consistently said that it is unconstitutional in the USA for

[14] *Zelman* v. *Simmons-Harris*, 536 US 639 (2002).
[15] A much longer account is in Kent Greenawalt, *Religion and the Constitution*, vol. I: *Free Exercise and Fairness* (Princeton: Princeton University Press, 2006), 261–89.
[16] *Watson* v. *Jones*, 80 US (1 Wall) 679 (1872).

courts to decide cases on the basis of faithfulness to church doctrine or on the basis of disputed claims of authority that rely on doctrine.[17] Rather, courts must rely on neutral principles, that is, principles based on secular documents that set out governing authorities, or they must defer to the highest adjudicative bodies within hierarchical churches and to the majorities within churches organized congregationally.

There is a good deal of complexity to all this that we need not examine, but we can draw two significant conclusions. The first is that this notion of abstention from resolving disputed issues of doctrine and governance is well suited for religious pluralism. For the foreseeable future, most state and federal judges will come from a Christian background, if they have any religious background. However ill-suited they may be to settle who is faithful to various Christian traditions, they will be even less competent to resolve similar disputes among Muslims, Hindus, and Buddhists, as these arise. Groups are much better off having to get their own affairs in order according to secular documents than trusting to civil courts to sort things out.

The second point here is more arguable than the analogous point about government expressions in respect to religious truth, and I shall settle for assertion rather than serious explanation. In respect to other groups that are engaged in internal disputes over the control of property or resources – say, trusts created to support modern art or cancer research – it is acceptable for courts to play a more active role in deciding if one faction, or a set of leaders, has deviated too far from underlying purposes. Perhaps groups set up to promote political ideologies, such as the ACLU, should be treated like religious organizations in this respect, but putting that possibility aside, this is another domain in which special treatment of religion is warranted.

Priest–penitent privileges. The same may be said about privileges not to disclose information revealed in confidence.[18] The law grants such privileges to lawyers, doctors, and secular therapists, as well as to clergy. But typically there is a difference. The other privileges are not absolute. Doctors and lawyers must reveal particular kinds of disclosures, ones in which the public interest is very strong. Priests and other clergy are not compelled to reveal communications made in confidence, whatever their nature. In most states, the so-called priest–penitent privilege fits the requirement of secrecy developed by the Catholic Church for its priests over the centuries. The law appropriately accommodates this practice without granting a

---

[17] The most recent Supreme Court authority with full opinions is *Jones* v. *Wolf*, 443 US 595 (1979).
[18] See Greenawalt, *Free Exercise and Fairness*, 246–60.

similar privilege to people whose non-religious roles do not demand absolute secrecy.

Accommodation and discrimination. One way in which religious exercise can be accommodated is to grant people with religious reasons to perform activities a liberty that most other people are denied. During Prohibition, Roman Catholics and some other Christians wanted, needed, to use wine for communion; during wartime conscientious objectors wanted an exemption from a military draft; members of the Native American Church have regarded peyote as the center of their religion and have needed to ingest peyote during worship in order to practice their religion; some Amish communities have wished to withdraw their children from standard schooling before they have reached the age when that would be allowed; some Muslim parents have wanted their children to be free to pray vocally at a time in the school day.

At first glance, it would appear that granting legal concessions to religious practice would benefit minority groups in a pluralist religious culture, and that indeed is what I think after many more glances, but there are some serious concerns. The main concerns are about tests of honesty, assessments of religious importance and public need, and unfairness to non-religious citizens with similar claims.

First, honesty. If officials or other citizens try to figure out whether someone is telling the truth, isn't this likely to work against unfamiliar minority religions? Members of a draft board may more easily understand and sympathize with a young Quaker who says he cannot fight than with a member of an unfamiliar Eastern religion who takes a similar stance. On examination, the worry about honesty is not serious if a privilege is sought for all members of a group that is not itself formed to evade a legal restriction (or all participants in a group activity) or is one that few people would be tempted to lie about. Wine for communion qualifies on both counts. Only participants in a service get the wine, and they get such a small amount no outsider would want to take the time to participate in order to get that small sip. Many people may wish to avoid jury service, but doing so is not important enough for them to be willing to lie about a religious conviction to achieve that end. When it comes to avoiding military service, however, or to avoid being sent away from one's home and family to a dangerous war one believes the country should never have embroiled itself in, people may lie. Some test of sincerity is needed.[19] Assessments of

---

[19] The test need not necessarily be whether the applicant is more probably telling the truth than not. There could be a presumption in his favor *or* some special burden to establish that he is not lying.

honesty may be required and these may work somewhat to the disadvantage of the unfamiliar, but what is the alternative?

In 1990, the Supreme Court abandoned a test of religious exercise it had adopted twenty-seven years earlier. According to the earlier test, if a law impinged on someone's religious exercise, the government could not apply the law against that person unless it had a compelling interest in doing so. Thus, a state could not deny unemployment compensation to a Seventh Day Adventist because she was unwilling to work on Saturday.[20] In the 1990 case of *Employment Division* v. *Smith*,[21] however, the Supreme Court announced that the Free Exercise Clause of the First Amendment conferred no such privilege on religious believers. Thus, a state law forbidding the use of peyote could be applied against members of the Native American Church. If religious believers have no privileges to be relieved of legal obligations, no test of sincerity is required, but this alternative is hardly more favorable to minority religions than the older approach.

Congress responded to *Smith* by adopting the Religious Freedom Restoration Act, a law that reinstates the older test as a matter of statutory law.[22] After the Supreme Court said that the law could not be applied against states and localities,[23] some states adopted their own similar laws.

One might object that any such law is unfair to non-believers, who should be respected along with the wide range of believers in a religiously diverse society. I agree with this critique up to a point; indeed, I think that equal treatment of non-religious conscientious objectors should be regarded as a constitutional requirement. But there are many claims that people are highly unlikely to make for non-religious reasons. Strong non-religious convictions that one needs a small sip of wine in a group or that one should withdraw one's children from school after eighth grade, or that one must not work on Saturday are very rare. I won't go through all the details, but I believe it is all right to limit exemptions to religious claimants, when the likelihood of similar non-religious ones is very slight or when the danger of fraud if one includes them is great.

I should note that including non-religious reasons does not eliminate the sincerity problem. Suppose the only test for a conscientious objector is sincere opposition to participation in war in any form. An applicant claims that according to his reading of the Bible, God enjoins us to be

---

[20] *Sherbert* v. *Verner*, 374 US 398 (1963).   [21] 494 US 872 (1990).

[22] 42 USC 2000 bb-1–200 bb-4 (2004). Congress subsequently enacted the Religious Land Use and Institutionalized Persons Act, 42 USC 2000 cc (2004).

[23] *City of Boerne* v. *Flores*, 521 US 507 (1997).

non-violent. Someone still must assess whether the applicant is being honest about his claim to possess that religious conviction.

Even more troubling than questions about honesty are ones about the degree of burden on a religious practice and the strength of the government's interest in not granting an exemption. There are some claims to special treatment that legislatures grant specifically. Thus, the federal government and states may provide that members of religious groups may use peyote in worship services. When this is done, neither executive officials nor courts have to delve into the practices of a religion or the possible government interest in denying an exemption. They just apply the statute. But when the courts have to apply a general standard like that of the Religious Freedom Restoration Act, they do need to make these difficult inquiries.

I shall say little about the strength of the government's interest. Suppose a tax is imposed, and religious citizens claim a right not to pay the tax out of honest religious conviction. Or an area is zoned to be purely residential, and members of a religion claim they should be able to build a church in the area. If the government's interest in uniform application of the law is very great as it is with most taxes, refusing to grant an exemption is acceptable. If the government's interest is slight, an exemption may be called for. How the test should be formulated and applied is difficult (and that problem would remain even were the possible exemption extended to non-religious claimants), but I shall focus instead on the issue of the burden on a religious individual or group.

The government should not have to accommodate every trivial religious claim. For example, suppose in the zoning situation, the members have no particular interest in building a church in the forbidden area, except that they can purchase property a little more cheaply. That is very different from members of an Orthodox Jewish congregation wanting to build near residences of their members, who must walk to worship services on the Sabbath.

How can administrators and courts possibly decide how important any particular activity is to a religious individual or congregation,[24] and if officials make such judgments, isn't that likely to work to the disadvantage of misunderstood minority religions? Yes, it is very difficult, and minority religions may suffer by comparison, but again what is the alternative?

We need to begin here with what a court's task should be if it does have to make such judgments. Obviously, judges should not be deciding what religious activities are really important or how any particular religion

---

[24] I explore a range of cases in Greenawalt, *Free Exercise and Fairness*, 201–32.

should really be understood. To do the first would be deciding a subtle question of religious truth; to do the second would be to determine the correct understanding of a religious tradition – inquiries we have already suggested that the state cannot make. Courts must judge importance as it is taken to be by members of the religion itself.

If the legal issue involves the claim of a particular individual – say the claims of a Jehovah's Witness not to work in a factory making turrets for tanks – the Supreme Court has rightly focused on the convictions of the individual involved.[25] If the claim is that a group should engage in an activity, such as using peyote during worship services, a court must do the best it can to discern how important the practice is for the members as a group. Judges should not insist that someone's religious conviction actually requires him to do something the state forbids, or forbids him from doing something the state requires, but they should demand proof that an important religious practice is being frustrated or that someone has a strong religious conviction that he perform an act that the government is discouraging.

Just to state this inquiry is to suggest how difficult and debatable the answer may be in many cases. Will it be harder for members of minorities to make their claims? Probably. A member of an unfamiliar religion *may* actually have one kind of advantage. A Presbyterian judge who supposes she already knows what is important for Christians, or for Presbyterians, may not be responsive to the claims of a Presbyterian with a view that differs from hers. She might actually be more open-minded about religious claims that are new to her. But often a distaste for the unfamiliar may cause judges to underrate the claims of importance of religions they regard as bizarre.

The obvious alternative is for courts and administrators *not* to make judgments about importance. That could mean rewarding those with religious reasons, however trivial, or not making any accommodations to religion. Of these two alternatives, by far the more likely scenario is the latter, the result the *Smith* decision reaches about the First Amendment. A regime of no accommodation to religious claims would be worse for members of minority religions than a legal standard that requires some preliminary investigation of importance.

There are other conceivable alternatives. One is to say that religious claims should be treated like non-religious claims but that sometimes a general right to be exempted on the basis of conscience should be

---

[25] *Thomas* v. *Review Board*, 450 US 707 (1981).

recognized – this could take care of conscientious objectors to military service. Another alternative is to say that sometimes a refusal to exempt religious claims would constitute forbidden discrimination against religion. (The law *could* adopt both these alternatives.) Since discerning whether a person has a conscientious objection is in fact one inquiry about how important not participating is for him, not so different from judging the importance of someone's religious claim, I shall concentrate here on the second possibility: discrimination. According to this view, the inquiry in a case like *Smith* should be whether members of the Native American Church suffered discrimination from the law that forbade use of peyote and did not make an exception for them. One claimed advantage of this approach is precisely that it avoids questions of importance and government interest.[26] But, unless the category of what counts as discrimination is very limited, this approach admits through the back door what it shuts out in front.

When the law itself is neutral on its face – treating everyone the same by allowing no one to use peyote – we could limit discrimination to circumstances in which lawmakers *intend* to harm a religion or treat its members worse than other citizens. In that event, the Native American Church would lose unless it could show that the failure of state legislators to make an exception for it was the result of their wish, their purpose, to treat their church badly. That is usually a very hard showing to make.

The protection against discrimination would become robust *only* if it included what we may call reckless or negligent disregard of the interests of a religion. An example of reckless disregard would be when legislators are aware that a law will impinge very badly on a religious minority but do not care – do not care in a way they would care about the effect on a more popular religion. Negligent disregard is when the legislators are unaware of such an effect although they should be. Thus, the Native American Church could argue that legislators would never have adopted a law with such drastic negative effects on a mainstream religion, and that their failure to show such concern for the Native American Church constitutes a form of discrimination.

I believe looking at these problems from the point of view of a broad notion of discrimination is promising – in part because it is one method to give effect to ideals of equality. But we would be fooling ourselves if we thought this was a way to avoid judgments either about burdens on religious

---

[26] Eisgruber and Sager, *Religious Freedom and the Constitution*.

individuals and groups or about government interest. Such judgments are implicated in the very process of assessing possible discrimination.

Judges are rarely going to be able to discern what exactly legislators were thinking when they adopted a general prohibition and did not make an exception. So judges will have to think about average or reasonable legislators. What would one suppose such a legislator would have had in mind? If the religious activity was of trivial importance *or* the government interest in stopping the activity across the board was very strong, such a legislator would not write an exception into a statute. If the religious activity was very important and the government interest in stopping that manifestation of the forbidden behavior was slight, an astute legislator would make an exception – just what I believe is true about the use of peyote by the Native American Church. But we can see it is just one's judgments about importance to the religion and about the government's interest in the prohibition that now underlie one's judgment about discrimination. That is how these inquiries enter by the back door.

Let me turn briefly to a special, troubling issue about discrimination. How far should religious institutions themselves be able to discriminate on the basis of grounds that are forbidden to other groups? It goes without saying that for positions of leadership, religious groups should be able to use religious criteria of choice. Baptists can choose ministers who embrace Baptist principles. Perhaps Congress has gone too far in allowing religious organizations to use religious criteria in choosing all employees,[27] rather than requiring a minimal showing that the religious views of a person in a position – say, a janitor – can matter for the flourishing of the religious endeavor.

The harder questions concern discrimination on other grounds – race, gender, or sexual orientation. At least if they can show some connection to their religious tradition and principles, religious groups should have a legal right to discriminate on these grounds in their core activities. A church that is committed to a male priesthood and that condemns homosexual activity as sinful should not have to hire as a priest a woman or a man who is openly gay.

A more difficult question is raised by tax exemptions. The Internal Revenue Service has decided that a religious university engaged in racial discrimination is not entitled to the status of a charitable activity, and that determination was upheld by the Supreme Court.[28] Some believe a

---

[27] The law was upheld in *Corporation of the Presiding Bishops of the Church of Jesus Christ of Latter-Day Saints* v. *Amos*, 483 US 327 (1987).
[28] *Bob Jones University* v. *United States*, 461 US 574 (1983).

similar fate should befall core religious institutions, churches, synagogues, mosques and so on, that engage in discrimination by race or gender. I disagree, but I do think such discrimination should be barred for personnel who are providing a service that is actually financed by government, such as a hospital or school.

These issues may prove most acute in relation to sexual orientation. Some religious groups believe that homosexual relations are sinful; they balk at hiring employees who openly engage in these sinful activities as part of the pattern of their lives. Maximum equality for gays is in conflict with the widest latitude for religious liberty. Federal law does not now bar discrimination according to sexual orientation, but some local governments do. Even in those areas I believe religious groups should be able to practice what they believe by taking an applicant's openly expressed sexual preferences and activities into account. But when a government does bar discrimination of this sort *in general*, it should not finance activities of religious groups that benefit the public – such as adoption agencies and hospitals – if the groups refuse to hire gays in the organizations that provide these benefits.

Defining religion. I have, thus far, neglected a final topic that concerns the treatment of religion – deciding what counts as religious. If religion is going to receive special treatment, whether it is receiving a benefit or being subject to restrictions that don't apply to other subjects, courts must be able to say whether a practice or claim is religious, or not. One may reasonably be worried that a definition of religion is itself likely to work to the disadvantage of the unfamiliar. To take a very simple example drawn from some earlier cases, a definition in terms of relation to a Supreme Being works fine for standard American religions but not so well for Buddhism. My own view is that rather than starting from a typical definition, courts should identify characteristics of what are undoubtedly religions in the world and ask whether the disputed instance shares many of the same characteristics.[29] This approach, instead of stating necessary and sufficient conditions, understands religion in the way that Ludwig Wittgenstein understood the category of games. A version of this approach was used by Judge Arlin Adams in a case deciding that a course in Transcendental Meditation could not be taught in New Jersey's public schools because it was religious.[30] To be sure, even this approach may be applied in a way that could be disadvantageous to the unfamiliar. But, again, what is the

---

[29] See Greenawalt, *Free Exercise and Fairness*, 124–56.
[30] *Malnak* v. *Yogi*, 592 F.2d 197, 207–10 (concurring opinion).

alternative? There can be no concessions to religious claims and religious groups as such, unless courts can use some approach to say whether or not a claim or practice is religious. And the law's method of categorization must be one that lawyers can feasibly use. This means it may be more or less close to how the boundaries of religion are understood in other disciplines.

CONCLUSIONS

In this chapter, I have offered many specific conclusions on difficult issues, without a full defense. Readers may reasonably disagree with various of these judgments. But the general lessons I draw from these inquiries are the following. First, religious liberty often coalesces with equal treatment. But sometimes aspects of religious liberty are in serious tension with aspects of equality. Second, the special treatment of religion in comparison with other subjects is, on balance, usually beneficial to minority religions, and thus promotes equality among religions. This is illustrated by the rule that government cannot engage in teaching religious truth. Third, the law must often settle for something less than an ideal. Legal standards of all sorts are often applied to favor dominant groups to the disadvantage of outsiders. Inquiries about sincerity, importance, and the boundaries of religion may work to the disadvantage of minority religious movements within a pluralist religious culture. But, by and large, the alternative of not engaging these inquiries will be that members of those groups will be subject to all the rules that apply to ordinary citizens, and they will be worse off. Some likely disadvantage in the applications of these standards is preferable to not having the standards used at all. Fourth, it would be a worthwhile endeavor in the coming decades to study just when the law should treat religion as distinctive and how the necessary legal inquiries may be undertaken as consistently with basic values of equality as is humanly possible.

RECOMMENDED READING

Ackermann, Bruce. *Social Justice in the Liberal State*. New Haven: Yale University Press, 1980.

Eisgruber, Christopher and Lawrence G. Sager. *Religious Freedom and the Constitution*. Cambridge, MA: Harvard University Press, 2007.

Greenawalt, Kent. *Religion and the Constitution*, 2 vols. Princeton: Princeton University Press, 2006–8.

"Viewpoints from Olympus," *Columbia Law Review* 96 (1996): 697–753.

Laycock, Douglas. *Collected Writings on Religious Liberty*, 4 vols. Grand Rapids, MI: Wm. B. Eerdmans, 2010–.

McConnell, Michael W., John H. Garvey, and Thomas C. Berg. *Religion and the Constitution*, 2nd edn. New York: Aspen Publishers, 2006.

Nurser, John. *For All Peoples and All Nations: Christian Churches and Human Rights*. Geneva: World Council of Churches Publications, 2005.

Stahnke, Tad and J. Paul Martin, eds. *Religion and Human Rights: Basic Documents*. New York: Columbia University Press, 1988.

Witte, John, Jr. and Joel A. Nichols. *Religion and the American Constitutional Experiment*, 3rd edn. Boulder, CO and London: Westview Press, 2010.

CHAPTER 12

Proselytism and human rights

Silvio Ferrari

The term "proselytism" as used in this article means the activity of communicating a religion or worldview through verbal communication or
through various related activities as an invitation to others to adopt the religion or worldview.[1] This "neutral" definition of proselytism is not the one
most frequently in use today. Proselytism is now a term that has acquired a
negative connotation in many religions: in Christian theological and legal
terminology, it frequently indicates a corruption of the Christian witness,
and it is often set against evangelization, meaning the announcement of
the good news, that is the redeeming message of Christ.[2]

The use of the term "proselytism" in a negative sense does, however, cause
some confusion. Indeed leaders of the Christian churches often speak of
"aggressive" proselytism,[3] and in its rulings the European Court of Human
Rights writes of "improper" proselytism.[4] Such terminology implies that
there is a "bad" (aggressive or improper) kind of proselytism and a "good," or
at least legitimate, kind. To avoid this confusion, I shall use the term "proselytism" in the neutral sense indicated at the beginning of this chapter.

The different uses of the term "proselytism" reflect deeper concerns
about the concept. First, there is the difficulty of distinguishing between
proselytism and evangelization. All Christian religious denominations
agree about excluding forms of coercion[5] and many improper means of

[1] This definition is taken from *Missionary Activities and Human Rights: A Code of Conduct for
Missionary Activities*, drafted by the Oslo Coalition on Freedom of Religion or Belief in March
2009 and available at www.oslocoalition.org/mhr.php.
[2] See Martin E. Marty, "Proselytizers and Proselytizees on the Sharp Arête of Modernity," in John
Witte, Jr. and Richard C. Martin, eds., *Sharing the Book: Religious Perspectives on the Rights and
Wrongs of Proselytism* (Maryknoll, NY: Orbis Books, 1999), 2.
[3] See, for example, the address of Benedict XVI at the meeting with the bishops of Brazil, May
11, 2007, in www.vatican.va/holy_father/benedict_xvi/speeches/2007/may/documents/hf_ben-
xvi_spe_20070511_bishops-brazil_en.html.
[4] See, for example, *Kokkinakis* v. *Greece* (Ser. A), 260-A (1993), ECtHR, 397–440.
[5] See, for the Catholic Church, canon 748 of the Code of Canon Law (1983), according to which "No
one is ever permitted to coerce persons to embrace the Catholic faith against their conscience."

inducing or persuading converts to the faith.[6] But that said, "one group's evangelization is another group's proselytism."[7] Second, these differences over proselytism are also due to the contrast that divides religions – and, within Christianity, its different denominations – over the question of changing religion. Some faiths consider change in religion, especially a conversion out of the faith, to be culpable and illegitimate, and they therefore always condemn proselytism. Other religions see conversion out of the faith as a licit act (albeit the result of a decision that is considered erroneous), and they condemn proselytism only when it utilizes improper means of persuasion. Understanding the causes of this difference, whose roots are to be found in the notion of religious membership, is the first step toward setting in order the complexity of the questions connected with proselytism.

Proselytism is not an activity that is restricted to religious communities. It also involves the states and their legal systems. A state can ignore the initiatives aimed at persuading its citizens to adopt or abandon a religion, or it can support them or oppose them. These options, which are often influenced by the religious and cultural background of a country, weigh upon the fundamental rights enjoyed by citizens and in particular on the right to religious freedom. To establish whether this right includes that of changing one's religion is one of the most controversial topics of international and constitutional law, as I shall address in the second part of this article.

PROSELYTISM IN THE MONOTHEISTIC RELIGIONS: THEOLOGICAL PRESUPPOSITIONS AND HISTORICAL AND LEGAL CONTEXT

The attitude to proselytism that has developed inside each religion is largely determined by each one's concept of religious membership. In the three principal monotheistic religions – Judaism, Christianity, and Islam – religious membership is defined according to different theological and legal criteria. Even a brief summary of these respective understandings is useful for understanding the meaning that these religions attribute to proselytism.

---

[6] A list of improper activities that can distinguish proselytism may be found in the document *The Challenge of Proselytism and the Calling to Common Witness: Study Document of the Joint Working Group Between the World Council of Churches and the Roman Catholic Church*, Sept. 25, 1995, n. 19.

[7] Cecil M. Robeck, Jr., "Mission and the Issue of Proselytism," *International Bulletin of Missionary Research* 20(1) (January 1996): 2.

One of the first differences is between the religions in which membership is understood as the result of a choice and the religions in which it is conceived as a fact that is independent from an expression of individual will. This is a distinction that should be taken with caution, as the personal dimension of the relationship between man and God is present in all of the religions considered here: in Christianity, however, it has a more marked impact on religious membership than it does in Judaism or Islam.

This last statement may be verified through an examination of the methods of entry into the three religions.[8] They all share the principle that one becomes Jewish, Muslim, or Christian through an act of conversion, that is, by personal choice. But the first two faiths provide that religious membership is also transmitted through birth – in a matrilineal way for Judaism, in a patrilineal way for Islam. According to Jewish law, the son of a Jewish mother is Jewish; according to Islamic law, the son of a Muslim father is Muslim irrespective of any expression of will. By contrast, according to the law of the Christian churches, religious membership descends from the fulfillment of a specific act, baptism, which requires a personal choice. The child of two Christian parents is not Christian until he or she has received baptism.

This first line of separation sets Judaism and Islam on the same side, among the religions that spread through descent, and Christianity, on the other side, among the religions founded on "assent."[9] This difference is important. If religious membership is something that the individual acquires by birth, he has no opportunity to abandon it. If, instead, it depends on personal choice, individual autonomy acquires greater prominence and the change in one's religion by means of a conscious act of choice may be considered a legitimate manifestation. In the first case, proselytism tends to be considered an activity that is always illegitimate; in the second case, the judgment may be different.

Also inside Christianity the notion of religious membership is not unambiguous, ranging from the religious denominations that emphasize the free adhesion of the individual and those that, in various ways, limit the importance of individual will. At one extreme are the denominations of Protestant origin which practice adult baptism: through this choice they

---

[8] Silvio Ferrari, *Lo spirito dei diritti religiosi. Ebraismo, cristianesimo e islam a confronto* (Bologna: Mulino, 2002), 203–27.

[9] Paul Morris, "Community Beyond Tradition," in P. Heelas, S. Lash, and P. Morris, eds., *Detraditionalization: Critical Reflections on Authority and Identity* (Oxford: Blackwell, 1996), 238–45. Other scholars speak, with reference to Christianity, of "intentional community." See Luke Timothy Johnson, "Proselytism and Witness in Earliest Christianity," in Witte and Martin, eds., *Sharing the Book*, 150.

emphasize that personal faith in Jesus Christ is the indispensable requirement for being baptized and becoming part of the Christian community.
At the other end of the spectrum, with significant differences in emphasis
between one religious group and another, may be found the denominations that practice infant baptism, considering that the salvific value of
baptism does not depend on the will to receive it. This is not membership
by birth, as in the case of Judaism and Islam, but nor is it a wholly personal
choice. The decision is not made by the person who is baptized but by his
parents. This difference is also reflected by the possibility of changing one's
religious membership. For some Christian churches, notably the Catholic
Church, baptism imparts on the subject receiving it an indelible sign that
the baptized cannot renounce even by a specific act of will: *semel catholicus, semper catholicus* ("once a Catholic, always a Catholic"). For others,
such as the Seventh-Day Adventist Church, it is possible to abandon the
community through a demonstration of will that corresponds, though in
an opposite direction, with the one by which the person entered it.[10]

It is evident that these different conceptions of entering and leaving the
church are reflected in proselytism. Generally speaking, the Evangelical
or Pentecostal groups, convinced that religious membership depends on
a conscious personal choice, do not hesitate to proselytize a person who
was baptized Catholic or Orthodox and who no longer practices his faith.
The Catholic or Orthodox communities, however, view these activities
with suspicion and aversion because they consider that any person who
has been baptized, even though he may live in a manner which is not consistent with his religious membership, is always a member of the church by
virtue of the baptism he received.

A second difference to take into account is between religions of a universal vocation and religions with a particular vocation. All Christian religious denominations share, albeit with different emphasis, the idea that
"the Church … has the duty and innate right, independent of any human
power whatsoever, to preach the gospel to all peoples."[11] This idea finds a
parallel in Islam but not, with the same clarity, in Judaism. For Jews the
first duty is not to spread their religion among all mankind but to ensure
that God's chosen people remain faithful.[12] Without exaggerating the

---

[10] For a short description of the theological concept and the legal discipline of baptism in the dif-
    ferent Christian denominations, see "Baptism," in *The Oxford Dictionary of the Christian Church*
    (New York: Oxford University Press, 1997), 150–3.
[11] Thus states can. 747 of the Code of Canon Law of the Catholic Church, translating into legal
    terms the commandment expressed in the Gospel according to Matt. 28:19.
[12] See Michael J. Broyde, "Proselytism and Jewish Law," in Witte and Martin, eds., *Sharing the
    Book*, 45.

importance of this distinction (since Jews did engage in intense proselytism in certain periods),[13] it signals a different tendency between "universal" and "particular" religions: the former emphasize the duty of their followers to preach their message, the latter the duty to maintain their own religion. A similar difference exists with religions that have strong ethnic connotations (think of the religions of the American indigenous peoples): their followers, who in the past were the object of intense proselytism by Christian missionaries, claim the right not to be induced to change their own religion. These demands have been echoed in the constitutional norms and in the rulings that subordinate the right to spread one's religion without impediment to respect of the "right to be left alone."[14]

This dialectic between the universal and the particular dimension, in its national or ethnic variants, occurs also in Christianity, where it has taken on different forms according to the historical and cultural context in which each religious denomination has developed. The Orthodox Churches are a good example of a community that has stressed the particular dimension of religious membership. The fall of the Byzantine Empire to Islam left the Orthodox Churches without a powerful central point of reference, favoring the tendency to create autonomous churches, united by the same faith but increasingly less by a common legal discipline. This process of differentiation led each church to develop in strict identity with its own people: the role played by the Russian Orthodox Church and by the Orthodox Churches of the Balkans in safeguarding the identity of their respective populations during the Mongol and Ottoman dominations accentuated this trend and favored the establishment of an increasingly close relationship between the church and nation and, in the last two centuries, between the church and national state. The particularly strong notion of the local church which was elaborated by Orthodox theology, according to which the identification of the faith with a certain people and a certain culture is the logical consequence of the incarnation, provided the context in which the ideas of "symphony" between church and state (far more intense and binding than the Catholic concept of cooperation between church and state) and of canonical territory took shape.

---

[13] See David Novak, "Proselytism in Judaism," in Witte and Martin, eds., *Sharing the Book*, 17.
[14] The Constitution of Zimbabwe, art. 19(5)(b) declares "the right to observe and practice any religion or belief without the unsolicited intervention of persons professing any other religion or belief." In the same regard, see the Constitution of Papua New Guinea (art. 45,3) and the ruling 510/1998 of the Constitutional Court of Colombia, discussed in Silvio Ferrari, "Globalization, Postmodernism and Proselytism," *Fides et Libertas* (1999): 22–3.

The Roman Catholic Church followed a different historical path. Unlike the Eastern Orthodox Churches, in the West the Roman Catholic Church established the power of the pope and, during medieval times, the local churches were progressively subjected to the control of the Holy See. A unitary corpus of Catholic canon law (in place of the many different canon laws of the Orthodox Churches) was applied to all Western Christianity, and this allowed the papacy to assert its dominance not only over theological matters and church life but also over the legal terrain. Without attempting to summarize in just a few lines the history of many centuries, at least one point should be underlined: in the West, the national states which emerged from the ashes of the Holy Roman Empire developed in opposition to the power of Rome and fought to wrest control of the local episcopacy and clergy from the papacy through the formation of national churches subject to a political sovereign. This contrast, which was only to be overcome in the twentieth century, prevented the Catholic world from developing that tight relationship between the church and national state that characterizes the Orthodox world.

The four coordinates that have been identified – voluntary or involuntary membership, in a universal or particular religion – combine in different ways inside each religion and contribute toward setting the scene in which each puts the question of proselytism.

PROSELYTISM IN CHRISTIANITY

All Christian denominations support, though with different emphases, the legitimacy of proselytism directed at people who do not profess any religion or who profess a religion that is not Christianity. In some countries this activity, especially when directed toward Muslims, may be self-restricted. But no Christian church can renounce spreading the Gospel and proposing it as the way of salvation for all those people who do not know it. For they all start with Christ's Great Commission: "Go ye, therefore, and make disciples of all nations, baptizing them in the name of the Father, Son, and Holy Ghost, teaching them to observe all that I have commanded you" (Matt. 28:19–20).

The question becomes more complicated in the relations between the Christian religious denominations. In this case there are different opinions not only about the opportunity but also about the licitness of conducting an activity which may lead a follower of one church to become a member of another church. Two examples – the first regarding Russia and the second Latin America – serve to show the causes and the consequences of this difference.

Intra-Christian proselytism is firmly rejected by the Orthodox Churches. Each of them has its own position which would require a separate examination, but all of them consider that proselytism is incompatible with the bond of unity that connects the sister churches. The strictest attitude has been assumed by the Russian Orthodox Church. The freedom of expression, of movement, and of religion recovered after the collapse of the Soviet regime, has allowed missionaries and followers of other Christian churches to enter and conduct activities in Russia, rapidly creating (or re-establishing) their own communities and organizational structures in Russian territory. The swift and unexpected expansion of these religious communities has generated, among Russian Orthodox Church leaders, the sensation of being under attack, convincing them that other Christian churches want to exploit the weakness of the Orthodox Church to swell their own ranks at its expense.[15] This conviction sparked a forceful reaction which went so far as to demand (and in more than one case to obtain) the state's support to limit the activity of proselytism.

It would, however, be a mistake to interpret the position of the Russian Orthodox Church only from this viewpoint, which – all things considered – was linked to contingent events: in reality it is more deeply rooted in a precise concept of the relations between the different Christian denominations. The point of departure for the Orthodox is the notion of canonical territory, based on the principle of "one city – one bishop – one church," which lies at the foundation of the model of organization adopted by the Christian churches since their origins.[16] This principle involves "the assignment of a certain ecclesiastical territory to one concrete bishop" and "the inadmissibility of violating the boundaries of ecclesiastical territories by bishops or clergy."[17] Consequently, "each local Orthodox Church

---

[15] See Metropolitan Kirill of Smolensk and Kaliningrad, "Gospel and Culture," in John Witte, Jr. and Michael Bourdeaux, eds., *Proselytism and Orthodoxy in Russia: The New War for Souls* (Maryknoll, NY: Orbis Books, 1999), 72–4.

[16] On the notion of canonical territory and on the conflict around this and the issue of proselytism that developed between the Russian Orthodox Church and the Catholic Church, see Johannes Oeldemann, "The Concept of Canonical Territory in the Russian Orthodox Church," in Thomas Bremer, ed., *Religion and the Conceptual Boundary in Central and Eastern Europe* (Basingstoke: Palgrave Macmillan, 2008), 229–35; see also Waclaw Hryniewicz, *The Challenge of our Hope: Christian Faith in Dialogue* (Washington, DC: Council for Research in Values and Philosophy, 2007), chap. 13.

[17] Bishop Hilarion of Vienna and Austria, "'One City – One Bishop – One Church': The Principle of Canonical Territory and the Appearance of 'Parallel Hierarchies'," *Europaica Bulletin* 84 (Jan. 23, 2006) in http://orthodoxeurope.org/section/14.aspx.

has its canonical territory, the integrity of which is recognized in principle by other Churches. Other Churches do not have the right to create parishes on this canonical territory."[18] According to the Orthodox doctrine, this rule applies not only to the relations between the various Orthodox Churches but also to those between different Christian Orthodox and non-Orthodox churches, which should therefore abstain from creating their own ecclesiastical hierarchies and structures in countries where the Orthodox Church is already rooted without the latter's authorization.

The representatives of the other Christian churches have often objected that, after decades of state atheism, many Orthodox people have kept a purely nominal connection with their church. But the leaders of the Russian Orthodox Church have countered these observations with "the idea of *traditionally Orthodox nations* – those in which the Orthodox Church is the Church of the majority of the population." In these countries the notion of "cultural canonical territory" is applied, according to which "the entire population of a country, which by its cultural roots belongs to the Orthodox tradition but lost contact with the faith of their ancestors for historical reasons, is the potential flock of the local Orthodox Church." Consequently, the other Christian churches should limit their pastoral activity to their own followers, avoiding any proselytism "to the detriment of the Orthodox Church."[19] In this perspective the Orthodox Christian who has lost his faith or who does not live according to it should be helped to recover his active affiliation with the Orthodox Church, without being induced to become a member of another Christian church.

This position of the Russian Orthodox Church, firmly stated in 2002 on the occasion of the re-establishment of the Catholic Church hierarchy in Russia, sparked off a polemic during which the authorities of the Church of Rome had the opportunity to clarify their points of disagreement with this theological and legal doctrine. First, the Holy See rejected the "division of the world into canonical territories," which was considered too rigid a form of church organization to reflect the ties that bind a church to the culture and tradition of its people. Second, they considered the position of the Russian Orthodox Church to be incompatible with human rights, in particular freedom of religion; indeed, in their view, it tended to "ensure the hegemony of the Russian Orthodox Church to the detriment not only

---

[18] *Ibid.*

[19] Bishop Hilarion of Vienna and Austria, "The Practical Application of the Principle of Canonical Territory," in *Europaica Bulletin* 87 (Feb. 17, 2006), in http://orthodoxeurope.org/section/14.aspx.

of the Catholic Church but also of personal liberty."[20] Finally, according to the authorities of the Catholic Church, the Russian Orthodox Church's position contradicted the "responsibility of proclaiming in fullness the Catholic faith to other Christians, who freely wish to receive it." Therefore "if a non-Catholic Christian, for reasons of conscience and having been convinced of Catholic truth, asks to enter into the full communion of the Catholic Church, this is to be respected as the work of the Holy Spirit and as an expression of freedom of conscience and of religion."[21]

The second example of intra-Christian proselytism regards Latin America, a continent which since its original colonization and evangelization in the sixteenth and seventeenth centuries has been solidly Catholic. In the last few decades, however, some Evangelical and Pentecostal religious movements have grown considerably and today 10–15 per cent of the population has abandoned the Church of Rome. This growth has worried many Catholic bishops who have protested and sometimes spoken of an anti-Catholic "plot" directed by US Protestant circles and sometimes accused these Protestant rivals of using improper means in conducting their activity of proselytism.[22]

As with post-Soviet Russia, so in this case it is useful to look beyond the contingent events and seek the theological and legal basis of the opposition between the Pentecostals and Evangelicals, on the one hand, and the Catholics on the other. The difference, again, lies in a different concept of church membership. For Pentecostals and Evangelicals, church membership is founded first of all on a conscious faith response; for Catholics, it is based on baptism. Much like their Russian Orthodox counterparts, Latin American Catholic leaders argued that all those who have been baptized, even if they do not practice their faith, are part of the Catholic Church and should not be led away from it but rather helped to recover a consistency of life within their own community of origin. For many Evangelical and Pentecostal movements instead it is legitimate for these "sleeping" Christians to be awakened to faith in another religious community; in their view, proselytism is excluded only if it is addressed to "committed"

---

[20] Walter Kasper, "Le radici teologiche del conflitto tra Mosca e Roma," *La Civiltà cattolica*, 1 (3642) (March 16, 2002): 541. Kasper was the President of the Pontifical Council for Promoting Christian Unity.

[21] Congregation for the Doctrine of the Faith, "Doctrinal Note on Some Aspects of Evangelization" (Dec. 14, 2007), n. 12, in www.vatican.va/roman_curia/congregations/cfaith/documents/rc_con_cfaith_doc_20071203_nota-evangelizzazione_en.html.

[22] See Paul E. Sigmund, ed., *Religious Freedom and Evangelization in Latin America: The Challenge of Religious Pluralism* (Maryknoll, NY: Orbis Books, 1999).

members of a religious community, but not to those who belong to it only nominally.[23]

The parallel between the conflict that pitted the Orthodox and Catholic Churches against each other in Russia and the one that divided Catholics, Evangelicals, and Pentecostals in Latin America is evident: in the latter case, however, it had a shorter and more limited impact. The elements that made the difference were first of all the notion of religious freedom, which was substantially shared by the Protestant Churches and by the Catholic Church after the Second Vatican Council. The principle that no one should "be forced to act in a manner contrary to his own beliefs"[24] brings with it the right for a Christian to freely choose "to join a different Christian community … after hearing a legitimate presentation of the Gospel."[25] Also important was that Catholics and Protestants both rejected the notion of a canonical territory, understood as a legal space in which only the members of one church may legitimately carry out activities of proselytism. Although the representatives of the Church of Rome had several times stressed the need to respect the Catholic tradition of Latin America, this appeal was never translated into a statement of illegitimacy of proselytism exercised by non-Catholic religious groups. Finally, the Second Vatican Council loosened the strict ties between the Catholic Church and the Latin American states which they had inherited from the Spanish domination.

PROSELYTISM AND STATE LAW

This last observation leads me to the final theme to be considered here: the attitude of states toward proselytism. The state can make proselytism easier or more difficult in many ways, without resorting to provisions that discipline it in explicit terms. State norms that prevent foreign missionaries from entering a country or limit the distribution of materials of a religious nature strike at the heart of proselytism, even though they are not called anti-proselytism laws. Conversely, state norms that provide for the access of a religion to radio and television may facilitate it. The assessment

---

[23] See Veli-Matti Karkkainen, "Proselytism and Church Relations," *The Ecumenical Review* (July 2000): 382–3; Robeck, "Mission and the Issue of Proselytism," 7.

[24] Second Vatican Council, "Declaration on Religious Freedom Dignitatis Humanae" (Dec. 7, 1965).

[25] "Evangelization, Proselytism and Common Witness: The Report from the Fourth Phase of the International Dialogue 1990–1997 Between the Roman Catholic Church and Some Classical Pentecostal Churches and Leaders," *Pneuma: The Journal of the Society for Pentecostal Studies* 21(1) (Spring 1999): V, 3, 95.

of all these laws would require a detailed analysis of the systems of relations between the state and the religions that are in force in each country. As it is not possible to conduct such a complex investigation here, I shall limit myself to considering the norms that most explicitly regard proselytism.

An examination of state legislation reveals that the regulation of proselytism is very varied.[26] At one extreme there are the countries that guarantee the freedom of religious propaganda, which includes proselytism.[27] Then there are the states which, although they avoid explicitly guaranteeing the right to propagate a religious faith, in their own laws omit any reference to proselytism, whether to allow it or to limit it or prohibit it: in these cases proselytism is guaranteed by the norms on freedom of religion and expression. Some countries do not forbid proselytism but they prohibit or make it difficult to change religion: this is the case, for example, of Nepal,[28] of some states of India,[29] and of some countries with a Muslim majority.[30] Others condemn proselytism when it is aimed at particular categories of persons (for example, minors) or is carried out using deceptive or improper means, such as the promise of material advantages in the case of conversion.[31] Although the general terms in which these norms are formulated may lend themselves to abuse, they are not considered to be in contrast with the international conventions that protect religious freedom.[32] More delicate is the case of countries that generally forbid proselytism that targets believers of a particular religion or of all religions.

---

[26] For an examination of the laws of some states, see Maria José Ciáurriz, *El derecho de proselitismo en el marco de la libertad religiosa* (Madrid: Centro de Estudios Politicos y Constitucionales, 2001).

[27] See, for example, the Constitutions of Italy (art. 19), Colombia (art. 19), and Nigeria (art. 38). Also the Constitution of India (art. 25,1) guarantees the right "to propagate religion," though the fact remains that proselytism is forbidden by the laws of some Indian states.

[28] See Interim Constitution of Nepal, art. 23,1.

[29] Thus, for example, art. 5 of the Gujarat Freedom of Religion Act n. 22 (2003) imposes on "whoever converts any person from one religion to another" to "take prior permission for such proposed conversion from the District Magistrate" and requires the "person who is converted" to "send an intimation to the District Magistrate." See also the Madhya Pradesh Freedom of Religion (Amendment) Act, 2006, art. 5.

[30] See Abdullah Saeed and Hassan Saeed, *Freedom of Religion: Apostasy and Islam* (Aldershot: Ashgate, 2004).

[31] Thus in Israel (see Criminal Law, sect. 174e 368) and in some states of India (see the Orissa Freedom of Religion Act, 1967, art. 3; the Gujarat Freedom of Religion Act, 2003, n. 22, art. 3).

[32] See European Court of Human Rights, *Larissis and others* v. *Greece* (Ser. A), 65 (1998-V), ECtHR, para 45. On the discipline of proselytism in international law, see Natan Lerner, *Religion, Beliefs, and International Human Rights* (Maryknoll, NY: Orbis Books, 2000), 80–118; Tad Stahnke, "Proselytism and the Freedom to Change Religion in International Human Rights Law," *Brigham Young University Law Review* (1999): 251–350.

In some cases this aversion toward proselytism may be traced to causes that are prevalently political: proselytism, especially if it is conducted aggressively, may create situations of conflict that can jeopardize peace and social cohesion. In these cases the prohibition or limitation of proselytism pertains to all religions, and it is aimed at guaranteeing peaceful coexistence among citizens of different religious faiths. An example of this attitude is provided by Article 5 of the Constitution of Chad (defined in art. 1 as a "secular State"), which forbids "all propaganda of an ethnic, tribalist, regionalist or religious nature, tending to affect the national unity or the secularity of the state."[33] In other cases, the aversion to proselytism may be traced to the religious character of the state. When a religion is declared a state religion or has a legally dominant position, it is possible that the activity of proselytism conducted by the followers of other religions may be viewed with disfavor. Thus the Constitution of Malaysia, where Islam is the state religion (art. 3), provides that the state "may control or restrict the propagation of any religious doctrine or belief among persons professing the religion of Islam" (art. 11,4).[34]

This political criterion, alone, does not explain all state norms that forbid proselytism. In countries with a state religion or dominant religion, some (such as Greece) forbid proselytism[35] and others (for instance, Denmark and Norway) allow it. This statement of fact reveals that the orientation of a state cannot be explained by referring only to its system of relations with the religions and without taking into consideration also the cultural and religious tradition. The Orthodox background of Greece helps explain the state's prohibition of proselytism; the Protestant background of Norway and Denmark explains the absence of such a prohibition. This observation is confirmed by the fact that, in the countries with a Christian majority, norms that prohibit or limit proselytism occur more frequently in the countries of Orthodox tradition[36] than in those with a Protestant or Catholic religious background.

---

[33] In the same regard see art. 18,2 of the Constitution of Azerbaijan (it too defined at art. 7 "a secular State") and art. 5 of the Freedom of Conscience Law of Uzbekistan (1998).

[34] See also art. 11,1 of the Ordonnance n° 06–03 du 29 Moharram 1427 correspondant au 28 février 2006 fixant les conditions et règles d'exercice des cultes autres que musulman, in *Journal Officiel de la République Algerienne* 12 (March 1, 2006): 24. Art. 2 defines Islam as the religion of Algeria, Art. 220 of the Moroccan penal code declares Islam is the official state religion of Morocco: cf. art. 6 of the Constitution.

[35] See art. 13,2 of the Greek constitution ("Proselytism is prohibited"). Art. 3,1 of the same constitution declares that "the prevailing religion in Greece is that of the Eastern Orthodox Church of Christ." Proselytism is prohibited also by law 1672 of 1939.

[36] Besides Greece, Armenia (cf. the "Law of the Republic of Armenia on the Freedom of Conscience and on Religious Organizations" [1991], art. 8).

CONCLUSIONS

The heated debates that have arisen around proselytism are to be seen in the light of the larger debate about religious freedom that started a few years ago. For decades, the individual dimension of religious freedom was prevalent, as can be seen in the great international codifications of human rights discussed in Jeremy Gunn's chapter. Today the collective dimension of this right has re-emerged forcefully, reaffirmed, for example, in the recent UN resolutions on the defamation of religion. In the first view, each individual has the right to choose or change his religion; in the second, each person receives his religion from the community into which he is born. Proselytism, if carried out in a correct manner, is always licit in the first case; it may not be in the second.

In the debate within Christianity, the weakest point of the criticisms leveled at proselytism by representatives of the Orthodox Churches lies in their underestimation of the personal dimension of the religious experience and, consequently, of the individual profile of religious freedom. The notion of individual religious freedom is not a consequence of medieval conceptions of natural law, nor of the philosophy of Enlightenment: it has a solid foundation in the passages of the Christian holy texts where it is stated that religion is first of all a fact of personal faith.[37] Christ's message summons the conscience of each person and urges an answer. The religious community – as well as the family, the ethnic group, the nation, and the state – cannot substitute for the individual in giving this answer nor determine its content. The demand by the Orthodox Churches to limit the proselytism of other Christian denominations does not adequately respond to this requirement and needs to be pondered so as not to restrict the freedom of each Christian.

Once this step has been taken it will be possible to recover the part of truth implicit in the Orthodox Churches' position. This is the reference to the bond of communion which, beyond whatever division, persists between the Christian churches and precludes every initiative that does not respect the relationship that there must be between sister churches. This bond cannot aim to limit the freedom of the individual member of one or another church, who must be free to follow the Christian message in the form most suited to his conscience. Its aim is different: it is directed at assuring that the existence of a common faith is revealed in the relationships binding the different Christian churches, inspiring their actions and

---

[37] See the chapter by David Aune herein.

behavior. In this light the choices made by the authorities of the Catholic Church to re-establish the Catholic hierarchy in Russia seem debatable. Indeed these decisions were made unilaterally, without respecting the dialogue that it is legitimate to expect between sister churches.

The road toward this objective is a long one, paradoxically longer today than some decades ago. A step in the right direction would be to avoid asking for the help of the state in the conflicts that set different Christian churches in opposition over proselytism. State support of one or another party in the dispute is not without a price and it responds to interests of a political nature which often exacerbate the tensions between churches. Restoring the issue of proselytism to its natural inter-church sphere would aid recognition that its solution lies in the maturation of the Christian faith of each church.

RECOMMENDED READING

An-Na'im Abdullahi Ahmed, ed. *Proselytization and Communal Self-Determination in Africa*. Maryknoll, NY: Orbis Books, 1999.

Lerner, Natan. *Religion, Beliefs, and International Human Rights*. Maryknoll, NY: Orbis Books, 2000.

Sigmund, Paul E. *Religious Freedom and Evangelization in Latin America: The Challenge of Religious Pluralism*. Maryknoll, NY: Orbis Books, 1999.

Stahnke, Tad. "Proselytism and the Freedom to Change Religion in International Human Rights Law," *Brigham Young University Law Review* (1999): 251–350.

Taylor, Paul M. *Freedom of Religion: UN and European Human Rights Law and Practice*. Cambridge: Cambridge University Press, 2005.

Witte, John, Jr. and Michael Bourdeaux, eds. *Proselytism and Orthodoxy in Russia: The New War for Souls*. Maryknoll, NY: Orbis Books, 1999.

Witte, John, Jr. and Richard C. Martin, eds. *Sharing the Book: Religious Perspectives on the Rights and Wrongs of Proselytism*. Maryknoll, NY: Orbis Books, 1999.

CHAPTER 13

Religious liberty, church autonomy, and the structure of freedom

Richard W. Garnett

We are used to thinking of religion – of religious belief and practice, ritual and worship, expression and profession – as an object of human rights laws; that is, as something that these laws protect, or at least aspire to protect. The leading human rights instruments confirm us in this entirely reasonable, if not quite complete, way of thinking. For example: "Everyone has the right to freedom of thought, conscience, and religion," the Universal Declaration of Human Rights (1948) proclaims, and political communities should "strive ... to promote respect for [this right]" and "to secure [its] universal and effective recognition and observance." Similarly, the European Convention on Human Rights (1950) declares that its signatories resolve to "secure [this right] to everyone within their jurisdiction." The Constitution of the United States, in typical fashion, frames the issue in terms of constraints on government, rather than charges to or aspirations for government, but it, too, puts religious liberty – the "free exercise" of religion – on the receiving end of the First Amendment's protection.

Provisions like these reflect a commitment – one that seems broadly shared today even if unevenly honored and imperfectly understood – to protecting the freedom of religion. It is one thing, though, to profess – even to entrench in law – such a commitment; it is another thing to operationalize or make good on that commitment. This latter, "walk the walk" task involves at least two related, but distinct, challenges. First, we need to identify the content of the "freedom of religion" that we are resolved to protect. This is easier said than done. "Everyone," we confidently and proudly declare, "has the right to freedom of religion," but what, exactly, are we talking about? What is "religion," anyway, and what does it mean for it to be "free"? Free from what? To do what? What does it mean to "have the right to freedom," of religion or anything else? What distinguishes "religious liberty" from plain-vanilla "liberty," and can this distinction be justified, assuming it can be captured in law? And so on.

Assume, for now, that we are able to find our way to plausible, attractive answers to these questions – answers that cohere with human nature, experiences, needs, and aspirations. With our "ends" in view, we turn next to the question of "means." We must decide, in other words, what are the legal and other mechanisms that we expect to sustain and vindicate, in practice, the commitment we have professed. Our hope, after all, is to erect more than what James Madison called "mere parchment barriers" to violations of religious freedom. Some mechanisms might be better (or less well) designed for the purpose and so might work better (or less well) than others; some actors and authorities might be more (or less) reliable and effective protectors than others. Our optimistic expectations for some processes might be unrealistic; our skepticism or even cynicism about others might be unfounded. The point is, the project of protecting human rights – including the right to religious freedom – involves reflecting on human goods and goals, but also wrestling with questions about institutional design and competence.

Now, with respect to the first challenge, it is easy to specify a few – though probably only a few – non-controversial, heartland propositions, around which we might build our understanding of the "freedom of religion." It would seem, for example, obviously to include, as the Supreme Court of the United States put it in *Employment Division* v. *Smith* (1990), "the right to believe and profess whatever religious doctrine one desires." Fair enough. But, what else? Skipping ahead to the second challenge, we would almost certainly point to judicially enforced, constitutionally entrenched constraints on government – constraints like those set out in the Bill of Rights – as a key means of translating our aspirations into practice. It is true, as Judge Learned Hand wisely warned, that "liberty lies in the hearts of men and women; when it dies there, no constitution, no law, no court can save it,"[1] but there is no need to deny that constitutions, laws, and courts are important to the effort. So far, so good. But again, what else? What other steps might we take, or tools might we use, to help religious liberty to flower, not only in the "hearts of men and women" but also in the rough-and-tumble world of scarcity, self-interest, compromise, and disagreement?

This chapter is an attempt to take on both of these challenges, that is, to consider both the content of religious freedom and the ways it is protected and promoted. I propose, first, that the "right to freedom of religion"

---

[1] Learned Hand, *The Spirit of Liberty: Papers and Addresses of Learned Hand* (New York: Knopf, 1952), 189–90.

belongs not only to individuals, but also to institutions, associations, communities, and congregations. Just as every person has the right to seek religious truth and to cling to it when it is found, religious communities have the right to hold and teach their own doctrines; just as every person ought to be free from official coercion when it comes to religious practices or professions, religious institutions are entitled to govern themselves, and to exercise appropriate authority, free from official interference; just as every person has the right to select the religious teachings he will embrace, churches have the right to select the ministers they will ordain. "Religion" is, Justice William Douglas observed in his *Wisconsin* v. *Yoder* (1972) dissenting opinion, "an individual experience," and it certainly is, but it is not only that. After all, as Justice William Brennan reminded us, in *Corporation of the Presiding Bishop* v. *Amos* (1987), "[f]or many individuals, religious activity derives meaning in large measure from participation in a larger religious community. Such a community represents an ongoing tradition of shared beliefs, an organic entity not reducible to a mere aggregation of individuals." Such "organic entities" are subjects, not just results or byproducts, of religious liberty. At the center of religious freedom, then, is what is called in American constitutional law "church autonomy," or what the American Jesuit and church-state scholar John Courtney Murray (and many others) called "the Freedom of the Church."[2]

This right to church autonomy – one dimension of religious freedom – is, again, an object of human rights law. It is also, however, a means – a structural mechanism – for protecting both the freedom of religion and human rights more generally. The relationship between the enterprise of protecting human rights and religious communities' right to self-determination is a dynamic, mutually reinforcing one. Human rights law, in other words, protects church autonomy – it protects the freedom of religious communities to govern and organize themselves, to decide religious matters without government interference, to establish their own criteria for membership, leadership, and orthodoxy, etc. – and, in turn, church autonomy promotes the enjoyment and exercise of human rights. This mechanism is, Murray thought, "Christianity's basic contribution to freedom in the political order."[3] If we understand and appreciate this contribution, we will better understand and appreciate that often misunderstood and misused idea, "the separation of church and state."

---

[2] John Courtney Murray, *We Hold These Truths: Catholic Reflections on the American Proposition* (Lanham, MD: Rowman & Littlefield Publishers, 2005), 186–90.
[3] *Ibid.*, 186.

THE CONTENT OF RELIGIOUS GROUP RIGHTS

Americans' thinking and talking about rights is thoroughly individualistic. Rights, we think, attach to particular people, and protect them, their privacy, their interests, and their autonomy from outside authorities. It should come as no surprise, therefore, that American judicial decisions and public conversations about religious freedom tend to focus on matters of individuals' rights, beliefs, consciences, and practices. However, as Mary Ann Glendon demonstrated almost twenty years ago in her compelling critique of American political discourse and of the legal regime that it reflects and produces, this focus is myopic and distorting.[4] It causes us to overlook and neglect the social context in which persons are situated and formed as well as the distinctive nature, role, and freedoms of groups, associations, and institutions. We make this mistake, it is worth noting, not only in the religious-liberty context. Frederick Schauer has shown that our law dealing with the freedom of expression, conscience, and belief has "been persistently reluctant to develop its principles in an institution-specific manner, and thus to take account of the cultural, political and economic differences among the differentiated institutions that together comprise a society."[5]

To be sure, the individual human person – every one – matters. He is "infinitely valuable, relentlessly unique, endlessly interesting."[6] Every person carries, in C. S. Lewis's words, the "Weight of Glory." "There are no ordinary people," he insisted:

You have never talked to a mere mortal. Nations, cultures, arts, civilizations – these are mortal, and their life is to ours as the life of a gnat. But it is immortals whom we joke with, work with, marry, snub, and exploit – immortal horrors or everlasting splendors.[7]

It is fitting, then, that the image of the lone religious dissenter, heroically confronting overbearing officials or extravagant assertions of state power, armed only with claims of conscience, is for us evocative and timeless. Think of St. Thomas More, as he is depicted in *A Man for All Seasons* (and perhaps also of those dissenters he helped to persecute). No account of

[4] Mary Ann Glendon, *Rights Talk: The Impoverishment of Political Discourse* (New York: Free Press 1991).
[5] Frederick Schauer, "Principles, Institutions, and the First Amendment," *Harvard Law Review* 112 (1998): 84, 110.
[6] Thomas L. Shaffer, "Human Nature and Moral Responsibility in Lawyer–Client Relationships," *American Journal of Jurisprudence* 40 (1995): 1, 2.
[7] C. S. Lewis, *The Weight of Glory and Other Addresses*, rev. edn, ed. Walter Hooper (New York: Macmillan Publishing Co., 1980), 19.

religious freedom would be complete if it neglected such clashes or failed to celebrate such courage.

Still, Glendon was right. Something goes missing when the freedom of religion is reduced to the individual's liberty of conscience, to her freedom of belief, or even to her right to engage in worship or religiously motivated action. A legal regime of human rights that is designed to protect only this reduced notion of religious freedom will leave vulnerable and unprotected important aspects of that freedom. Such a regime will misfire because it describes and categorizes the world in an incomplete and perhaps even distorted way, passing over and leaving out things that matter. We should want our laws – and perhaps especially our human rights laws – to capture faithfully what is significant, and what really matters, about the real world that these laws govern and to which they speak. We should want, in other words, our human rights laws to "see," and so to respect and protect, the freedom that belongs rightfully to religious groups, associations, institutions, and communities.

What is this freedom, then, that complements and helps to sustain individuals' enjoyment of their rights to religious liberty? It makes sense to begin by returning to the basic proposition that, in Murray's words, the Constitution guarantees religious freedom not only to individual believers but also "to the Church as an organized society with its own law and jurisdiction."[8] What the United States Supreme Court has called "ecclesiastical right[s],"[9] no less than individuals' rights, are protected by the First Amendment, as well as by other human rights instruments. These rights are not – at least, they should not be regarded as – merely derivative of or proxies for individuals' rights; their protection is not simply a vehicle for securing individuals' liberties.[10]

It should be emphasized, also, that the American Constitution's protections for "ecclesiastical rights" are not idiosyncratic or anomalous. That religious freedom has a communal, corporate aspect, and includes a right to autonomy and self-determination for religious communities, is acknowledged in many other nations' domestic laws and in international human rights litigation, decisions, and instruments.[11] In fact, it seems – for

---

[8]   Murray, *We Hold These Truths*, 80.

[9]   *Kedroff v. St. Nicholas Cathedral*, 344 US 94, 119 (1952).

[10]   Brett Scharffs has noted, however, that – at least in the context of the European Court of Human Rights – "religious institutions still do not have standing in their own rights, but only as an aggregation of the rights of their members." Brett G. Scharffs, "The Autonomy of Church and State," *Brigham Young University Law Review* (2004): 1217, 1277–8.

[11]   See generally, for example, Gerhard Robbers, ed., *Church Autonomy: A Comparative Survey* (Frankfurt am Main: Peter Lang, 2001). As John Witte has observed, the principle of "religious

a number of historical, cultural, and philosophical reasons – that the church-autonomy principle sits more easily in European law and practice than in their American counterparts.

Like the human rights project generally, lawyers' thinking about and legal protection for religious communities' rights have been shaped heavily by Christianity, and by Christian claims about the person, the church, and the state. Of particular interest is the landmark *Declaration on Religious Freedom*, which Pope Paul VI promulgated at the close of the Second Vatican Council and which famously affirmed the right of the human person to worship in accord with his or her conscience. The Declaration opened with the powerful proposal that "[t]he right to religious freedom has its foundation in the very dignity of the human person," not "in the subjective disposition of the person but in his very nature."[12] That is, attached to our "very nature" is the desire – and responsibility – of persons to seek, find, and adhere to the truth and, at the same time, a moral immunity from external coercion in matters of religious conscience. James Madison, in his famous *Memorial and Remonstrance Against Religious Assessments* (1785), advanced a similar claim.

The Declaration did not stop, though, with an affirmation of the freedom of religious conscience, understood as immunity for individuals from external coercion. Nor did it stop with the insistence – though it did insist – that individuals have a right to associate for religious purposes and to express their religious beliefs in community through worship and otherwise. The claim was stronger: "Religious communities," the document contends, "are a requirement of the social nature both of man and of religion itself." And, these communities "rightfully claim freedom in order that they may govern themselves according to their own norms, honor the Supreme Being in public worship, assist their members in the practice of the religious life, strengthen them by instruction, and promote institutions whereby they may join together for the purpose of ordering their lives in accordance with their religious principles." They "also have the right not to be hindered [by law] in the selection, training, appointment, and transferal of their own ministers, in communicating with religious authorities and communities abroad, in erecting buildings for religious purposes, and in the acquisition and use of suitable funds or properties."[13] It is not – to

group rights" has "long been recognized as a basic norm of international law." "Introduction: The Foundations and Frontiers of Religious Liberty," *Emory International Law Review* 21 (2007): 1, 9. See further chapters by T. Jeremy Gunn and Kent Greenawalt herein.

[12] Pope Paul VI, *Declaration on Religious Freedom* (*Dignitatis Humanae*) ¶2 (1965). See further the chapter by Bryan Hehir herein.

[13] *Dignitatis Humanae* ¶4.

underscore the point – simply that religious faith and experience have a communal dimension. The freedom to be enjoyed by religious communities is not defended merely as an incident of individuals' religious exercise, but as these communities' moral right, a right that is rooted – as the right to religious freedom more generally is rooted – in the dignity of the person and in God's plan for the world.

So, the law of human rights, in the United States and elsewhere, recognizes and protects the appropriate exercise of religious authority, the autonomy of religious institutions, and the right to self-determination of religious communities. It is not entirely settled what exactly are the content and textual home in the American Constitution for the church autonomy principle, but it nevertheless seems clear that the freedom of religion which the Constitution protects is enjoyed by institutions as well as individuals. What, then, is the specific content of this protection? What, exactly, is "church autonomy," and what does it mean, "on the ground" and in practical terms, for a religious community to have the "right to self-determination"? Gerard Bradley has argued that "church autonomy" is the "flagship issue of church and state," the "litmus test of a regime's commitment to genuine spiritual freedom."[14] What would a regime hoping to pass this "test," and accord appropriate significance to this "flagship issue," need to do, or refrain from doing?

The church autonomy principle is at least potentially implicated in a wide variety of disputes and contexts: the supervision of diocesan finances by a bankruptcy court or administrative agency, a requirement that religiously affiliated organizations pay for employees' contraception or that doctors in religiously affiliated hospitals perform abortions, litigation regarding church discipline proceedings or membership requirements, the division of church property after a schism or split, the application of non-discrimination laws to churches' and religious schools' decisions about the hiring and firing of clergy and teachers, and efforts by governments to control or regulate churches' selection of their leaders, to mention just a few. The principle is probably not reducible to any single "test," though there would seem to be several non-controversial, core propositions around which a broader right to self-determination can be constructed. (Recall the litany of specific applications, mentioned earlier, in the *Declaration on Religious Liberty*.) In many ways, the church-autonomy "doctrine" is less a rule than a grab-bag of holdings, or a collection of themes, animated

---

[14] Gerard V. Bradley, "Forum Juridicum: Church Autonomy in the Constitutional Order," *Louisiana Law Review* 49 (1987): 1057, 1061.

by a "spirit of freedom for religious organizations."[15] We know that the First Amendment does not permit state action that creates or requires "excessive entanglement" between the government and religious institutions, practices, teachings, and decisions.[16] It commands that the "secular and religious authorities … not interfere with each other's respective spheres of choice and influence."[17] The Justices have refused to "undertake to resolve [religious] controversies" because "the hazards are ever present of inhibiting the free development of religious doctrine and of implicating secular interests in matters of purely ecclesiastical concern."[18] The Supreme Court has affirmed, time and again, the "fundamental right of churches to 'decide for themselves, free from state interference, matters of church government as well as those of faith and doctrine'."[19] And so on.

In Bradley's view, "church autonomy" means "the issue that arises when legal principles displace religious communities' internal rules of interpersonal relations." The principle has been said to preclude "civil court review" of "internal church disputes involving matters of faith, doctrine, church governance, and polity."[20] And Justice Brennan (following Douglas Laycock) put the matter in a particularly helpful way, observing that religious organizations' "autonomy in ordering their internal affairs" includes the freedom to "select their own leaders, define their own doctrines, resolve their own disputes, and run their own institution."[21] This formulation captures nicely a wide and reasonably complete range of the challenges to religious institutions' freedom and of the circumstances in which they arise.

THE MEANS OF PROTECTING RELIGIOUS GROUP RIGHTS

I suggested earlier that following through on a stated commitment to the freedom of religion requires thinking both about the content of that

---

[15] Kedroff, 344 US at 116.
[16] *Lemon* v. *Kurtzman*, 403 US 602, 613–14 (1971).
[17] Laurence H. Tribe, *American Constitutional Law*, 2nd edn (Mineola, NY: Foundation Press, 1988), §§14–12, at 1226.
[18] *Presbyterian Church* v. *Mary Elizabeth Blue Hull Mem'l Presbyterian Church*, 393 US 440, 449 (1969).
[19] *EEOC* v. *Catholic Univ. of America*, 83 F.3d 455, 462 (D.C. Cir. 1996) (quoting Kedroff, 344 US at 116).
[20] *Bryce* v. *Episcopal Church in the Diocese of Colorado*, 289 F.3d 648, 655 (10th Cir. 2002).
[21] *Corp. of Presiding Bishop* v. *Amos*, 483 US 327, 341–2 (1987) (Brennan, J., concurring) (quoting Douglas Laycock, "Towards a General Theory of the Religion Clauses: The Case of Church–Labor Relations and the Right to Church Autonomy," *Columbia Law Review* 81 [1981]: 1373, 1389).

freedom – about, in other words, what it is we are committed to protecting – and about the means and mechanisms to be employed. So far, I have tried to make the case that the "freedom of religion" has a communal, corporate, public dimension, as well as a private one. It is enjoyed by and safeguards the rights of institutions as well as individuals. How can this freedom, so understood, effectively be preserved and promoted?

One way is obvious (especially to lawyers): today, most well-functioning political communities both express and advance their commitments to fundamental human rights, including the right to religious liberty, by "entrenching" these rights in their constitutions – thereby putting them, at least to some extent, beyond the reach of ordinary politics – and by authorizing courts to declare invalid the actions of governments and officials that invade these rights.[22] Certainly, as was noted at the outset of this chapter, this approach is reflected in the Constitution of the United States, as well as in other nations' constitutions and in foundational international human rights instruments. The *Declaration on Religious Freedom* also highlighted the importance of "constitutional limits on the powers of government, in order that there may be no encroachment on the rightful freedom of the person and of associations." It is good advice to "put not our trust in princes," but it nevertheless makes sense to enlist the political authority, including its judicial arm, in the work of protecting human rights.

It takes nothing away from the importance of constitutionally entrenched and judicially enforceable human rights provisions to propose that other, complementary, structural mechanisms are helpful, even necessary, to ensure that religious freedom flourishes. We protect human rights not only by listing various things that governments may not do, but also by designing and situating governments in such a way that they are less likely, and less able, to do such things. Constitutionalism is about more than composing a litany of aspirations; it is also the enterprise of ordering our lives together and promoting the common good by categorizing, separating, structuring, and limiting power in entrenched and enforceable ways.

The United States Constitution provides a helpful illustration. As (we should hope) every law student learns, and as Madison famously explained in *The Federalist*, those who designed and ratified the Constitution believed that political liberties are best served through competition and cooperation among plural authorities and jurisdictions, and through structures

---

[22] Michael J. Perry, *Constitutional Rights, Moral Controversy, and the Supreme Court* (Cambridge and New York: Cambridge University Press, 2009), 23–30.

and mechanisms that check, diffuse, and divide power. The United States Constitution is more than a catalogue of rights; our constitutional law is, in the end, "the law governing the structure of, and the allocation of authority among, the various institutions of the national government."[23] The US constitutional experiment reflects, among other things, the belief that the structure of government matters for, and contributes to, the good of human persons. There is no need to belabor even a point as fundamental as this one: "The genius of the American Constitution" – of American *constitutionalism* – "lies in its use of structural devices to preserve individual liberty."[24]

In the earlier discussion of "church autonomy," I said that included in the freedom of religion – in the content of the human right to which we are committed and that we aim to protect – is the right of religious institutions to govern themselves and to exercise appropriate authority without interference from governments. This right, no less than the immunity of individuals' religious conscience from coercion, reflects and is rooted in the dignity of the human person, which is the foundation for the morality of human rights more generally. Add now to this claim another one, namely, that church autonomy is – like federalism, like the separation of powers, like "checks and balances" – a structural principle, whose operation enables self-determining religious communities to play a structural role. These communities are protected, but also protectors; they enjoy and exercise religious freedom rights for themselves, but also – through that enjoyment and exercise – contribute to the enjoyment and exercise of these rights by others. This is true today, and has been true for a millennium.

Not many today know much about an eleventh-century monk named Hildebrand, who eventually reigned as Pope Gregory VII. However, the three days in late January 1077, when the excommunicated German emperor, Henry IV, stood barefoot in the snow doing penance outside the castle at Canossa of Countess Matilda of Tuscany, are as important to the development of Western constitutionalism as the later events at Runnymede, or Philadelphia. Hildebrand led a "revolution" that, as the great legal scholar Harold Berman described, worked nothing less than a "total transformation" of law, state, and society.[25] The battle cry for

---

[23] Gary Lawson, "Prolegomenon to Any Future Administrative Law Course: Separation of Powers and the Transcendental Deduction," *St. Louis University Law Journal* 49 (2005): 885.
[24] Steven G. Calabresi and Kevin H. Rhodes, "The Structural Constitution: Unitary Executive, Plural Judiciary," *Harvard Law Review* 105 (1992): 1153, 1155.
[25] Harold J. Berman, *Law and Revolution: The Formation of the Western Legal Tradition* (Cambridge, MA: Harvard University Press, 1983), 23.

this papal revolution – the idea that would serve as the catalyst for what Berman regarded as "the first major turning point in European history" and as the foundation for nearly a millennium of political theory – was *libertas ecclesiae*, the "freedom of the church."[26]

It is, of course, beyond the scope of this chapter to provide a comprehensive account of the Investiture Crisis, the Papal Revolution, and their aftermath. For present purposes, though, a quick sketch will do. We should begin with what was, as Robert Wilken has observed, a "capital fact of ecclesiastical life in the early Middle Ages … [namely,] that the affairs of the church were managed by kings and princes."[27] These authorities – it is probably anachronistic to call them "secular," given the way we use that word today – did not think of themselves as reaching across a boundary between "religion" and "politics." The emperor would have assumed that the care of Christians' souls and the good functioning of Christ's Church fitted comfortably in his God-given portfolio. Nevertheless, it was this "fact" that was the target of Hildebrand's ambitious revolution. Building on but moving well beyond a century of reform efforts and attacks on corruption, Pope Gregory VII issued in 1075 a ringing, harsh condemnation of secular control over the selection and investiture of bishops. The emperor, Henry IV, was unmoved, to say the least, by the pope's claims and legal arguments, and responded, "I, Henry, king by the grace of God, do say unto you, together with all of our bishops: Go down, go down, to be damned throughout the ages."[28]

The dramatic confrontation at Canossa that followed, after Henry's excommunication, was hardly the end of the matter. The Wars of Investiture soon broke out, and raged for several decades; Henry eventually appointed a pope of his own; and Gregory died in exile, quoting the Psalmist and lamenting, "I have loved justice, and hated iniquity; for that reason I die in exile." The Concordat of Worms, in 1122, calmed things for a time, and represented a kind of compromise; it was a compromise, though, out of which emerged "Western political science – and especially the first modern Western theories of the state and secular law."[29] As George Weigel has put it:

Had the emperors succeeded in making the Church an administrative and spiritual subdivision of the empire, more would have been lost than the *libertas*

[26] *Ibid.*, 87.
[27] Robert Louis Wilken, "Gregory VII and the Politics of the Spirit," in Richard J. Neuhaus, ed., *The Second One Thousand Years: Ten People Who Defined a Millennium* (Grand Rapids, MI: Wm. B. Eerdmans, 2001), 6.
[28] Berman, *Law and Revolution*, 96.
[29] *Ibid.*, 111.

ecclesiae, the capacity of the Church to order its own internal life. The possibility of institutional pluralism in the West might have been lost or, at the very least, delayed.[30]

It takes nothing away from the "revolutionary" character of Gregory VII's claims and achievements to recall that their animating proposition – the "freedom of the church" – was not his own invention. In the year 494, for example, Pope Gelasius had written to the Byzantine emperor Anastasius I, insisting, "[t]wo there are, august Emperor, by which this world is ruled on title of original and sovereign right – the consecrated authority of the priesthood and the royal power."[31] Nor should we think that the idea's importance is diminished by the fact that, just under one hundred years after the pope's challenge to Henry IV, King Henry II and Thomas Becket clashed in England after the former reclaimed royal supremacy over the church, or by the obvious challenges posed to Hildebrand's vision by the Protestant Reformation, the Peace of Augsburg, the French Revolution, and nineteenth-century anti-clericalism.

"Well," we might ask, "so what?" What is the relevance of medieval clashes between ambitious emperors and popes to contemporary conversations about religious liberty or to the present-day enterprise of protecting human rights through law? Just this: the Investiture Crisis, and Pope Gregory VII's aggressive, expansive account of the "freedom of the church," illustrate the crucial connections between pluralism and constitutionalism, between the autonomy of religious institutions and the rights of individuals. John Courtney Murray explored and emphasized these connections with care, and his thinking is reflected in the *Declaration on Religious Liberty*. In his view, we are not really free – none of us, whether a religious believer or not, is really free – if "[our] basic human things are not sacredly immune from profanation by the power of the state." The challenge, then, is and has long been to find the limiting principle that can "check the encroachments of civil power and preserve these immunities." And, he thought, "Western civilization first found this norm in the pregnant principle, the freedom of the Church." This principle supplied, in other words, what Murray called the "new Christian theorem," namely,

---

[30] George Weigel, *The Cube and the Cathedral: Europe, America, and Politics Without God* (New York: Basic Books, 2005), 100.
[31] The text of this letter is available through the Internet Medieval Source Book, at: www.fordham.edu/halsall/source/gelasius1.html. John Witte has described this "two powers" passage as "a locus classicus for many later theories of a basic separation between pope and emperor, clergy and laity, regnum and sacerdotium." *Religion and the American Constitutional Experiment*, 2nd edn (Boulder, CO: Westview Press, 2005), 6.

that the church "stood between the body politic and the public power, not only limiting the reach of the power over the people, but also mobilizing the moral consensus of the people and bringing it to bear upon the power." For Murray, it was the freedom of the church that furnished a "social armature to the sacred order," within which the human person could be "secure in all the freedoms that his sacredness demands."[32] He believed that "the protection of ... aspects of life from the inherently expansive power of the state ... depended historically on the freedom of the Church as an independent spiritual authority."[33]

SEPARATION OF CHURCH AND STATE

It might seem strange at first, but constitutionalism depends for its success on the existence and activities of non-state authorities. It should protect, but it also requires, self-governing religious communities that operate and evolve outside and independent of governments. It is a mistake, then, to regard "religion" merely as a private practice, or even as a social phenomenon, to which constitutions respond or react. Instead, we should understand the ongoing enterprise of constitutionalism as one to which religious freedom contributes. Human rights depend for protection and flourishing not only on enforceable constraints on government but also on the structure of the social order. The autonomy that religious institutions enjoy, with respect to matters of polity, doctrine, leadership, and membership contributes to, even as it benefits from, that structure.

All of this goes to show how it is that the "separation of church and state" in fact supports – as many strongly believe but just as many forcefully deny – the freedom of religion. Of course, in contemporary public debates, "separation" is often regarded, both by its opponents and many of its self-styled defenders, as a policy that mandates a public square scrubbed clean of religious symbols, expression, and activism. It is thought, or feared, that the separation of church and state requires religious believers to keep their faith strictly private and to wall off their religious commitments from their public lives and arguments about how we ought to order society. On this view, separation serves the enterprise of human rights protection, if at all, by constraining religious believers and institutions, and by reducing the potential for social conflict and persecution.

---

[32] Murray, *We Hold These Truths*, 204–5.
[33] Francis Canavan, S.J., "Religious Freedom: John Courtney Murray and Vatican II," *Faith and Reason* 8 (1987), reprinted in Robert P. Hunt and Kenneth L. Grasso, eds., *John Courtney Murray and the American Civil Conversation* (Grand Rapids, MI: Wm. B. Eerdmans, 1992), 167–80.

There is, however, another, better view: the "separation of church and state", properly understood, is a structural arrangement in which the institutions of religion are distinct from, other than, and meaningfully independent of the institutions of government. It is a principle of pluralism, of multiple and overlapping authorities, of competing loyalties and demands. It is a rule that limits the state and thereby clears out and protects a social space, within which persons are formed and educated, and without which religious liberty is vulnerable. So understood, "separation" is not an anti-religious ideology, but an important component of any worthy account of religious freedom under and through constitutionally limited government. "Fundamental to Christianity," Pope Benedict XVI recently reaffirmed, "is the distinction between what belongs to Caesar and what belongs to God ... in other words, the distinction between Church and State."[34] In a similar vein, he has emphasized that it was Christianity that "brought the idea of the separation of Church and state into the world. Until then the political constitution and religion were always united. It was the norm in all cultures for the state to have sacrality in itself and be the supreme protector of sacrality." Christianity, however, "deprived the state of its sacral nature ... In this sense," he has insisted, "separation is ultimately a primordial Christian legacy."[35]

CONCLUSIONS

Churches and other religious communities enjoy, as they should, a broad freedom to organize, govern, and direct themselves and their affairs, in accord with their own teachings and doctrines. I have suggested that this freedom not only benefits from, but also contributes to, the enterprises of human rights law and of constitutionalism more generally. That said, there is no avoiding the fact that church autonomy principles and premises are vulnerable and, in some contexts, under attack. The right clearly exists, but its scope and foundations are, increasingly, contested.

This vulnerability is connected, no doubt, to the link that is sometimes asserted and that many perceive between church autonomy principles, on the one hand, and, on the other, sexual abuse and corrupt activity by clergy, venality and mismanagement by bishops, and dioceses' declarations of bankruptcy. It is common for the critics of religious communities' self-

---

[34] Pope Benedict XVI, *Deus Caritas Est* 28(a) (2005).
[35] Joseph Ratzinger, *The Salt of the Earth: The Church at the End of the Millennium* (San Francisco: Ignatius Press, 1997), 238, 240.

determination rights to misunderstand these rights, and the church autonomy principle, as entailing the implausible and unattractive assertion that churches and clergy are somehow "above the law," entirely unaccountable for wrongs they do or harms they cause. In addition, the freedom of religious associations, communities, and institutions is made more precarious by the limited and dwindling appeal in contemporary discourse of the very idea of religious "authority." To the extent the church autonomy principle is thought to privilege institutions over individuals, or structures over believers, its purchase diminishes, given that people today tend to think about faith – and, by extension, about religious freedom – more in terms of personal spirituality than of institutional affiliation, public worship, and tradition. To the extent we approach religious faith as a form of self-expression, performance, or therapy, we are likely to regard religious institutions as, at best, potentially useful vehicles or, more likely, stifling constraints and bothersome obstacles to self-discovery. This, however, would be a mistake.

RECOMMENDED READING

Berman, Harold J. *Law and Revolution: The Formation of the Western Legal Tradition.* Cambridge, MA: Harvard University Press, 1983.

Bradley, Gerard V. "Forum Juridicum: Church Autonomy in the Constitutional Order," *Louisiana Law Review* 49 (1987): 1057–87.

Chopko, Mark E. and Michael F. Moses. "The Freedom to be a Church: Continuing Challenges to the Right of Church Autonomy," *Georgetown Journal of Law & Public Policy* 3 (2005): 387–452.

Garnett, Richard W. "The Freedom of the Church," *Journal of Catholic Social Thought* 4 (2007): 59–86.

"Do Churches Matter? Toward an Institutional Understanding of the Religion Clauses," *Villanova Law Review* 53 (2008): 273–96.

"The Story of Henry Adams's Soul: Education and the Expression of Associations," *Minnesota Law Review* 85 (2001): 1841–84.

Glendon, Mary Ann. *Rights Talk: The Impoverishment of Political Discourse.* New York: Free Press, 1991.

Laycock, Douglas. "Towards a General Theory of the Religion Clauses: The Case of Church–Labor Relations and the Right to Church Autonomy," *Columbia Law Review* 81 (1981): 1373–417.

Maritain, Jacques. *Man and the State.* Chicago: University of Chicago Press, 1951.

Murray, John Courtney. *We Hold These Truths: Catholic Reflections on the American Proposition.* Lanham, MD: Rowman & Littlefield Publishers, 2005.

Robbers, Gerhard, ed. *Church Autonomy: A Comparative Survey.* Frankfurt am Main: Peter Lang, 2001.

Scharffs, Brett G. "The Autonomy of Church and State," *Brigham Young Law Review* (2004): 1217–348.

Serritella, James A. *et al.*, eds. *Religious Organizations in the United States: A Study of Identity, Liberty, and Law.* Durham, NC: Carolina Academic Press, 2006.

Tierney, Brian. *The Crisis of Church and State: 1050–1300.* Englewood Cliffs, NJ: Prentice-Hall, 1964.

CHAPTER 14

Christianity and the rights of children: an integrative view

† Don S. Browning

I address two questions in this chapter: how should we conceptualize and ground the rights of children, especially with reference to the rights of parents? And what can Christianity contribute to an adequate answer to the first question? I primarily address what should be law's *prima facie* answer to these questions. I also show why Christianity, and the tradition of natural law which it carries, emphasizes yet also relativizes the biological relatedness and marriage of a child's parents as central to children's rights – both legal and religious. This suggests that law and religion should cooperate in guiding adults to exercise their reproductive rights in ways that guarantee that children will be raised by the parents who conceive them and that this happens within a legally institutionalized marriage.

I argue for an integrative view of children's rights. This perspective is only slightly visible in contemporary family-law theory in the United States. It is more prominent, however, in the major documents of the international human rights tradition, especially the 1948 Universal Declaration of Human Rights (UDHR) and the 1989 United Nations Convention on the Rights of the Child (UNCRC), as well as the deeper intellectual tradition, significantly influenced by Christianity, that fed these statements. This tradition has held that natural parents have the *prima facie* right to raise their own offspring and that children have a right to be raised by the parents who conceive them, unless there are contingencies that make this impossible or negative for the well-being of the child.

The integrative tradition was central to most Western family law long before it influenced these modern human rights documents. It began with the later Plato and Aristotle, was fed by the doctrine of creation in Judaism and Christianity, appeared in later patristic theory, got synthesized first in Ulpian's natural-law theory in Roman law then in the moral theology of Thomas Aquinas, and was later transmitted to secular family law during the early years of the Protestant Reformation. This tradition was revived in Roman Catholic social teachings in the late nineteenth and early twentieth centuries, and was mediated by Charles Malik and Jacques Maritain to the committee that wrote the UDHR.

In contrast to the integrative tradition that held marriage and reproduction together, much modern family-law theory in America and elsewhere promotes what is commonly called the adult right of "private ordering." This is defined as the right of adults to organize their intimate lives as they see fit without the guidance of law or the governance of the state. This private ordering ethic includes the right of adults to conceive and raise children as they wish so long as no direct harm is done.[1] This ethic, and the forces of modernization that have inspired it, have introduced a variety of separations into the modern domestic sphere – separations between marriage and sexual intercourse, marriage and childbirth, marriage and child rearing, childbirth and parenting, and (with the advent of assisted reproductive technologies) childbirth from sexual intercourse and biological filiation. Many sociologists and legal scholars hold that the separations born of these modernizing forces are both inevitable and mostly benign; rather than resisting them, they claim that law and public policy should accommodate and try to order the consequences. In this chapter, I suggest otherwise, and call for a renewal of the integrative tradition that emphasized law's obligation intentionally to channel, in cooperation with other institutions, adult behavior to conform to the normative requirements of the legal marriage that in the past has regulated procreation, parenthood, and children's rights.

THIN VIEWS OF THE CHILD'S RIGHTS

The idea of the rights of the child, in recent legal theory, often correctly includes the right to basic nurturance and physical care or, at other times, the child's right to economic and social capital.[2] A powerful legal trend, however, has narrowed the child's rights and best interests to a thin and one-dimensional affective intersubjective relationship. This is especially true, as we will later see, in the American Law Institute's (ALI) report on reforming family law, entitled *Principles of the Law of Family Dissolution* (2002).[3] In this influential document, there is a strong emphasis on the

---

[1] Martha Ertman, "Private Ordering under the ALI *Principles*: As Natural as Status," in Robin Wilson, ed., *Reconceiving the Family: Critique of the American Law Institute's Principles of the Law of Family Dissolution* (Cambridge: Cambridge University Press, 2006), 284.

[2] James Coleman, "Social Capital and the Creation of Human Capital," *American Journal of Sociology* 94 (1988): 95–120.

[3] *Principles of the Law of Family Dissolution: Analysis and Recommendations* (Newark, NJ: Matthew Bender & Co., 2002).

child's need for and right to continuity of relationships in the midst of the multiple separations in the sexual field that I listed above. In some custody disputes, the ALI emphasis on defining the child's rights as a continuity of relationships leads courts to give visitation rights to long-term caregivers not related to the child by biology or marriage. Sometimes legal parent-hood is granted to third-party caregivers, thereby providing the child with three or more parents. I argue that the modern legal movement in this direction overlooks other crucial institutional, cultural, and biological factors deserving consideration in determining the rights of children.

I believe that family law should be guided, in both family formation and dissolution, by a thick multi-dimensional model of the rights and needs of the child. The rights of the child should entail simultaneously working to actualize the basic goods (sometimes called the premoral goods) needed for the child's flourishing and respecting the child's emerging per-sonhood. This view is both Aristotelian in valuing the teleological goods required for healthy development and Kantian in its emphasis on respect for the child. Both views found their place amidst the thick perspective on human action found in Christian jurisprudence, even though respect for the person of the child was grounded in the theological narrative that all children are born children of God and should be valued as extensions of the divine goodness.

THE RIGHTS OF CHILDREN IN UNCRC AND THE UDHR

Contemporary American family law has overlooked how the inte-grative tradition helped define the rights of the child in modern inter-national human rights law. The 1989 UN Convention on the Rights of the Child (UNCRC) is considered the definitive international document on children's rights. It was profoundly influenced by the 1948 Universal Declaration of Human Rights (UDHR). There is, however, a poorly understood Christian tradition that shaped both the UDHR and the UNCRC that also functioned with a more multi-dimensional view of the rights of children than can be found in most of contemporary American legal theory.

The UDHR spends much of its space on the rights of the family, rather than the rights of individual parents. It firmly establishes the priority of family rights and responsibilities when it states in Article 16.3: "The fam-ily is the natural and fundamental group unit of society and is entitled to protection by society and the State." This statement became a mantra in subsequent human rights statements. It can be found in Article 10 of the International Covenant on Economic, Social, and Cultural Rights (1966) and Article 23.1 of the International Covenant on Civil and Political Rights (1966).[4] But what does it mean, and what is its broader historical context?

The UDHR was significantly influenced by the Christian integrative tradition.[5] Charles Malik, the highly influential and articulate Lebanese Christian philosopher and statesman, was the source of the Declaration's emphasis on the family as the "natural and fundamental group unit of society." Originally, he hoped to insert the sentences: "The family deriving from marriage is the natural and fundamental group unit of society. It is endowed by the Creator with inalienable rights antecedent to all positive law and as such shall be protected by the State and Society."[6] Malik believed that the words "natural" and "endowed by the Creator" assured that the marriage-based family would be seen as endowed by its own "inalienable rights" and not viewed as a human invention subject to the caprice of either the state or current public opinion.[7] In this formulation, he preserved several important ideas: the priority of the rights of natural parents, the importance of marriage-based parenthood, the *prima facie* rights of children to be raised by their natural parents, and a larger narrative about God's good creation that sanctioned and stabilized these values.

Two of these values were lost in the final formulation in the UDHR – the importance of marriage-based parenthood and reference to the religious narrative historically used to support this institution. Malik was able, however, to retain the emphasis on the "family as the natural and fundamental group unit of society," and this phrase influenced statements about both parental and children's rights in the UNCRC. It asserted that it was the role of the state to protect the family and the respective rights of children and parents. It also implied that the state did not create the family and the rights of parents and children; the family has preexisting rights resident in its very nature.

NATURAL LAW AND KIN INVESTMENT

Malik's formulation suggests that natural parents, on average, show more investment in their children than the state or other parental substitutes.

---

[4] Ian Brownlie, *Basic Documents on Human Rights* (Oxford: Clarendon Press, 1992), 125.
[5] *Ibid.*
[6] Johannes Morsink, *The Universal Declaration of Human Rights: Origins, Drafting, and Intent* (Philadelphia: University of Pennsylvania Press, 1999), 254.
[7] *Ibid.*, 255.

It also maintained the rights of children in principle to be raised by those most likely to be invested in their well-being – the individuals who conceive them. This line of thinking drew not only on Roman Catholic social teachings but also on the ancient theory of kin altruism. Aristotle provided much of the naturalistic and philosophical language for the centrality of kin altruism in the family theory of Western philosophy, law, and religion. Aristotle's arguments also influenced the powerful theory of subsidiarity that constituted the philosophical core of Roman Catholic social teachings on the relation of family and state.

Aristotle had considerable insight into what evolutionary psychologists today call "kin altruism" – our tendency to invest more in those with whom we are biologically related. In his *Politics*, Aristotle wrote: "In common with other animals and with plants, mankind have a natural desire to leave behind them an image of themselves."[8] With this in mind, Aristotle rejected Plato's idea in the *Republic* that civic health would be improved if competing nepotistic families were undermined by removing children from their procreating parents and raising them in anonymity with nurses appointed by the state.[9] Aristotle believed that if the state separated natural parents from their offspring, parental love would become "watery" and diluted. The energy that fueled parental care would be lost.[10] Violence would grow because the inhibiting factor of consanguinity would be removed. From the perspective of the developing child, Aristotle believed that the family is more fundamental than the state.[11] Aristotle was an early champion of the UDHR's assertion that the family is the basic group unit of society.

This Aristotelian idea appeared again in the natural law thinking of Ulpian, the great third-century Roman jurist who influenced much of subsequent Western secular and religious law. He once wrote, "Natural right is that which nature has taught all animals."[12] To illustrate the natural inclinations humans share with other animals, Ulpian referred to the sexual union of male and female and the natural tendency of parents to care for their offspring. A millennium later, the Roman Catholic theologian Thomas Aquinas synthesized the thinking of Aristotle and Ulpian with his theology of creation. He stated the role of this natural kin altruism

[8] Aristotle, *Politics*, in *The Basic Works of Aristotle* (New York: Random House, 1941), bk. I, ii.
[9] Plato, *The Republic* (New York: Basic Books, 1968), bk. V, par. 462.
[10] Aristotle, *Politics*, bk. II, iv.
[11] *Ibid.*, bk. I, ii.
[12] Justinian, *Justinian's Institutes*, trans. and ed. Peter Birks and Grant McLeod (Ithaca: Cornell University Press, 1987), bk. I, 1.2.

in family formation and marriage with a double language that was simultaneously bio-philosophical and religious. His bio-philosophical view was informed by Aristotle and Ulpian and the religious language principally came from Genesis and New Testament commentary on Genesis.[13] Aquinas's full argument about the grounds of parental care was not solely dependent on the Bible. The religious language functioned to stabilize insights gained from natural observation and philosophical arguments, a point legal scholars should observe before rejecting Christian arguments as dogmatic, arbitrary, and unfit for grounding human rights.

Aquinas's naturalistic view of parenthood recognized that human mothers attach more easily to their infants because they carry them for months and expend enormous energy in giving birth to them. Human males attach to offspring because the long and burdensome period of human infant dependency makes human mothers turn to their male consorts for help.[14] Men are more likely to attach to their infants if they have a degree of certainty that the infant is actually theirs and therefore continuous with their own biological existence.[15] Aquinas also believed human males attach to their offspring because of the mutual assistance and sexual exchange they receive from the infant's mother. We should notice that these natural conditions listed by Aquinas almost perfectly parallel those now held in the field of evolutionary psychology to have led humans, in contrast to most other mammals, to form long-term attachments between fathers and mothers for the care of their infants and children.[16]

The narratives that constitute the Christian idea that marriage is a sacrament or covenant should be understood as building on and consolidating these classic Aristotelian–Ulpianic–Thomistic understandings of the natural factors that go into family and marital formation. But this tradition never held that the inclinations of nature were sufficient in themselves to

---

[13] Thomas Aquinas, "Supplement," *Summa Theologica* III (London: T. & T. Washbourne, 1917), q. 42, A. 3.

[14] *Ibid.*, q. 41, A. 1.   [15] *Ibid.*

[16] For a summary of these four conditions as they can be found in the literature of evolutionary psychology, see Don Browning *et al.*, *From Culture Wars to Common Ground: Religion and the American Family Debate*, 2nd edn (Louisville, KY: Westminster John Knox Press, 2000), 111–13. See also Don Browning, *Marriage and Modernization: How Globalization Threatens Marriage and What to Do about It* (Grand Rapids, MI: Wm. B. Eerdmans, 2003), 109–11. For a quick summary by the leading evolutionary psychologists, see Martin Daly and Margo Wilson, "The Evolutionary Psychology of Marriage and Divorce," in Linda J. Waite, ed., *The Ties that Bind* (New York: Aldine de Gruyter, 2000), 91–110. For a more directly biological account as to why biological fathers are more sensitive to the emotional cues of their offspring in contrast to non-biological offspring, due to hormonal reactions in the biological fathers, see A. S. Fleming *et al.*, "Testosterone and Prolactin are Associated with Emotional Responses to Infant Cries in New Fathers," *Hormones and Behavior* 42 (2002): 399–413.

produce long-term commitment between parents and their children. This is why Malik wanted to support the idea of the family as the natural group unit of society with the reinforcements of marriage and the will of the Creator, something he failed to accomplish in the UDHR.

Malik's sources do not end with Aquinas. His more proximate source was the theory of subsidiarity that began to take shape in the writings of Pope Leo XIII at the end of the nineteenth century, especially his 1891 *Rerum Novarum*, an anchor text of modern Catholic social teachings. The concept of subsidiarity was a philosophical idea nestled within a theological context but also analytically independent of it. Leo XIII believed it to be a law of nature – one found in Aristotle and Aquinas – that humans should have certain *prima facie* rights and responsibilities to both the fruits of their bodily labor *and* the issue of their procreative labor. With regard to natural parents, this was true because they by nature would see themselves in their children and thereby be more invested in them. In a similar way, infants and children gradually would come to see themselves in their parents of conception and be more inclined to attach, develop, and follow their lead. Therefore, parents should have both the right to discharge this care, and children should have the right to be raised by those who conceive them and are likely to have this investment.[17] The meaning of subsidiarity is that both the state and the market should give support (*subsidium*) to both intact and disrupted families when they are in distress, but that neither of them should do anything to disturb or usurp the natural inclinations and powers of parents and children to care for one another. In taking this stand, a position amplified later by Pius XI in *Casti Connubii* (1930) and *Quadragesimo Anno* (1931), the tradition of Roman Catholic social teachings critiqued the two contemporary and competing grand solutions to the world domestic crises – the family dominated by the state and the family dominated by the market.[18]

SUBJECTIVE RIGHTS, OBJECTIVE RIGHTS

It is now time to ask, do the rights of children and parents depend on some understanding of human nature or some narrative about the purpose of life? If it is the former, must a theory of subjective rights based on

---

[17] "Rerum Novarum," in Michael Walsh and Brian Davies, eds., *Proclaiming Justice and Peace: Papal Documents from Rerum Novarum through Centisimus Annus* (Mystic, CT: Twenty-Third Publications, 1991), paras. 11 and 12.
[18] Pius XI, *Casti Connubi* (1930), in Claudia Carlen, ed., *The Papal Encyclicals: 1903–1939* (Wilmington, NC: McGrath Publishing, 1981), 391–5.

a natural law (*lex naturae*) concept of a human faculty (*facultas, potestas*) be invoked to ground the respective rights of children and parents? If the latter, from where do we derive our guiding narrative about the purpose of life? I argue that human rights, particularly the rights of children, require both an understanding of the subjective powers that humans have a right to exercise and some narrative about the purpose of life. Narratives about the purpose of life coordinate and pattern potentially conflicting subjective powers and rights.

Brian Tierney tells us that when first elaborated in Western thought, *subjective* natural rights had to do with the exercise of our individual powers. On the other hand, *objective* natural rights were understood as the correct ordering of a "pattern of relations" between subjective rights.[19] From this perspective, the idea of the family as the "natural and fundamental group unit of society" is an objective right. It coordinates into a mutually reinforcing pattern the subjective rights of parents to their children and the subjective rights of children to care by their parents of conception because of their likely higher investment.

This theory of objective right, however, is not revealed by a direct analysis of a list of individual subjective rights, although this is relevant. A narrative view of the purpose of life is required for subjective powers to find their fully proper relation to one another in a theory of objective right. Nature gives hints of this objective order, but no theory of natural law, even when informed by contemporary scientific theories of nature, can by itself provide a theory of objective rights sufficient to define the respective rights and obligations of parents, children, and the state.

Tierney believes that theories of objective natural rights were elaborated by Aristotle and Thomas Aquinas. But he claims that, first, eleventh- and twelfth-century Roman Catholic canonists and, then two centuries later, nominalist philosopher, William of Ockham, introduced a theory of subjective natural rights as well. This helped to establish the individualistically oriented rights tradition that obtains in much fuller form today. This suggests that the doctrine of private ordering so prominent in American family law today is a contemporary manifestation of the tradition of subjective rights.[20] Unlike medieval rights talk, however, which rooted subjective rights talk in objective right order, modern human rights thinking often ignores or obscures the doctrine of objective rights. This, unfortunately, leaves us with a disconnected and often contradictory list of

---

[19] Brian Tierney, *The Idea of Natural Rights* (Atlanta, GA: Scholars Press, 1997).
[20] *Ibid.*, 39–42.

subjective rights that can function as tools of manipulation by interest groups to accomplish their political and legal goals. Both the UDHR and the UNCRC come closer to the earlier theory of objective rights understood as a pattern of mutually reinforcing subjective rights, rooted in certain starting assumptions about the nature of persons and society.

CRITICALLY GROUNDING HUMAN RIGHTS

Modern human rights thinking pertaining to children and adults largely stands devoid of critical grounding. The historically most influential tradition conveying human rights to the modern world – the natural rights and natural law traditions of Aristotle, Stoic philosophy, Roman law, and the early Roman Catholic canonists – has been generally rejected in the United States in spite of its influence on the two major human rights documents I have analyzed.

To advance this tradition of commentary, I want to review two commanding models of human rights thinking. One is the theory advanced by Larry Arnhart in his recent *Darwinian Natural Right: The Biological Ethics of Human Nature* (1998).[21] The other is implicit in the model of parent and child rights found in Aquinas's view that combines a theory of natural law with a narrative view of the purpose of life.

Arnhart grounds human rights, including the rights of children, in human nature. Human nature – more specifically its biological structure of needs and desires – gives rise to natural rights that humans are justified in pursuing. Arnhart tells us that, "According to the ancient Greek notion of 'natural right,' which appears in Aristotle's writings, human beings, like all natural beings, have natural ends, so that whatever fulfills those natural ends is naturally good or right for them." Furthermore, although Aristotle and Charles Darwin held very different worldviews, Arnhart believes that modern biology projects a similar view of human nature to the one held by Aristotle. It is one that sees self-preservation, self-protection, sociality, parental bonding with offspring, infant bonding with parents, conjugal attachment between mothers and fathers, group attachments, and aspirations for status as pervasive natural tendencies and powers in human beings and the true ground for human rights.

Arnhart, however, is enough of an Aristotelian to understand that these natural desires and capacities also must be guided by habits, customs,

---

[21] Larry Arnhart, *Darwinian Natural Right: The Biological Ethics of Human Nature* (Albany, NY: State University of New York, 1998), esp. 3–6, 46.

virtues, laws, and traditions of practice. Arnhart contends that balancing these needs and rights within ourselves and with those of others over an entire life cycle is the task of Aristotelian *phronêsis*, prudence, or practical reason. This practical reason shapes both custom and law. This practical wisdom is not an abstract universal principle such as Kant's categorical imperative.[22] It is, according to Aristotle and Arnhart, a delicate judgment. Nonetheless, even prudence is informed by human nature and natural rights. He tells us that the natural desires of human beings constitute a universal source of morality, law, and politics. But even then, according to Arnhart, they provide no universal rules for what should be done in particular circumstances.

Arnhart makes no distinction between subjective and objective natural rights. But he should. Although his list of needs and rights is grounded in objective human nature, he also acknowledges that they are multiple, can conflict, and require a higher ordering. Arnhart needs a narrative about the purpose and goal of the human life cycle that would help prioritize the cluster of interacting needs that he makes central. To illustrate how this can work, and indeed did work in the tradition of human rights thinking shaping the UDHR and the UNCRC, I turn once again to the thought of Thomas Aquinas, who was so formative to the line of thought that eventually did, in fact, shape these great international documents, via the insights of Charles Malik.

Aristotle and Aquinas stood in the background of Malik's formulation of the human rights tradition. Aquinas and Aristotle are close to Arnhart in the belief that morality emerges out of the struggle to realize human desire and satisfy human need. A close reading of Aquinas, however, demonstrates that the needs of children are assigned central weight in giving objective form to the relation of parents' and children's rights and the institutional pattern that they should take. This is dramatically different from the privileging of adult rights implicit in the contemporary legal doctrine of private ordering.

For Aquinas, the central need that controls matters of sexuality and affection between men and women is, as we saw above, the long period of dependency that characterizes the human infant. Because of this long period of human infant vulnerability, the human child both requires and *has a right* to the long-term bonding of his parents and, indeed, its institutionalization in matrimony. But Aquinas tells us that the response of

---

[22] Immanuel Kant, *Foundations of the Metaphysics of Morals* (New York: Bobbs-Merrill, 1959), 18.

procreating parents to the needs of their offspring varies from species to species. He wrote,

> Yet nature does not incline thereto in the same way in all animals; since there are animals whose offspring are able to seek food immediately after birth, or are sufficiently fed by their mother; and in these there is no tie between male and female; whereas in those whose offspring need the support of both parents, although for a short time, there is a certain tie, as may be seen in certain birds. In man, however, since the child needs the parents' care for a long time, there is a very great tie between male and female, to which tie even the generic nature inclines.[23]

There is in this paragraph a theory of both subjective and objective natural rights. It is the subjective need (and hence a subjective right) of the infant for care that puts pressure on the parents to form a "very great tie" – a tie that will, among other results, create the needed care for the infant. But, as we saw above, there is a subjective need (and hence a subjective right) of both mother and father to care for that child which they recognize as continuations of their own existence. That parental recognition, as both Aquinas saw and evolutionary psychologists acknowledge today, is easier to achieve for mothers than fathers. When it is consolidated, however, it forms the grounds for a bond – an attachment, to use the language of the great John Bowlby – that meets the infants' deep needs for security, continuity, and affirmation at the point of family formation and only at the point of family dissolution as much of family-law theory holds today.[24]

When viewed correctly, these two sets of subjective rights of children and parents should work synergistically to produce the *objective natural right* that the UDHR had in mind when it called the family the "natural and fundamental group unit of society" that would ideally, at least for Malik, be founded on marriage. Only marriage can pattern institutionally the subjective needs and rights of parents to attach to their offspring, the subjective needs of children to attach with their parents, and the subjective need of parents for an intimate and bonding relation with another.

But Aquinas added a narrative that gave these naturalistic insights a new meaning and order. He knew that the natural inclinations of human beings had their limits. He noticed that humans, in spite of their inclination to care for offspring that they recognize as theirs and because of their

---

[23] *Summa Theologica: Complete English Edition in Five Volumes*, trans. Fathers of the English Dominican Province, 5 vols. (New York: Benziger Bros., 1947–8), vol. V: Supp., III, q. 41.
[24] John Bowlby, *Attachment and Loss* I (London: Hogarth Press, 1969).

sexual bonding with their mates, still had inclinations to wander away from these attachments. He observed that they had many other conflicting tendencies such as desires "to indulge at will in the pleasure of copulation, even as in the pleasure of eating" and the tendency to fight one another for access to females as well as resisting "another's intercourse with their consort."[25] The affections and attachments of humans, especially males, are easily distracted. They are unstable. So, on the basis of natural inclinations alone, even parental attachments are likely to be unstable. So what more is needed?

For Aquinas, the more that was needed is the institution of marriage and a narrative that justified and supported its presence in the life of the father, mother, and child. In short, the marital institution stabilizes human inclinations so that subjective rights can find form in objective rights – so that parents' rights, children's rights, and the corresponding rights and responsibilities of the state can be consolidated, signaled, and forcefully communicated from the beginning of family formation. As is well known, Aquinas, like Peter Lombard before him, absorbed marriage into the sacramental system of the Roman Catholic Church. This led the medieval church to make marriage a spiritually empowered and unbreakable sacrament. It is now well known by scholars that this absorption was based on a mistake in translation when the famous words of Ephesians referring to Christian marriage as a great "mysterion" (Eph. 5:32) were rendered in the Latin Vulgate as *sacramentum* (sacrament) rather than mystery, which would have been more accurate to the original meaning. Although recognizing this undercuts the Catholic view that Christianity must, to be authentic, make marriage an unbreakable sacrament, it does not invalidate the deeper view, widely accepted in Judaism, Christianity, and other great religious and cultural traditions, that marriage should be like an enduring covenant. The long-term dependency needs of the child both contributed to and yet were consolidated by a narrative about the covenant status of marriage – a covenant that was increasingly seen as not only between the husband and wife, but between the couple and society, the couple and their religious community, and the couple and whatever transcendent power they held as sacred. Although most Protestant countries after the Reformation rejected the Roman Catholic sacramental view of marriage, they retained the idea that marriage was a special covenant or status which served the needs and rights of both adults and children.

---

[25] Thomas Aquinas, *Summa Contra Gentiles* (London: Burns, Oates & Washbourne, 1928), III, ii, p. 117.

MODERN TRENDS VERSUS THE INTEGRATIVE MODEL

For several reasons, contemporary law has drifted away from this integrative view of child and parental rights and toward the doctrine of adult private ordering of their sexual and reproductive rights. This is due to law's preoccupation with the law of family dissolution instead of formation, its pretension that law must be morally neutral about the norms of family formation, and its tendency to hold that modernization by necessity promotes private ordering.

The modern dominance of adult and parental rights over the rights of children can be seen in the American Law Institute's *Principles of the Law of Family Dissolution*. This report reflects mainline legal thinking on parent and child rights today, which also can be found in the writings of prominent family-law scholars such as Martha Ertman, Martha Fineman, June Carbone, and many others. The report is famous for two salient moves relevant to parental rights and children's rights. At the moment of family dissolution, it renders legal marriage and cohabiting relationships equivalent before the law. At the same time, it thinks about children's rights mainly from the angle of family disruption; it seeks to preserve the continuity of the child's relationships with various caregivers in order to minimize stress to the child at family breakdown and change. It does this to the point of legalizing multiple parent-like figures with either decision-making authority or visitation rights.

Chapters 2 and 6 of the ALI *Principles* are relevant to the best love, care, and rights of the child. To advance the rights and best care of the child at the time of family dissolution, the ALI *Principles* says this means "predictability in the concrete, individual patterns of specific families."[26] In situations of family dissolution, the continued participation in the life of the child of estoppel and *de facto* parents may be "critically important for the child's welfare."[27] This emphasis on the continuity of caretakers leads the report to formulate one of its strongest provisions – that dissolving families with children must file a "parenting plan" that outlines the role that both biological and other caretakers will take in the child's life on legal rights, decision-making rights, visitation rights, where the child will live, and how to solve conflicts.

This plan is highly contextual and reflects what moral philosophers call a "situation ethics."[28] It is fine-tuned for the best interests of the child

---

[26] *Principles of the Law of Family Dissolution*, 3.   [27] *Ibid.*, 5; see also p. 7.
[28] William Frankena, *Ethics* (Englewood Cliffs, NJ: Prentice Hall, 1973); Joseph Fletcher, *Situation Ethics* (San Francisco: Harper and Row, 1966).

at the point of family dissolution and reconfiguration. Even here the ambiguous borderline between what the report sometimes calls moral neutrality and at other times calls "fairness" requires that the plan be enacted without regard to "race, ethnicity, sex, religion, sexual orientation, sexual conduct, and economic circumstances of a parent."[29] At this point, a moral philosopher would notice the tension between the report's situational ethic when considering the rights of children and its Kantian-Rawlsian ethic of fairness when weighing the rights of adults. However this tension is resolved, the ALI *Principles'* claims to moral neutrality seem spurious.

In dealing with the stress of family dissolution, Chapter 6 of the ALI *Principles* begins directly to reshape the normative context of parenting and children's rights by addressing family formation. It makes recommendations on the rise of domestic partnerships. In an effort to induce fairness between separating cohabiting partners and parents, it virtually imposes, without the consent of the couple, the same laws of dissolution applicable in legal marriage.[30] In effect, this makes cohabiting partners and married couples almost equivalent before the law.[31]

The ALI *Principles* presents this proposed equivalence without acknowledging that the differences are also huge, thereby obscuring the signaling power of the institution of marriage. Marsha Garrison points out that in marriage, in contrast to cohabitation, couples publicly *elect and consent* to the rules and in most cases treat marriage as a covenant of great seriousness to which they bind themselves before family, friends, community, and the state.[32] The work of Garrison is vastly different from the proposals of the *Principles*. The *Principles* injects into family formation and childrearing a world of contingency without conscious intentions, commitments, promises, and covenants witnessed publicly by friends, community, and whatever metaphysical reality the couple might assume. Whatever this does to enhance adult subjective rights in the questionable doctrine of private ordering, it stunningly disconnects the pattern of subjective rights between parents and children that made up the objective family rights implicit in the UDHR and the UNCRC.

---

[29] *Principles of the Law of Family Dissolution*, 12.
[30] *Ibid.*, 913, 915.
[31] *Ibid.*, 916. It should be noted that this chapter does not make cohabiting couples equivalent before interstate agencies and the federal government.
[32] Marsha Garrison, "Marriage Matters: What's Wrong with ALI's Domestic Partnership Proposal," in Wilson, ed., *Reconceiving the Family*, 307–10.

MARGARET BRINIG: RETURN OF
THE INTEGRATIVE VIEW

While the ALI *Principles of Family Dissolution* represents a dominant perspective among modern American family-law scholars, several modern legal scholars on marriage have emerged to offer alternative Christian perspectives.[33] Notre Dame law professor Margaret Brinig is a good example of a Christian jurist who has taken several steps toward a revised integrative view of children and parental rights. Her proposals are realistic about the challenges of contemporary families, parents, and children at both family formation and dissolution. Brinig is the leading family-law scholar bringing together legal theory with empirical research. This gives her family-law scholarship a rich double language that both describes and retrieves the classical marital concepts of covenant and one-flesh union while also explaining their social functions with empirical data interpreted by the new institutional economics. On the basis of these resources, Brinig opposes the ALI *Principles'* concern to make domestic partnerships equivalent to legal marriage and to think about the rights of children almost exclusively from the perspective of the child's need for continuity during family dissolution at the expense of the child's rights for family formation built around marriage.[34]

Brinig preserves in fresh terms the accomplishments of older Jewish and Christian traditions of jurisprudence without, however, becoming apologetic for them as such. On the other hand, her position is theologically sensitive. For instance, it is consistent with the integrative model found in the classics on marriage and childcare found in Augustine and Thomas Aquinas and the latter's influence on the UDHR and the UNCRC.

She does this by first developing a phenomenology of covenant – a description of the model of marriage that historically has dominated Western thinking in law, culture, and religion. She then secondarily employs both the new institutional economics and evolutionary psychology in ways analogous to how Aquinas used the psychobiology and

---

[33] For samples of their views, see Mary Ann Glendon, *The Transformation of Family Law: State, Law, and Family in the United States and Western Europe* (Chicago: University of Chicago Press, 1989); Helen Alvare, "Catholic Teachings and the Law Concerning the New Reproductive Technologies," *Fordham Urban Law Journal* (Nov. 1, 2002); Scott Fitzgibbon, "A City without Duty, Fault, or Shame," in Wilson, ed., *Reconceiving the Family*, 28–46; "Procreative Justice and the Recognition of Marriage," in M. Obi, ed., *Family and the Law in the 21st Century* (Toykyo: Hogakushoin Publishing Co., 2007).

[34] Margaret Brinig and Steven Nock, "Legal Status and Effects on Children," *Legal Studies Research Paper* No. 07–21 (Notre Dame, IN: Notre Dame Law School, 2007), 1–32.

institutional theory of Aristotle to shape Roman Catholic marriage theory and much of the later Western legal tradition of marriage.[35] She does this to illustrate how covenant thinking can be translated into secular law's rightful concern with the hard procreative, economic, and health realities of parents and children.

Brinig argues that the post-Enlightenment contractual model of marriage that sees it as a freely chosen agreement is inadequate to both our experience of marriage and our past legal understandings of the institution. Phenomenologically and historically, Western marriage has been viewed as a solemn agreement to a union of "unconditional love and permanence" through which the "parties are bound not only to each other but also to some third party, to God or the community or both."[36] After developing the received tradition, she then gives a further economic account of its concrete institutional implications.

To do this, Brinig turns to what is commonly called the "new institutional economics." This perspective both builds on, yet goes beyond, the rational-choice view advocated by Nobel Prize-winning economist Gary Becker and the prolific law and economics theorist, Judge Richard Posner. Marriage, she argues, is more like a firm than it is an individualistically negotiated contract. A firm is an association organized to perform a specific function, achieve economies of scale, capitalize on special talents of individual participants, and relate to external parties as a collective unit. A firm is based on a prior agreement – something like a covenant – between the parties involved and the surrounding community about the purpose of the corporate unit. Brinig says this about the analogy between firms and covenantal marriage: "This agreement does not purport to anticipate all future transactions among the firm members. In fact, one of the goals of the firm is the elimination of explicit interparty contracting and account keeping."

The new institutional economics helps us see things in the firm and in marriages (especially marriages with children) that the older individualistic rational-choice economic model missed. It helps us see the "channeling," "signaling," and "reputational" aspects of firm-like marriages. The firm model enables us to grasp how marriages formed by settled public commitments (covenants) to each other, potential children, and society develop identifiable social patterns that convey trusted information,

---

[35] John Witte, Jr., *Law and Protestantism* (Cambridge: Cambridge University Press, 2002), 210–14, 230–40.

[36] Margaret Brinig, *From Contract to Covenant* (Cambridge, MA: Harvard University Press, 2000). Quotations hereafter are from *ibid.*, 6–9, 28–9, and 133.

dependable access to known and valued goods, and valued reputations both within the marriage and between the marriage and the wider community. Marriages that result in children, however, are more like a particular type of firm called franchises. This analogy between marriage with children and the franchise is especially important for the rights of children. A set of imposed responsibilities comes from the needs (the subjective rights, to use the older terminology) of the child that cannot be totally dissolved even with legal divorce. Brinig believes that the inextricable one-flesh union and the shared family history do "not disappear" when the marriage ends or the child turns eighteen. She points out something that the ancient "one-flesh" model of marriage profoundly understood but that the ALI *Principles* and much of contemporary family law misses, namely, that divorcing or separating couples with children "never completely revert to a pre-marriage state. Nor do children leaving home entirely free themselves from their parents or siblings." Brinig insists that "marriage persists to a certain degree in spite of divorce. To the extent that it persists, the family still lives on as what I call the franchise."

Brinig's phenomenology of covenant and her institutional economics is supported by empirical research. Her empirical studies with Steven Nock lead her to assert that, in contrast to much of contemporary legal theory, the status of parents in legal marriage is a leading positive asset for the well-being of children and has important implications for children's rights. They allude to the abundant number of studies from both the United States and Europe showing that cohabiting partnerships, even with children, are less stable. They write that when legally married couples "know they are in a long-term relationship ('until death do us part' or at least until the age of emancipation), they have incentive to 'specifically invest' in the relationship and in the other party to it." In addition, "legal recognition provides a signal for the provision of all kinds of outside support for the family, whether by government, by extended family, or by other affinity groups." These investments and subsequent benefits "should accrue to children as well as adults."[37] In other words, they should be part of the rights of children.

---

[37] *Ibid.*, 6. Brinig and Nock arrived at these conclusions through an analysis of the University of Michigan Panel Survey of Income Dynamics and its Child Development Supplement. They analyzed the large longitudinal database of these surveys with standard social-science scales measuring child well-being. Keeping children with natural mothers (both married and unmarried) constant, they measured child well-being from the perspective of the independent variables of income, family structure, and legal relation of parents (unique to their study). For these data, see "Legal Status and Effects on Children," *Legal Studies Research Paper*, 1–32.

Her position has many concrete implications relevant to the rights of children. For instance, she believes rendering cohabitation and marriage largely equivalent before the law, as the ALI *Principles* proposes, would end in undermining the signaling and channeling functions of marriage. This would mean a significant loss for guiding men into aligning and integrating their sexuality, affection for sexual partner, and commitment to children. Brinig is fully aware – as was Aristotle, Thomas Aquinas, evolutionary psychologists, and other empirical social scientists – that men are more likely to attach and commit to children if they know the child is theirs, spend time with the child as it grows, get invested in the child through ongoing experience, and have a satisfying relation with the mother of the child – all of which are facilitated by the channeling functions of legal marriage. They agree that fathers are good for children, and children have a right to their fathers.

In view of the witness of both tradition and the contemporary social sciences, Brinig contends that law should not hesitate to do what it can to encourage the marital franchise with children as the defining center of family formation. Marriage can be encouraged through the law, she suggests, by not giving legal recognition to cohabitation, not undermining the signaling power of the marital institution, and by greatly increasing the social and cultural rewards of marriage. She holds it is worth taking seriously the Louisiana, Arizona, and Arkansas experiments in "covenant marriage."

I make no claim that Brinig's view is the only example of the integrative perspective in contemporary law and the rights of children. But in Brinig's perspective, we have a jurisprudence of marriage that is argued on rational legal grounds, yet is both influenced by and broadly compatible with the outlines of the classic integrative view of marriage and the objective rights of parents and children in marriage. Her position helps bridge the social space between secular law and the dominant models of love, marriage, and the rights of children functioning historically in Western societies and shaped by the multi-dimensional views of the complex Christian heritage.

RECOMMENDED READING

Arnhart, Larry. *Darwinian Natural Right: The Biological Ethics of Human Nature.* Albany, NY: State University of New York, 1998.

Aquinas, Thomas. "Supplement," *Summa Theologica* III. London: T. & T. Washbourne, 1917.

Aristotle. *Politics*, in *The Basic Works of Aristotle*. New York: Random House, 1941.

Bowlby, John. *Attachment and Loss.* London: Hogarth Press, 1969.

Brinig, Margaret. *From Contract to Covenant.* Cambridge, MA: Harvard University Press, 2000.

Browning, Don. *Marriage and Modernization: How Globalization Threatens Marriage and What to Do about It.* Grand Rapids, MI: Wm. B. Eerdmans, 2003.

Browning, Don, Bonnie Miller-McLemore, Pamela D. Couture, Brynolf Lyon, and Robert M. Franklin. *From Culture Wars to Common Ground: Religion and the American Family Debate*, 2nd edn. Louisville, KY: Westminster/ John Knox Press, 2000.

Brownlie, Ian. *Basic Documents on Human Rights.* Oxford: Clarendon Press, 1992.

Daly, Martin and Margo Wilson. "The Evolutionary Psychology of Marriage and Divorce," in Linda Waite, ed., *The Ties that Bind.* New York: Aldine de Gruyter, 2000, 99–110.

Garrison, Martha. "Marriage Matters: What's Wrong with ALI's Domestic Partnership Proposal," in Robin Wilson, ed., *Reconceiving the Family: Critique of the American Law Institute's Principles of the Law of Family Dissolution.* Cambridge: Cambridge University Press, 2006, 307–33.

Morsink, Johannes. *The Universal Declaration of Human Rights: Origins, Drafting, and Intent.* Philadelphia: University of Pennsylvania Press, 1999.

Principles of the Law of Family Dissolution: Analysis and Recommendations. Newark, NJ: Matthew Bender & Co., 2002.

Witte, John, Jr. *Law and Protestantism: The Legal Teachings of the Lutheran Reformation.* Cambridge: Cambridge University Press, 2002.

CHAPTER 15

Christianity and the rights of women

M. Christian Green

"Wives, be subject to your husbands, as to the Lord. For the husband is the head of the wife as Christ is the head of the church."   (Eph. 5:22–4)

"Let a woman learn in silence with all submissiveness. I permit no woman to teach or to have authority over men; she is to keep silent."
(1 Tim. 2:11–12)

"There is neither Jew nor Greek; there is neither slave nor free; there is neither male nor female; for you are all one in Christ Jesus."   (Gal. 3:27–8)

Former United States President Jimmy Carter and other members of the group of political and religious leaders known as "The Elders" have recently embarked on a worldwide initiative on "Equality for Women and Girls." Grounded in the language of the Universal Declaration of Human Rights – particularly the guarantee, "Everyone is entitled to all the rights and freedoms set forth in this Declaration, without distinction of any kind, such as race, color, *sex*, language, *religion*, political or other opinion, national or social origin, property, birth or other status,"[1] as well as such subsequent international conventions as the Convention on the Elimination of Discrimination against Women (CEDAW) – the Elders have called for religious leaders, in particular, to examine their own records when it comes to the rights of women and girls. As the mission statement for the initiative proclaims, "Religion and tradition are a great force for peace and progress around the world. However, as Elders, we believe that the justification of discrimination against women and girls on grounds of religion or tradition, as if it were prescribed by a higher authority, is unacceptable … We especially call on religious and traditional leaders to set an example and change all discriminatory practices within their own religions and traditions."[2]

[1] Universal Declaration of Human Rights (1948), accessible at www.un.org/en/documents/udhr (emphases added).
[2] The Elders, "Equality for Women and Girls," July 2, 2009, accessible at www.theelders.org/womens-initiatives.

For his own part, President Carter has stated even more pointedly, "The truth is that male religious leaders have had – and still have – an option to interpret holy teachings either to exalt or subjugate women. They have, for their own selfish ends, overwhelmingly chosen the latter. Their continuing choice provides the foundation or justification for much of the pervasive persecution and abuse of women throughout the world."[3] This concern for women's rights has recently prompted Carter to leave the Southern Baptist Convention after sixty years of membership. In their global initiative, the Elders echo an earlier call made by then First Lady Hillary Rodham Clinton at the Fourth World Conference on Women in Beijing in 1995, when she emphasized, likely drawing on the social principles of her United Methodist faith: "Every woman deserves the chance to realize her own God-given potential. But we must recognize that women will never gain full dignity until their human rights are respected and protected … It is time for us to say here in Beijing, and for the world to hear, that it is no longer acceptable to discuss women's rights as separate from human rights … If there is one message that echoes forth from this conference, let it be that human rights are women's rights and women's rights are human rights once and for all."[4]

Christianity, like other religious traditions, has often had an ambivalent relationship to women's rights. While some passages in the New Testament prescribe for women a posture of submission, subjection, silence, and subordination, others hold out the tantalizing prospect of equality. When it comes to the rights of women, Christianity is rife with dualities of subordination and liberation, equality and difference, sacrifice and virtue, creation and redemption. In this chapter, I provide a brief historical overview of how Christian women, both comfortably ensconced and sometimes alienated from the tradition, have addressed, resisted, and reconciled these tensions. I relate these historical struggles to the ongoing evolution of women's rights in the international human rights frameworks established in the Convention on the Elimination of Discrimination against Women (CEDAW) in 1981, the International Conference on Population and Development at Cairo in 1994, and the Fourth World Conference on Women at Beijing in 1995. From these historical and contemporary tensions between Christianity and the human rights of women, I distill

[3] Jimmy Carter, "The Words of God Do Not Justify Cruelty to Women," *The Observer*/guardian.co.uk, July 12, 2009.
[4] Hillary Rodham Clinton, "Remarks to the UN 4th World Conference on Women Plenary Session," Beijing, China, Sept. 5, 1995, accessible at www.americanrhetoric.com/speeches/hillary-clintonbeijingspeech.htm.

some key tensions in the relationship between Christianity and women's rights that continue to be present, even as Christian women around the world today are advocating both for women's rights and wider frameworks of "third-generation" human rights with the potential to benefit all humanity.

While a more extended treatment of Christianity and women's rights could draw on biblical examples and the medieval mystical women who have recently drawn considerable attention in theology and women's studies, it was in the Renaissance that Christian women's calls for rights began to take on a modern flavor resonant with the ongoing struggle for women's human rights today. Christine de Pisan (1363–1434)[5] wrote treatises against the misogyny of male writers in her time, but she is best known for *The Book of the City of Ladies* and *The Treasure of the City of Ladies* (also known as *The Book of the Three Virtues*) in which she chronicled the contributions of women to society and outlined the process for cultivating virtues necessary to counter misogyny.[6] Christine argued, "The man or the woman in whom resides greater virtue is the higher; neither the loftiness nor the lowliness of a person lies in the body according to the sex but in the perfection of conduct and virtues."[7] She also provided concrete advice for women of all walks of life, from princesses to prostitutes, the latter of whom she assures, "You ought to know that without doubt no woman is so low that if she sincerely wishes to renounce sin with the good intention of never returning to it or falling again, if she repents and begs God's mercy, God will protect and preserve her from all those who wish to dissuade her good intentions."[8] Christine's writings commend virtues of chastity and restraint, but in the interest of women's self-determination and spiritual salvation.

---

[5] For general biographical information and analysis of Christine de Pisan, see Christine de Pisan, *The Vision of Christine de Pizan*, trans. Glenda McLeod and Charity Cannon Willard (Cambridge: D. S. Brewer, 2005); Laurel Thatcher Ulrich, *Well-Behaved Women Seldom Make History* (New York: Knopf, 2007); Bonnie A. Birk, *Christine de Pisan and Biblical Wisdom: A Feminist-Theological Point of View* (Milwaukee, WI: Marquette University Press, 2005); Deborah L. McGrady and Barbara K. Altmann, eds., *Christine de Pisan: A Casebook* (New York: Routledge, 2003).

[6] Christine de Pisan, *The Book of the City of Ladies*, rev. edn trans. Earl Jeffrey Richards (London: Penguin, 1998); Christine de Pisan, *The Treasure of the City of Ladies*, trans. Sarah Lawson (Harmondsworth and New York: Penguin, 1985).

[7] Christine de Pisan, *Book of the City of Ladies*, I, 9.3, 24.

[8] Christine de Pisan, *Treasure of the City of Ladies*, 172.

As the Renaissance gave way to early modernity, advocacy of women's rights often took on a more secular and rationalistic tone, but religious underpinnings remained evident in the work of Christian women writers. Catholic writer Marie de Gournay (1565–1645),[9] for example, became known as an opponent of the Protestant movement in the French wars of religion and as an advocate of women's rights through two treatises, *The Equality of Men and Women* (1622) and *The Ladies' Grievance* (1626).[10] The divine roots of her argument for "mere equality" of the sexes hinged on the argument that "the virtue of man and virtue of woman are the same thing, since God bestowed on them the same creation and the same honor: *masculum et feminam fecit eos.*" Both men and women, in de Gournay's view, required the intermediation of the church in their scriptural hermeneutics.

On the other side of the English Channel, Mary Astell (1666–1731) was another proto-feminist writer who sought to articulate women's rights from within the Christian faith.[11] Particularly for her advocacy of women's education, she has come to be known as the "first English feminist." Her best-known books, *A Serious Proposal to the Ladies, for the Advancement of Their True and Greatest Interest* and *A Serious Proposal, Part II*, recommended the establishment of new institutions for women's religious and secular education.[12] A subsequent work, *Some Reflections on Marriage* (1700), argued for the extension of women's vocation beyond the traditional options of mother or nun.[13] Astell saw women's education

---

[9] For more general biographical information and analysis of Marie de Gournay, see *L'Ombre Discourant de Marie de Gournay* (Paris: Editions Champions, 2006), esp. chaps. II, 2 and II, 3 on the feminist and moral dimensions of her work; Michèle Fogel, *Marie de Gournay: Itinéraires d'une femme savante* (Paris: Fayard, 2004), esp. chap. 8 on religion and sex equality; Marjorie Ilsley, *A Daughter of the Renaissance, Marie le Jars de Gournay, Her Life and Works* (The Hague: Mouton, 1963); Peggy Preston Holmes, "The Life and Literary Theories of Marie Le Jars de Gournay" (Ph.D. thesis, University of London, 1952).

[10] Marie Le Jars de Gournay, "The Equality of Men and Women" (1641) and "The Ladies' Complaint" (1641) in Marie Le Jars de Gournay, *Apology for the Woman Writing and Other Works*, ed. and trans. Richard Hillman and Colette Quesnel (Chicago: University of Chicago Press, 2002).

[11] For general biographical information and analysis of Mary Astell, see William Kolbrenner and Michal Michelson, eds., *Mary Astell: Reason, Gender, Faith* (Aldershot: Ashgate, 2007); Patricia Springborg, *Mary Astell: Theorist of Freedom from Domination* (Cambridge and New York: Cambridge University Press, 2005); Christine Sutherland, *The Eloquence of Mary Astell* (Calgary: University of Calgary Press, 2005).

[12] Mary Astell, *A Serious Proposal to the Ladies, for the Advancement of Their True and Greatest Interest, Parts I and II* (1694, 1697), ed. Patricia Springborg (Ontario: Broadview Literary Texts, 2002).

[13] Mary Astell, "Reflections on Marriage" (1700), in *Astell: Political Writings*, ed. Patricia Springborg (Cambridge: Cambridge University Press, 1996).

as essential not only to the expansion of women's vocational possibilities, but also to their equal opportunity for salvation through understanding of God. Of the social conventions that conspired to limit women's vocational and spiritual development, she observed, "One wou'd therefore almost think, that the wise disposer of all things, foreseeing how unjustly Women are denied opportunities of improvement from *without*, has therefore by way of compensation endow'd them with greater propensions to Vertue and a natural goodness of Temper *within*, which if duly manag'd would raise them to the most eminent pitch of heroick Vertue."[14] In a further development of her own understanding of divine matters, she entered into a written correspondence with British theologian, John Norris, who published their correspondence, under the title *Letters Concerning the Love of God*, with Astell's name omitted.[15] Apparently, her nominal invisibility was not enough to conceal her authorship from those who knew her work and the volume drew praise for its rhetoric and theological insight.

The examples above and the ones to follow in the Enlightenment and modern periods come from the Catholic and Anglican branches of Christianity. In the Reformed Protestant branches of the tradition, certain figures, such as Martin Luther's notable wife, Katharina von Bora, come to mind as feminine faces of the Reformation. Nevertheless, it appears that the study of women's distinctive contributions to the Reformation, particularly as concerns any distillation of a Reformed version of women's rights, is in its infancy. Kirsi Stjerna, the author of one recent study, argues, "The Reformation for women was not necessarily in every regard the same as it was for men. The 'good news' proclaimed about the gospel and the structures built around it were not necessarily equally good for men and for women."[16] Reasons offered for the absence of a women's rights movement in the Reformation tradition include the closing of convents as an alternative vocation for women, the valorization and sanctification of the roles of wife and mother, the privatization of that domestic role, the absence of a visionary and prophetic (as opposed to devotional) literary tradition among Reformed women writers, and the theological focus on the individual that prevented Reformed women from conceiving of themselves as a class or category within the overall Reformation.[17] Still, Stjerna suggests that Marie

---

[14] *Ibid.*, 57.
[15] Mary Astell, *Mary Astell and John Norris: Letters Concerning the Love of God*, ed. E. Derek Taylor and Melvyn New (Aldershot: Ashgate, 2005).
[16] Kirsi Stjerna, *Women and the Reformation* (Oxford and Malden, MA: Blackwell Publishing, 2009), 4.
[17] See especially Stjerna's concluding chapter for an assessment of the Reformation in feminist terms.

Dentière of Geneva and Argula von Grumbach of Bavaria offered distinctively feminist arguments for women's rights to preach and teach and that
the writings of other women included in her survey can be construed as
proto-feminist in their arguments and mutual support.[18]

ENLIGHTENMENT FEMINISTS

In the heady days of the eighteenth-century Enlightenment, religion was
increasingly viewed as an obstacle human rights As the revolutionary
and anti-clerical fervor rose to a peak in late eighteenth-century France,
leading French feminist, Olympe de Gouges (1748–93),[19] wrote widely
on gender equality, human rights, and the abolition of slavery. Her
Declaration of the Rights of Woman and the Female Citizen (1791), a feminist rejoinder to the recently promulgated "Declaration on the Rights
of Man and Citizen" in France, challenged male authority and female
inequality. It began with a moral and political challenge to patriarchy:

> Man, are you capable of being just? It is a woman who poses the question; you
> will not deprive her of that right at least. Tell me, what gives you sovereign empire
> to oppress my sex? … Man alone has raised his exceptional circumstances to a
> principle. Bizarre, blind, bloated with science and degenerated – in a century of
> enlightenment and wisdom – into the crassest ignorance, he wants to command
> as a despot a sex which is in full possession of its intellectual faculties; he pretends
> to enjoy the Revolution and to claim his rights to equality in order to say nothing
> more about it.[20]

In the notably Deist terms of the Enlightenment, de Gouges defended
women's rights with arguments of natural laws handed down by a
"Supreme Being," whose treasures men and women were to share equally.
De Gouges's indefatigable activism on behalf of women's rights ended
when she was guillotined during the Reign of Terror.

If Mary Astell was England's first feminist, Mary Wollstonecraft (1759–
97),[21] a contemporary of de Gouges, would become her better-known

---

[18] Stjerna, *Women and the Reformation*, 42, 216.
[19] For general biographical information and analysis of Olympe de Gouges, see Lisa Beckstrand, *Deviant Women of the French Revolution and the Rise of Feminism* (Madison, NJ: Fairleigh Dickinson University Press, 2009); Sophie Mousset, *Women's Rights and the French Revolution: A Biography of Olympe de Gouges*, trans. Joy Poirel (New Brunswick: Transaction Publishers, 2007).
[20] Olympe de Gouges, "Declaration of the Rights of Woman and the Female Citizen" (1791), in Darline Gay Levy, Harriet Branson Applewhite, and Mary Durham Johnson, eds., *Women in Revolutionary Paris, 1789–1795* (Urbana, IL: University of Illinois Press, 1980), 87–96.
[21] For a comparison of the work of both, see Regina James, "Mary, Mary, Quite Contrary, or, Mary Astell and Mary Wollstonecraft Compared," *Studies in Eighteenth Century Culture* 5

successor. In *A Vindication of the Rights of Women* (1792), Wollstonecraft responded to Edmund Burke's conservative political treatise, *Reflections on the Revolution in France* (1790) and to Jean-Jacques Rousseau's proposals in France to limit women's education to the domestic arts.[22] She argued that women are not naturally inferior to men, but appear to be only because of their lack of education and the way in which education and social conventions equally distorted men's views of such matters. Of the latter, she observed, "Men, in general, seem to employ their reason to justify prejudices, which they have imbibed, they can scarcely trace how, rather than to root them out … [T]he imperfect conclusions thus drawn, are frequently very plausible, because they are built on partial experiences, on just, though narrow, views."[23] Wollstonecraft proposed that both men and women would benefit from an education and a social order based on reason. She further argued that society as a whole depends on the education of women, since mothers are the primary educators of young children. Such feminine virtue could only come through freedom. As Wollstonecraft put it, "Liberty is the mother of virtue, and if women be, by their very constitution, slaves, and not allowed to breathe the sharp invigorating air of freedom, they must ever languish like exotics, and be reckoned beautiful flaws in nature."[24] Having learned some hard life lessons through two rather exploitative romantic relationships prior to her eventual marriage to the poet Percy Bysshe Shelley, one of which produced an out-of-wedlock child, Wollstonecraft defended such traditional notions as sexual modesty and the sanctity of marriage, but she also challenged the prevailing double standard that did not require these equally of men as of women.

MODERN MOVEMENTS AND GLOBAL DIRECTIONS

In nineteenth-century America, the movement for women's rights was contemporaneous and often collaborative with the movement to abolish slavery. Both the suffrage and abolitionist movements also drew on ideas of equality and justice that were often religiously grounded. Elizabeth Cady Stanton (1815–1902) was one of the signature voices in the suffrage

---

(1976): 121–39. For general biographical information and analysis of Mary Wollstonecraft, see Lyndall Gordan, *Vindication: A Life of Mary Wollstonecraft* (New York: HarperCollins, 2005); Diane Jacobs, *Her Own Woman: The Life of Mary Wollstonecraft* (New York: Simon and Schuster, 2001); Janet Todd, *Mary Wollstonecraft: A Revolutionary Life* (New York: Columbia University Press, 2000).

[22] Mary Wollstonecraft, *A Vindication of the Rights of Women* (1792), ed. Miriam Brody (London: Penguin Classics, 2004).

[23] *Ibid.*, 92.   [24] *Ibid.*, 122.

movement, with a decidedly ambivalent relationship to organized religion. Elizabeth Cady Stanton and her husband, Henry Stanton, had a marriage of forty-seven years that produced seven children. The couple had a long history of activism, including work in the temperance and abolition movements even before the movement for women's suffrage. Stanton's convictions regarding women's rights crystallized while attending the 1840 International Anti-Slavery Convention in London with her husband on their honeymoon. Separate seating of men and women at the conference prompted considerable debate, particularly when leading abolitionist William Lloyd Garrison opted to sit with the women. Stanton and other women in attendance subsequently organized the first women's rights convention at Seneca Falls, New York, in 1848. There, Stanton authored and read a "Declaration of Sentiments," modeled on the Declaration of Independence, proclaiming men's and women's equality, and demanding women's suffrage.

It was shortly after the Seneca Falls conference, in 1851, that Stanton was introduced to Susan B. Anthony, who would become her staunch ally in the women's rights movement.[25] Convinced that women were entitled to vote as "citizens" under the Fourteenth Amendment, the women and their collaborators began a campaign of going to the polls and demanding the franchise. Stanton also began to advocate a broader definition women's rights – including women's parental and custody rights, divorce rights, employment rights, income rights, property rights, and birth control – that eventually led to a split between Stanton and Anthony's National Women's Suffrage Association (NWSA) and the more conservative and religiously based American Women's Suffrage Association (AWSA). When the two groups later unified under the name National American Women Suffrage Association, Stanton assumed the presidency of the organization at Anthony's urging, but not without continued reservations about some of the conservative religious leanings of some of the AWSA leadership.

In the 1890s Stanton began to give voice to her long-simmering concerns about the status of women in Christianity in her two-volume work, *The Woman's Bible*.[26] Therein, Stanton provided a feminist interpretation of the Bible and challenged sexism in the organized church and its relegation of women to a subordinate position in both church and society. "From the

---

[25] For general biographical information and analysis of Susan B. Anthony and her relationship with Elizabeth Cady Stanton, see Mary D. Pellauer, "Susan B. Anthony," in *The Teachings of Modern Christianity on Law, Politics, and Human Nature*, vol. I, ed. John Witte, Jr. and Frank S. Alexander (New York: Columbia University Press, 2006).

[26] Elizabeth Cady Stanton, *The Woman's Bible* (1895) (Mineola, NY: Dover Publications, 2002).

inauguration of the movement for women's emancipation the Bible has been used to hold her in her 'divinely ordained sphere',", Stanton argued. "Marriage for her was to be a condition of bondage, maternity a period of suffering and anguish, and in silence and subjection, she was to play the role of a dependent on man's bounty for all her material wants, and for all the information that she might desire on the vital questions of the hour, she was commanded to ask her husband at home. Here is the Bible position of women briefly summed up."[27] At the same time, she maintained, "There are some general principles in the holy books of all religions that teach love, charity, justice, and equality for all the human family, there are many grand and beautiful passages, the golden rule has been echoed and reechoed around the world."[28] In 1892, ten years before her death, Stanton testified before the United States Congress, in an address titled *Solitude of Self*,[29] to the central value of the "individuality of each human soul," the "Protestant idea" of the "right of individual conscience and judgment, our republican idea, individual citizenship," and the "rights of ... what belongs to her as an individual, in a world of her own, the arbiter of her own destiny."[30]

Many of the moral and spiritual themes in Stanton's *Solitude of Self* at the dawn of the nineteenth century would reappear in *The Long Loneliness*, Dorothy Day's (1897–1980) mid-twentieth-century autobiography. Day's autobiography conveys a sense of spiritual struggle as she moved through an early period of socialist and anarchist activism for peace and women's suffrage into a later period of spiritual awakening and conversion to Roman Catholicism.[31] Day would fold her concern for women's rights into a theology of solidarity, maintaining, "We have all known the long loneliness and we have learned that the only solution is love and that love comes with community."[32] Day would become most famous for cofounding the Catholic Worker movement, which pursued non-violent and pacifist action and established "houses of hospitality" to aid and advocate for

---

[27] *Ibid.*, 7.   [28] *Ibid.*, 12.

[29] Elizabeth Cady Stanton, *The Solitude of Self* (Ashfield, MA: Paris Press, 2001). See also Vivian Gornick, *The Solitude of Self: Thinking about Elizabeth Cady Stanton* (New York: Farrar, Straus, and Giroux, 2007).

[30] From the complete address reproduced at the excellently resourceful website of the documentary *Not for Ourselves Alone: The Story of Elizabeth Cady Stanton and Susan B. Anthony*, dir. Ken Burns (1999), accessible at: www.pbs.org/stantonanthony.

[31] For general biographical information and analysis of Dorothy Day, see Deborah Kent and David Gregory, "Dorothy Day," in Witte and Alexander, eds., *The Teachings of Modern Christianity*. See also the excellent documentary film *Dorothy Day: Don't Call Me a Saint*, dir. Claudia Lawson (Los Angeles: One Lucky Dog Productions, 2006).

[32] Dorothy Day, "The Final Word Is Love," *The Catholic Worker* (May 1980), 4.

the poor and homeless. Women's rights were thus connected to a wide web of other economic, social, and political rights in her work. Day famously requested, "Don't call me a saint – I don't want to be dismissed that easily!" Nevertheless, in 2000, Pope John Paul II designated Day a "Servant of God," the first of four stages of canonization.

In the nineteenth century, connections were made between women's rights and the abolitionist movement. In the twentieth century, these connections extended to worker's rights and poverty rights movements. In each case, the struggle for women's rights was linked to other struggles against oppression. In the twenty-first century, two recent winners of the Nobel Peace Prize, Rigoberta Menchú and Wangari Maathai, have linked women's rights to concerns of indigenous, environmental, and land rights at the local and global levels. Rigoberta Menchú won the Nobel Prize in 1992 for her work promoting the rights of indigenous peoples who suffered greatly during Guatamala's thirty-plus years of civil war. In her autobiography, *I, Rigoberta Menchú*,[33] she describes the role of a biblically based liberation theology in that movement, noting, "We began to study the Bible as our main text ... The important thing for us is that we started to identify that reality with our own ... We began studying more deeply and we came to a conclusion. That being a Christian means thinking of our brothers around us, and that every one of our Indian race has a right to eat."[34] Menchú draws on natural and cultural maternalism as well as religion in her arguments for indigenous rights, specifically that "something important about women in Guatemala, especially Indian women" is their "relationship with the earth" and "responsibilities they have, which men do not have."[35] At the same time, Menchú has resisted an exclusive focus on women's rights, arguing, "For the time being, though, we think that it would be feeding machismo to set up an organization for women only, since it would mean separating women's work from men's work. Also we've found that when we discuss women's problems, we need the men to be present, so that they can contribute by giving their opinions of what to do about the problem. And so that they can learn as well. If they don't learn, they don't progress."[36]

In 2004, the Kenyan environmental and political activist Wangari Maathai became the first African woman to win the Nobel Peace Prize. Maathai's work has drawn attention to the connections between

---

[33] Rigoberta Menchú, *I, Rigoberta Menchú: An Indian Woman in Guatemala* (London: Verso, 1984).
[34] *Ibid.*, 131–3. [35] *Ibid.*, 220. [36] *Ibid.*, 222.

peace, democracy, and sustainable development. Her United Nations-supported project, Envirocare, put unemployed Kenyans to work planting trees to conserve the environment, eventually leading to the Green Belt Movement that would provide Kenyan women with small stipends to plant nurseries and trees. Maathai's Green Belt Movement attained international visibility in 1985 at the Third World Conference on Women in Nairobi, but it also led to persecution at home. Maathai and her organization were denounced by the Kenyan government throughout the 1980s and 1990s for preaching democracy along with environmentalism. In 1992 Maathai was arrested with other pro-democracy activists drawing international condemnation, including statements from Vice President Al Gore and Senator Edward Kennedy in the United States. Upon her release, Maathai participated in a hunger strike by a group of Kenyan mothers on behalf of those still in prison. After being broken up and beaten up in incidents of police violence, the protesters relocated to All Saints Cathedral, the seat of the Anglican Archbishop in Kenya, whose hospitality to the protesters reconfirmed, for Maathai, the power of the church to act for justice.[37] In 2002 Maathai was elected to the Kenyan Parliament with 98 per cent of the vote and was subsequently appointed Assistant Minister in the Ministry for Environment and Natural Resources, before assuming the inaugural presidency of the African Union's Economic, Social and Cultural Council in 2005. She has continued to draw international honors and international attention, including a visit from then Senator Barack Obama, during which Maathai and Obama planted a tree at Uhuru Park, the central Nairobi park that had been the site of many democratic and environmental protests by Maathai and her fellow activists.

As the twentieth century moved into the twenty-first, women's rights activists increasingly connected women's rights to a variety of other civil, political, economic, social, and cultural rights, as well as to the concerns of women around the world. Just as Christianity is increasingly a religion of the global South, the activism of women like Menchú and Maathai is increasingly the face of global women's activism. One crucial venue for such activism has been the United Nations, which has had a significant recent history of attention to women's rights in its international conventions and conferences.

---

[37] Wangari Maathai, *Unbowed: A Memoir* (New York: Knopf, 2006), 224.

CHRISTIANITY AND THE INTERNATIONAL WOMEN'S HUMAN RIGHTS FRAMEWORK

Despite the history of Christian women's struggles for women's rights and of Christian contributions to the development of international human rights, the Christian response to secure *women's rights as human rights* has been one of ambivalence, contestation, and sometimes outright antagonism. Christian groups have variously lobbied for and against women's rights conventions, beginning with CEDAW and more recently at the conferences at Cairo and Beijing, and the proceedings related to the Convention on the Rights of the Child. In recent years, the opposition to these various conventions by conservative Christians, often joined by Muslim groups, has tended to drown out the voices of mainline and progressive Christian supporters of women's rights. The "strange bedfellows" coalition of conservative Christians and Muslims, which drew considerable attention at the Cairo and Beijing conferences, is the most recent example of religious opposition to women's rights, and it is an opposition that has become increasingly globalized in recent years.

CEDAW was adopted by the United Nations General Assembly in 1979, entered into force as an international treaty in 1981, and has been ratified by over a hundred nations.[38] The Convention was a result of more than thirty years of work by the United Nations Commission on the Status of Women, which was established in 1946 to monitor the situation of women and to promote women's rights. It is the primary international human rights instrument on the rights of women.[39] Only the United States and a handful of Muslim nations have yet to ratify the agreement.[40] Though framed in the somewhat minimalist, negative-rights language of non-discrimination, CEDAW, in fact, promotes a broad vision of sex and gender equality. The convention defines "discrimination against women" as encompassing "any distinction, exclusion or restriction made on the basis of sex which has the effect or purpose of impairing or nullifying the

---

[38] See the text and associated documents at: www.un.org/womenwatch/daw/cedaw.

[39] For more information on the drafting of and debates surrounding CEDAW, see Hanna Beate Schopp-Schilling and Cees Flinterman, eds., *The Circle of Empowerment: Twenty-Five Years of the UN Committee on the Elimination of Discrimination Against Women* (New York: The Feminist Press of the City of New York, 2007); Diana G. Zoelle, *Globalizing Concern for Women's Human Rights: The Failure of the American Model* (New York: St. Martin's Press, 2000), esp. chap. 2.

[40] CEDAW has been signed and ratified by 185 countries. CEDAW was signed by President Carter in 1980, but has never been ratified by the USA. The only six UN member states that have not signed CEDAW are the Islamic states of Iran, Somalia, Sudan, and the Pacific island nations of Nauru, Palau, and Tonga. The Vatican, as Permanent Observer to the UN, has also withheld its signature.

recognition, enjoyment or exercise by women, irrespective of their marital status, on a basis of equality of men and women, of human rights and fundamental freedoms in the political, economic, social, cultural, civil or any other field" (art. 1). It commits state parties to the enactment of "all appropriate measures, including legislation, to ensure the full development and advancement of women, for the purpose of guaranteeing them the exercise and enjoyment of human rights and fundamental freedoms on a basis of equality with men" (art. 3). The specific provisions of CEDAW fall into three general categories: (1) standard civil and political, and economic, social, and cultural rights; (2) reproductive rights; and (3) recognition of the ways that culture and tradition may restrict women's rights.

CEDAW guarantees women a number of specific rights in the categories of "first-generation" civil and political rights and "second-generation" economic, social, and cultural rights. Under the category of civil rights and the legal status of women, women are guaranteed the rights to vote, to hold public office, and to exercise public functions (art. 7), to represent their countries at the international level (art. 8), to statehood, irrespective of their marital status (art. 9), and to equality with men in matters of rights and obligations with regard to choice of spouse, parenthood, personal rights, and property rights in marriage and family relations. Under the category of economic, social, and cultural rights, women are guaranteed non-discrimination in education, employment, and economic and social activities (arts. 10, 11, and 13); access to the means and benefits of rural development (art. 14); and to equal rights to conclude contracts and to administer property, and to equal treatment in all stages of procedure in courts and tribunals (art. 15).

CEDAW also contains a number of provisions in the perennially controversial arena of reproductive rights. Article 12 calls on state parties "to eliminate discrimination against women in the field of health care in order to ensure, on a basis of equality of men and women, access to health-care services, including those related to family planning" and, further, "to ensure to women appropriate services in connection with pregnancy, confinement and the post-natal period, granting free services where necessary, as well as adequate nutrition during pregnancy and lactation." In a subsequent provision, women and men are guaranteed the "same rights to decide freely and responsibly on the number and spacing of their children and to have access to the information, education and means to enable them to exercise these rights" (art. 16e). The gender neutrality of these guarantees of reproductive health and reproductive freedom and the absence of any reference to the religiously contested issue of abortion are both significant.

Elsewhere, the treaty specifies that special measures aimed at protecting maternity shall not be deemed discriminatory (art. 4), while at the same time advocating "a proper understanding of maternity as a social function and the recognition of the common responsibility of men and women in the upbringing and development of their children" (art. 5). While these provisions might be read as an instance of conflicting principles of special protection and equal treatment of women in their maternal role and function, they might also be read as acknowledging the different, but common, responsibilities that men and women share in procreation.

CEDAW provisions also recognize the ways that culture and tradition may restrict women's rights. The preamble insists "that a change in the traditional role of men as well as the role of women in society and in the family is needed to achieve full equality of men and women." State parties are urged "to modify the social and cultural patterns of conduct of men and women, with a view to achieving the elimination of prejudices and customary and all other practices which are based on the idea of the inferiority or the superiority of either of the sexes or on stereotyped roles for men and women" (art. 5). Resistance to sexist prejudices is particularly commended in the realm of education, where state parties are urged to pursue the "elimination of any stereotyped concept of the roles of men and women at all levels and in all forms of education by encouraging coeducation and other types of education which will help to achieve this aim and, in particular, by the revision of textbooks and school programs and the adaptation of teaching methods" (art. 10c). As the introduction to the CEDAW text puts it: "[C]ultural patterns which define the public realm as a man's world and the domestic sphere as women's domain are strongly targeted in all of the Convention's provisions that affirm the equal responsibilities of both sexes in family life and their equal rights with regard to education and employment. Altogether, the Convention provides a comprehensive framework for challenging the various forces that have created and sustained discrimination based upon sex."[41]

The opposition to CEDAW by conservative Christian groups outside of the circle of UN member states and permanent observers began to percolate in the 1970s and 1980s and continues to the present day. One reason for this is that the United States has yet to ratify the agreement; every election raises the prospect that a favorably disposed President and Senate might move forward with ratification. Phyllis Schlafly, a Christian conservative and leading opponent of an Equal Rights Amendment to the

---

[41] CEDAW, Introduction.

United States Constitution in the 1970s, has argued as recently as 2007, "Ratification of CEDAW would be craven kowtowing to the radical feminists, exceeded only by the treaty's unlimited capacity for legal mischief."[42] Fellow Christian conservative and population-control critic and reproductive-rights opponent, Steven Mosher, has maintained, "The pompously named CEDAW, the Convention on the Elimination of All Forms of Discrimination Against Women, sounds on its face not to be too bad, just clumsy and utopian. Yet it is a totalitarian piece of social engineering that aims to do everything from legalize abortion-on-demand worldwide to abolish Mother's Day (no joke)."[43] A report on international conventions on women's and children's rights by the Family Research Council, the research arm of the Christian group Focus on the Family, concludes, "The United Nations has become the tool of a powerful feminist–socialist alliance that has worked deliberately to promote a radical restructuring of society."[44] The author of an anti-UN blog with a conservative Christian following concludes, "CEDAW forbids us to recognize – or celebrate – that men and women are fundamentally different."[45] That Christian conservatives continue to register objections to CEDAW, nearly thirty years after its enactment, is striking.

The attention of both conservative and progressive Christian groups to issues of women's rights was even more evident fifteen years after CEDAW at the Cairo and Beijing conferences – huge international gatherings designed to promote the rights of women.[46] It was at these conferences and their five-year review meetings in 1999 and 2000 that the coalition of Catholic, Muslim, Mormon, and Evangelical Christian groups around issues of abortion, contraception, family, and gender became especially vocal.[47] At Cairo, Catholics, doctrinally opposed to abortion, contraception, and sterilization, were joined by Muslims, who objected to sexual

---

[42] www.eagleforum.org/psr/2007/mar07/psrmar07.html.

[43] www.pop.org/20070210731/cedaw-makes-a-comeback.

[44] Patrick F. Fagan, William L. Saunders, and Michael A. Fragoso, "How UN Conventions on Women's and Children's Rights Undermine Family, Religion, and Sovereignty," accessible at: http://downloads.frc.org/EF/EF09E38.pdf.

[45] http://screwtheun.blogspot.com/2007/03/un-mandate-for-womens-rights-no-more.html.

[46] For the "Programs of Action" and other documents related to the Cairo and Beijing conferences, see the comprehensive websites at: www.un.org/popin/icpd2.htm and www.un.org/women-watch/daw/beijing/fwcwn.html.

[47] For an insightful analysis of these coalitions, see Michelle Goldberg, *The Means of Reproduction: Sex, Power, and the Future of the World* (New York: The Penguin Press, 2009), particularly chap. 4 on Cairo and Beijing and chap. 6 on the globalization of the culture wars over reproduction. See also Doris Buss and Didi Herman, *Globalizing Family Values: The Christian Right in International Politics* (Minneapolis, MN: University of Minnesota Press, 2003) and Kathryn Joyce, *Quiverfull: Inside the Christian Patriarchy Movement* (Boston: Beacon Press, 2009), esp. chap. 18, on the globalization of the Christian Right's family and gender views.

conduct outside of marriage, as well as to reproductive rights viewed as individual rights. The Catholics and Muslims were joined by Mormons, Evangelical Christians, and other conservative religious groups who opposed abortion and who instead advocated sexual abstinence outside of marriage. At Beijing, the conservative coalition continued to oppose reproductive rights, definitions of "gender" that could be construed as affirming homosexuality, definitions of women's rights seen as denigrating motherhood, and any provisions deemed to constitute a threat to the family, particularly the authority of parents over their children. Mainline and progressive Christian groups who largely supported CEDAW and the Cairo and Beijing platforms were also vigorous participants in these debates, but their work was often given less attention in the media than the conservative religious alliance.[48]

In hindsight, it is arguable that the focus at Cairo and Beijing and their successor meetings on issues of reproductive rights, gender, and family deflected attention from other issues of women's rights on which there is greater potential for agreement and collaboration. Human trafficking for sex and labor, the feminization of the global migrant economy, mass rape in situations of conflict and genocide, persistent and shocking rates of maternal mortality in childbirth, differential effects of global pandemics (such as HIV/AIDS) and environmental degradation on women's lives and livelihoods, children's rights, the role of women in development – all of these are the persistent issues for women's rights today. These issues involve and implicate much larger structures of injustice that religions, including Christianity, should have a profound interest in addressing. These and similar women's rights and their connection to the "third generation" of human rights against poverty, war, and environmental destruction – while not eliding important quests for reproductive health and rights – seem destined to be a focus of women's human rights advocacy by women of Christian and other faiths going forward.

CHRISTIAN FEMINIST TENSIONS IN WOMEN'S RIGHTS AS HUMAN RIGHTS

What do we learn from the history of Christian women's advocacy for women's rights and the participation of Christians in international human rights debates? First, we see women drawing on the resources of

---

[48] For the perspective and analysis of one of the leading Progressive Protestant participants with a particularly good account of religious activity at UN meetings following on Cairo and Beijing, see Jennifer Butler, *Born Again: The Christian Right Globalized* (London and Ann Arbor, MI: Pluto Press, 2006).

Christianity, but with a distinctively critical hermeneutic of the tradition. This tradition can lead, after all, to *subordination or liberation*. Biblical equality and natural law are bases for women's rights, but they also serve a hermeneutical function in assessing whether the larger tradition is meeting the demands of justice. Neither can stand as a Christian foundation for women's rights without concrete assessments of their actual realization in women's lives and the life of the church. Equality in the image or eyes of God must be actualized in equality in human relations. Nature and natural law can serve as a basis for women's rights, particularly those rights derived from women's status as mothers, but they cannot be viewed in isolation from the way in which our human understandings of nature, even the most fundamental categories of biology and biological relations, are considerably shaped by culture.

Second, Christian understandings of women's rights continue to grapple with the age-old feminist dilemma of *equality or difference* as the proper framework for women's rights. It is notable that many of the women whose struggles are catalogued above never married, had sexual relationships outside of marriage, or experienced periods of turmoil or doubt within their marriages. Most had no children, but those who did embraced their maternal roles heartily, though not without ambivalence. Marriage and motherhood continue to be both cherished experiences and stumbling blocks for many women. The question of whether women and men should be recognized as equals or whether women's distinctive experience of motherhood is a difference that matters continues to present itself regularly in feminist inquiries, including those concerning Christian theories of women's human rights.

Third, we see a discourse of *virtue and sacrifice*. Women are to perfect their own virtue first, before they can transmit it to others, particularly to children. The family is to be a school of virtue, but it must also be a school of justice. Education enables choices in life, and choice enables virtue. Women's education has been defended as fundamental both in the history of women's activism and in struggles for women's human rights and international development today. As the Elder and Mozambican women's and children's rights activist, Graça Machel, has put it, "Education is the single most important foundation for women to reach equality and to extend choice over their bodies and lives."[49] With education and choice as the conditions for virtuous action, women become not just victims of oppression, but agents of change.

---

[49] The Elders, "Equality for Women and Girls," "Education," July 2, 2009, accessible at: www. theelders.org/womens-initiatives.

Finally, we see an ever-broadening notion of women's rights as inter-related with other concerns for peace, poverty, indigenous rights, global health, and environmental sustainability – the "third generation" of human rights. Practically, women's rights have increasingly intersected over time with a variety of groups on a variety of issues. Politically, women's rights advocacy has expanded beyond fundamental civil and political rights, to economic, social, and cultural rights, and increasingly toward this more global understanding. It seems no coincidence that women like Menchú and Maathai, winning their Nobel Peace Prizes for concerns beyond the usual war and peace issues, have managed both to advance women's rights and to expand the basic definitions of peace and human rights. Theologically, it can be said that the effort of these Christian women in human rights tracks another new direction in Christian feminist theology beyond nature and *creation* to grace and *redemption*. Christian women are transforming women's rights and transforming the world. Women's rights are, indeed, human rights.

RECOMMENDED READING

Bayes, Jane, and Nayeri Tohidi. *Globalization, Gender, and Religion.* New York: Palgrave Macmillan, 2001.

Boden, Alison L. *Women's Rights and Religious Practice.* Basingstoke: Palgrave Macmillan, 2007.

Concilium Foundation, ed. *The Rights of Women.* London: SCM Press, 2002.

Cook, Rebecca J., ed. *Human Rights of Women.* Philadelphia: University of Pennsylvania Press, 1994.

Howland, Courtney. *Religious Fundamentalisms and the Human Rights of Women.* New York: St. Martin's Press, 1999.

Peters, Julie and Andrea Wolper, eds. *Women's Rights, Human Rights.* New York and London: Routledge, 1995.

Schopp-Schilling, Hanna Beate, and Cees Flinterman, eds. *The Circle of Empowerment: Twenty-Five Years of the UN Committee on the Elimination of Discrimination Against Women.* New York: The Feminist Press of the City of New York, 2007.

Zoelle, Diana G. *Globalizing Concern for Women's Human Rights.* New York: St. Martin's Press, 2000.

CHAPTER 16

Christianity, human rights, and a theology that touches the ground

Robert A. Seiple

It is always fashionable to quote French philosopher and theologian Jacques Maritain when discussing the birth of the international human rights movement, specifically, the Universal Declaration of Human Rights forged in 1948. Acknowledging the plurality of opinion during that exercise, Maritain differentiated between the "what" and the "why" of human rights. The strength of that document is anchored in the agreement as to the "what," but, as Maritain came to realize, "with the 'why', the dispute begins."[1]

The "dispute" was ameliorated when the rationale for human rights, for all intents and purposes, was put aside. Political expediency, the art of the possible, carried the day. But as most knowledgeable observers of that founding document would agree, today's environment for human rights would likely not allow even the "what" of this document to be written and approved. The Universal Declaration has been consigned to selective implementation at best and, at worst, lip service within the international community. This begs the question: is the vagueness of the rationale for human rights a contributor to the uneven and, at times, ineffective presentation of these rights today? Does the lack of a "why" dilute the power of the "what?"[2]

Insofar as this was a mistake in formulating human rights agreements in the past, it is one that can be, and must be, avoided in this book. Christianity has had 2,000 years to define its orthodoxy, to clarify its principles, to articulate its authority – and to create a theology that touches the ground, a practical theology that meets people where they live. Christianity and human rights provide for, and demand, an underlying

---

[1] Jacques Maritain, *Man and the State* (Chicago: University of Chicago Press, 1951), 77.
[2] See Elizabeth M. Bucar and Barbra Barnett, eds., *Does Human Rights Need God?* (Grand Rapids, MI: Wm. B. Eerdmans, 2005), 2: "is it possible that the current failure of human rights protection stems from this concerted effort to avoid addressing the rationale for human rights?" The book was put together to correct this issue.

foundation that speaks to the timeless importance of an embrace of human dignity and of human rights everywhere.

In this chapter I offer a partial sketch of a Christian foundation for human rights, based on the character of God and his Son. Using the Bible as a legitimizing source for a Christian understanding of human rights, I then discuss three critically important components of any human rights regime: human value, human choice, and human hope.

While these three components are essential to every form of human rights, my principal focus in this chapter is on economic and social rights – the basic rights to food and drink, shelter and protection, health care and education, and other rights that are essential to preserving and enjoying the most basic right to human life and human dignity. These "second-generation rights," as they are often called today, are captured most authoritatively and elaborately in the United Nation's International Covenant on Economic, Social, and Cultural Rights (1966), but they are also reflected in many other international and domestic instruments. My principal preoccupation with economic and social rights in this chapter, however, is practical, showing how they are made real in tangible and touching human acts. And my starting-point for considering these rights is biblical, showing how the Bible is fundamentally concerned about the poor, the widow, the orphan, the sojourner, and the needy in our midst.[3] Christ makes concern for "the least of these" a fundamental responsibility of the Christian in his famous exposition on the Day of Judgment:

When the Son of Man comes in his glory, and all the angels with him, he will sit on his throne in heavenly glory. All the nations will be gathered before him, and he will separate the people one from another as a shepherd separates the sheep from the goats. He will put the sheep on his right and the goats on his left.

Then the King will say to those on his right, "Come, you who are blessed by my Father; take your inheritance, the kingdom prepared for you since the creation of the world. For I was hungry and you gave me something to eat, I was thirsty and you gave me something to drink, I was a stranger and you invited me in, I needed clothes and you clothed me, I was sick and you looked after me, I was in prison and you came to visit me."

Then the righteous will answer him, "Lord, when did we see you hungry and feed you, or thirsty and give you something to drink? When did we see you a stranger and invite you in, or needing clothes and clothe you? When did we see you sick or in prison and go to visit you?" The King will reply, "I tell you the truth, whatever you did for one of the least of these brothers of mine, you did for me."

---

[3] See chapters by David Novak and David Aune herein.

Then he will say to those on his left, "Depart from me, you who are cursed, into the eternal fire prepared for the devil and his angels. For I was hungry and you gave me nothing to eat, I was thirsty and you gave me nothing to drink, I was a stranger and you did not invite me in, I needed clothes and you did not clothe me, I was sick and in prison and you did not look after me."

They also will answer, "Lord, when did we see you hungry or thirsty or a stranger or needing clothes or sick or in prison, and did not help you?" He will reply, "I tell you the truth, whatever you did not do for one of the least of these, you did not do for me." Then they will go away to eternal punishment, but the righteous to eternal life. (Matt. 25:31–46)

HUMAN RIGHTS AND THE CHARACTER OF GOD

The passage that reveals a portion of God's character is John 3:16, unarguably the best-known verse in the entire New Testament. Similarly, the character of Jesus, his Son, is vividly portrayed in Philippians 2:6–8. The passage from John demonstrates a love, grace, and mercy that an omnipotent God freely provides for humanity. Eternal salvation awaits those who believe.

For God so loved the world that he gave his one and only Son, that whoever believes in him shall not perish but have eternal life.[4] (John 3:16)

In the Philippians passage, the rights that are offered in John 3:16 are balanced with the responsibility inherent in a suffering servant.

Who, being in very nature God, did not consider equality with God something to be used to his own advantage; rather, he made himself nothing by taking the very nature of a servant, being made in human likeness. And being found in appearance as a human being, he humbled himself by becoming obedient to death – even death on a cross! (Phil. 2:6–8 [NIV])

This balance of rights and responsibilities – inherent in the nature of God, and, by extension, in the nature of humans who represent God's image on earth – is critically important in how one approaches human rights. Consider the following vignette, my exit interview with Ambassador Thomas Pickering, upon leaving the State Department in the fall of 2000. Tom clearly had something on his mind as the interview began. To paraphrase the discussion, "There's a part of the human rights exercise that is not particularly helpful. You get the philosophy right. Your righteous

---

[4] All biblical passages are taken from the New International Version of the Bible.

indignation puts you on the right side of history. But the rhetoric doesn't translate easily into geo-political realities. If, for whatever reason, those rights come without a practical implementation strategy, the high sounding rhetoric becomes frustratingly hollow, very quickly."[5] Tom wanted to see more pragmatism, a workable philosophy of human rights, a theology that touched the ground.

As a starting-point to this balancing act, John 3:16 cannot stand alone. This beautiful articulation of the very character of God would be meaningless if the words were not incarnated in God's Son. That Son introduced a methodology of obedience, an obedience that could not bypass suffering, the ultimate identification with, and embrace of, a suffering humanity. As we shall see, the familiar words captured in John's Gospel elevate humanity by providing a gift, the description of which is embodied in the Son. In the words of Pope John Paul II, "these two aspects – the affirmation of the person as a person and the sincere gift of self – not only do not exclude each other, they mutually confirm and complete each other."[6]

The linkage of rights and responsibilities produces a very difficult human rights ethic than often attends modern human rights talk. If we hear of a child starving in Somalia, for example, that fact is now part of our knowledge base, and we are accountable for what we know. If we can do something to alleviate the condition of suffering, we are now also responsible for what we do. If we both know and can help, yet do nothing, our crime is as heinous as the conditions that created a starving Somalian child in the first place. This may seem to be a harsh ethic, but this inescapable linkage ultimately will give credibility to the entire human rights exercise.

Returning more specifically to John 3, there is much to be teased out of the use of the word, "whoever." It is a word that transcends bias, an impartial statement that applies to every human being. This is where equality is defined. No one is left out. Any may apply. Enrollment is open. All who believe, according to this verse, can participate in a program that is free of distinctions. Humanity is elevated to the same starting-point, and, if desired, the same end.

Think for a moment if the concept of "whoever" were mandated in our world. India's caste system, for example, would totally disappear. The infanticide brought on by China's "one-child" initiative, where the overwhelming majority of destroyed babies were girls, would never have

[5] At the time, Pickering was the Undersecretary of State for Political Affairs, the #3 officer at State.
[6] John Paul II, *Crossing the Threshold of Hope* (New York: Alfred A. Knopf, 1994), 202.

happened. Romania's "Home for the Unrecoverables," a testimony to a morally and medically bankrupt country of the 1990s, would have been precluded. One religion would never be more important than another. Racial differences would not create invidious distinctions. Genocidal tendencies, driven by the height of one's cheek bones (Rwanda) or the spelling of a last name (Bosnia), or the African/Arab divide in the Nuba Mountains of Sudan, would be eliminated. Differences would give way to human dignity.

But this is another important aspect of "whoever." The program for spiritual redemption is not mandated. Everyone has the right to believe, or not. There is no coercion here. Much of human dignity comes from the mystery of an omnipotent God allowing for the free will of his creation. At the heart of Christianity there is the understanding that for faith to be authentic, it needs to be freely embraced. The choice is not God's. It belongs to the "whoever." John 3:16, then, is also a statement of human rights, the freedom to choose. Free to us, but costly in its initial implementation.

The Philippian passage underscores the cost of that which was freely given. Here the Apostle Paul provides one of the richest, and most vivid, descriptions of Jesus as both God and man. For our purposes, our focus will only be on Jesus's human identity and the character made visible in implementing the redemption plan. Jesus's life is a statement of faithfulness, total obedience, the active embrace of humiliation, and an ongoing pattern of self-renunciation. As an understatement, it is a life of servanthood that transcends pedigree. Succinctly stated, Jesus was born to die. The suffering of his death would complete the suffering of his life. While it is difficult to suggest suffering as a methodology, or pain as a plan, there is no question that the "rights" of John 3:16 cannot be fully realized apart from the human injection of servanthood, regardless of the cost. Jesus's life was more than advocacy on behalf of an oppressed humanity. It was the life of an activist who would give up all of his advantages to secure the final advantage of those he came to serve. In the Christian faith, this is the ultimate source of human dignity, the ultimate demonstration of love of neighbor, the clearest example of responsibility met.

So, in the character of God, we have a firm answer to the "why" of human rights, the rationale for Christianity and Christians to embrace the human rights of all. God speaks from a position of power. Jesus's life and death create his authority. The proper use of power and authority to right wrongs, to overcome negative distinctions, to satisfy grievances, is a good working definition of justice.[7] The Christian faith is based on the power of the crown and the authority of the cross, and although Ambassador Pickering did not say it quite this way, there is no crown without a cross. Christians know the source of human dignity and, by extension, human rights. Equally known is the difficult cost of securing those rights.

HUMAN VALUE: VALUING GOD'S IMAGE, MAKING RIGHTS REAL

Christianity is more than a divine plan of redemption for humanity. With the words, "made in the image of God," Christianity also finds its social obligation, the maintenance of values between and among people, the enhancement of the human condition regardless of context. The Christian responsibility is to elevate others to that "image" no matter how difficult or extreme the environment may be. Unfortunately, life unfolds in a fallen world, and many times even the thought of human value is put at risk.

When I first met Boshorro, a nine-year-old Somali girl, she was sitting on a gurney in stunned silence. Her pencil-thin arms hung weakly at her sides. In a culture where little girls may be the last to be fed, the famine that racked Somalia had taken its toll on Boshorro. She also had a gaping hole in her stomach, from which the hospital staff had just drained a cupful of pus. As if famine were not enough, a horrific civil war had broken out in Somalia. Boshorro had been caught in its crossfire and now suffered the twin ravishes of limited food and armed conflict.

But the pathetic image before me exhibited one more indignity. I noticed that the sleeves of her dress had been cut out. When I inquired as to why this was done, a medical staffer replied without emotion. "We had to reduce her value. If the dress were whole, she would have been vulnerable to the bad elements of our society. We had to reduce her vulnerability by reducing her value."

In Romania's orphanages, I witnessed the same devastations on human life. When a sick child was approaching death, the first thing that was done was to take the child's name off his or her bed. Nameless, the child would then be taken down into the basement of the orphanage, to die alone. Alone and nameless, once death claimed the child's life, the body was removed in much the same manner that we would take out the

---

[7] See Robert A. Seiple, *Ambassadors of Hope: How Christians Can Respond to the World's Toughest Problems* (Downer's Grove, IL: InterVarsity Press, 2004), chap. 7, where I expound on this definition of justice.

garbage. When the ground behind the orphanage softened in springtime, the body would be buried. In winter, the frozen ground made that impossible, so the remains were left on top of the ground where marauding dogs performed the final indignity. Human value, during that time, proved to be very illusive.

I experienced my first hostile gas attack in Gaza. We rushed into a nearby hospital and ultimately found ourselves in the ICU portion of the building. Patients were lying on beds positioned close to the windows because there was no air conditioning. Life was a struggle, an attempt to continue breathing, aided by the limited machines and technology available for that part of the world. The struggle was now made more difficult by the gases that were drifting in from the open windows, challenging lives already vulnerable. When we finally left the hospital, I found one of the gas canisters used in the attack. It was made in Johnstown, Pennsylvania. It was a statement of values.

At 9:15 every morning, the Assistant Secretaries of State hold their daily meetings in the State Department. I was always intrigued when the inevitable clash of national interests and national values would rear its head. National interests were almost always defined in economic or military terms – keeping sea routes open, maintaining security in a global economy, and so on. These were the "hard" issues, realpolitik, maintaining America's position as the last remaining superpower, continuing its role as the indispensable nation. National values were represented by moral imperatives, the so-called "soft" issues, human rights, and my issue, religious freedom. False choices were allowed, however, and most often national values gave way to national interests. I felt then, and continue to believe, that smart people can negotiate the "hard" issues. But the "soft" issues, they are the ones that people are prepared to die for. We neglect such issues at our considerable peril. It is all about values.

Sometimes devaluation takes a more insidious turn. One of the most destructive elements we have in our society today is the easy categorization of people. We create a "one size fits all" category, an intellectually lazy exercise that masks human distinctions by lumping people together. Once a category is created, it is easy to stereotype those that fall within it. Once stereotyped, it is equally easy to demonize those who have been stereotyped. Left unchecked, demonization can lead to hatred and, in many parts of the world that live with only a rudimentary rule of law, violence can soon follow. Evangelicals, for example, come in multiple stripes. Many see only the category, not the individuals who are as varied as those in any other religious grouping. Similarly, Muslims have found themselves characterized as one. Islam has one-and-a-half-billion adherents. We have taken a "cliff notes" approach to Muslims, and now have a category that links the whole with the destructive hints of terrorism, a characteristic of only a few. Such exercises are value statements, negatively applied.

Perhaps the most insidious approach is the devaluing of something important by claiming to be working in its best interests. We see this in the outworking of religious freedom issues in the United States. The separation of church and state is the backdrop for this exercise. If there is a religious element in the public square that offends, some feel obliged to remove it. Christmas trees in the Seattle airport, crosses in college chapels, crèches and menorahs in public view – if someone is offended, freedom *from* religion carries the day, and the purportedly offensive symbol is removed. If we do not like the way a prayer ends, or how many times a day one prays, or in what direction one offers those prayers, we remove it from the public square. In the name of good governance, we keep church separated from state, and run the risk of destroying the varied and rich tapestry provided by religion in America.

A more positive approach, and a more sustainable exercise, is the cultivation of respect between and among people of faith. Respect is partially a function of knowledge. We cannot respect that which we do not know. Knowledge, in turn, is a function of delving more deeply into relationships, eschewing superficiality, listening better, hearing more. As respect grows, the things that offend tend to fade away. A different value takes over.

It is important to differentiate respect from mere tolerance. Respect elevates. Tolerance seeks a lower common denominator. Respect ultimately comes from the heart. Tolerance is an exercise of the intellect. Respect celebrates humanity. Tolerance allows for a cheap form of grace to be applied to people we do not especially like. It is forbearance, not equality.[8] Tolerance is a lesser value. Those who reflect "the image of God" must demonstrate respect.

Gratefully, there are also examples of positive human values at work in difficult places. I observed a cataract operation, conducted outdoors, just south of Danang, Vietnam. The necessary power for the operation came from the headlight of a motor bike. The person destined to receive her sight that day was an eighty-six-year-old grandmother. Given the very limited resource available, the question asked by one of the bystanders, was inevitable. "Why would you operate on an eighty-six-year-old woman?"

---

[8] Stephen L. Carter *The Culture of Disbelief: How American Law and Politics Trivialize Religious Devotion* (New York: Basic Books, 1993), 93.

The implication was clear (and one we hear in American hospitals as well), why "waste" medical efforts on the aged, especially when resources are so scarce? The doctor answered quietly, "This is an eighty-six-year-old woman. She deserves to see her grandchildren at least once before she dies." It is all about value.

In Ethiopia a clinic was established about twenty-five years ago to treat fistulas in women. A tear has taken place, sometimes following pregnancy but possibly also as a consequence of female genital mutilation. The tear does not heal, and now there is a constant, uncontrollable urine drip. This seepage is both uncomfortable and humiliating. Women who have this condition, for example, are kicked off public transportation, are precluded from hotel stays. Many times they are quickly divorced by their husbands. It takes only a very minor operation to correct this problem, and the clinic exists to do just that. But there is more than physical healing at stake. Self-esteem needs to be created as well. Following the healing process, and before they are discharged, the women are each given a brand new dress. Life begins anew. It is a value statement.

In Mauritania, the issue is one of literacy. Women want to be able to read and write. One rationale offered to me was particularly sad, "I want to be able to read my husband's divorce papers." On a more positive note, female literacy is the most important element empowering sustainable development. Once women can read and write, they insist that those skills are made available to their children – and a positive development process begins. This is the kind of development that has lasting value. That value is seen today in Mauritania.

Human value is one of the great "take aways" from a God who loved and a Christ who died. It is where the Christian gets both worth and marching orders, for as theologian Miroslav Volf sums up human responsibility, "what happens to us must be done by us."[9] The key commandment to love God and love neighbor, a commandment articulated in the Old Testament and reinforced in the New Testament, produces the responsibility for the Christian to be active in the world providing value-added human rights.

HUMAN CHOICE: FREEDOM AND DIGNITY

Human rights are at least partially based on a uniform understanding that all peoples should have the potential to make good choices. The precise

---

[9] Miroslav Volf, *Exclusion and Embrace: A Theological Exploration of Identity, Otherness, and Reconciliation* (Nashville: Abingdon Press, 1996), 129.

language in the preamble to the 1966 International Covenant for Civil and Political Rights lends itself to this thought: "all members of the human family" enjoy these rights derived "from the inherent dignity of the human person." This "inherent dignity" suggests that choices are made from a position of strength, a position shared with all of humanity. The human family provides both "universal respect" for the rights and the "responsibility to strive for the protection" of these rights. Acknowledging the difficulty in achieving this, however, the language of the preamble becomes very practical. These rights and, by extension, our ability to choose from strength, "can only be achieved if conditions are created" that foster human dignity. Consider the following "condition."

We encountered a new mother in Chad, a woman who had just recently given birth to twin boys. Unfortunately, the boys were born in the midst of a famine, and the mother realized immediately that she did not have the resources to keep both of her children alive. She had to choose which child would live and which child would die. By the time we got there, the choice had already been made, and it was irreparable. One of the children was bouncy, robust, and had good color. The other was sallow, listless, thin, and frail, and made more so by frequent vomiting. It would only be a few hours before "conditions" would claim a young life.

Granted, this is an extreme example, but unfortunately it is played out over and over again in a world where local context does not support "inherent dignity," where the very environment works against choosing from strength. This mother's choice was made not from strength but from abject poverty, the kind of poverty that can now be defined as a condition that precludes ethical considerations. In a world where most of us reflect only briefly over choices of clothes to wear, foods to eat, cars to drive, and schools to attend, it is legitimate to worry over the health of "all members of the human family."

One of the strengths of the international human rights covenants is the inherent assumption of mutual accountability. We hold each other accountable for creating the conditions that will optimize human rights. This is not always understood. When I first sat across the table from Ye Xiawen, head of the Religious Affairs Bureau in China, his initial question was "Who made you the international morality cop?" And in the question-and-answer period that followed my 2006 talk to the Foreign Affairs Institute in Vientiane, Laos, I was similarly asked, "By what authority are you here to tell us about human rights?" (The question was sharpened considerably by my known role in the so-called "secret" bombing in Laos during the Vietnam War.) In each case, I emphasized the same thought, namely, the concept of mutual accountability inherent in the human rights documents. We are not only challenged to point out each other's shortcomings, however, we are also challenged to work together to create better conditions on the ground for the practical implementation of human rights.

In this exercise of creating a better environment within which good choices are possible, there are two very important areas for discernment. The first discernment concerns the actual abuses taking place, the obstacles that may exist in a country, obstacles that preclude the realization of a human right. This point of discernment is normally surprisingly easy. When people are oppressed, when rights are denied, when human dignity is being diminished, it is fairly obvious to all. Facts are facts, and the global reach of communication uncovers and exposes these human threats quickly. When a pastor is jailed in a remote section of Laos, for example, that information makes it to the internet within hours.

The second level of discernment is far more complicated. Is the abuse in question an isolated incident? Were government officials involved? Was it a function of government intentionally or has the government created and condoned an environment of impunity? What right has been violated? (It is important to differentiate rights, as reporting of violations is sometimes a function of legal resources available, or what rights groups will make the most noise. Religious freedom, for example, experiences this all the time.)

Complicating this second level of discernment is the strategy for reform. How might this problem be fixed? It is here that international differences in the implementation of human rights need to be taken into consideration. As Ye Xiawen reminded me during that memorable visit, "We have different cultures, different histories, and different systems of governance." He is right, and this requires immense amounts of sensitivity and great discernment as the human family is contextualized by national boundaries. The desire to produce a common expression for "inherent dignity" has now been made profoundly more difficult.

The human rights community needs to be vigilant in terms of the individual "effects" of abusive practices even as it seeks to ameliorate the long-term "causes" by bringing sustainable change to the conditions on the ground. How might the Christian faith inform such an exercise?

Perhaps the best known of Jesus's parables is the Parable of the Good Samaritan (Luke 10:25–37). The parable was designed to answer a lawyer's question, "Who is my neighbor?" The lawyer knew he was supposed to love his neighbor, but this commandment was far too general for his legally trained mind. He was looking for boundaries. In the parable, a man was beaten and robbed, and is now lying close to death on the side of the road. A Levite and a rabbi both, in turn, pass this man. Each has a choice to make. Both know what has happened to the man, and one can assume that each passerby can do something to help. The ethic discussed earlier, the accountability of knowing and the responsibility for acting, was quickly and totally ignored, and the two move on, "passing on the other side of the road." A choice was made, and backs were turned on a vulnerable human being. Then an unusual source of help happens on the scene. A despised Samaritan, a foreigner, the "other," sees the exact same reality but reacts completely differently. Immediate help is provided. The beaten man's wounds are bound up on the spot. Long-term care is put in place as the Samaritan takes the man to an inn, providing food and shelter for him. Finally, the Samaritan underwrites the cost of his compassion and guarantees the financial resource necessary to completely restore the unnamed victim back to health. With that the answer to the lawyer's question is provided and the loving of neighbor takes on new and profound meaning.

Obviously this parable and its implications are useful for today's human rights activist. There are, however, two additional implications that must be taken into account. First, how do we handle today's "Jericho Road"? The knowledge explosion on the information highway makes us all too aware of the numbers, and conditions, of beaten humanity found along that road. Our understanding of an enormously fragile humanity is only limited by the band width we can afford for our computers. How can we preclude the paralysis of sheer numbers as we individually walk this Jericho Road?

Second, when do we do more than simply patch up today's problems? When, for example, do we go up into to the mountains and roust out the robbers? How do we change the underlying causes that allow for individuals to be beaten and robbed of their humanity? How do we fix cultures, redeem institutions, and change structures so that a day might come when the vulnerability of the individual is reduced? How do we properly use both power and authority to right wrongs, to settle grievances, to make justice a reality for "all members of the human family"?

This is a challenge that we enter into both individually and collectively, through the individual passion of the abolitionist Wilberforce, for example, to the collective strength of the United Nations, from the obedience of one to the faithfulness of many, from indigenous church outreach ministries to the comprehensive holism of an international aid organization like World Vision, from recognizing both the star over a manger as well as the light that floods a city on a hill. All of our resources need to be harnessed with a common purpose in mind: create the conditions where positive options for life are strengthened, and proper choices can be made from an elevated position of strength.[10]

Often the missing ingredient in human rights is the role that hope plays. Bette Bao Lord, a long-time human rights activist from Washington, DC, tells the story of a young boy in China. Every day the boy gets up, goes out to a large grassy field, and flies his kite. He flies it as high as he can, each and every day. He follows this regime every day, because on the edge of this large field is a prison. And in that prison sits his father. The son gets up every day to fly his kite so that his father will see the kite and know he is being remembered, that there are people on the "outside" who love him, that wait expectantly for his release.

Hope might be a future concept, but hope is legitimated by tangible signs in the present. The kite is tangible, a sign that there is reason to believe in a different future, a reason to be hopeful. Human rights, regardless of the motivating source, need to be infused with hope. The absence of hope can be just as destructive as the absence of food and water. People can literally die, when all hope is gone.

This definition of hope – the promise of a future reality made credible through a tangible present – is further illustrated in the Old Testament book of Jeremiah. The Babylonians have laid siege to Jerusalem. Time is running out. Food and water are increasingly scarce. With what appears to be a strange sense of timing, God commands Jeremiah to go out and buy a field. Enter the real estate market! Buy the field, pay cash, get a clear title, bring along someone to witness the transaction. Why? Why now? The gates are about to fall. The pagans will scale the wall. Jerusalem will be destroyed, and a long painful exile will begin for those who survive. The answer is hopeful. "For in seventy years, my people will return. They will reconstitute their vineyards and rebuild their homes" (Jer. 32:6–44). It can be assumed that during the darkest days of the exile, the purchase of this field, this tangible down-payment on a future reality, will provide hope for the people of Israel.

---

[10] I realize this is an all-too-brief statement of what can be done. See further my *Ambassadors of Hope*, esp. chap. 9 where I treat this issue in greater depth.

My father was seventy-five-years old when he planted a number of small fruit trees on his property in Harmony, New Jersey. I reacted verbally, and somewhat mockingly said to him, "You have to be the biggest of optimists, planting trees at your age." My father passed away several years ago, and now, when I return to the old homestead, I have a choice to make. I can go to the cemetery and brood over his grave, or I can pick the fruit from his trees and reflect on someone who knew a great deal about hope.

Hope is a critical component, and sometimes a surprise consequence, of actions designed to protect human rights. In 1998, the United States unanimously passed the International Religious Freedom Act. The Act provided a religious freedom office in the State Department, an Ambassador-at-large to head up that office, and an annual report on religious freedom abuses worldwide. When that Act was signed into law, countless nameless, largely faceless, people around the world were filled with hope. The persecuted might still feel oppressed, but now they knew that someone important was taking their side. In the halls of power, the last remaining superpower was standing up and providing a voice for those who were unable to speak for themselves. Perhaps the future reality of those most oppressed would change. Given the very tangible mechanism put into place by the Act, hope in the future was now made credible.

How does Christianity anchor and augment human hope? What does Christianity have to offer human rights dependent on this concept of hope? At the heart of Christian witness, there is hope. Peter's words are brief but far-reaching, "We bear witness to the hope that lies within us" (1 Pet. 3:15). This is the role and this is the task of the committed Christian. This should also be the core competency of the Christian. In the myriad of ways that this can be communicated, Christians bear responsibility for being agents of hope. In the loving of neighbor, in aiding the man beaten and robbed on the side of the road, in taking on the challenges of changing structures, systems, and cultures that oppress, Christianity has the responsibility of providing tangible hope in the present. As represented in Christian teaching, tangibility has been achieved. God is still sovereign, the grave is still empty, and the "gates of hell have not prevailed" against His church.

Events that have taken place in the past bear witness to credible hope for the future. Again, emanating from Christianity's core beliefs, a King has come. A Kingdom has been established. The Sermon on the Mount is a Kingdom sermon. The Lord's Prayer is a Kingdom prayer. From his birth to his death, from the wise men's visit to Herod to Pilate's sign over the cross, Jesus is acknowledged as a King.

But not fully. There is the mystery of the "already" but "not yet." The fullness of the Kingdom awaits Jesus's Second Coming. At that time, hope will be vindicated. Tangible expressions will become real. Awaiting that final fulfillment, Christians remember, and sustain their hopes, in a communion ceremony, where bread and wine bear witness to a body broken and blood that was shed.

Christianity has much to offer the provision of human hope. Christians fly kites. They buy land, plant trees, and make laws favoring the oppressed. They announce Kingdoms, break bread, and drink wine. All of this is done to keep hope alive, to make hope tangible, credible, relevant, and legitimate.

Human value, human choice, and human hope are derived from the fundamental beliefs of the Christian faith. Human rights, and the vigorous pursuit of these rights, are part of the inescapable tapestry of Christianity. The rationale for Christian involvement in the human rights arena is one of the most natural understandings to emerge from this religion.

RECOMMENDED READING

Bucar, Elizabeth and Barbra Barnett, eds. *Does Human Rights Need God?* Grand Rapids, MI: Wm. B. Eerdmans, 2005.

Carter, Stephen L. *The Culture of Disbelief: How American Law and Politics Trivialize Religious Devotion*. New York: Basic Books, 1993.

Gregorian, Vartan. *Islam: A Mosaic, Not a Monolith*. Washington, DC: Brookings Institution Press, 2003.

Hasson, Kevin Seamus. *The Right to be Wrong*. New York: Encounter Books, 2005.

John Paul II. *Crossing the Threshold of Hope*. New York: Alfred A. Knopf, 1994.

Meacham, Jon. *American Gospel: God, the Founding Fathers, and the Making of a Nation*. New York: Random House, 2006.

Nasr, Seyyed Hossein. *The Heart of Islam: Enduring Values for Humanity*. San Francisco: Harper, 2002.

Seiple, Robert A. *Ambassadors of Hope: How Christians Can Respond to the World's Toughest Problems*. Downer's Grove, IL: InterVarsity Press, 2004.

Swaine, Lucas. *The Liberal Conscience: Politics and Principle in a World of Religious Pluralism*. New York: Columbia University Press, 2006.

Thomas, Scott M. *The Global Resurgence of Religion and the Transformation of International Relations: The Struggle for the Soul of the Twenty-First Century*. New York: Palgrave Macmillan, 2005.

Volf, Miroslav. *Exclusion and Embrace: A Theological Exploration of Identity, Otherness, and Reconciliation*. Nashville: Abingdon Press, 1996.

CHAPTER 17

A right to clean water

John Copeland Nagle

Environmental law has developed apart from ideas of rights. It emerged from the common law of property and torts, exploded into a multitude of statutes, and has expanded into international law. Only recently have notions of human rights related to the environment gained traction, and their impact remains modest.

Environmental law has also developed apart from Christian teaching. Indeed, one famous essay blamed Christianity for the world's worsening environmental problems.[1] Since then, numerous Christian writers have articulated thoughtful expositions of the lessons of biblical and Christian teaching regarding care for the world that God created. These writings, though, devote little attention to the relationship of Christian environmental teaching to public policy or law generally, or to claims of environmental rights in particular.

In this chapter, I use the idea of a right to clean water to illustrate the role that rights play in environmental protection. Christianity and other value systems agree that clean water is perhaps the most fundamental environmental need for humans and other creatures alike. Both the law and voluntary organizations – including many Christian relief organizations – work aggressively to provide clean water throughout the world. They do so, however, with scant assistance from the legal construct of rights. Little is lost from such reliance upon a legal framework that operates outside the context of human rights, and Christian teaching has much less to say about the possible value of adding rights claims to environmental law debates than it does about the need to make environmental progress, however we do so.

---

[1] See Lynn White, Jr., "The Historic Roots of Our Ecologic Crisis," *Science* 155 (1967): 1203–7.

Christianity and creation. Christian environmental thinking begins
with the innumerable biblical texts involving the creation of the earth
and all of its creatures, the relationship of the people to their often hostile environment, the rules for treating animals and the land, and the rich
imagery contained in the psalms and other books. Eight themes about
God's creation emerge from the Bible's teaching.[2]

God created the world. The opening sentence of the Bible states that "in
the beginning God created the heavens and the earth" (Gen. 1:1). The balance of the first chapter of Genesis records how God created plants, fish,
animals, birds – and finally men and women. That chapter also describes
how God brought order to the world by separating light from darkness,
land from water, and the earth from the heavens. The way in which God
did all of this is notable in two respects. First, God created the world out
of nothing. As the apostle John later wrote, "[t]hrough him all things were
made; without him nothing was made that has been made" (John 1:3).
Second, God created by His word. The creation story repeatedly describes
how God spoke and "it was so" (Gen. 1:7, 9, 11, 15, 24). There is, of course,
another notable feature of the creation story – God created the world in six
days – but the debates that have centered on how that happened are not
especially relevant to environmental issues today.

God pronounced the creation to be good. When God created each part
of creation, He "saw that it was good" (Gen. 1:10, 12, 18, 21, 25). These
statements suggest three interconnected explanations for the goodness of
creation: creation is good because God created it, creation is good because
God proclaimed that it was so, and creation is intrinsically good as shown
by God's response to it. Creation reflects God and it honors God. Today
creation suffers the consequences of the entry of sin into the world, as discussed below, but that simply shows that the current state of creation does
not reflect the original goodness that God saw.

God is the owner of all creation. David wrote that "[t]he earth is the
Lord's, and everything in it" (Ps. 24:1). The idea of God as the owner of
creation pervades the creation account, the Old Testament saga of the
people of Israel, and the parables that Jesus told in the New Testament.
God charges humanity with certain responsibilities for creation, but God's

---

[2] Much of this section is taken from John Copeland Nagle, "Christianity and Environmental Law,"
    in Michael McConnell, Robert Cochran, and Angela Carmella, eds., *Christian Perspectives on the
    Law* (New Haven: Yale University Press, 2001), 435–52.

authority and control over His creation supersedes both the creation itself and humanity's role in it.

God gave humanity dominion over creation. The most controversial verses in the Bible for environmentalists appear at the end of the first chapter of Genesis, where God gives men and women "dominion" over all other creatures and commands humanity to "fill the earth and subdue it" (Gen. 1:26, 28). Historically, these commands have been cited to justify actions that treat the provision of resources needed – or wanted – by humanity as the only purpose of creation. Much of the recent Christian environmental scholarship questions that understanding. Indeed, the word "dominion" is used elsewhere in the Bible to describe a peaceful, servant rule (Lev. 25:43; Ezek. 34:4; 1 Kings 4:24). Moreover, God exercises dominion Himself, and the examples of God's rule – and His rule of creation in particular – belie any suggestion that dominion equals exploitation. Three models of dominion – servanthood, kingship, and stewardship – support a Christian obligation to actively care for creation.

God charged men and women with the responsibility of caring for creation. God placed Adam in the Garden of Eden so that Adam could "tend and keep it" (Gen. 2:15). What it means to "keep" creation is illustrated by the priestly request that "the Lord bless you and *keep* you" (Num. 6:24) and by God's placement of an angel at the east of Eden to "guard" the garden after the fall into sin (Gen. 3:24). The obligation to care for creation is further demonstrated by the understanding of the command to exercise "dominion" described above. The story of Noah obeying God by saving all species from the flood, God's subsequent covenant with the entire creation, and God's encouragement of all creatures to multiply and fill the earth provides yet another example of our duty to care for creation. Conversely, the Bible teaches that God will judge those who injure the earth (Rev. 11:16–18).

God alone is worthy of worship. The first commandments that God gave to Moses on Mount Sinai were that "[y]ou shall have no other gods before me" and that "[y]ou shall not make for yourself an idol in the form of anything in heaven above or on the earth beneath or in the waters below. You shall not bow down to them or worship them" (Ex. 20:3–4). The Scriptures then recount numerous instances where people violated those commands by worshiping a variety of other beings: golden calves, Baal, silver and gold gods, angels, the starry host, and unknown gods. In short, people "exchanged the glory of the immortal God for images made to look like mortal man and birds and animals and reptiles" (Rom. 1:23). The consequences that befell the people who worshiped the creation instead of the creator demonstrates the seriousness with which God takes these commands.

Creation has suffered the effects of the entry of sin into the world. The fall of humanity that occurred when Adam and Eve sinned affected the rest of creation, too. The immediate result was God's curse of the ground so that it produces thorns and thistles and so that much more work is required to obtain food from the land. The fall also alienated people from other creatures, with later passages describing how God used animals to exercise His judgment against humanity (Lev. 26:22; Num. 21:6; Ezek. 5:17). Animals, plants, and the rest of creation suffer themselves because of human actions and because of God's judgment against human sin.

God will redeem His creation. The entire creation is included in many of the covenants that God announces throughout the Bible. For example, God established a covenant with Noah, his descendants, *and* every living creature on earth that never again would a flood destroy all life on earth (Gen. 9:8–11). In his Letter to the Romans, Paul writes that:

> The creation waits in eager expectation for the sons of God to be revealed. For the creation was subjected to frustration, not by its own choice, but by the will of the one who subjected it, in hope that the creation itself will be liberated from its bondage to decay and brought into the glorious freedom of the children of God. We know that the whole creation has been groaning as in the pains of childbirth right up to the present time. (Rom. 8:19–22)

Other passages describe how this earth will be destroyed on the day of judgment, only to be replaced by a new earth (2 Pet. 3:7, 10; Rev. 21:1).

Christianity and water. Christian teaching has a lot to say about water in particular. Water plays a central role in the Bible. The Old Testament Prophets promise water as a blessing for people and other creatures in the desert (Isa. 35:6; 43:19–20; 44:3–4). Jesus promised a reward to those who provide a cup of water to those who are thirsty (Matt. 10:42). The cleansing power of water is evident throughout the Scriptures, both in the physical sense (Mark 7:3; John 9:7; 13:5) and in the spiritual sense of baptism. The Bible also emphasizes the importance of pure water. Numerous passages describe the consequences of polluted water (Ex. 15:23; 2 Kings 2:19–22; Jer. 8:14; Ezek. 32:2, 13). Throughout the Bible, water sustains human health, enables plants to grow, and serves ceremonial purposes. Yet the Israel of biblical times often suffered from a lack of water, so the people relied upon wells, cisterns, and channels to collect and keep necessary water supplies.[3]

---

[3] See Sampson M. Nwaomah, "Water in the Bible in the Context of the Ecological Debate in the Nigerian Delta," *Journal of Faith, Spirituality, and Social Change* 1 (2008): 187, 188–91.

This biblical teaching has begun to inspire Christian writings about the importance of water and the need to protect it. Christian ethicist John Hart observes that "[w]ater is intended by the Creator to be a sign and mediation of the Spirit's immanence and solicitous care for the living."[4] Hart adds, "When water is pure, its life-giving role can be fulfilled. When water is polluted, it endangers health and life not only for humankind, but for all the biotic community."[5] Nigerian religious studies professor Sampson Nwaomah calls for Christians to address the threats to clean water in the Niger Delta by organizing and creating awareness, awakening and sustaining the government's attention, galvanizing community efforts, and boycott oil and gas industries if necessary.[6] There are also Christian writers who would place greater emphasis upon global clean water than on the problems of climate change. Calvin Beisner, for example, argues that "[a] billion dollars invested in waste water treatment plants and municipal water systems would improve the health and life expectancy of many times more people than an equal amount invested in" the "most acclaimed problems" of climate change, species extinction, and deforestation.[7]

THE RIGHT TO CLEAN WATER

Much of the debate about rights and what Christians regard as God's creation concerns animal rights. Christian teachings that regard humanity alone as created in the image of God, and thus distinct from animals and the rest of creation, provoke hostile reactions among many animal rights scholars and activists, even though Christian teaching offers different justifications for animal welfare efforts. Besides animal rights, much environmental writing considers whether other features of the natural environment should be afforded legal rights. Christopher Stone advanced that argument in a famous 1972 article entitled "Should Trees Have Standing?," which Justice Douglas embraced while dissenting from the court's holding that the opponents of a proposed ski resort lacked standing to litigate the project's compliance with the substantive commands of environmental law.[8] Such debates about animal rights and rights for

---

[4] John Hart, *Sacramental Commons: Christian Ecological Ethics* (Lanham, MD: Rowman & Littlefield, 2006), 80.

[5] *Ibid.*, 79.

[6] Nwaomah, "Water in the Bible," 202–4.

[7] E. Calvin Beisner, *Where Garden Meets Wilderness: Evangelical Entry into the Environmental Debate* (Grand Rapids, MI: Acton Institute, 1997), 74–5.

[8] See *Sierra Club* v. *Morton*, 405 US 727, 742 (1972) (Douglas, J., dissenting), citing Christopher Stone, "Should Trees Have Standing? – Toward Legal Rights for Natural Objects," *Southern California Law Review* 45 (1972): 450–501.

natural objects continue, but they are not debates about *human* rights. So let me turn to that issue now.

Christian teaching is hardly unique in its recognition of the importance of clean water. But clean water's importance has not yielded an express right to clean water in international law, American law, or the laws of most nations. The following sections describe the debate concerning the existence of a right to clean water, discuss the alternative means of achieving clean water, and consider whether the establishment of a right would make a difference.

The existence of a right to clean water. International law does not contain an express right to clean water. One online petition would address that absence by adding a new Article 31 to the Universal Declaration of Human Rights to provide that "[e]veryone has the right to clean and accessible water, adequate for the health and well-being of the individual and family, and no one shall be deprived of such access or quality of water due to individual economic circumstance."[9] Meanwhile, some find a right to clean water implicit in other existing human rights. The Committee on Economic, Social and Cultural Rights of the UN Economic and Social Council drafted the most extensive defense of an implied right to water in its General Comment No. 15 in 2002.[10] The sources of that purported right include the rights to life, an adequate standard of living, the highest attainable standard of health, and adequate housing and food. The committee asserted that the normative content of a right to water includes a sufficient quantity of water, safe water quality, freedom from arbitrary disconnections, physical and economic accessibility, information regarding water issues, and non-discrimination in water services.[11] Three years later, a human rights subcommission of the UN Economic and Social Council asserted that "the right to drinking water and sanitation is unquestionably a human right," and it elaborated on state duties to "[e]stablish a regulatory system" and to "establish water-quality standards on the basis of the World Health Organization guidelines."[12] Speaking of the World Health Organization (WHO) in 2003 it issued a report on "The Right to Water"

---

[9] See Freeflo, Article 31: The Right to Water, http://freeflo.org/article31.

[10] United Nations Economic and Social Council, Committee on Economic, Social and Cultural Rights, Substantive Issues Arising in the Implementation of the International Covenant on Economic, Social and Cultural Rights: The Right to Water (arts. 11 and 12 of the International Covenant on Economic, Social and Cultural Rights), General Comment No. 15 (2002) (hereinafter General Comment No. 15).

[11] *Ibid.*, 4–6.

[12] United Nations Economic and Social Council, Commission on Human Rights, Sub-Commission on the Promotion and Protection of Human Rights, Economic, Social and Cultural Rights: Realization of the Right to Drinking Water and Sanitation 5, 6, 8 (July 11, 2005).

that begins with UN Secretary-General Kofi Annan's assertion that "[a]ccess to safe water is a fundamental human need and, therefore, a basic human right."[13]

Several Christian organizations have joined the campaign for a right to clean water. The Pontifical Council for Justice and Peace provided the most extensive Christian defense of a right to clean water in 2003. The Council's note "Water, An Essential Element for Life," advances three arguments for a right to water. First, the note observes that "water is a precondition for the realization of other human rights." Second, the note offers the familiar argument regarding the importance of water: "Water is an essential commodity for life. Without water life is threatened, with the result being death. The right to water is thus an inalienable right." The note's third argument asserts that "[t]he dignity of the human person mandates" the acknowledgment of a right to water.[14] Each of these three arguments draws support from numerous governmental and secular organizations as a justification for a right to clean water, as well as from Christian teaching.

Yet the existence of an international right to clean water is the subject of continuing debate. The submission of the United States to the UN High Commissioner of Human Rights in June 2007 expresses many of the concerns with recognizing a right. Initially, the USA "strongly supports the goal of universal access to safe drinking water." But the USA denies that the importance of clean water yields a legal right to clean water, and it disputes the General Comment 15's effort to tease such a right out of other rights contained in international instruments. Instead, "while there is no 'right to water' under international law, as a matter of policy and good government it is manifest that water is essential for the life and all individuals, and indeed for all life on earth."[15] Similarly, the Finnish submission to the UN High Commissioner describes the existence of a right to water as "controversial," noting the reluctance of many nations "to approve the rights-based approaches" to water.[16]

Domestic laws show a similar pattern. South Africa's Constitution contains a right to water. India's Supreme Court has interpreted its

---

[13] World Health Organization, The Right to Water 6 (2003).

[14] Pontifical Council for Justice and Peace, Note: Water, An Essential Element For Life, www.vatican.va/roman_curia/pontifical_councils/justpeace/documents/rc_pc_justpeace_doc_20030322_kyoto-water_en.html (March 2003).

[15] Views of the United States of America on Human Rights and Access to Water 1, 5 (June 2007).

[16] Permanent Mission of Finland to the United Nations, Finland's Human Rights Policy, Access to Water 1 (Apr. 20, 2007).

Constitution to contain a right to clean water. By contrast, in Canada, British Columbia has held that the law does not recognize such a right.[17] In the United States, many state constitutions guarantee a right to a clean environment. Several even guarantee a right to clean water.[18] But such constitutional rights have had little direct effect because most courts have declined to interpret them as judicially enforceable.

Achieving clean water. The effort to provide clean water has proceeded despite the absence of a right to clean water. Governmental regulation of activities that interfere with clean water, government funding of projects that are necessary to provide clean water, and the support of private organizations – including Christian organizations – all contribute to the quest for clean water. I will review each method in turn.

Regulation. In the United States, environmental law pursues clean water without relying upon the rubric of rights. Water quantity is primarily the province of state water law, which assigns rights to use water to those who live next to it (in Eastern riparian law states), to those who use it first (in Western prior appropriation law states), or through hybrid regulatory schemes (for groundwater). Federal law intervenes to guarantee sufficient water for protected wildlife and protected lands, but not for human uses.

Water quality has become primarily the province of federal environmental law. The environmental statutes that Congress enacted during a frenzy of activity during the late 1960s and the 1970s form the heart of environmental law in the United States. The Clean Water Act (CWA) of 1972 mandates that anyone discharging pollutants into the water must employ the leading water-pollution control technology identified by EPA. The Safe Drinking Water Act (SDWA) establishes nationwide minimum drinking-water protection standards. Those federal statutes, however, do not employ the language of environmental rights. There are a few stray references to a right to clean water in discussions of American environmental law, but they all occur in rhetorical statements rather than in legal prescriptions or decisions.[19] Instead, the CWA and the SDWA focus on

---

[17] See Constitution of the Republic of South Africa, Art. 27(1)(b) (1997); *AP Pollution Control Bd.-II v. Prof. MV Nayudu (Retd) & ORS*, Civ. App. Nos. 368–373 (India Dec. 1, 2000); *Red Mountain Residents & Property Owners Asss'n* v. *Simpson*, 2000 BCTC LEXIS 1958, *8 (B.C. Sup. Ct. 2000); *Slocan Forest Prods. Ltd*. v. *Doe*, 2000 BCTC LEXIS 1377, *9 (B.C. Sup. Ct. 2000).

[18] Massachusetts Constitution, Art. II, §3 (providing "the right to clean … water"); Pennsylvania Constitution, Art. I, §27 (providing "a right to … pure water").

[19] The examples include HR Doc. No. 387, 89th Cong., 2nd Sess. 9 (1966) (statement of President Johnson supporting a "creed" that would proclaim "[t]he right to clean water – and the duty not to pollute it"); *Water Pollution Control Legislation, 1971: Hearing Before the House Public Works & Transp. Comm.*, 92nd Cong., 1st Sess. 346 (1971) (testimony of EPA Administrator William

the quality of the water rather than the rights of water users. Both laws empower individuals to bring citizen suits to remedy violations of the substantive commands of the law, but even those citizen suit provisions decline to identify a right to clean water.

Funding. Money is key to providing clean water. The CWA contains numerous provisions that authorize the expenditure of federal funds to build municipal sewage treatment facilities and to develop other water-pollution control programs. The SDWA authorizes similar expenditures. Annual spending on water-pollution control programs in the United States rose from $9.1 billion in 1972 (the year of the CWA's enactment) to $50 billion in 2000.[20] Yet many advocates insist that the government needs to spend much more money to achieve clean water throughout the United States.

The world community recognized the need to devote more resources to providing clean water when it recognized access to safe drinking water as one of the Millennium Development Goals. Adopted by the United Nations General Assembly in 2000, one of the goals is to "[h]alve, by 2015, the proportion of the population without sustainable access to safe drinking water and basic sanitation."[21] The goal prompted numerous agencies to increase funding and coordinate their efforts to provide clean drinking water throughout the world. By 2009, the world was "ahead of schedule in meeting the 2015 drinking water target," though "884 million people worldwide still rely on unimproved water sources for their drinking, cooking, bathing and other domestic activities."[22]

The United States also pursues global clean water through funding and diplomacy. In his inaugural address, President Obama told "the people of poor nations, we pledge to work alongside you to … let clean waters flow."[23] Toward that end, the United States spent more than $1 billion on global water and sanitation efforts in ninety-five countries in 2008.[24] The law encourages such diplomacy. Congress enacted the Senator Paul Simon Water for the Poor Act of 2005 in order to emphasize water and sanitation

---

Ruckelshaus) (observing that "[s]ome believe there should be a constitutional right to clean air and clean water"); *Water Pollution – 1970, Part 5: Hearing Before the Subcomm. on Air & Water Pollution of the Senate Pub. Works Comm.*, 91st Cong., 2nd Sess. 1674 (1970) (statement of David R. Zwick) (describing the federal government "as protectors of the people's right to clean water").

[20] See William L. Andreen, "Water Quality Today – Has the Clean Water Act Been a Success?" *Alabama Law Review* 55 (2004): 537, 574.

[21] United Nations, *The Millennium Development Goals Report* 2009, 45. [22] *Ibid.*, 46.

[23] 155 *Congressional Record* S669 (daily edn Jan. 20, 2009) (inaugural address of President Obama).

[24] US Department of State, *Senator Paul Simon Water for the Poor Act: Report to Congress*, iii, 4 (2009) (citing fiscal year 2008 statistics).

assistance in countries that are in the greatest need of such assistance. The act "requires that access to clean water become a cornerstone of America's foreign assistance efforts"[25] and codified "one of the Millennium Development Goals in US law for the first time."[26] A proposed new 2009 version of the act calls upon the United States to "lead a global effort to bring sustainable access to clean water and sanitation to poor people throughout the world" by providing clean water to 100 million people for the first time.[27]

Private Christian NGOs. Many international non-governmental organizations (NGOs) target the need to provide clean water to those who do not enjoy it throughout the world. The role of the Christian NGOs is especially telling given the focus of this paper. At a recent congressional hearing, Representative Smith praised the work of Living Waters International, "a Christian ministry that implements water development through training, equipping and consulting."[28] Living Waters prioritizes the use of appropriate technologies, which is necessary because "drilled wells with hand pumps are the best solution for rural communities" because such pumps "are simple to repair, and replacement parts can easily be found." Living Waters also emphasizes community involvement and "seeing people manage their own water solutions to the greatest extent possible."[29] The organization spent $13 million on clean-water projects in 2008, which is a proverbial drop in the bucket to what is needed. Numerous other Christian NGOs contribute significant funds and resources toward providing clean water throughout the world.[30] Yet Living Waters refuses to estimate how many billions of dollars it would take to "solve the world's water crisis," in part "because what is lacking are competent, responsible implementers" of new and existing water projects.[31]

---

[25] Senator William H. Frist, MD, "Medicine as a Currency for Peace Through Global Health Diplomacy," *Yale Law and Policy Review* 26 (2007): 209, 222. See also 155 *Congressional Record* E936 (daily edn Apr. 22, 2009) (statement of Rep. Blumenauer) (explaining that the act "established investment in safe and affordable water for the world's poorest as a major goal of US foreign assistance").

[26] 151 *Congressional Record* H9707 (daily edn Nov. 5, 2005) (statement of Rep. Blumenauer).

[27] Senator Paul Simon Water for the World Act of 2009, S. 624, 111th Cong., 1st Sess. §§3 and 4(a).

[28] *Africa's Water Crisis and the US Response: Hearing Before the Subcomm. on Africa & Global Health of the House Foreign Affairs Comm.*, 110th Cong., 1st Sess. 35 (2007) (prepared statement of Rep. Smith).

[29] Living Waters, Our Approach, www.water.cc/about-lwi/our-approach/.

[30] See, for example, Compassion, Water Facts, www.compassion.com/child-advocacy/find-your-voice/quick-facts/water-quick-facts.htm; Samaritan's Purse, A Thirsty World Needs Clean Water, www.samaritanspurse.org/water/; World Vision, Water and Sanitation, www.worldvision.org/content.nsf/learn/ways-we-help-water.

[31] Living Waters, What Would It Take? How Much Money Would Solve the World's Water Crisis, www.water.cc/water-crisis/related-news/.

WOULD A RIGHT TO CLEAN WATER YIELD
GREATER ACCESS TO CLEAN WATER?

Clean water has been a top international priority despite the absence of a right to clean water. Most countries accord clean water similar priority in their domestic laws, again even in the absence of such a right. And additional funding, rather than additional regulation, is most needed to provide greater access to clean water. What difference, then, would a human right to clean water make in the effort to provide clean water? The arguments for such a right can be restated into four claims that I will address in this section: a right to clean water would (1) add substantive protections to efforts to provide clean water, (2) provide access to judicial remedies for violations of the right, (3) enable the regulation of international organizations and governments, and (4) counter the push for privatizing water resources.

The substantive scope of a right to clean water. A right to clean water, say its supporters, will provide specific legal protections to those whose access to clean water is threatened. That depends, however, on the precise content of a right to clean water. "The challenge," as the Pontifical Council puts it, "remains as to how such a right to water would be realized and enforced at the local, national, and international levels."[32] The Finnish government is more skeptical, observing that "the question of the right to water as a human right seems much more complex" when it is applied to specific water quality and water-quantity claims, rather than stating an abstract goal.[33]

Consider some of the questions that have arisen under the SDWA in recent years. Is regulation of a proposed uranium mine entrusted to the federal government or to the native tribal community? What is the permissible amount of sewage pathogens that may be injected underground? What is the appropriate treatment technique to eliminate the parasite cryptosporidium from drinking water? Can apartment owners meter and bill their tenants for water purchased by the owners but distributed to and actually used by the tenants?[34] These are not the kinds of questions that are

---

[32] Pontifical Council, see n. 14, above.
[33] Permanent Mission of Finland to the United Nations, *supra* note 26, at 2.
[34] See *Hydro Res., Inc.* v. *United States EPA*, 562 F.3d 1249 (10th Cir. 2009) (holding that EPA has the authority to regulate the uranium mine), reh'g en banc; *Miami-Dade County* v. *United States EPA*, 529 F.3d 1049 (11th Cir. 2008) (deferring to EPA's underground injection rule); *City of Portland* v. *EPA*, 507 F.3d 706 (D.C. Cir. 2008) (rejecting the complaints of New York City and Portland that EPA's required treatment of Cryptosporidium is too expensive); *Manufactured House. Inst.* v. *United States EPA*, 467 F.3d 391 (4th Cir. 2005) (upholding EPA's rule allowing apartment owners to meter and bill water).

susceptible to resolution by the assertion of a right to clean water. Instead, the SDWA provides the answers based upon the detailed requirements that Congress wrote into the law and that EPA developed through its delegated responsibility to adopt implementing regulations. The premise of the SDWA and other environmental statutes is that the legislature and the executive are best positioned to develop the substantive provisions related to clean water, rather than expecting the judiciary to craft a clean-water jurisprudence akin to judicial efforts to flesh out the right to free speech or the right to bear arms.

Access to judicial remedies. The proponents of constitutionalizing environmental rights contend that such an action would better enable individuals to sue to remedy any environmental harm. Much of the discussion of a proposal federal environmental constitutional amendment occurred in the context of facilitating such lawsuits. The constitutional proposal failed, but the citizen suits that Congress added to the CWA and most other environmental laws afforded a statutory right for "any person" to bring a citizen suit to remedy any violation of environmental law.[35] Citizen suits have become an integral tool in the enforcement of the substantive commands of the CWA and the SDWA (as well as environmental statutes aimed at resources besides the water).

The statutory authority for citizen suits, however, is limited by the constitutional limits of federal courts to decide cases and controversies. Environmentalists blame the Supreme Court's standing doctrine for unnecessarily preventing individuals who seek to enforce the commands of the CWA and the SDWA from pursuing a judicial remedy. The proponents of a constitutional right to clean water believe that such a right would overcome these kinds of obstacles imposed by current standing doctrine. But such a right is no assurance that clean water will actually be provided. The experience of the many foreign nations that guarantee environmental rights in their constitutions is telling. China's Constitution, for example, guarantees that the government "protects and improves the environment" and "prevents and controls pollution,"[36] yet individual citizens lack access to administrative and judicial remedies for water pollution and instead often suffer persecution if they seek such remedies. Likewise, the Sudanese government recognizes a human right to access to clean water,[37] but it has

---

[35] 33 USC §1365.

[36] Constitution of the People's Republic of China, Art. 26 (2004).

[37] See El Khutma Awad Mohammed, "Scope and Content of the Relevant Human Right Obligations Related to Equitable Access to Safe Drinking Water and Sanitation" 1 (Apr. 2007) (report prepared for the Sudanese Ministry of Environment and Physical Development Higher Council for Environment and Natural Resources).

been unable or unwilling to guarantee that right even as the country's lack of clean water has become an international issue.

What the champions of a constitutional right to clean water really object to is the inadequate enforcement of the CWA, the SDWA, and other environmental regulations by the government. Citizen suits can prompt government regulators to act, or they can replace governmental action if necessary. It is less clear, though, whether a constitutional right to clean water would give individuals broader access to the courts. And to the extent it does, it is unclear how the courts would decide the kinds of substantive questions that they already face under the CWA and the SDWA. Christian environmental teaching offers little insight into this debate about the institutions that are best positioned to produce clean water.

Controlling governments and international organizations. Clean water is sometimes compromised by entities that are beyond the control of domestic governments. One environmental NGO emphasizes the need to regulate the activities of international financial institutions as they relate to clean water.[38] Or the government itself may be the problem. For example, one submission accused the Botswana government of "repeatedly us[ing] denial of water as a means to force the Gana and Gwi Bushmen off their land in the Central Kalahari Game reserve, and to prevent them from returning to that land."[39] An internationally recognized human right to clean water would prohibit governments from using water as a strategic weapon. It is conceivable, though, that other human rights relating to the right to life and prohibitions on war crimes already address that scenario. In any event, a negative right to be protected against hostile government denials of a right to clean water is more modest than the affirmative obligations that attach to most calls for a right to clean water.

Privatization of water. The proponents of a right to clean water also contend that such a right will block efforts to privatize water supplies. Efforts to transfer the responsibility for managing water systems from the government to private parties have generated substantial controversy throughout the world. Christians have been involved in that debate, often on the side of those opposing privatization. John Hart asserts that "[w]hen water is privatized and allocated only to those people(s), industries, or commercial purposes determined by its owners, the role of water

---

[38] See "Preliminary Submissions of the Council of Canadians Blue Planet Project," in re United Nations Human Rights Council Decision 2/104: Human Rights and Access to Water 17–22 (Apr. 2007).

[39] "Survival for Tribal Peoples, Survival International Submission to UN Human Rights Council on Indigenous Peoples and Access to Water" 1 (Apr. 11, 2007).

as a common good and the function of water to provide for the common good are eliminated."[40] Philosophy Professor Normal Wirzba agrees that a "corporate view of water … is immoral precisely because it makes abstract (a tradable commodity) what is a practical necessity for all life forms."[41] And the Pontifical Council's statement advises that "[w]ater by its very nature cannot be treated as a mere commodity among other commodities. Catholic social thought has always stressed that the defense and preservation of certain common goods, such as the natural and human environments, cannot be safeguarded simply by market forces, since they touch on fundamental human needs which escape market logic."[42]

But the relationship between a right to clean water and objections to privatization is uncertain. Does Christian teaching suggest that water should be free? The WHO supports a right to clean water, but it also acknowledges that citizens may have to pay for clean water.[43] Moreover, there is a tension between the presumed implications of a right to clean water and the use of economic tools and technological improvements to promote sustainable development. Again, it is unclear how the language of rights helps to resolve such questions.

CONCLUSIONS

Christian teaching counsels care for God's creation, including the abundant fresh waters with which we are blessed. It is more difficult to identify the unique contribution of Christian environmental teaching regarding the proper tools – including legal tools – to achieve clean water throughout the world. Those questions turn more on questions of rights than they do about creation, and so Christians who are concerned about water should become conversant with the rich literature that addresses the role of human rights and how they contribute to various social goods. It is also useful to consider why the expansion of international human rights has not produced a similar turn toward rights to resolve environmental problems. Consider J. B. Ruhl's explanation:

The correct environmental policy is not as clear-cut as, say, our convictions that free speech is vital and slavery is evil. The latter are not characterized by large gray areas or competing social values. But environmental policy, like economic policy,

[40] Hart, *Sacramental Commons*, 79.
[41] Normal Wirzba, *The Paradise of God: Renewing Religion in an Ecological Age* (Oxford: Oxford University Press, 2003), 161.
[42] Pontifical Council, "Note: Water, An Essential Element For Life."
[43] World Health Organization, "The Right to Water," 32.

education policy, welfare policy, and most of social policy in general, is defined by hard choices and complicated, multidimensional problems. The reason the Environmental Protection Agency has over ten thousand pages of rules is because that's how many it takes to tackle the problem. To think that environmental policy can be summed up in two sentences thus seems naive, if not ludicrous … We made a choice, over two centuries ago, to craft an operational blueprint for government that would adopt social policy sparingly and only when it was clear that the policy could and would be delivered. Constitutions of other nations loaded with aspirational statements and promises of good housing and jobs have become the subject of jokes because they fail to deliver. They fail to deliver because, in the end, how can they? Few social policy goals can be expressed as more than aspirations, something we work toward by using the institutional tools made available under the constitutive scheme.[44]

The international character of human rights raises further questions about the role of sphere sovereignty and subsidiarity, both of which favor local and private approaches to problems when that is possible. Such approaches already play a critical role in the effort to provide clean water throughout the world. Perhaps a right to clean water will provide some additional marginal benefits, but much of the public and private work to provide clean water will progress even without such a right.

RECOMMENDED READING

Bouma-Prediger, Steven. *For the Beauty of the Earth: A Christian Vision for Creation Care.* Grand Rapids, MI: Baker Academic, 2001.

Fisher-Ogden, Daryl and Shelley Ross Saxer. "World Religions and Clean Water Laws," *Duke Environmental Law & Policy Forum* 17 (2006): 63–117.

Hart, John. *Sacramental Commons: Christian Ecological Ethics.* Lanham, MD: Rowman & Littlefield, 2006.

Kravchenko, Svitlana and John Bonine, *Human Rights and the Environment: Cases, Law, and Policy.* Durham, NC: Carolina Academic Press, 2008.

Nwaomah, Sampson M. "Water in the Bible in the Context of the Ecological Debate in the Nigerian Delta," *Journal of Faith, Spirituality & Social Change* 1 (2008): 187.

Pontifical Council for Justice and Peace, Note: Water, An Essential Element For Life, www.vatican.va/roman_curia/pontifical_councils/justpeace/documents/rc_pc_justpeace_doc_20030322_kyoto-water_en.html (March 2003).

United Nations, Economic and Social Council, Committee on Economic, Social and Cultural Rights. Substantive Issues Arising in the Implementation of the International Covenant on Economic, Social and Cultural Rights: The

---

[44] J. B. Ruhl, "The Metrics of Constitutional Amendments: And Why Proposed Environmental Quality Amendments Don't Measure Up," *Notre Dame Law Review* 74 (1999): 245, 281.

Right to Water (Arts. 11 and 12 of the International Covenant on Economic, Social and Cultural Rights), General Comment No. 15 (2002).

US Department of State, Senator Paul Simon Water for the Poor Act: Report to Congress (2009), www.ehproject.org/PDF/ehkm/wfp2009.pdf.

Wirzba, Normal. *The Paradise of God: Renewing Religion in an Ecological Age.* Oxford: Oxford University Press, 2003.

World Health Organization, The Right to Water (2003), www.who.int/water_sanitation_health/rtwrev.pdf.

The final word: can Christianity contribute to a global civil religion?

Robert N. Bellah

I will begin with two caveats. I have decided to leave the bulk of this chapter as it was written in 2007, representing the atmosphere in the United States and the world at a time we considered "normal," and then in conclusion append a brief discussion of how later events have forced a change in everyone's thinking. Second, I have cited Christianity in my title because it is the religion with whose impact on global culture I am most concerned here, but I do not mean to privilege Christianity. A genuine global cultural consensus will need the contribution of all the religions.

In my essay "Civil Religion in America," first published in *Daedalus* in 1967, I discussed toward the end the possibility of what I called a "world civil religion."[1] Naive though it may sound today, the idea of a world civil religion as expressing "the attainment of some kind of viable and coherent world order," was the imagined resolution of what I then called America's third time of trial (the first time was concerned with independence; the second with slavery), an idea later developed in my book *The Broken Covenant*.[2] The third time of trial, as I then put it, was concerned with America's place in the world, and indeed what kind of world it would have a place in. That "viable and coherent world order" for which I hoped, would, I believed, require "a major new set of symbolic forms." So far, I argued, "the flickering flame of the United Nations burns too low to be the focus of a cult, but the emergence of a genuine transnational sovereignty would certainly change this."

This extraordinary vision might make it seem that my essay of forty-plus years ago was hopelessly out of touch with reality, unless one realizes that much of the actual text of that essay was a severe criticism of an America that had gone badly astray and was not helping the world toward a viable

---

[1] "Civil Religion in America" has been most recently reprinted in Robert N. Bellah and Steven M. Tipton, eds., *The Robert Bellah Reader* (Durham, NC: Duke University Press, 2006), 225–45.

[2] Robert N. Bellah, *The Broken Covenant: American Civil Religion in Time of Trial*, 2nd edn (Chicago: University of Chicago Press, 1992 [1975]).

and coherent world order at all. I included a long quotation from Senator J. William Fulbright about "the arrogance of power." Nor does the United States seem to have learned very much from Vietnam. We have continued to treat the world with arrogance many times since, though especially during the administration of George W. Bush.

One thing I learned from the complex discussion of the 1967 essay is that, for many, particularly religious believers but also secularists, the idea of "a civil religion" is viewed as a threat, one religion competing with and threatening to displace other religions. Although that was never the way I intended the term to be used, in order to avoid endless definitional argument I stopped using the term "American civil religion." Since the idea of a global civil religion could reignite that argument over terminology, I have decided to leave the term in my title as an attention getter, but in the text itself to speak of a global cultural consensus with a religious dimension as a less provocative description of what I want to discuss.

For the creation of a viable and coherent world order, a world civil society is surely an essential precondition, and, I would argue, any actual civil society will have a religious dimension, will need not only a legal and an ethical framework, but some notion that it conforms to the nature of ultimate reality. The biggest immediate problem is the strengthening of global civil society, and it is on that that I want to focus in this chapter. But I will have some hints and suggestions that perhaps the religious communities of the world may have something to contribute to that global civil society, and, indeed, that their participation may be essential for its success.

But first I think I have to raise the serious question, one not on the table in 1967, as to whether we do not already have a global civil religion. Harvey Cox raised this issue starkly in his 2002 essay "Mammon and the Culture of the Market." In his first paragraph he says, "My thesis is that the emerging global market culture – despite those who do not, or choose not to, see it – is generating an identifiable value-laden, 'religious' worldview." The market, Cox argues, is not seen as a human creation, but as a power beyond human control. In this view the market is omnipotent, omniscient, and omnipresent. All we have to do, as individuals or nations, is to bow down to it. Its demands are beyond question.[3]

---

[3] Harvey Cox, "Mammon and the Culture of the Market: A Socio-Theological Critique," in Richard Madsen *et al.*, eds., *Meaning and Modernity: Religion, Polity, and Self* (Berkeley: University of California Press, 2002), 124–35. The best treatment I have seen of what Cox calls the emerging global market culture is David Harvey's *A Brief History of Neoliberalism* (Oxford: Oxford University Press, 2005).

Cox calls for a Christian theological critique of this god who is no god and reminds us of Jesus's words, "You cannot serve God and Mammon" (Luke 16:13). Although many are suffering under the rule of this new deity, those who celebrate it can be found all over the world, in China and India as well as the West, and, for the moment, they seem without serious opposition. But if the worship of Mammon is the new global religion, it is not one that can create a viable and coherent world order or a global civil society that might make that possible. On the contrary, it seems to make our grave problems, environmental catastrophe and the greatest inequality in human history, worse, not better. Can we understand what is happening, and can we see any alternative?

I want to use some statements of Michael Walzer as a foil for my argument. I have learned much from him, have taught some of his books, so it was with some surprise that I found myself raising serious questions about his book *Thick and Thin: Moral Argument at Home and Abroad*. I was amazed to learn from him that humanity in effect does not exist. He writes:

Societies are necessarily particular because they have members with memories not only of their own but of their common life. Humanity, by contrast, has members but no memory, and so it has no history and no culture, no customary practices, no familiar life-ways, no festivals, no shared understanding of social goods. It is human to have such things, but there is no singular human way of having them.[4]

And later in the book he writes, "our common humanity will never make us members of a single universal tribe. The crucial commonality of the human race is particularism: we participate, all of us, in thick cultures that are our own."[5] This is especially news to me since I have spent much of my life, particularly the last ten years, writing the history of humanity in a book tentatively entitled "Religion in Human Evolution." And I have argued that the fact that religion has characterized all human societies means that religion is a kind of common culture, religion in the singular as I learned from my teacher Wilfred Cantwell Smith, even though it is also, as is all human culture, at the same time indelibly particular.

---

[4] Michael Walzer, *Thick and Thin: Moral Argument at Home and Abroad* (Notre Dame, IN: University of Notre Dame Press, 1994), 8.

[5] *Ibid.*, 83. For a recent and much more balanced treatment of the relation between universalism and particularism, see Michael Walzer, "Morality and Universality in Jewish Thought," in William M. Sullivan and Will Kymlicka, eds., *The Globalization of Ethics* (Cambridge: Cambridge University Press, 2007), 38–52.

What I would question in Walzer's position is the idea that the global and the particular are mutually exclusive, that one lives in one and
only one community, which, were it true, would surely make the idea of
membership in "a single universal tribe" impossible. I would argue, on the
contrary, that humans have almost never lived in one and only one community, that we almost always, and in modern times necessarily always,
live in many overlapping communities, and, under the rule of Mammon,
none of them may be particularly thick. To affirm that humanity has no
memory, no history, and no culture, seems to me remarkable at a time
when there is widespread popular interest in human origins, in human
evolution, and, since the pioneering work of William McNeill, in world
history. And if the Olympic Games and, for much of the world, the World
Cup, aren't global festivals, what are they? According to *Wikipedia*, 715
million people watched the 2006 World Cup.

Harold Berman has eloquently argued for the existence of world law,
which necessarily implies at least the beginnings of world politics and
world civil society.[6] While we have no world state, and would not want
one, the paranoid fantasies of American nativists about the black helicop-
ters of the United Nations suggest that even that is widely present in the
imagination. But the beginnings of world governance, which is not the
same thing as a world state, we certainly have. A remarkable example is
the fact that air-traffic control and the rules for landing and taking off at
airports, even the language used between pilots and controllers, are the
same all over the world. Even more obviously, our global economy would
be impossible were there not a plethora of rules, some legal, some customary, governing global trade and capital transfers. We will need to sort out
what is ominous and what is promising in this growing array of world law
and world regulation, but that world society does not exist and each of us
is stuck in his or her particularistic tribe, as Walzer affirms, seems to me
remarkably far from the truth.

That there is no world culture seems to me an idea that can come only
from the reification of the nation-state. World culture can be traced all
the way back. The bow and arrow, for example, had been adopted everywhere except in Australia, long before history. Stith Thompson has traced
motifs in folklore that can be found in every continent. There has never
been a time when human culture has not been shared; we do not come

---

[6] See, for example, Harold J. Berman, "World Law," *Fordham International Law Journal* 18(5)
(1995): 1617–22, and Berman, "Faith and Law in a Multicultural World," *Journal of Law and
Religion* 18(2) (2002–3): 297–305. See also Daniel Philpott, "Global Ethics and the International
Law Tradition," in Sullivan and Kymlicka, eds., *The Globalization of Ethics*, 17–37.

in hermetically sealed boxes. Even the nation-state is a cultural form that has been transmitted with remarkable fidelity over the entire world since the nineteenth century as the work of John Meyer and his associates has abundantly shown.[7] Wilfred Smith has traced shared stories and practices throughout the world religions, most of which themselves have been disseminated over very wide areas and have influenced and been influenced by those they have not converted.[8] Hinduism spread throughout Southeast Asia, leaving, for example, a remarkable degree of Sanskrit vocabulary in modern Indonesian. Buddhism spread throughout East Asia, as well as Southeast Asia, and had a considerable impact on Chinese Confucianism, acting as a stimulant to the formation of Neo-Confucianism. Christianity and Islam have spread all over the world and mutually influenced all the cultures they contacted. Nonetheless, global culture, which I would insist is a deep feature of human history, is not the same thing as global civil society or global governance. World empires, beginning with the Achaemenid Persian empire in the middle of the first millennium BCE, have played a significant role in human history, but have never succeeded in becoming the universal empires that they aspired to be. Civil society is a relatively late idea, only emerging for the first time in the West in the eighteenth century.

It is worth noting that world trade, often the carrier of world culture, can be traced back into the deepest recesses of human history, but was growing in importance since classical times when China and India were linked in a variety of ways with the Middle East and Europe. After the European discovery of the New World, trade truly became global. The degree to which market economies were embedded in states and societies has been a subject of wide-ranging historical argument that I do not need to get into, but a principled independence of the market from state and guild monopolies was a feature of the early modern period, pioneered by Britain, but rapidly diffusing to other societies and making possible the emergence of modern capitalism.

Developing only slightly later, but overlapping the disembedding of the economy, was the emergence of civil society or the public sphere, a realm of thought, argument, and association independent of the state, but leading to the formation of what came to be called public opinion, which politicians could ignore at their peril. Jürgen Habermas's

---

[7] See, for example, George M. Thomas *et al.*, *Institutional Structure: Constituting State, Society and the Individual* (Newbury Park, CA: Sage, 1987).
[8] Wilfred Cantwell Smith, *Towards a World Theology* (Philadelphia: Westminster Press, 1981).

early work, *The Structural Transformation of the Public Sphere*, helped us understand this newly independent realm.[9] Whereas Hegel tended to use civil society, which he defined as the system of needs, as referring to the economy, and Marxists still follow that usage to some extent, more recent writers, such as Habermas, while recognizing the relation of the new economy to the emerging civil society, nonetheless saw it as independent not only from the state but, in principle, from the market as well.

I will use "civil society" as virtually synonymous with "public sphere" in a way that has become common in recent writings to refer to forms of communication and association that have been disembedded from the state and are not directly controlled by the market. In the eighteenth century the main problem was to achieve independence from the state, and the institutionalization of human rights was the essential precondition for an independent civil society. The First Amendment to the American Constitution guaranteeing freedom of religion, speech, press, and assembly is the legal basis that makes civil society possible and similar developments have followed, not without much struggle and backsliding, elsewhere ever since, even where such rights, though included in constitutions, are consistently violated in practice. This again suggests that culture and even law have spread where institutions and practices have not as yet fully developed.

Civil society, though oriented to the discussion and advocacy of political issues, lacks the capacity to make binding decisions. Nonetheless it is closely related to another eighteenth-century idea, the sovereignty of the people. It was Robespierre who first gave the idea of democracy a positive meaning after centuries during which it was usually a pejorative term. Democracy as a way of exercising the sovereignty of the people, gave civil society the right, not to make political decisions, but to elect those who would. This idea has now achieved global legitimacy even when it is often honored in the breach.

Most writing about civil society has taken the nation-state as the basic frame of reference, though of late there has been quite a bit of discussion of global civil society. Alejandro Colas has made the useful point that civil society was international virtually from the beginning. Though it may have originated in Britain in the eighteenth century, it was already disseminated to the American colonies, whose actions in turn were widely influential

---

[9] Jürgen Habermas, *The Structural Transformation of the Public Sphere: An Inquiry into the Category of Bourgeois Society* (Cambridge, MA: MIT Press, 1989 [1962]).

on the continent, as were British practices.[10] In fact, all the great modern ideologies – liberalism, nationalism, and socialism – were international and involved not only cross-national communication of a variety of sorts, but many international associations. We may think of nationalism as antithetical to globalism, but nationalism has always been an international phenomenon. Colas cites the interesting example of Giuseppe Mazzini, the most important theorist of Italian nationalism, establishing in 1847 the People's International League whose objectives he defined as:

to disseminate the principles of national freedom and progress; to embody and manifest an efficient public opinion in favour of the right of every people to self-government and the maintenance of their own nationality; to promote a good understanding between the peoples of every country.[11]

While many have argued that the rapid growth of NGOs since World War II is an indication of the growth of global civil society, Colas suggests the limitations of NGOs in that they represent only limited memberships and are usually oriented to single issues rather than to structural problems, whereas social movements that cross national boundaries more closely approximate a genuine global civil society. His examples include socialism, feminism, and environmentalism.

Mass communications, but particularly the internet, have made possible the organization of global public opinion to a degree unimaginable only a few years ago. Adam Lupel has described a remarkable event:

On 15 February 2003 across North America, Europe, the Middle East, Asia and Australia as many as 30 million people took to city streets to express opposition to the planned invasion of Iraq. It seemed an extraordinary moment for global civil society, perhaps for the first time living up to its name. The anti-war movement appeared to accomplish in a day what four years of transnational activism against neo-liberal globalization could not. It brought together constituencies from East and West, North and South into a broad-based movement with a common clear objective: stop the US-led drive for war. The next weeks saw what was perhaps a Pyrrhic victory for global civil society. The protests no doubt contributed to the Bush Administration's defeat in the UN Security Council. But in the end they also contributed to the heightened sense that the United Nations and global civil society were impotent next to the hegemonic power of the United States.[12]

---

[10] Alejandro Colas, *International Civil Society: Social Movements in World Politics* (Cambridge: Polity, 2002), 49–58 and *passim*.

[11] *Ibid.*, 55.

[12] Adam Lupel, "Tasks of a Global Civil Society: Held, Habermas and Democratic Legitimacy Beyond the Nation-State," *Globalizations* 2(1) (2005): 117–18.

Using this example in both its positive and negative aspects as a starting-point, we can ask where are we? Granted that there is a global economy, global culture, global law, global civil society, even global festivals, why are global institutions both so promising and so weak? I will turn to Jürgen Habermas, Europe's leading social philosopher, for help, particularly in his remarkable essay of 1998, "The Postnational Constellation and the Future of Democracy."[13] Habermas organizes his discussion around the tension between two central facts in our present situation: (1) the nation-state is the largest form of society that has been able to create a sense of common membership powerful enough to convince a majority of its citizens that they have a responsibility for all, including the least advantaged, thus giving rise to significant redistribution in what we have come to call the welfare state; and (2) the rise of the global neo-liberal market ideology and practice has everywhere threatened the capacity of nation-states to carry out the responsibilities inherent in the notion of common membership. Habermas begins his essay with an epigraph from Robert Cox that sums up the present dilemma:

All politicians move to the centre in order to compete on the basis of personality and of who is best able to manage the adjustment in economy and society necessary to sustain competitiveness in the global market ... The possibility of an alternative economy and society is excluded.[14]

What Habermas is describing is a double disparity between economics and politics: economics is seen as the realm of the natural, not the social, whereas politics is the sphere of intentional social choice. But when nations are the sole locations of effective politics and the economy has become global, then the disparity in power between global economy and even the strongest state means that it is the economy that will in the end determine outcomes. In this situation Habermas asks whether "we can have a politics that can catch up with global markets" in order to avert the "natural" disaster that an uninhibited market economy seems to entail.[15] That idea is opposed by those who view the economy not as a human creation but as a force of nature, as something that can only be accommodated, never controlled, ideas that make global market culture into a god that can only be worshiped. Habermas sees this as an enormous challenge to citizens of all countries to form a global civil society: "Only the transformed consciousness of citizens, as it imposes itself in areas of domestic policy, can pressure

---

[13] Jürgen Habermas, "The Postnational Constellation and the Future of Democracy," in *The Postnational Constellation: Political Essays* (Cambridge, MA: MIT Press, 2002 [1998]), 58–112.
[14] *Ibid.*, 58.   [15] *Ibid.*, 109.

global actors to change their own self-understanding sufficiently to begin to see themselves as members of an international community who are compelled to cooperate with one another, and hence to take one another's interests into account." What we need, he argues, is "an obligatory cosmopolitan solidarity."[16] He stresses the need for a "world domestic policy," because we are now living in a world, not in nation-states alone, and the world market requires such a policy.[17]

As a practical example, though one with implications for even larger forms of political cooperation, he takes the European Union and the difficulties it has faced in becoming something more effective than a mere currency union. Habermas uses the example of what he calls the modern state as a constitutional republic, no longer a nation in the sense of a particular ethnic group, but including people of various ethnic, religious, and linguistic backgrounds, yet united in what he calls an abstract constitutional patriotism, such that its members can still identify with each other and even sacrifice some of their own advantages for the common welfare. He points out that an effective European Union would require that "Swedes and Portuguese are willing to take responsibility for one another."[18] To the degree that the EU has given special advantages to its poorer members this has actually begun to happen, with apparent public support. But he points out that the neo-liberal economy not only pressures all nations to lower wages and decrease benefits, but also to lower taxes to the point where the state no longer has the resources to carry out its social programs. A really effective EU would be able to stop or reverse this tendency by setting minimum wages and higher taxes across the Union. Ultimately, of course, a global union would be necessary to reverse the neo-liberal drive to the bottom.

The most fundamental question that Habermas is raising is whether a global civil society and some forms of global governance are possible, a civil society and governance that would not replace nation-states but would place some limits on their autonomy, as the global economy already does. And here there is a question of what kind of people we are. Could Americans accept the notion of common global membership such that we would be willing to give up something of ours for the sake of Somalians or Vietnamese? It is at this point that I think we have to ask what are the cultural resources for thinking of global citizenship that would go along with global economics and moderate its excesses? Is abstract constitutional

[16] *Ibid.*, 55.   [17] *Ibid.*, 54.   [18] *Ibid.*, 99.

patriotism enough? It is here that we have to consider philosophical and religious resources for thinking about membership in global civil society, membership that would entail at least short-term sacrifice, though as we look at global warming and the growing numbers of failed states, the Tocquevillian idea of self-interest rightly understood is not to be ignored.

Since we actually have, in the UN Universal Declaration of Human Rights and its subsequent elaborations, something that can be called a global ethic, sometimes referred to as a human rights regime, we can ask how much help we can derive from this consensus, one that is not simply an ideal but that has significant legal weight, though by far not enforceable everywhere, not even in the original home of legal human rights, the USA.[19] And we can ask whether the questions raised by non-Western and non-Christian thinkers about the adequacy of an exclusive emphasis on human rights can be answered, as well as the question whether an exclusive focus on human rights may not be part of our problem, however much in the end it must surely be part of a solution.[20]

To the extent that human rights as we understand them have significant Christian historical roots (something many supporters of human rights may not be aware of or care to be aware of), it is also worth remembering that Christianity is now a global phenomenon. Webb Keane in his powerful book *Christian Moderns* has pointed out that at the beginning of the twenty-first century one-third of the world is now Christian and that one-third of those Christians live in former colonies.[21] He further points out that many of the leaders of non-Western countries (often formerly leaders of independence movements) were educated in missionary schools even though they were not converts. One could add that reform movements in Buddhism, Hinduism, and Islam have been to more than a small degree a response to Christian, especially Protestant, examples. So if there is a relation between Christianity, modernity, and human rights, it has for some time been global and can no longer be dismissed as Western.

Let me return to the way Habermas poses the problem: how can we create a global civil society that will have the same capacity of citizens to identify with the plight of fellow citizens as already exists in nation-states, and

---

[19] See Jeremy Waldron, "Is This Torture Necessary?" *New York Review of Books* 54(16) (Oct. 25, 2007): 40–1, 44. See further the chapter by Waldron herein.

[20] Hans Küng drafted the Chicago Declaration toward a Global Ethic, endorsed by the Parliament of the World's Religions in 1993; for the text, see Sullivan and Kymlicka, eds., *The Globalization of Ethics*, 236–46. Küng has developed his thought further in *A Global Ethic for Global Politics and Economics* (Oxford: Oxford University Press, 1998).

[21] Webb Keane, *Christian Moderns: Freedom and Fetish in the Mission Encounter* (Berkeley: University of California Press, 2007), 43.

to his example of the immediate task of creating such a civil society that would include the whole European Union. While accepting Habermas's framework, let me offer a couple of caveats. First, under the regime of the neo-liberal market, it is not always easy to get even the citizens of the same nation to identify with all other citizens (in the United States it has never been easy). Second, the situation in which such identification has been most effective has usually been war: we are all in this together because we have a mortal enemy that we must defeat. If we cannot assume the ability to identify with all fellow members of civil society even in advanced democracies and the conditions that have made that possible have usually involved war, we can see that the task of generalizing such identification beyond the nation-state will never be easy.

It is for these reasons that I wonder if Habermas's abstract constitutional patriotism will ever be enough. It is one thing to believe in abstract principles. It is another to mobilize the motivation to put those principles into institutional practice. Hans Joas has recently pointed out, following the pioneering work of Georg Jellinek, that, though ideas about human rights go way back in Western history, and include classical, Catholic, Lutheran, and Calvinist thinking, it was only when the American sectarian Protestants in the eighteenth century, mainly the Baptists and Quakers, were willing to insist on them that they got included in the American Constitution.[22] Religious fervor is always problematic because it has so often been used for evil as well as good purposes, but it may be that only such powerful motivation could make human rights genuinely practical. And though Christianity has a big contribution to make, it surely is not alone. Confucians hold on the basis of the *Analects of Confucius* that "all within the four seas are brothers." Buddhists identify not only with all human beings but with all beings in the universe, natural as well as human – all have the Buddha nature. For millennia these deep commitments have been held but never effectively institutionalized. Can the world's religions now mobilize their commitments so that they can at last have genuine institutional force?

Moving to the next question as to whether human rights as vested exclusively in individuals are enough, we may ask whether Kantian moral universalism alone can provide sufficient guidance. Perhaps it will

---

[22] Hans Joas, "Max Weber and the Origin of Human Rights," in Charles Camic, Philip S. Gorski, and David M. Trubek, eds., *Max Weber's Economy and Society: A Critical Companion* (Stanford: Stanford University Press, 2005), 366–82, at 371. Jellinek's book, *The Declaration of the Rights of Man and of Citizens: A Contribution to Modern Constitutional History*, was published in German in 1895 and in English translation by Henry Holt in 1901.

require substantive religious motivation to see that human rights without a humane and caring society will be empty, incapable of fulfillment. And there remains the question of some functional equivalent to the powerful mobilization of human aggression by nation-states as a basis for solidarity. Early in the twentieth century William James raised the question of the moral equivalent of war.[23] We have seen the use of war as a metaphor in such things as the war on poverty, the war on drugs, and so forth, but the metaphor never seems to be as effective as real wars. I suppose it would be too much to ask if we could mobilize a religious war against selfishness, ignorance, and sinfulness in each of us according to our own faith, in part because, I suppose, we have been fighting that war all along. In any case there are enormous threats on the horizon and a popular culture that seems more apprehensive than at any time in my life, with fear of the future replacing the certainty of progress. But anxiety and fear have often fueled extremely regressive movements, and there is no certainty that they will move people in the right direction. There is also the great danger that anxiety and fear can immobilize rather than stimulate to action. It is a delicate balance.

Surely secular philosophies have ways of dealing with the fragility of solidarity, even at the national level, and the ease with which humans can be frightened into a negative solidarity against alleged enemies. But if, as I have argued, the world's religions may have capacities to strengthen and generalize a sense of solidarity so that it reaches truly global proportions, they can do so only in and through self-criticism. Let me say plainly what I have already implied and what earlier chapters in this volume have already made clear: Christianity, and especially Protestant Christianity, has contributed significantly to the institutionalization of human rights and human solidarity. I have given the American example of the religious roots of the Bill of Rights, but I must add the significant role of Evangelicals in leading the social gospel movement that helped (with the assistance of Catholics motivated by Catholic social teachings) to create in the middle years of the twentieth century what became the beginnings of a welfare state in the USA. Yet Christianity and especially Protestant Christianity have contributed to an emphasis on individual piety that makes the secular notion of radical autonomy attractive. Max Weber saw the relation between "the Protestant ethic and the spirit of capitalism." Webb Keane has shown the relation between global Protestantism and

---

[23] William James, "The Moral Equivalent of War," first published in February 1910 in William James, *Writings 1902–1910* (New York: Library of America, 1987 [1910]), 1281–93.

neo-liberal economics. It is in these regards that I have said that religion is part of the problem as well as part of the solution. And if Christianity can make a contribution to the creation of global solidarity only through self-criticism, such is the case with all the other religions, and secular philosophies as well. There is no way of sorting out the good guys from the bad guys in our present world crisis. We all need each other, but we need critical reason and profound faith reinforcing each other.

What the world requires that we do now must go on at many levels, religious, ideological, and political at the global, national and local levels. But one thing Habermas's scenario requires is very evident, however difficult to achieve. We must now turn the idea of being citizens of the world into a practical citizenship, willing to be responsible for the world of which we are citizens. I truly believe that there are millions of citizens of the world in every country, willing to make the necessary commitments. Whether they are anywhere in the majority so that the politicians will listen to them instead of pandering to the short-term interests of their constituents is doubtful. What we need is to turn a growing minority into an effective majority.

For those of us in the United States a classical example might be instructive. As far as I know, the first usage of the idea of being citizens of the world originated with the Stoic philosophers in the ancient Mediterranean. They thought of themselves as *kosmou politai*, literally citizens of the world. But for us it is worth remembering that even the Roman Stoics always used the term in Greek – there was no Latin translation. Sheldon Pollock speculates, following Ovid, that this was because the Romans thought their task was "to transform the *kosmos* into their *polis*, or rather to transform the *orbis* into their *urbs*, the vast world into their own city."[24] If one looks at George W. Bush's *National Security Strategy* of September 2002 one can see that he claims the oversight of the entire world for the United States, which might explain why Americans have been relatively hesitant about becoming citizens of the world. It is the world that must recognize our primacy, not we that must recognize the primacy of the world.

Because I see neo-liberalism as the source of our deepest global problems it might be thought that I am opposed to it altogether. That would be as foolish at this point in history as to be opposed to capitalism altogether. What I worry about is the destructive consequences of the naturalization of neo-liberalism so that it has no effective challenge. I agree with

[24] Sheldon Pollock, *The Language of the Gods in the World of Men: Sanskrit, Culture, and Power in Premodern India* (Berkeley: University of California Press, 2007), 276.

Habermas that world politics needs to catch up with the world economy so that an effective structure of regulation can be created that will protect the environment and the vulnerable of the earth who are paying the price while only a few are reaping the benefits. If this is a political challenge it is also a religious challenge. I am convinced that religious motivation is a necessary factor if we are to transform the growing global moral consensus and the significant beginnings of world law into an effective form of global solidarity and global governance.

AFTER THE DELUGE

I want to add just a few reflections in early 2009 to what I have written above. In our present situation much of what I wrote two years ago seems prescient. I cited Habermas in describing "the 'natural' disaster that an uninhibited market economy seems to entail." We are now living in the midst of that disaster, which only seems natural if we are still worshiping Mammon and cling to neo-liberal fundamentalism. What is surely the most severe recession since World War II, and what some observers believe will be an actual depression rivaling in intensity and duration the Great Depression of the 1930s, is already producing serious social problems everywhere in the world. The economy and society are too intertwined for a breakdown in one not to have grave consequences in the other. As a result Mammon seems a much less appealing deity than recently he did.

The economic collapse coincided with a major political transition in the United States, and we have yet to see what kind of political changes other nations may undergo. Looking at the Great Depression we have no reason to believe that such changes will necessarily be benign. Yet emergency conditions can make possible positive social reforms that have long been delayed in "normal" times. They can also enable significant changes in ideology. In the United States the Obama administration marks significant changes in both thought and action. Barack Obama has used the language of the common good in a way far more central than have American leaders in a long time, and his programs, at this moment as yet to be enacted, appear to embody that kind of thinking. He is also seeking cooperation with the rest of the world in a way that is unprecedented in America in recent times.

There is clearly a religious dimension to this shift in thought and action: the biblical and civic republican traditions in America are providing significant alternatives to utilitarian and expressive individualism as dominant cultural orientations that we have not seen for decades. It is far too soon to say whether parallel shifts will occur in other nations, Western and non-Western, and deriving from a variety of roots in the major world religious traditions. All I can say now is that this period of grave national and international crisis, fraught with danger though it is, could make possible the forging of a new global cultural consensus on issues of the environment, human rights, and social justice, and drawing from religious insights from a variety of traditions. It is possible, though by no means certain, that the present crisis might provide the environment for a major step forward in the creation of a global civil society and a global cultural consensus with a religious dimension.

RECOMMENDED READING

Bellah, Robert N. "Civil Religion in America [1967]," in Robert N. Bellah and Steven M. Tipton, eds., *The Robert Bellah Reader*. Durham, NC: Duke University Press, 2006, 225–45.

The Broken Covenant: American Civil Religion in Time of Trial, 2nd edn. Chicago: University of Chicago Press, 1992 [1975].

Berman, Harold J. "World Law," *Fordham International Law Journal* 18(5) (1995): 1617–22.

"Faith and Law in a Multicultural World," *Journal of Law and Religion* 18(2) (2002–3): 297–305.

Colas, Alejandro. *International Civil Society: Social Movements in World Politics*. Cambridge: Polity, 2002.

Cox, Harvey. "Mammon and the Culture of the Market: A Socio-Theological Critique," in Richard Madsen *et al.*, eds., *Meaning and Modernity: Religion, Polity, and Self*. Berkeley: University of California Press, 2002, 124–35.

Habermas, Jürgen. *The Structural Transformation of the Public Sphere: An Inquiry into the Category of Bourgeois Society*. Cambridge, MA: MIT Press, 1989 [1962].

"The Postnational Constellation and the Future of Democracy," in Habermas, *The Postnational Constellation: Political Essays*. Cambridge, MA: MIT Press, 2002 [1998], 58–112.

James, William. "The Moral Equivalent of War," in William James, *Writings 1902–1910*. New York: Library of America, 1987 [1910], 1281–93.

Joas, Hans. "Max Weber and the Origin of Human Rights," in Charles Camic, Philip S. Gorski, and David M. Trubek, eds., *Max Weber's Economy and Society: A Critical Companion*. Stanford: Stanford University Press, 2005, 366–82.

Keane, Webb. *Christian Moderns: Freedom and Fetish in the Mission Encounter*. Berkeley: University of California Press, 2007.

Küng, Hans. *A Global Ethic for Global Politics and Economics*. Oxford: Oxford University Press, 1998.

Lupel, Adam. "Tasks of a Global Civil Society: Held, Habermas and Democratic Legitimacy beyond the Nation-State," *Globalizations* 2(1) (2005): 117–33.

Smith, Wilfred Cantwell. *Towards a World Theology.* Philadelphia: Westminster Press, 1981.

Walzer, Michael. *Thick and Thin: Moral Argument at Home and Abroad.* Notre Dame, IN: University of Notre Dame Press, 1994.

Biblical index

Index

Abraham, God's covenant with, 54
accommodation of religious beliefs, 244–9
accountability for human rights, mutuality of, 329–30
Ackermann, Bruce, 251
ACLU (American Civil Liberties Union), 211
Act of Uniformity (1559, England), 28
Adams, Arlin, 250
Adams, John, 153
adult baptism, 29, 255
Advisory Panel of Experts on Freedom of Religion or Belief, OSCE, 208
Aeterni Patris (1879), 24
Africa, role of Protestant missionaries in, 31–2
African [Banjul] Charter on Human and People's Rights (1981), 208
African Charter on the Rights and Welfare of the Child (1999), 208
African Commission on Human and Peoples' Rights, 208
agapist rejection of natural rights theory, 157–8, 168
Ahmed, An-Na'im Abdullahi, 266
AI (Amnesty International), 210, 211
Albericus de Rosate, 103
Alexander, Frank S., ix
Alfeyev, H., 189
ALI (American Law Institute), 196, 284, 295–6, 299
Alston, Philip, 211
Althusius, Johannes, 146–8, 154
Altmann, Alexander, 234
America. *See* United States
American Civil Liberties Union (ACLU), 211
American Convention on Human Rights (1969), 207
American Declaration of the Rights and Duties of Man (1948), 207
American Jewish Committee, 196

American Law Institute (ALI), 196, 284, 295–6, 299
American Women's Suffrage Association (AWSA), 309
Amish communities, withdrawal of children from standard schooling, 244
Amnesty International (AI), 210, 211
Anabaptists, 28, 29
Anastasius I (Byzantine emperor), 278
Anglicanism
    individual freedom, emphasis on, 29
    nationalization of faith in, 28
Anglo-Saxon law, 20
Annan, Kofi, 341
Anthony, Susan B., 309
anti-Semitism, as negative impact of religion, 7
apocalyptic. *See* eschatology
Appiah, Anthony, 218
Aquinas. *See* Thomas Aquinas
Arab Charter on Human Rights, 208
Arab Human Rights Committee, 208
Arab League, 208–10
Arbour, Louise, 208
Arianism, 174
Aristotle
    children's rights, integrative tradition of, 283, 285, 287–9, 291, 292, 298, 300
    community, human need for, 119
    on human personality, 2, 179
    judicial equity, concept of, 140
    justice
        equality, relationship to, 162–5, 169
        Roman Catholic use of theory of, 124
    neo-scholastic natural rights law based on, 22
    on objective natural rights, 290
    Politics, 300
    on slavery, 2, 90
Arnhart, Larry, 291–2, 300
Ashoka (Japanese emperor), edicts of, 212
Asian Legal Resource Center, 211

370